The Making of the Third Republic

The Making of the

THIRD REPUBLIC

Class and Politics in France, 1868-1884

SANFORD ELWITT

Louisiana State University Press
BATON ROUGE

ISBN 0–8071–0077–3
Library of Congress Catalog Card Number 73–90866
Copyright © 1975 by Louisiana State University Press
Manufactured in the United States of America

This book was designed by Dwight Agner and
set in Linotype Garamond by Heritage Printers,
Charlotte, North Carolina.

Contents

⟦ *Preface*

RECENTLY, a group of French historians, of which I was one, met in informal seminar to consider the question: "The Third Republic, What Price Survival?" The question itself testifies to the durability of a regime in a country whose revolutions, counterrevolutions, monarchies, empires, and a dozen constitutions between 1791 and 1875 puzzled her contemporaries and have intimidated historians working to make sense of an apparently chaotic past. The question also carries with it the unstated assumption that the Republic merely "survived," as if it had sustained a protracted state of siege mounted by a progression of intractable enemies. Adolphe Thiers said that the Republic divided men least, that it came into existence *faute de mieux*.

This book stands Thiers' epigram on its head. It appears that a more useful hypothesis may be that the Republic united men most. And yet, how could that adequately account for the durability of a regime that, by most accounts, rested on a class base—as had all previous regimes. The aforementioned seminar of historians concluded that the essence of the Republic lay in its successful postponement of social reform. We all agreed that its record on that score was a disgrace. Yet, again, that conclusion rests upon a categorical imperative—the promise unfulfilled—and assumes that a program of serious social reform would have constituted a dagger aimed directly at the heart of the Republic itself. Indeed it would have, had not the foundations of the bourgeois Republic been constructed of solid material, had not those who made the Republic been clearly conscious of their task and been properly armed to carry it out.

Thus, questions relating to survival and durability must be subsumed beneath more immediate and fundamental problems, particularly the contradictory nature of the French Republic, which was at once the heir of a democratic tradition and the embodiment of bourgeois class rule. Viewed from this perspective, the history of France since the collapse of the *ancien régime* to the foundation of the Third Republic may be interpreted as a continuing struggle to resolve the contradiction by providing the material foundations and mobilizing the ideological resources upon which a class-conscious bourgeoisie rose to displace a mixed collection of "notables." The contradiction found its own resolution in the triumph of republican democracy that simultaneously became an instrument of class rule. The time was ripe for the tradition itself to serve as a weapon to legitimate and reinforce the ideological and political hegemony of a ruling class. For there existed no real contradiction between the most durable ideals of the French Revolution and their fulfillment in the bourgeois state. Hence, the Republic was born unburdened with social promises to be fulfilled. The Communards of Paris in 1871 understood this very well and with great heroism against overwhelming odds fought to the death to defend their social Republic.

The answer to the question, "What price survival?" then must be: the sacrifice of a just social order. But we would be fools indeed to demand of those who had grasped power to make that sacrifice and participate in their own liquidation—fools, that is, unless we possessed sufficient ideological and political firepower to enforce such a demand. Paradoxically, those who made the Republic did so in full confidence that their construction provided for a just social order. Not incidentally, they possessed the power to back up their conception of such an order. We may disagree with their conception, but we cannot ask them to have constructed an alternative order in violation of their very natures. Let us then take them on their own terms, which does not mean suspending critical analysis. Rather, it means, in Eric Hobsbawm's words, recreating the "material and historical environment" within which the republican leadership formulated a social ideology and an accompanying social policy. Then, perhaps, we shall understand more completely not so much the "price of survival," but the dynamics of a system that, for several generations, either arrogantly ignored the challenge or dealt with it on its own terms.

To take such an approach requires that much of the traditional historiography of modern France be reexamined and new paths charted. In this effort, I have drawn on the advice and criticism of several good friends, colleagues, and comrades.

First, I have had the good fortune to receive the continuing counsel of Professor Edward Whiting Fox, under whose direction I began this project, in an earlier truncated form, as a doctoral dissertation at Cornell University. His support and friendship have helped to smooth the rough road I have traveled.

A number of colleagues read the entire manuscript, offered valuable criticism, and, most nourishing for my spirit, gave good words of encouragement: Charmarie Blaisdell, John Cairns, John Cammett, Leslie Derfler, Eric Hobsbawm, Joseph Moody, George Rudé, Albert Soboul, and Peter Stearns. In most cases they put aside their own work on short notice to read it under pressure conditions. For that I am most grateful.

Others read part of the manuscript or just talked history with me over the years, thereby helping me to better understand what I was doing and reinforcing my conviction in the indivisibility of history as it takes shape in the hands of such skilled craftsmen as Emile Karafiol, Donald Kelley, Henry Shapiro, and Warren Susman. My colleagues at the University of Rochester, Dean Miller, John Waters, and Mary Young, also share in whatever merits this book might possess. My students at Rochester, Laura Frader, Richard King, Bonnie Smith, Laura Strumingher, and Donald Young, taught me as I taught them.

I also thank the editors of *French Historical Studies* and *Science and Society* for permission to use excerpts from articles previously published in their journals.

A special *salutation fraternelle* to those comrades who are very special to me: Elizabeth Fox-Genovese, Eugene Genovese, and John Laffey, who read the manuscript and subjected it to their unique analytical scrutiny; Alan Adamson, Charles Bertrand, Ella Laffey, and G. David Sheps, who were spared the reading, but who, along with the Genoveses and John Laffey, share with me a priceless relationship of mutual comradeship, respect, and trust.

To those who are dearest to me I reserve special mention: my sons, Jonathan and Sammy, with whom I have enjoyed and will continue to enjoy tenderness, love, and just plain fun; and Marcia, who has shared with me the pain of the bad times and the joy of the good, who has labored in the archives and in the libraries at my side, who has helped me translate awkward prose into good English, and whose love has stood as a rock and sustained me.

January, 1974
Rochester, New York

The Making of the Third Republic

▐ Introduction

THIS BOOK SEEKS to establish the social and ideological foundations of the Third French Republic in its formative years, 1868–1884.
It consciously avoids the traditional approach, in which a concentration on Paris politics, on the shifting patterns of parliamentary groups,
and on the general climate of greed and corruption all too often ob-
scures the processes by which the Republic was forged. I have chosen
a different path. Guided by a flexible yet consistent class analysis, I
argue that an alliance of capitalists and petty producers, mobilized
under the banner of republican democracy, developed the ideological
perspectives and social policies that expressed the essential nature of
the Republic. The capitalist fraction provided the leadership for that
alliance. Its spokesmen fashioned the ideological weapons to neutralize
the disparate and frequently antagonistic elements in the republican
coalition. The story of those years, then, reveals the tensions and the
struggles associated with the creation of a stable bourgeois social order
in France.[1]

1. General surveys of the entire period include François Goguel, *La Politique des
partis sous la troisième république* (Paris: Editions du Seuil, 1956); Jacques Chastenet,
L'Enfance de la troisième, 1870–1879 (Paris: Hachette, 1952); Robert David, *La
Troisième république: Soixante ans de politique et d'histoire* (Paris: Plon, 1934);
Georges Bourgin, *La Troisième république* (Paris: Colin, 1939); David Thomson,
Democracy in France (Oxford: Clarendon Press, 1955); Guy Chapman, *The Third
Republic of France: The First Phase, 1871–1894* (London: Macmillan, 1962); Em-
manuel Beau de Loménie, *Les Responsabilités des dynasties bourgeoises* (4 vols.; Paris:
Denoël, 1946–63), Vol. I, Chaps. 5–7, Vol. II, Chap. 1; from the socialist point of view,
A. Zévaès, *L'Histoire de la troisième république* (Paris: Editions Georges-Anquetil,

Each chapter constitutes an individual study forming a constituent element of the total work. The several studies fall into two categories that bear a reciprocal relationship to one another: social ideology and socioeconomic policy. Indeed, the entire emphasis falls on the interplay between two aspects of a single reality. The first two chapters establish the contours of a republican ideology and its class base as they took shape in the political struggle against the Second Empire and, subsequently, in the construction of a national republican movement after 1871. These chapters also portray republican ideological values in action through examples drawn from local history. The remaining chapters pick up the story after 1875 and treat public works, education, the rise of economic nationalism, and imperialism.

In choosing these subjects I have been guided by the leading political figures of the time and lesser known but equally important local leaders. The issues discussed in this book arrested their attention and consumed their energies. To chart their responses, solutions, and compromises is to develop a clearer view of the material foundations, the social relations, and the ideological constructions that went into the making of the Third French Republic. I have chosen to begin in 1868 because that year marked the appearance of a republican movement that defined itself in terms of a coherent social outlook and offered a viable alternative to the prevailing political order. By 1884, the principal social and economic policies that characterized the republican order had been realized.

The Great Revolution of 1789 established the foundations of the bourgeois state. However, capitalist production had not yet transformed French society—a fact that separates the experience of France from that of England, where, during the previous century, the capitalization of agriculture came to dominate the landscape. In France, the Napoleonic regime both hardened the fractionalization of rural property

1926); for the republicans see Jacques Kayser, *Les Grandes batailles du radicalisme* (Paris: Rivière, 1961) and Georges Weill, *Histoire du parti républicain en France, 1814–1870* (Paris: Alcan, 1928).

and, by establishing the Bank of France, confirmed the concentration of mobile capital atop an economy based mostly on petty production. Thus, the revolution remained unfinished.

Economic and social developments during the subsequent half century turn on the distinctions and relationships among capitalism, industrialization, and industrial revolution. I will use the term *capitalism* in two related senses: as a way of characterizing social production and human relationships and as a stage in the historical process. Capitalism, as Marx and Weber saw in different ways, predated industrialization but was immensely strengthened by it during the course of the nineteenth century.

In France the subordination of production to capitalist relations and the triumph of an industrial bourgeoisie proceeded in measured stages without the powerful generating force of an industrial revolution. During the two generations following Waterloo, investment capital remained concentrated in the hands of a small number of major bankers, who presided over an economic system in which investment in the state debt and in foreign securities effectively blocked the flow of large amounts of capital into domestic industrial production. An industrial revolution did not occur. Manufacturing did not eclipse all other sectors of the political economy, nor did it suddenly and catastrophically transform the rhythm of life and work for a majority of the population.

Nevertheless, industrial production expanded steadily, if not dramatically, within a capitalist framework. Most enterprises were of modest size and could be found in numerous regions of France: Alsace, the north, Normandy, the Nivernais, the Aveyron, Languedoc, the Lyonnais, and the Saint-Étienne basin. Textiles, metallurgy, and mining predominated. All such enterprises (and there were some large ones among them) extended the domain of capitalist production as they multiplied. French capitalism did not wait for industry to give it life, but industry gave to capitalism new energy. Thus, although France had not become fully industrialized and although industry made its initial impact regionally, rather than nationally, capitalist productive relations came to dominate important sectors of social and economic life.[2]

Contemporary observers of the French scene between 1815 and 1850 confirmed that capitalist social relations had encroached upon traditional society and, in the process, that definite social classes had formed. Jean Sismondi and Alexis de Tocqueville expressed, for different reasons, hostility to and trenchant criticism of the new order. Others, like Saint-Armand Bazard and Lorenz von Stein, accepted its implications and attempted to provide a tough ideological discipline in the form of sociology—the "new science of society." Still others reacted hysterically. Saint-Marc Girardin in 1831 likened the revolutionary workers of Lyon to "Tartar barbarians" sweeping westward from the steppes of central Asia to engulf all civilization. None of these men had any doubt that progressive industrialization would strengthen French capitalism as well as deepen class antagonisms. Yet—and here the distinction between a social system and a technological transformation becomes evident—none of them witnessed a French industrial revolution, for the simple reason that it did not happen.[3]

Michel Chevalier, entrepreneur, Saint-Simonian, and future economic adviser to Napoleon III, sketched his own perception of France's class structure. He wrote in 1835 that "it is universally recognized that the middle class rules in France." This "bourgeoisie" consisted of "ac-

2. Industrial development up to 1850 and the rise of credit institutions are covered well in Arthur Dunham, *The Industrial Revolution in France, 1815–1848* (New York: Exposition University Books, 1955); Rondo Cameron, *France and the Economic Development of Europe, 1800–1914* (Princeton: Princeton University Press, 1961); Maurice Lévy-Leboyer, *Les Banques européennes et l'industrialisation dans la première moitié du xix siècle* (Paris: S.E.V.P.E.N., 1965); Bertrand Gille, *La Banque et le crédit en France, 1815–1848* (Paris: Presses universitaires de France, 1952); Henri Sée, *Histoire économique de la France* (2 vols.; Paris: Colin, 1951); Guy Thuillier, *Aspects de l'économie nivernaise au xix siècle* (Paris: Colin, 1966); Paul Leuilliot, *L'Alsace au début du xix siècle* (3 vols.; Paris: S.E.V.P.E.N., 1959), II; and, on a more specialized level, Claude Zarka, "Un exemple de pôle de croissance: L'Industrie textile du Nord de la France, 1830–1870," *Revue économique* (1958), 65–106.

3. Jean Sismondi, *Nouveaux principes d'économie politique* (Paris: Rignoux, 1819); Alexis de Tocqueville, *Recollections* (Cleveland and New York: World, 1960); Daniel Halévy and Céléstin Bouglé, *La Doctrine saint-simonienne: L'Exposition de 1829* (Paris: Rivière, 1925); Lorenz von Stein, *History of the Social Movement in France from 1789 to Our Own Time* (New York: Bedminster Press, 1960); the quote from Girardin is from the *Journal des débats*, December 8, 1831, quoted in Jean Bruhat, *Histoire du mouvement ouvrier français* (Paris: Editions sociales, 1962), 243.

tive" producers, manufacturers, and farmers. Chevalier recognized another kind of bourgeois, one who exists "without active employment" and who "derives an income from his estates by rent or sharing the produce with the cultivator without attempting to increase it." Finally, his comment on the state of the working classes was terse: "The laborers are nothing."[4]

Class polarization did not, in fact, occur with such stark suddenness. French society consisted of a much more complex mixture that was to endure even in the face of advancing capitalist industrial production. Capitalist property, even if it appeared to be the wave of the future, coexisted with large sectors of an economy organized on the basis of private property, especially in rural France. Chevalier himself recognized, in passing, "mechanics and small proprietors," adding that their increasing numbers followed the growth of the bourgeoisie.[5]

Cultural and ideological elements added to the diversity. Joseph Schumpeter, properly rejecting a strictly economic determinist definition of class, views class identity and class relationships in broader terms:

A class is aware of its identity as a whole, sublimates itself as such, has its own peculiar life and characteristic "spirit. . . ." Class members behave toward one another in a fashion characteristically different from their conduct toward members of other classes. They are in closer association with one another; they understand one another better; they work more readily in concert; they close ranks and erect barriers against the outside; they look out into the same segment of the world, with the same eyes, from the same viewpoint, in the same direction.

Schumpeter adds another observation that is particularly relevant: "It is common for nonmembers of a class to work with and on behalf of that class, especially in a political sense, while members of a class may actually work against it."[6] Hence, persons belong to a class as a

4. Michel Chevalier, *Society, Manners, and Politics in the United States: Letters from North America* (Ithaca: Cornell University Press, 1969), 380–82.
5. *Ibid.*, 382.
6. Joseph Schumpeter, *Imperialism, and Social Classes* (Cleveland and New York: World, 1955), 107, 110.

function of their social relations with other persons, not as a reflex of social origins or as a function of narrow economic relationships.

A class of industrial capitalists appeared simultaneously with the development of capitalist production. Its importance before mid-century can easily be overstated, but its impact, particularly regarding class formation, cannot be discounted. The most striking development of this period, to take one observation (that of Robert Nisbet), consisted of the rapid expansion of "an industrial bourgeoisie" that steadily asserted its dominance in society. The French experience did not constitute an exception to this general tendency, only a variation on it in terms of scope and pace. Jean Bouvier calls attention to the hegemonic ambitions of the French bourgeoisie to organize the total victory of capitalism by propagating *"for all of society"* an ideological system consistent with its own outlook. Those hegemonic ambitions manifested themselves most obviously among industrial bourgeois, who confronted workers on the one hand and the "old" financial bourgeoisie on the other.[7]

The political consequences of such a position first became apparent in 1848, when the industrial bourgeoisie made its maiden voyage into politics. Its first assault against the entrenched bourgeois notables ended in a defeat in which the republicans (as they now called themselves) were indeed accomplices. Faced with the challenge from below —the first bout of class warfare—the republicans preferred to scuttle the democratic Republic in favor of a Bonapartist dictatorship. (We should recall in this connection that Louis Napoleon won election to the presidency of the Second Republic on a program reaffirming "republican order.") To explain this sudden transformation we need only recall that the industrial bourgeoisie was relatively weak and scattered and, as a class, unsure of itself as an independent political force. Its brief opportunistic romance with workers in the February days sealed off any solid alliance with petty producers. Its principal interest, and its only course, consisted of defending capitalist social

7. Robert Nisbet, *The Sociological Tradition* (New York: Basic Books, 1966), 22, 26, 58, 179–81; Jean Bouvier, *Histoire sociale et histoire économique* (Geneva: Droz, 1968), 32–33.

relations. Thus, the bourgeoisie's weakness propelled it toward the Party of Order and, ultimately, into the arms of Bonaparte. "Radical" republicanism constituted a risk that the bourgeoisie could not afford to take.[8]

A generation passed, and within that time the bourgeois position in society became immensely strengthened. During two decades of imperial rule, France's industrial development entered its most dynamic phase. An enlarged and transformed banking system led the way, making its heaviest impact in the construction of the second (main line) railway network. Heavy industry and textiles also flourished. A national market appeared in outline. Within this market the previously established base of capitalist industrial, commercial, and agricultural property underwent significant expansion. An enlarged bourgeoisie emerged whose dependence upon the Empire's program of capital accumulation and essential public works decreased as its own economic position became consolidated.[9]

By the mid-1860s, when economic crisis forced a recasting of political positions, especially in commercial policy and social policy,

8. Marx's two essays, *The Class Struggle in France* (many editions) and *The Eighteenth Brumaire of Louis Bonaparte* (many editions), remain classics of political and social analysis. See also André-Jean Tudesq, *Les Grands notables en France, 1840–1849* (2 vols.; Paris: Presses Universitaires de France, 1964), II, and Philippe Vigier, *La Région alpine pendant la seconde république* (2 vols.; Paris: Presses universitaires de France, 1963). A host of local studies may be found in the several series of the Bibliothèque de la révolution de 1848.

9. A synthesis of French economic development under the Second Empire and beyond to the end of the century awaits its historian. Meanwhile, there are many specialized works, including Claude Fohlen, *L'Industrie textile au temps du second empire* (Paris: Plon, 1956); Louis Girard, *La Politique des travaux publics du second empire* (Paris: Colin, 1951); Georges Duveau, *La Vie ouvrière en France sous le second empire* (Paris: Gallimard, 1946), Chap. 1; A. Turgan, *L'Industrie en France* (10 vols.; Paris, 1862–74); Émile Levasseur, *Histoire de l'industrie et de la classe ouvrière en France, 1814–1870* (Paris: Rousseau, 1901); Bertrand Gille, *La Sidérurgie française au xix siècle* (Geneva: Droz, 1968); Jean Bouvier et al., *Le Mouvement du profit en France au xix siècle* (Paris: Mouton, 1965); Rondo Cameron (ed.), *Essays in French Economic History* (Homewood, Ill.: Irwin, 1970), 201–370; Tom Kemp, *Economic Forces in French History* (London: Dobson, 1971); Maurice Lévy-Leboyer, "La Croissance économique en France au xix siècle," *Annales: E.S.C.*, No. 4 (July-August, 1968), 788–808; Pierre Léon, "L'Industrialisation de la France en tant de facteur de croissance économique du début du xviii siècle à nos jours," *Première conférence internationale d'histoire économique: Contributions* (The Hague: Mouton, 1960), 163–205; and, finally, the several quantitative studies of Markovitch, Marczewski, and Toutain published in the *Cahiers de l'Institut de science économique appliquée* (Paris: I.S.E.A., 1960–65).

the regime's unwillingness to broaden its base to include provincial industrialists, its continued support of financial privilege and monopoly, and its active courting of workers appeared—from the perspective of the industrial bourgeoisie—to constitute a menace to a stable social order. Class interest and political commitment fused. What I will henceforth call the "republican bourgeoisie" emerged as a distinct sociopolitical movement in opposition to the Empire. These republican bourgeois included both figures active in various aspects of capitalist production and their spokesmen in the public arena. At times, the two combine in the same person, as was the case with Jules Ferry of Saint-Dié, Nicholas Claude of Épinal, Jules Siegfried and Félix Faure of Le Havre, Pierre Dorian of Saint-Étienne, Joseph Magnin of Dijon, Jules Deregnaucourt of Roubaix, and many others of lesser fame.

By 1868 the signs multiplied that the Bonapartist political structure had lost its power and its flexibility. The regime depended upon mass peasant support to produce its huge quinquennial electoral pluralities, but its promotion of capitalist industry generated alien and disruptive forces that intruded into the traditional world of petty production. The question that remained was not if, but when the authoritarian Empire would give way to some form of constitutional system. That happened quickly. In 1869 the "liberal Empire" made its debut, characterized by a more independent legislature with serious controls over the budget. During that same year, legislative elections brought out a strengthened opposition that exposed the weakness of the imperial political apparatus. The established opposition, formed originally in 1863, was dominated by political figures known as "Orleanists," a label that reflected less their attachment to the cadet branch of the Bourbons than a direct affiliation to the big financial bourgeoisie that had shared power under Louis-Philippe's umbrella. Their commitment to constitutional government, however, remained questionable, since many had collaborated with the Bonapartist regime and had profited handsomely from the association.[10]

10. Theodore Zeldin, *The Political System of Napoleon III* (Oxford: Clarendon Press, 1960); Robert Schnerb, *Rouher et le second empire* (Paris, 1938); Jean Lhomme,

The republican opposition possessed more impressive credentials to receive the legacy of political power. The republicans, like the Orleanists, represented a fraction of the French bourgeoisie, but, unlike the Orleanists, accepted an ideology that emphasized democratic, egalitarian, and secular values. They had no quarrels with the prevailing socioeconomic order and subsequently demonstrated that their rule, rather than that of the Empire, promised the stabilization of that order. The imperial regime had given birth to the forces of popular government which were incompatible with its own continued existence.

The advance of capitalism not only created the conditions for expanded entrepreneurship, but also tended to raise the degree of industrial concentration and to accelerate the growth of the proletariat. Both these consequences of industrial expansion, successfully obscured during the heyday of plebiscitary democracy, threatened the security of petty producers who feared for the liquidation of their greengrocer's paradise. Consequently the republican bourgeoisie, if it intended to grasp command of political power, was forced to take into account the world of petty production, whose interests opposed its own, but with whom a political alliance was essential.

An alliance of industrial capitalists, substantial farmers, and petty producers suggests a complex social movement that embraced classes and fractions of classes. Clearly, such an alliance held within it traps and dangers. The leadership of the republican movement had a distinct bourgeois coloration and spoke in unmistakable bourgeois accents. Nevertheless, that leadership formulated ideological positions that produced sympathetic vibrations among petty producers. Republicans managed to resolve the difficulties of their position by appeals to equality, property (of all sorts), and entrepreneurial freedom—all of which appeared to promise opportunity to energetic capitalists and security to small producers. To consolidate their political alliances and yet remain true to their own interests, bourgeois republicans were forced to mark out a narrow path between defense of the capitalist

---

La Grande bourgeoisie au pouvoir (Paris: Presses universitaires de France, 1960); and, for a further economic picture, Jean Bouvier, *Le Crédit lyonnais: Les Années de formation d'une banque de dépôts, 1863–1882* (2 vols.; Paris: S.E.V.P.E.N., 1961).

order and radical criticism of its current political constitution. They succeeded, where they had failed in 1848, because a secure industrial base and a strong sense of purpose permitted them to mobilize a "radical" political movment without fear of losing control of it. Similarly, they had no use for "the man on horseback" and his peasant multitudes. A broad-based political movement, with a solid class core, could contend for power on its own terms. It is a measure of the strength and the vision of the republican bourgeoisie that such moderate men of order seized the opportunity to turn the movement for egalitarian democracy into a stable bourgeois system fortified against both aristocratic reaction and social revolution.

I do not mean to imply that these "moderate men of order" used the movement for egalitarian democracy cynically and in violation of their own deeply felt principles. No doubt some did. Nor do I call for approval of those principles and the class perspective from which they sprang. Within the French bourgeoisie, as within other bourgeoisies, we can locate numerous examples of political radicalism closely associated with the most fervent pursuit of capitalist profit. Frequently, the latter was a condition of the former. Radical democracy and capitalist production, under certain conditions and at certain times, have not been mutually exclusive. We need only recall similar events elsewhere during the same period as recounted by such scholars as Bernard Semmel for Britain, Robert Sharkey for the United States, Giuliano Procacci for Italy, and C. A. M. Hennessy for Spain.[11]

Bonaparte's sudden collapse following the disaster at Sedan created a temporary political vacuum. In the time-honored manner, the politicians proclaimed the Republic from the balcony of the Hôtel de Ville in Paris to the cheers of the assembled throng. Many waved red flags. They were to return later in greater force to establish the Commune. In the meantime, however, the decisive action occurred elsewhere. A

---

11. Bernard Semmel, *The Rise of Free Trade Imperialism* (Cambridge: Cambridge University Press, 1970); Robert Sharkey, *Money, Class, and Party* (Baltimore: Johns Hopkins University Press, 1959); Giuliano Procacci, *History of the Italian People* (New York: Harper and Row, 1972); C. A. M. Hennessy, *The Federal Republic in Spain* (Oxford: Clarendon Press, 1962).

Government of National Defense, hastily organized, took command of the political machinery of the state. While some of its members remained in Paris to attempt to head off the impending uprising of workers, the majority, led by Léon Gambetta, established the government's operating headquarters in unoccupied territory—first in Tours and then, as the Prussian army approached the Loire, in Bordeaux. Initially, they were mostly preoccupied with organizing the defense of France, a lost cause, as they came to recognize. More and more, during the winter of 1870–1871, the provisional republican leadership turned its attention to establishing the provincial bases for the republican movement. Many who had laid the foundations for, in Henri Allain-Targé's words, the "Republic under the Empire," devoted themselves to this effort.[12]

National elections held in February, 1871, brought out of the backwoods men with vague monarchist inclinations. Their views separated them from the mass of the people who had sent them to Versailles only to put an end to the war with Prussia. The monarchists, however, remained for four years, much to their own surprise. Despite their royalist sympathies, they made Adolphe Thiers provisional President of the Republic. Thiers had impeccable credentials as a man of order. His name had been cursed in the working-class quarters of Lyon since 1834, and in May, 1871, he surpassed himself in organizing the slaughter of the Communards. While Thiers was engaged in that task, the leaders of the republican bourgeoisie remained, for the most part, silent. During his two years in power, Thiers presided over the steady political advance of the republicans and moved toward an alliance with them. For that reason, he was overthrown in May, 1873, and replaced by Marshal Patrice MacMahon.

During the four years that France functioned without a formal constitution, the possibility of a royalist restoration was widely debated. In fact, the installation of MacMahon in power sealed off the possi-

12. Henri Allain-Targé, *La République sous l'empire: Lettres, 1864–1870* (Paris: Grasset, 1939); Daniel Halévy and Émile Pillias (eds.), *Lettres de Gambetta, 1868–1882* (Paris: Grasset, 1938); J. P. T. Bury, *Gambetta and the National Defense* (London: Longman, 1936); H. Stannard, *Gambetta* (London: Methuen, 1921). Other references will be found in the notes to Chapter I.

bility. That may seem paradoxical since he drew his support from Orleanists, headed by the prime minister, Duc Albert de Broglie. However, "Orleanist" stood for the established financial bourgeoisie, whose members expected to establish the rule of their faction and had no need of divine right to legitimate their pursuit of power. Beau de Loménie and Arthur Loth, in their books on the restoration that never happened, go so far as to assert that the Orleanist bourgeoisie sabotaged the efforts of the serious monarchists.[13] The Orleanists need not have bothered. There were a few dozen deputies in the Assembly, members of the Réunion des reservoirs, who openly boasted of their intention of installing the Bourbon pretender, the Comte de Chambord, on the throne as Henri V. They, however, constituted a general staff without troops. In any event, Chambord refused to claim his inheritance except on his own terms, insisting specifically that he could not reign under the *tricolore* of the Revolution. No settlement was acceptable to him unless the lilies of the Bourbons were adopted as the national standard. While the various deputies of the royalist right negotiated frantically between Chambord and his cousin, the Comte de Paris, the former remained inflexibly bound to his principles. He made several trips to France from his château in Austria. After the last of them, in the spring of 1873, Chambord saw no chance for a restoration. He recognized that he did not belong in bourgeois France and, to his credit, recognized that fact before any of his supporters.

Although royalism as a political force died in 1873, the republicans made considerable capital out of the whole affair (see Chapter II). Also, the agitation helps to account for the relative sterility of national politics between 1871 and 1875 and for the feeling of general exhaustion and relief that greeted the final ratification of the constitutional laws of 1875. Not that those years passed without some productive activity: military reform was undertaken; the German indemnity was paid off eighteen months ahead of schedule; the bureau-

13. E. Beau de Loménie, *La Restauration manquée* (Paris: Editions des portiques, 1932); Arthur Loth, *L'Echèc de la restauration monarchique* (Paris: Perrin, 1910); René Rémond, in *La Droite en France de 1815 à nos jours* (Paris: Aubier, 1954), makes a dubious case for including the monarchist movement in the general category of right-wing political sects.

cracy submitted to much-needed streamlining and rationalization; and the competence of local government bodies was expanded.

Thiers' two years in power and MacMahon's succession were marked by a series of extraordinary episodes of Byzantine parliamentary politics as various factions (we can hardly call them parties) maneuvered for position. The narratives of Frank Brabant, Émile de Marcère, Anatole Claveau, and Gabriel Hanotaux cover that ground well. Yet, curiously enough, few historians, with the exception of Daniel Halévy, have noticed that during Thiers' administration and that of MacMahon up to 1875 the republican bourgeoisie made steady advances toward eventual national power.[14] The lesson to be learned is that a focus on the Paris-Versailles nexus can obscure our vision, for it diverts attention from events in the provinces that helped shape the character of the Republic. A series of by-elections took place between July, 1871, and 1874. We will examine several representative ones in Chapter II. They demonstrated that the "monarchists," of whatever complexion, did not faithfully represent the popular will. Such monarchists as remained miraculously transformed themselves into "conservatives" and "men of order," thus explicitly recognizing the existence of the Republic and doing battle against the republicans on the latter's chosen terrain. The net effect of these elections was progressively to strengthen the republican movement and prepare for its assumption of national power once the opportunity presented itself.

Two major consequences followed from this series of elections. First, the republican bourgeoisie made impressive gains in recruiting the masses of rural petty producers to their ranks. This followed directly from the campaign of 1869, in which the leading republicans constructed an ideological case for the solidarity of capitalist property and

14. Frank Brabant, *The Beginning of the Third Republic in France* (London: Macmillan, 1940); Émile de Marcère, *L'Assembleé nationale de 1871* (Paris: Plon, 1904) and *Histoire de la république, 1873–1879* (2 vols.; Paris: Plon, 1908–10); Gabriel Hanotaux, *Histoire de la fondation de la troisième république* (2 vols.; Paris: Plon, 1925–26); Anatole Claveau, *Souvenirs politiques et parlementaires d'un témoin* (2 vols.; Paris: Plon, 1913–14); Daniel Halévy, *La Fin des notables* (Paris: Grasset, 1930) and *La République des ducs* (Paris: Grasset, 1937); Roger Winnacker, "French Elections of 1871," *Papers of the Michigan Academy of Science, Arts, and Letters*, XXII (1936), 477–83.

other private property. Chapter I explores in detail what I call this "democratic myth." It proved to be a formidable weapon against aristocratic reaction on the right and independent workers' movements on the left.

Second, the politics of the early and mid-1870s defined the republican coalition as a party of both "movement" and "order." Here I borrow François Goguel's terminology but reject his rigid separation of movement and order in a synchronic model.[15] The republicans clearly stood for movement insofar as republican social ideology incorporated elements of egalitarian democracy, emphasized industrial development, and promoted the institution of the secular state. But the republicans presented themselves as a party of order as well, for they represented specific class interests and the defense of the prevailing social order, while providing the opportunities for its expansion and fulfillment in a stable system insulated against shocks from either the right or the left. During these early years of the Republic, the right appeared to present the more serious threat; thus the savage struggles associated with the *seize mai* crisis. Later they turned their attention to the rise of the workers' movement and successfully blunted its edge.

The constitutional laws of 1875 gave the Republic its legal and institutional framework, but did not specify who would rule or under what conditions. The determination of that question dominated political struggles for the next two years, but consolidation of republican strength in the provinces already had virtually settled the question.

National elections in 1876 produced a republican majority. However, MacMahon, with the old established financial bourgeoisie at his side, struggled to stem the republican tide. In May, 1877, he dismissed the republican government of Jules Simon, thus precipitating the famous *seize mai* crisis. Strictly speaking, MacMahon had the constitutional power to dismiss Simon's cabinet despite its support by a parliamentary majority. But the republicans were not prepared to be charitable on constitutional grounds. In June they mobilized 363 of their number to vote "no confidence" in the Duc de Broglie, Simon's successor. MacMahon's coup not only threatened the republicans' po-

15. Goguel, *La Politique des partis*.

litical position, but, because the events of the *seize mai* were inter-
woven with the intraclass struggle of financial and industrial capital,
larger stakes were at issue.[16]

The character of the intraclass struggle will be examined in a
study of the confrontation over a national railroad policy, which precipitated the political crisis of the *seize mai* (Chapters III and IV).
The railroad question pitted the interests of the republican bourgeoisie, representing industrial and agrarian capital, against those of the
financial bourgeoisie. The specific point of conflict focused on whether
the latter's control of the six major railroad companies would be maintained, thereby stifling expansion of the national market. This was not
just a question of business, in the narrowest terms. The ideological
edifice of the republicans threatened to crumble should they prove unable to deliver the social and economic goods. Successful resolution of
the issue in favor of national industrial interests provided the opportunity for expanded production to serve a broader domestic market.
Further, the development of new rail lines strengthened the bonds between the world of petty production and the major centers of capitalist
production. This tended to complement the political alliance of the
two groups (which had made possible the defeat of the bankers in the
first place) while exposing the ascendancy of industrial capital and
the continued strength of the financial bourgeoisie's economic position; this was something the republicans had accepted once they had
broken the bankers politically.

The political defeat of the financial bourgeoisie paved the way for
the elaboration and execution of the Freycinet Plan, a comprehensive
public works program, the core of which was the completion of the
French railway network and the consequent consolidation of the national market.[17] However, rails alone did not suffice to give social

16. The *seize mai* and subsequent events are all treated, to varying degrees, in
the general works cited above. The only useful account of the politics of the *seize mai*
is Fresnette Pisani-Ferry, *Le Coup d'etat manqué du 16 mai 1877* (Paris: Grasset, 1965).
17. A recent article, which I came across after finishing this book, confirms in all
important respects what I said about the Freycinet Plan and adds the point that the
plan should be viewed in the context of the general economic crisis: Y. Gonjo, "Le 'Plan
Freycinet,' 1878–1882: Un Aspect de la 'grande depression' économique en France,"
Revue historique, CCXLVIII (July-September, 1972), 49–86.

cohesion to that market. National educational reform took the process one step further.

Republican bourgeois wanted not only free access to the national market. They also demanded the security that comes only when the mass of the population, regardless of class, accepts the established social order. Education, fashioned in the mold of bourgeois ideological values, effectively served that purpose. The establishment of universal secular primary education in 1884 marked the culmination of nearly two decades of effort by industrialists, prosperous farmers, and their spokesmen, who constituted the core of the republican bourgeoisie. Just as they fought to forge the iron and steel sinews of a national economic system, they exerted equal energy to develop educational weapons to reinforce ideologically their conquest of social power (Chapter V). The frequency with which railroad and educational reform were linked together and the similarity in the justifications for each provide a striking illustration of the principal concerns of the republican bourgeoisie: national solidarity and the neutralization of class antagonism. Universal education promised to provide the necessary mobility—to pave the way for entrepreneurial freedom—that constituted the heart of the "democratic myth." Beyond that, the positivist ideology of solidarity embedded in educational theory and practice raised duties above rights and opposed common citizenship to class identity. Secular education thus fitted perfectly the interests of a class of industrialists. Its twin emphases on practical training and loyalty to the Republic and the social order for which it stood placed in the hands of the republican bourgeoisie potent weapons to enforce its ideological hegemony.

Developments on other fronts exposed both the importance and the fragility of the republican alliance of capitalists and small producers. The world economic crisis had made its initial impact on French production by 1877. French industrialists began to campaign for tariff protection and worked hard to make the cause of protection a national republican cause. They made certain limited gains by 1881 but could not push through their entire program. Small producers cared less about the rate of profit than about the price of commodities. The republican bourgeoisie chose not to break up the coalition on this issue. Instead it sought refuge in further efforts to discipline the working class and integrate it into the republican system, thereby keeping the factories busy and the streets peaceful. The methods employed were by no means entirely repressive. Republicans recognized the advantages in agreeing to allow workers the legal right to associate before the workers took it for themselves. The consequent legislation of 1884 was designed to associate workers in a common effort with employers to develop national production and to limit the number of potential recruits for the war of labor against capital (Chapter VI).

Imperial expansion added yet another foundation stone for the Republic to rest on. It united those whom the campaign for protection had divided. Building on the initiatives of previous regimes, successive republican governments expanded the French empire in North Africa, in West Africa, and in the Far East. French imperialism, like that of other countries, was a bourgeois enterprise. However, it quickly became a national endeavor and was presented as essential to the very survival of the Republic itself. Although imperial policy thrust outward from the metropolis, its success hinged on its practical and ideological benefits for the domestic social order: hence, my use of the term "social imperialism" (Chapter VII). Fundamental unity of purpose behind the pursuit of empire did not exclude the emergence of different points of view that reflected different economic concerns. Industrialists for the most part linked empire to an expanded protected market. They joined forces with elements of the financial bourgeoisie to promote capital export. France also had its free-trade imperialists, but, aside from bankers, port merchants, and manufacturers of export products, these imperialists were of a curious variety. They came from the ranks of left-wing democrats (*démocrates avancés*) and combined the most outspoken domestic radicalism with strident appeals to chauvinism and imperialism. Ironically, these "radical democrats" and their once-hated *haut bourgeois* antagonists found themselves in the same camp. Again we witness the spectacle of the intersection of radical politics and bourgeois interests.

Less than a decade separated the republican triumph of 1877 from the formulation and execution of these social and economic policies. Yet, the ground had been well prepared. Thus, the late 1860s and the early 1870s may be viewed as years of preparation, whereas the half-dozen years following the *seize mai* were years of consolidation and stabilization. Those latter years witnessed the movement onto the national stage of men who dominated French political life for the subsequent two decades and who laid the foundations for the republican social and ideological order: Jules Ferry, Charles de Freycinet, René Waldeck-Rousseau, Maurice Rouvier, Henri Brisson, Félix Faure, Sadi Carnot, Charles Floquet, and the dozens of local political leaders whose anonymity should not shroud their importance. Although some called themselves radicals and others, opportunists or conservatives, they shared a fundamental class outlook and consolidated the coalition of capitalists and petty producers that stood at the heart of the Republic.

Chapter I

⟦ *The Republican Revolution*

TWO REVOLUTIONS occurred in France during the transition from the Second Empire to the Third Republic. One, the violent social upheaval of the Commune that was drowned in blood in May, 1871, has become the object of much historical study and the source, for better or worse, of socialist myths and hopes. Without in any way slighting the importance of the Commune, this chapter will have little to say about it. Its course and outcome did not divert the main currents of republican social and ideological development. Republican attitudes toward the "social question" become brutally clear before the terrible events of May, 1871.

The other revolution, which I call the republican revolution, brought forth the Republic from the ruins of the Empire. The struggles that attended its birth should be understood as the political manifestations of the tensions imbedded in the making of French bourgeois society. The use of the term revolution in this second context carries with it a good deal of ambiguity and a certain amount of irony; for the revolution fashioned by the republicans, though no mere change of regime, did not challenge the fundamental social relations governing French society. Indeed, it grew out of and confirmed those relations and, in the process, stifled the social revolution. The republicans preempted the revolution, organized it, and set its limits. They could not have done so had they not acted from a firm foundation of capitalist and private property that had been consolidated during the waning years of the Second Empire. The political positions taken by the republicans not only marked off the boundary between themselves and the imperial regime, but also described the social and ideological limits within which the Republic evolved.

Every political movement has its proper moment. Its characteristics are shaped according to the interests, perceptions, and culture of those who march under its banner. Thus it was with the republicans, the ideological content of whose program reflected their position in a changing society. In this sense, the Republic grew from the ground up and awaited only formal recognition of its existence. The crisis of the Empire provided that opportunity. The subsequent crusade for democratic liberty, expressed in ideological terms, challenged the regime on economic and social issues: credit, taxes, public works, industrial and financial monopolies. Whatever the appearance of the debate and however radical the rhetoric, the fundamental nature of the economy rarely came under attack. Bourgeois class rule did not disappear with the Empire. Quite the contrary, it widened and became more securely established under the Republic.

Let us look closely at some of those issues and at the ideological context within which they emerged. We will discover that the republicans did not indulge themselves merely in political opposition, but articulated an alternative social program that bore their distinct stamp and struck deeply into the heart of France—a new France, in many ways, thanks to the efforts of the previous regime. The story will proceed along two paths that repeatedly cross: ideological statement and social action.

The Republic Under the Empire

Before, during, and after the election campaign of 1869, the opposition's attack on Napoleon III translated into personal terms what was in fact an assault against the entrenched fiscal-economic system.[1] In

1. The recent appearance of a number of local and regional studies by French scholars now makes possible a comprehensive view of the political scene in the late 1860s. *Cf.* René Amanieu, "Hommes et suffrages dans deux cantons toulousains en 1869," *Revue d'histoire économique et sociale,* XLI (1963), 183–212; André Armengaud, *Les Populations de l'Est-Aquitaine au début de l'époque contemporaine* (The Hague:

this way the republican bourgeoisie maintained a broad national coalition of capitalists, petty producers, and peasants. Insisting that their alliance purposely cut across classes, the republicans repeatedly warned of the dangers of class polarization. They argued that capitalist concentration, of which they were the chief beneficiaries, disrupted a comfortable balance of social classes. While among the upper classes "luxury abounded without restraint or limit . . . misery ruled below." They pointed to an emerging confrontation of "two enemy nations" and an explosive "class antagonism."[2] Political democracy promised a solution within the framework of the existing political economy. "There is no question of equalizing wealth; we must only narrow the gaps so as to give everyone the chance to escape misery and to put within reach of everyone an existence of modest comfort."[3] The realization of this ideal carried with it a democratic imperative, as Eugène Pelletan pointed out: "the right of the worker and farmer to enjoy the effective and inalienable exercise of power."[4]

Henri Allain-Targé's pamphlet, *Les Déficits,* set the tone for republican ideology, pointed to the elaboration of a coherent republican social policy, and defined the process by which "class antagonism" would be smothered. Allain-Targé's polemic against imperial fiscal policy denied the possibility of future prosperity without radical political change. The Empire had originally fulfilled a necessary function as the mainspring of growth, but in its declining years had degenerated

Mouton, 1961), Pt. 3, Chap. 5; André Brandt and Paul Leuilliot, "Les Elections à Mulhouse en 1869," *Revue d'Alsace,* XCIX (1960), 104–28; Joseph Decheneau, "Les Elections de 1869 dans le département de la Maine-et-Loire" (Diplôme d'études supérieures, Université de Poitiers, 1958); Louis Girard (ed.), *Les Elections de 1869* (Paris: Rivière, 1960); Paul Guichonnet, "Jules Favre et la bataille pour les élections de 1869 en Haute-Savoie," *Cahiers d'histoire,* I (1956), 65–102; Paul Leuilliot, "Politique et religion: Les Élections alsaciennes de 1869," *Revue d'Alsace,* C (1961), 67–101; Jacques Lovie, *La Savoie dans la vie française de 1860 à 1875* (Paris: Presses universitaires de France, 1963); Robert Marlin, "Les Elections législatives de 1869 dans le Doubs," *Cahiers d'histoire,* VII (1962), 65–83; J. Merley, "Les Elections de 1869 dans la Loire," *Cahiers d'histoire,* VI (1961), 59–93; Robert Vandenbussche, "Aspects de l'histoire politique du radicalisme dans le département du Nord, 1870–1905," *Revue du Nord,* XLVII (April-June, 1965), 223–69.
2. Eugène Spuller, *Histoire de Napoléon III* (Paris: Chevalier, 1872), 13.
3. Léonce Ribert, *La Gauche, la situation, le programme démocratique* (Paris: Chevalier, 1869), 73.
4. Quoted by the attorney general of Nîmes in a report to the minister of justice, December 19, 1868, in BB (18) 1795, Archives nationales, hereinafter cited as AN.

into a holding company for special interests. Much of the progress produced by "free and honest labor" in the 1850s had been wiped out by the "wild speculation" of the succeeding decade. In its wake, this speculation left an enormous state debt financed by periodic orgies of massive borrowing which, as he wrote in another place, "devours the future after having chewed up the present."[5] Only the upper stratum of the bourgeoisie profited from this state of affairs, appropriating a share of the national wealth grossly out of proportion to its numbers. Thus, although the Empire provided the material means by which prosperity was available to all, its political and economic authoritarianism denied popular access to power. Interposed between the people and the productive resources of the nation, the Empire, surrounded by the church and the big bourgeoisie, had forfeited its legitimacy.

Following his thoughts on the state of fiscal affairs, Allain-Targé extended his view to embrace the entire political economy. He formulated a democratic myth that illuminated a particular perception of the world. Central to this theme was the notion that the perpetuation of a narrow, class-oriented economic policy raised the long-term threat of social disintegration and, its inevitable consequence, internal violence.

The stabilization of an equitable social order, Allain-Targé went on, required the infusion of political liberty into a body politic drained of vitality during twenty years of dictatorship. The establishment of liberty, in the halls of the legislature and in the marketplace, would clear the way for the pursuit of justice and equality. He held up the experience of the United States as proof of his assertion, for it was generally agreed that there "political equality" produced "order and prosperity." Allain-Targé introduced a solidarist and socially conservative conception of the Republic in unmistakable terms. At the root of democratic institutions, providing the indispensable nourishment and greatest strength, was the "union of the bourgeoisie and the people." The justification for democracy lay in its built-in barrier to class struggle and social disintegration. The creation of "a society of equals, of

5. Henri Allain-Targé, *Les Déficits* (Paris: Chevalier, 1868), 24, and *Revue politique*, June 27, 1868, p. 63.

free citizens," would provide the opportunity for honest men "to gather their savings and acquire property—which is the aim of all who labor." Braced by this declaration of faith, Allain-Targé projected a lyrical vision of a Republic bound up in the solidarity of "men from every background and from all walks of life" united "under the common flag."[6]

For that reason he attacked *grand bourgeois* oligarchs whose vision did not extend beyond their short-range interests. He recognized that social politics that stifled freedom, mobility, and opportunity carried within it the sources of national liquidation:

The bourgeoisie which has dominated society by its yoke of servile and insolent bureaucrats, on a solid base of military authority and the absolute ignorance of the greatest number, this bourgeoisie resists our efforts. It does not want to lose its privilege. It wants to retain its electoral monopoly, —it does not want free and *serious* education which would be open to all: it does not want to exercise power through liberty, but rather prefers to stifle the nation under the administrative centralization from which it derives all of the wealth, the power, and the influence through its alliance with authority.[7]

Allain-Targé thus defended the interests of the bourgeois social order by attacking the big bourgeois-imperial alliance. He condemned the bourgeoisie for refusing to "exercise power through liberty," while his popular perspective with its ideological egalitarianism promised exactly that. For he could not imagine class rule except through liberty. His radicalism, the path of legal revolution, looked for the goals of solidarity and class harmony to be achieved without social revolution— that is, without any upheaval in the arrangement of social relations.

As if concerned that the subtlety of his discussion obscured his main point, Allain-Targé warned of the consequences should the logic of his argument go unappreciated. In the absence of republican institutions to act as a safety valve, violence would surely follow. Who could tell where that would end? "The CLASSES in French society

6. Allain-Targé, *Les Déficits*, 26–27.
7. Henri Allain-Targé, *La République sous l'empire: Lettres, 1864–1870* (Paris: Grasset, 1939), 24–25.

have lived together, side by side, without seeing each other, communicating or interacting ... The bourgeoisie should know that, alongside it, the forces of democracy have grown during the Second Empire. It will find these forces ... so solidly entrenched that it would be crazy to renew war against it." His meaning seems clear enough. The ruling classes should not be shocked to discover that their recapitulation of the tragic errors of the July Monarchy would produce equally tragic results. In order to reinforce his plea for common sense and to soften the threat implicit in it, Allain-Targé discounted the fear that democracy opened the way to revolution. The people "have had time to reflect upon the ideas of 1848. They have abandoned utopias, empiricism, illusions; but in fulfilling their electoral responsibilities, they have become fully aware of its [universal suffrage] essential conservatism as well as its power."[8]

However much Allain-Targé's democratic myth may be put down to wishful thinking, variations on his theme became embedded in republican social gospel. These pronouncements represented the diffusion of bourgeois ideological values throughout the ranks of the middle classes or, in other words, the clothing of liberal ideology in radical garb. The emerging ideology served two purposes. It provided the necessary ideological framework for the political unity of antagonistic elements of the bourgeoisie; it replaced class conflict with the equality of all men in the marketplace by focusing on exchange rather than production as the decisive determinant in the economy.[9]

An anonymous pamphleteer, writing during the hiatus between the collapse of the Empire and the crushing of the Commune, made more explicit what Allain-Targé was getting at. He blamed the immi-

8. Allain-Targé, Les Déficits, 25.
9. A statement from Marx's Grundrisse helps us here: "In these simple forms of the money-relation, all the immanent contradictions of bourgeois society appear extinguished, and that is why bourgeois democrats take refuge within them ... to justify the existing economic relationships. In truth, so long as a commodity of labor is seen only as an exchange-value, and the relations between them are seen only as exchange relations, as equilibration of these exchange-values, then the individuals, the subjects between whom this process takes place, are merely partners in exchange. There is absolutely no formal difference between them. ... Each subject is a partner in exchange; that is, each has the same relation to the other as the other has to it. Thus, as subjects of exchange, their relationship is one of equality." Quoted in Martin Nicolaus, "The Unknown Marx," New Left Review (March-April, 1968), 44, italics in the original.

nent social crisis on previous state intervention into the social question, which hardened class lines rather than obliterated them. He preferred solidarity to antagonism: "The big quarrel between capital and labor is basically only a quarrel over words. The brain power, the force, and the talent which the worker brings to industry constitutes his true capital. There is thus a close relationship between this sort of capital and that which the entrepreneur furnishes." State intervention, in the form of the promotion of monopolies, tended to distend the economy and disrupt the equilibrium of the marketplace. Under the regime of economic liberty, the distribution of products would be equitable and the economy self-balancing. He proposed the maximum freedom to permit association for self-improvement and denied that "workers' associations, people's banks, the association of capital and labor" had any resemblance to "socialist systems." These projects promised an extension of entrepreneurial freedom rather than its limitation. As for workers and small producers, "all that can be done ... is to guarantee the most complete liberty and to abolish the most hateful indirect taxes on consumption goods."[10]

Antoine Malardier, taking the analysis one step further, wrote a pamphlet called *République et socialisme*, in which he demonstrated how the Republic could get along without socialism. He confronted the logic of modernization and its consequences for the small proprietor and worker and produced an ostensibly alternative model for the social order. Recognizing that "small property" was "in danger of being swallowed up by big property," Malardier proposed a marriage of individualism and collectivism. Large enterprises were to be placed under the joint control of owners' and workers' associations. Small

10. *Notes et chiffres concernant l'organisation de la république* (Paris: Chevalier, 1871), 5, 7–11, iv. Along the same lines, Charles Laterrade, in *Le Libre-échange et la démocratie à Bordeaux* (Bordeaux: Lavertujon, 1869), 15, attacked the proponents of free trade as being accomplices of imperial despotism and thus acting against the establishment of a healthy economic climate and entrepreneurial freedom: "Le libre-échange, c'est la libre disposition du fruit de son travail et de ses capitaux. C'est le droit pour chacun d'acheter et de vendre ce qu'il lui plaît, où lui plaît et comme il lui plaît; c'est le droit de se procurer une marchandise quelconque où il lui convient d'acheter, sans avoir à payer chose que le prix de la marchandise librement débattu avec le vendeur, et le frais de transport." Laterrade's outburst suggests less of an attack on free trade than on a laissez-faire devil-take-the-hindmost policy by which the small entrepreneur is left with the hindmost.

enterprises were to be reconstituted along lines recalling a variation of the guild system. These ideas were not startlingly new. Louis Blanc had proposed a similar scheme in the *Organisation du travail*, as had Pierre Joseph Proudhon in his speeches before the National Assembly in 1848. Like the projects of his predecessors, Malardier's plan avoided the hard questions of social relations in an advanced industrial environment. He made a stab at going beyond purely political solutions and balanced on the thin edge separating institutional from social reform. But he hedged his collectivist propositions within a traditional liberal framework, supported by hortatory appeals to moral rearmament. The result, finally, was a retreat to the democratic myth, which, as in the case of Allain-Targé, ultimately served conservative purposes:

DEMOCRATIC-SOCIALIST INSCRIPTIONS

Property
    Every citizen ought to own property
    Every property owner ought to be a citizen
Liberty
    Property guarantees liberty
Religion
    Any nation which delivers its children to clerical education is a nation lost

   . . . .

Education
    Scientific education makes men
    Secular education makes democrats
    Civic education makes citizens
    Rationalist education makes republicans
Labor
    The uniqueness of the personality forms the foundation of all human activity[11]

Defense of individual liberty and private property was the mainspring of what Maurice Hess called "social democracy." As the state delivered the public welfare into private hands so did it suppress individual freedom: "Large stocks of capital, placed at the disposal of

11. Antoine Malardier, *République et socialisme* (Paris: Chevalier, 1870), 7–10, 19.

monopolies, producing profits for the privileged few, always crush individual production, whether of the cooperative sort or not."[12] Instead of expending capital resources to encourage a wider distribution of property and prosperity through the promotion of small, viable enterprises, the government stunted the growth of individual initiative. The Bank of France, the argument went, made no effort to organize the extensive distribution of credit at low interest rates, and the "Crédit foncier and Crédit agricole . . . squander their capital in banking deals and loans to foreign governments, instead of serving agriculture which is in such desperate need."[13] The solution was neither redistribution of wealth nor other comparably drastic schemes of social renovation. A democratic Republic, governed by the representatives of business and agriculture and pledged to low taxes and low expenditures, would suffice: "We must have a thrifty government."[14]

The republican bourgeoisie kept its distance from sweeping programs of social reform. It consciously avoided raising the "social peril" as an overture to a replay of the tragedy of 1848. At that time, as Bernard Lavergne pointed out in 1869, the confusion of the "republican idea" with the "socialist idea" drove farmers and businessmen into the conservative camp.[15] Eugène Spuller made the same point in a self-critical analysis of the Second Republic: The failure of the democratic Republic in 1848 resulted largely from the inability of the politicians who operated in the rarified atmosphere of Paris to consider the *classes moyennes* in the provinces. The republicans in 1848, said Spuller, offered nothing in defense of property and material interests and thus exposed themselves to a conservative counterattack which swept to victory in the imperial dictatorship.[16]

They did not make the same mistake again. At every step of the way republicans declared themselves to be representative of legitimate

---

12. Maurice Hess, *La Haute finance et l'empire* (Paris: Chevalier, 1869), 14.
13. Henri Merlin, *Lettre à un électeur rural: Huit années de politique impériale* (Paris: Chevalier, 1868), 13–14.
14. *Manifeste électorale du comité démocratique de l'arrondissement de Vervais et des cantons de Rozoy et Marle* (Guise, 1869).
15. Quoted in Armengaud, *Les Populations de l'Est-Aquitaine*, 432.
16. Eugène Spuller, *Histoire parlementaire de la séconde république* (Paris: Chevalier, 1868), 16.

authority. Accordingly, they formed the political avant-garde supplied and supported by a broad coalition of urban and rural property owners. They did not form the new party of opposition so much as give it voice. Their moment had arrived, and they knew how to take advantage of it. Revolutionaries of the past had become stanch defenders of order. Conservatives of the past had become revolutionaries. Jules Grévy, campaigning in the Jura, represented himself as the candidate of "order." Grévy accused his Bonapartist opponent of being a "revolutionary." He made the distinction on clearly practical grounds: "You have the choice between the government's candidate and an independent . . . the one, a puppet of the policies which have burdened us with big armies, disastrous adventures, crushing budgets, mindless borrowing . . . the other, a dedicated partisan of policies aimed at cutting down the military and reducing taxes." Allain-Targé carried the democratic message into the region of his birth, the Maine-et-Loire, where he appeared "at once radical and conservative." He transmitted to local businessmen and landowners his conviction that from the "point of view of financial, commercial, and industrial interests . . . only radical democratic solutions henceforth provide true and lasting guarantees."[17]

A composite of these "radical democratic solutions" reveals little more than specific criticism of the existing tax structure and budget. Eugène Pelletan, campaigning in the Midi, dwelt heavily on the iniquities of the tax structure, as did Adolphe Crémieux, Armand Duportal, and Jules Simon.[18] Significantly, these charges were frequently coupled with charges of economic *dirigisme* and active discrimination by the imperial fiscal and public works administration against small producers, businessmen, and industrialists. Edmond Laroche-Joubert, a liberal supported by republicans, won his campaign in the Charente on a program that included abolition of railroad monopolies, elimina-

17. *Tribune française*, August 16, 1868, December 27, 1869.
18. Attorney general of Nîmes to the minister of justice, December 19, 1868, in BB (18) 1795, AN; attorney general of Grenoble to the minister of justice, prefect of the Gironde to the minister of the interior, February 9, 1869, in BB(18) 1795 9803 (a), AN; attorney general of Toulouse to the minister of justice, May 11, 1869, in BB(18) 1795(2) 9803(b), AN.

tion of octrois and indirect taxes, and the establishment of an income tax.[19] While the government continued to favor the interests of big capital, provincial producers mobilized in opposition. In the Doubs, for example, considerable discontent among various kinds of entrepreneurs led to a coalition of local capitalists with the traditionally democratic, even anarchistic, watchmakers. Robert Marlin describes how the former turned this discontent to their political advantage: "If there was not serious misery in the Doubs in 1869, a good deal of discontent, chiefly economic, was distilled and exploited by the industrial bourgeoisie who were driven as much by doctrinal conviction as by material interest, more or less well understood . . . this bourgeoisie, which led the principal assault, accepted even the risk of supporting the small revolutionary party."[20] Their ranks were swelled by the addition of a number of small metallurgical entrepreneurs whose archaic establishments, fueled with charcoal, had failed to maintain a solid position in the market. They had suffered a 50 percent decline in production since 1864.[21] Such experiences denied the expectations of universal prosperity implied in the capitalist adventures of the 1850s.

Specific abuses were cited as evidence of the sabotage of healthy enterprise. A republican newspaper in Gascony exposed in detail how the government had abandoned regulation of the canals of the southwest and sold newly developed waterways to the Péreire interests of the Midi Railroad, which then proceeded to raise the rates on the canals in order to force shippers to use their railroads.[22] Jeanne Gaillard has shown that protests against transportation monopolies had increased in intensity since the late 1850s. The voices of complaint multiplied after the signing of the Conventions of 1859. It had become apparent that "differential rates operated solely for the benefit of big producers

19. *Tribune française*, November 29, 1868.
20. Marlin, "Les Elections législatives," 81.
21. *Ibid.*, 67–70. The recently published work of Jean Vial, *La Sidérurgie française de 1815 à 1864* (Paris: n.p., 1967), confirms this interpretation. He shows that the period of most rapid transformation was during the 1850s, followed by a brusque retrenchment in the following decade. The firms most able to support a decline in demand possessed the most efficient plants, whereas small or obsolete plants had little prospect of holding their own in a sharply narrowed market.
22. *Messager du sud-ouest* (Agen), April 22, 1869, in BB (18) 1795 (1) 9803 (a), AN.

[while] middling and small enterprises could only stand aside in anger against a system which operated against them. Many at that time suddenly faced the fact that the era of *boutiquiers* had ended."[23] All warned of the disaster that awaited the small producer if the free-spending imperial government continued to funnel the public wealth into "big salaries for high bureaucrats" while "salaries for small officials . . . particularly rural officials" languished.[24] Fiscal officials, prefects, justices of the peace carried on their duties in tight alliance with the interest of big capital.[25] In the Gironde, local officials pledged to impartiality, such as the justices of the peace, conspired to deny small farmers the opportunity to profit from the sale of large parcels of public land.[26]

The rhetoric of rural populism appeared frequently and not accidentally in republican propaganda. Of the generation that first saw action in the campaign of 1869, Eugène Spuller said: "We found ourselves agreed on what appeared to us . . . the essential and primary point of republican policy: I refer to the overriding necessity of winning to the republican cause those masses of Frenchmen whom the Revolution of 1789 had made citizens and owners of the land and whom the Revolution of 1848 had made voters."[27] In 1848, French peasants, driven by fear of *partageux*, turned their votes against their benefactors and rallied to Bonaparte. Twenty years of imperial rule grounded in universal (rural) suffrage seemed to confirm the not uncommon view of the peasantry as an "inert mass in the hands of prefects." Such a mood reinforced a persistent urban chauvinism in which the outcome of the struggle for the Republic, and the social peace it promised, depended upon the leadership of a class-conscious bourgeoisie: "In this area of decomposition and revolutionary change, the

23. Jeanne Gaillard, "Notes sur l'opposition au monopole des compagnies de chemin de fer entre 1850 et 1860," *1848*, XLIV (December, 1950), 239.
24. Report from the attorney general of Orléans to the minister of justice on a meeting held in Ferrières (Loiret) on May 5, 1869, in BB(18) 1795(1) 9803(a), AN.
25. Édouard Lockroy, *À bas le progrès!* (Paris: Pairès, 1870), 65–73.
26. Report from the prefect of the Gironde to the minister of the interior, February 9, 1869, in BB(18) 1795(1) 9803(a), AN.
27. Eugène Spuller, *Conférences populaires* (2 vols.; Paris: Dreyfous, 1879–81), I, 9. Speech delivered on October 25, 1875.

bourgeoisie represents the only solid ground on which the future and the past may meet . . . the bourgeoisie is both that superior status toward which all popular ambitions reach and the milieu in which the aristocracy becomes purified. . . . Against monarchical parasitism, against the brute apathy of peasants, against the insane dreams of socialism," only the bourgeoisie stand firmly in the breach between a renewal of tyranny and total social disintegration.[28] This attitude did nothing to advance the republicans' aim of beating the imperial machine at its own game: ideological domination of the countryside. Although the regular business of politics would fall to urban members of the liberal professions—the only ones who had the time and training for such matters—the mass of small farmers, by the sheer weight of their numbers, possessed sufficient strength, if mobilized, to sabotage the Republic. Ideological unity, therefore, became a matter of urgent political necessity. This requirement produced both the radical tone and the conservative substance of the republican message.

Henri Brisson summoned the republican bourgeoisie to cultivate rural fields.[29] Taking to the electoral trail in 1869, he and his associates in the high councils of republicanism generated a campaign to link rural conservatism with middle-class radical democracy. In so doing, they were led to deliver the familiar sharp attacks on the fiscal apparatus of the Empire: the high price of credit, the abuses of monopolists, and the arrogance of finance capital.[30] But these radical attacks always returned to stirring pleas for the rights of the individual producers. And why not? After all, the provincial businessmen and their lawyer spokesmen, stalwarts of "legal revolution" (to borrow John Womack's phrase), were not above making popular alliances to gain their political ends. It would not be the first time that a portion of the bourgeoisie embraced radicalism, and the alliances it imposed, to put themselves in power. And if they could carry on that campaign under the banner

28. D. R., *Les Paysans et le suffrage universel: Études sociales et politiques* (Paris: n.p., 1869), 19–20, 114.

29. Henri Brisson, "La Tyrannie au village," *Libéral du centre* (Limoges), March 10, 1869.

30. Attorney general of Nîmes to the minister of justice, February 16, 1869, in BB(18) 1795(2) 9803(b), AN.

of solidarity and combine radical political reform with social defense, then surely they would gain the best of both worlds.

Pierre Joigneaux, the voice of the wine producers of the Côte-d'Or, returned in 1869 after twenty years in the wilderness to preach the republican message on his home ground. He for one was unwilling to write off the peasantry, for to do so would be to invite disaster. Universal suffrage, he insisted, "implies understanding of political rights and duties; this understanding must be spread around immediately." From this position, Joigneaux proceeded to a radical critique of prevailing economic policy. He aimed his hardest blows at budgetary excesses and oppressive taxes which he considered not so much unjust in the abstract as destructive of the good and simple life and obstacles to the material improvement of agriculture and business. He linked all social ills to the abuses of high finance and big business which crowded out of the marketplace the decent, hard-working man anxious only to profit modestly from the sweat of his brow. Joigneaux did not suggest that the economy be overhauled or its natural progress rerouted. He did make explicit that the republican political line necessarily had to accommodate farmers as well as bourgeois, whose common concerns made them natural allies in the struggle for entrepreneurial freedom.[31]

Jules Simon, running for election in the Hérault, echoed Joigneaux's message. His wholly unwarranted reputation as a *partageux* grew in proportion to his distance from Paris. The traditionally legitimist winegrowers in the villages surrounding Béziers, shaken by low prices for their crop, were in a mood to listen to republicans and even to self-proclaimed oracles of "advanced democracy." But, being small farmers and property owners, they instinctively recoiled at "subversive ideas about property." Simon, fully aware of these nuances, stressed the fact that he was a republican, that is, an opponent of the regime, "but not a communist or even a socialist."[32] Similarly, Alphonse Dréo and Étienne Garnier-Pagès, in the heart of the conservative west in

31. Electoral message to the voters of the Côte-d'Or, 1869, in B/a 1128, Archives de la préfecture de police de la Seine, hereinafter cited as APP.

32. Attorney general of Montpellier to the minister of justice, March 31, 1869, in BB (18) 1795 (1) 9803 (a), AN.

Laval, raised social and economic issues in the form of slogans, "liberty, order, peace and economy," which, for all their vacuity, reproduced accurately and simply the essence of the republican message.[33] Alphonse Gent in the Vaucluse pledged himself to liberty, including liberty of conscience, and specifically repudiated "violence and brutal revolution."[34]

Republicans paid special attention to progressive farmers whose entrepreneurial appetites had been sharpened in the marketplace and whose relative wealth had liberated them from the tyranny of the chatelain.[35] Thus the prefect of the Gers refused to attend the closing banquet of the annual agricultural fair in Condom, organized by the leading citizens of the region, because he feared a hostile reception. He linked this state of affairs to the agitation in "cafés and wineshops" where presumably the same people devoured newspaper articles that "indict the rich, the government, and the priests as enemies of the people."[36] Nowhere is there any evidence that these people intended the destruction of the established social order.

These episodes reveal a tactical pattern of which the 1869 elections were but the initial stage. Beyond tactics, however, there was doctrine and the formulation of a social ideology that proceeded in harmony with the nature of the republican electorate. André Lavertujon of Bordeaux urged his fellow republicans to undertake the task of establishing a common program for property owners, regardless of class. He considered the traditional view of an insurmountable barrier separating town from country to be a myth and, worse, a recipe for defeatism. For "between these two categories of voters [no] radical difference exists in talent and intelligence; only information separates them. I have no doubt that if the people of the countryside learn the

---

33. Attorney general of Angers to the minister of justice, May 6, 1869, *ibid.*
34. A. Autrand, *Statistique des élections parlementaires et des partis politiques en Vaucluse de 1848 à 1928* (Vaison-la-Romainé: n.p., 1932), 58–59.
35. In the Deux-Sèvres, for instance, the republicans Ricard, Delavault, and Antonin Proust (Allain-Targé's son-in-law) found considerable support among the farmers "de la plaine de Niort et de Malle, très aisés, et par suite plus libres." Georges Picard, *Histoire du département des Deux-Sèvres, 1790–1927* (Niort: Baussay, 1928), 225–34.
36. J. Dagnan, "Le Gers sous le second empire," *1848*, XXIV (1930), 213.

facts about foreign, domestic, and economic policy, rural and urban voters will vote as one."[37]

Armand Duportal's campaign in Toulouse drew more attention than most republican campaigns. His performance provided a critical test of whether an urban radical, closely identified with the working class, could relate successfully to semirural and middle-class property owners. Duportal's efforts ended in apparent disaster. In the second electoral district of the Haute-Garonne, including the southern and western quarters of Toulouse and the arrondissements of Muret and Saint-Gaudens, he ran a poor third to the Bonapartist candidate, Campaigne, and the liberal, Rémusat.[38] But the statistics tell substantially less than the full story. It turns out that Duportal did not pursue his campaign in vain. He discovered surprising strength among the semirural *jardiniers* (workers with attachments to rural property), who were concentrated in that part of the city and its environs. Peasant kulaks voted Bonapartist or, less often, liberal, whereas their less affluent neighbors voted republican.[39] Clearly Duportal had not closely identified sufficiently with conservative patterns, although the activity surrounding his campaign shows that this was the direction in which he was moving. Gambetta made several trips to Toulouse in April, and the two of them scoured the countryside in a handshaking and speechmaking campaign. At every stop they repeated their commitment to a conservative economic order: low taxes, a sharply reduced military budget, elimination of fiscal monopolies, and the inviolable rights of property. The team of Duportal and Gambetta made a definite impression on the farmers, who expressed genuine admiration for their good sense and sound ideas.[40]

Édouard Lockroy, in his polemic written shortly after the 1869 elections, distilled into concentrated vitriol the fury of farmers who had become conscious of systematic government discrimination. *Down*

37. *Tribune française*, August 9, 1868; attorney general of Bordeaux to the minister of justice, June 1, 1869, in BB(18) 1795(1) 9803(a), AN.

38. The figures were: Campaigne, 16,801; Rémusat, 12,418; Duportal, 3,915. *Avenir national* (Paris), June 9, 1869.

39. Amanieu, "Hommes et suffrages," 203–209.

40. Attorney general of Toulouse to the minister of justice, April 13 and May 11, 1869, in BB (18) 1795 (2) 9803 (b), AN.

With Progress! exposed what Lockroy claimed were the deadly effects of imperial social and economic policy. A wider distribution of wealth and opportunities for enhanced material security were stifled by a regressive and burdensome tax structure. "In taking items of basic necessity, the regime oppresses peasants, workers, bourgeois; the hard-working and intelligent classes: the real nation!" Whereas the big landowner paid an infinitesimal tax in proportion to his wealth, the small farmer, vulnerable to the annual vicissitudes of climate, paid a fixed rate unrelated to the state of his land or the volume of his harvest. While salaries for redundant officeholders skyrocketed and big businessmen stuffed their pockets from the public treasury, no money was made available for agricultural credit. Farmers, above all, paid for the dishonesty of government credit policies. "To encourage commerce and industry is certainly an excellent idea. Nevertheless, may we not ask if agriculture does not deserve . . . some encouragement. I recognize that it has the Crédit foncier which loans its capital to stock market manipulators. That will not do." The rerouting of capital initially assigned to the Crédit foncier from agricultural credit to Turkish bonds and the French-controlled Banque ottomane struck Lockroy as a particularly odd way for Napoleon III to deliver on his promise to bring prosperity to the farmer.[41]

Lockroy's closing message abandoned irony and analysis for the passionate rhetoric of the moralist: "You [referring to the imperial government] have promoted and organized speculation. You have created a barony of bankers. You have encouraged stock exchange manipulations. You are involved in every shady operation. You have deified money."[42] Notwithstanding its evocative title, Lockroy's pamphlet did not condemn modernization in the manner of those *fin de siècle* Frenchmen whose hankerings after a bucolic paradise fed into a right-wing and fascist ideology.[43] His quarrel with finance capitalism

41. Lockroy, *À bas le progrès!*, 27, 34–38, 65–73, 41.
42. *Ibid.*, 126.
43. Maurras, Péguy, Daniel Halévy, among others. Proudhon was their spiritual ancestor. To that they grafted on various corporatist cuttings from Renan, Taine, Le Play, secular positivists, and classical sociologists. It is no accident that Halévy, author of *Visites aux paysans du centre*, wrote an admiring biography of Proudhon, *La Vie de Proudhon*.

focused on its failure to set aside narrow interests in favor of an even development of the economy. It was, at the same time, clearly designed to rebut certain principles of liberalism, notably free trade. Lockroy's radicalism, it should be emphasized, had nothing in common with socialist collectivism. His fervent pleas in defense of the rights of the individual producer should erase any misleading impressions read into his anticapitalist rhetoric. Events in Alsace and in Marseille further demonstrate the point.

East and South

In Alsace, the emergence of a republican opposition precipitated a fraternal struggle within the tightly woven fabric of textile, machinery, and chemical entrepreneurs of the Haut-Rhin. By 1869, a massive defection from the imperial standard was underway, led by members of the Mulhouse-Colmar-Thann *patronat*.

Industrial and social action in this area had always maintained an inner consistency guided by the twin principles of profit making and paternalism, each of which was employed in the service of the other. Unlike much of the French *haute bourgeoisie*, a number of Alsatians embraced republicanism at a time when to do so entailed certain risks. Jacques Kœchlin dabbled in *charbonnerie* conspiracies in the 1820s, surreptitiously turned out *tricolores* in his cloth factory, and grudgingly accepted the July Monarchy, but maintained his preference for "the Republic, bourgeois, moderate, founded on the principles of liberty and order."[44] The same Kœchlin family manufactured textile machinery as well as textiles, promoted railroads, and entered a variety of other enterprises, all profitable in a protected market.[45]

Within this framework, Alsatians promoted a host of social service institutions characteristic of their outlook. They founded pension funds, savings banks, retirement homes, nurseries, and workers' compensation funds. The Société industrielle de Mulhouse, organized in

44. Henri Laufenburger and Pierre Pflimlin, *Cours d'économie alsacienne, II: L'Industrie de Mulhouse* (Paris: Sirey, 1932), 312–17.
45. Société industrielle de Mulhouse, *Histoire de l'industrie de Mulhouse* (Mulhouse, 1902), 666–70.

1826 originally to encourage technical studies related to textile production, widened its scope to include discussion and implementation of good works.[46] The fact that they supported political opposition to Napoleon III did not prevent them from cooperating with the regime in social action. For his part, Napoleon III understood the significance of such achievements: "If their example were taken up everywhere, what a sobering effect it would have and what an eloquent reply [it would be] to socialism."[47]

Whatever identification the Alsatian industrialists might have had with the regime—and this was a question of class interest—they operated independently of it with enough confidence in their own strength to take an independent political line. Their brief infatuation with the Empire in the 1850s, based on a common interest in modernization, did not survive the decade.[48] Neither the Empire's frank antiliberalism nor its economic *dirigisme* was compatible with the dominant Alsatian moods of Protestant individualism and laissez faire. Many of the Alsatian notables easily embraced republicanism, in which they found much to admire: anticlericalism, opposition to monopolies, and most important the solidarity of capital and labor.[49] Adherence to the republican position did not in any way contradict either the social interests or the cultural outlook of the Alsatian entrepreneurs. Indeed, the opposite is true. Republican politics, in this region as well as in other areas, took on the coloration of those who made the republican opposition a political instrument of their own class interests.

The campaign of 1869 in Alsace followed predictable lines. The candidate of the emperor (no longer official) was Jean Dollfuss, a manufacturer of printed cloth, champion of free trade, and one

46. Marie-Joseph Bopp, "L'Oeuvre sociale de la haute bourgeoisie haut-rhinoise au xix siècle," *La Bourgeoisie alsacienne* (Strasbourg: n.p., 1967), 387–99; Georges Duveau, *La Vie ouvrière en France sous le second empire* (Paris: Gallimard, 1946), 130.
47. Ferdinand graf Eckbrecht-Duerckheim, *Erinnerungen aus alter und neuer Zeit* (Stuttgart, 1887), II, 69ff, quoted in Bopp, "L'Oeuvre sociale," 393.
48. This modernization was internally financed and resulted in the conversion of half the *imprimeries* in Mulhouse to steam power. Robert Lévy, *Histoire économique de l'industrie cotonnière en Alsace* (Paris: n.p., 1917), 164–70.
49. Auguste Scheurer-Kestner, "Souvenir d'un républicain alsacien," I, 189, in 12706, Bibliothèque nationale, nouvelles acquisitions françaises, hereinafter cited as BN NAFr.

of the negotiators of the Cobden-Chevalier Treaty. Producers of cotton thread and cloth mobilized against him, for they ascribed their declining profits to the introduction of such goods into France.[50] Their candidate in the Mulhouse constituency was Albert Tachard, nephew of André Kœchlin who was, in turn, Dollfuss' brother-in-law. Tachard's credentials, aside from his family connections, apparently rested on his abundant leisure time for politics. A gentleman farmer, he was characterized locally as a place seeker, flatterer of the multitude, and millionaire fair-weather friend of workers. His task was to galvanize a patron-worker political alliance in the best paternalist tradition. His campaign speeches stressed the curiously defensive flavor of the republicans' offering on the social question: "Distrust these apostles bearing instant solutions to great social problems, or appealing to the worst instincts in order to mobilize a clientele of malcontents."[51] Tachard employed his talents to secure the republicans' left flank and also fully exploited the resentment of artisans, mechanics, and small businessmen against *le gros capitalisme*, of which Dollfuss was an outstanding example. He also enlisted rural support on the basis of Dollfuss' notorious indifference to local demands for cheap agricultural credit.[52] Under the umbrella of such an alliance, radical in its attack on the Empire while conservative in its basic formulations, Jacques Kœchlin's descendants and their associates moved closer toward his ideal of a *République bourgeoise*.

Gambetta campaigned for election in the first district of Marseille, where he confronted as opponents Thiers and Ferdinand Lesseps. In Marseille Gambetta was as remote in spirit as in distance from his working-class base of Belleville. Marseille was mired in "economic stagnation." Small businessmen, mechanics, artisans, and industrialists spoke with bitterness of the gap between the government's claims of prosperity and the reality of their own situation. They blamed the

---

50. *Journal des économistes*, XXIV (December, 1871), 438–39.
51. Quoted in Brandt and Leuilliot, "Les Elections à Mulhouse," 112.
52. *Ibid.*, 109–17. "Tachard fut retenu par la crainte de mécontenter ceux des industriels qui le protégeaient en leur rendant le mauvais service d'ameuter les passions populaires. 'Il ne fera de la démocratie contre les patrons.'"

crisis on imperial fiscal policies, specifically the national debt swollen by the cost of public works, the Mexican expedition, and the military establishment. Gambetta's program articulated the grievances as well as the aspirations of the middle classes. "I am," he said, "a candidate of democracy which, precisely because it is radical, is that much more devoted to order, the fundamental basis of all societies, and to liberty, which provides the indispensable guarantee necessary to protect the dignity and the rights of all."[53] In a district with a heavy concentration of workers (nearly 40 percent), Gambetta took little notice of specific social questions. But he clearly marked out the route of democratic social policy within the limits of liberal principles and national requirements, with an emphasis on traditional solutions. The Marseille bourgeoisie surely found ample comfort in Gambetta's assurances that "radical democracy . . . aims only at the enhancement of justice and liberty and of solidarity among men." They took even more pleasure in Gambetta's emphatic commitment to "the close alliance of radical politics and business."[54]

Solidarity in practice meant coalition between republican politicians and the Marseille middle classes for whose interests, there as elsewhere, the republicans stood. Disappointed by Thiers' weak performance in the first round of the election, the Marseille establishment swung behind Gambetta in the second round. They quietly subsidized his campaign and financed Gustave Naquet's left-wing newspaper, *Le Peuple*. Naquet repaid the gesture by joining with the liberal *Sémaphore* in attacking "anarchists" (a code word for working-class agitators) for sabotaging the joint liberal-democratic assault on the Empire.[55] The workers abandoned their efforts, but not without rancor. One of their leaders, André Bastélica, bitterly denounced republican demagoguery: "Universal suffrage was a red herring and counted for nothing in such a hostile milieu. . . . The democratic union that every-

53. Undated clipping (but certainly 1869) from Marseille, in B/a 917, APP.

54. Joseph Reinach (ed.), *Discours et plaidoyers politiques de Gambetta* (11 vols.; Paris: n.p., 1881–85), I, 426–67.

55. Émile Gaidan, *Étude sur le mouvement électoral de 1869 à Marseille: Élection Gambetta* (Marseille: Clapier, 1869), 12–21.

body calls for is nothing but liberal doubletalk."[56] Bastélica's conclusions were absolutely accurate. Gambetta stood, not as the champion of the *populares*, but as the candidate of an emerging national coalition of property owners, "whom he took care to reassure about the close ties between the democratic Republic and their interests."[57] Writing shortly after the elections, in early 1870, Gambetta elaborated his position: "We must restate, and demonstrate that for us the victory of democracy with its free institutions means security and prosperity for material interests, everybody's rights guaranteed, respect for property, protection of the legitimate and basic rights of laborers, the raising up morally and materially of the lower classes, but without conflict and without compromising the position of those favored by wealth and talent . . . our single goal is to bring forth justice and social peace."[58]

Gambetta's performance in Marseille should be taken neither as evidence of a callous disregard of social issues nor as elaborate pretense. Rather, he and his republican colleagues refused to consider such issues in other than a national solidarist context that they insisted must coincide with the bourgeois commitment to property, as articulated in the republican social program. They rejected any suggestion that the interests of workers could not be harmonized with the interests of everyone else within the sweeping embrace of universal suffrage under democratic leadership. Democracy, Gambetta insisted, "will make us politically free, intellectually more acute, economically more comfortable, morally more righteous, socially more equal, and it will establish order on the basis of the harmony of rights and interests."[59] This popular alliance under bourgeois leadership in defiance of class di-

56. Quoted in Girard (ed.), *Les Elections de 1869*, 99. Bastélica was probably unaware of Prévost-Paradol's cynical assessment of the advantages of universal suffrage, but he would have recognized the argument: "On ne peut rien inventer ni proposer au delà pour séduire l'imagination populaire, et . . . les agitateurs ne peuvent revendiquer aucun moyen plus radical de connaître et satisfaire la volonté du plus grand nombre. Le suffrage universel est, donc, de ce point de vue, un secours pour l'ordre matériel et la paix publique . . . [et] le sentiment des classes populaires, tandis qu'il se fortifie et devient plus éveillé dans les régions de pouvoir." Prévost-Paradol, *La France nouvelle* (Paris: Michel-Lévy, 1869), 51–52.

57. Report to the Paris police from Marseille, in B/a 917, APP.

58. Quoted in Joseph Reinach, *La Vie politique de Léon Gambetta* (Paris: Alcan, 1918), 9.

59. Reinach (ed.), *Discours*, I, 426.

visions faced its severest test in republican contacts with workers and in their response to the "social question."

Republicans and Workers

The frequency with which bourgeois republicans stood with workers against the common imperial opponent was deceptive. Collaboration extended only to a tactical alliance. Such political alliances generally do not survive the first decisive breach in the common opponent's defenses. Thus, we should look at the social program of the republicans and at their idea of the revolution to see just where that idea contradicted the popular alliance being built up. Republicans—and not only the most conservative of them—often spoke loudly of political revolution, the legal revolution in institutions, in order to silence those who would demand a hearing on the social question. Egalitarian democracy, after all, transcended class frontiers.

Republicans dealt with social issues largely within the context of legal reform which reflected their own distinct class perspective. Jeanne Gaillard has described how members of the republican opposition, liberals and radicals both, sponsored producers' cooperatives and people's banks. One of them, called Le Crédit au travail, was launched by the liberal economist Jules Clamageran, the industrialist Charles Dollfuss, the educational reformer Jean Macé, and the farmers' publicist Pierre Joigneaux. The purpose of the bank was to stimulate workers' participation in industry. It was run according to classic free enterprise capitalist principles. Gaillard's judgment on the political implications of such an enterprise bears quoting: "Its makeup paralleled the politics of a party which sought less specifically a working class clientele than a popular clientele."[60] In the *Almanach coopérateur*, written for a popular audience by republican publicists, we encounter much of the same. One of the future leading politicians of the Republic, Henri Brisson, warned: "Let us not forget politics!" As one who sought the path toward social order in the midst of political uncertainty, he had

---

60. Jeanne Gaillard, "Les Associations de production et la pensée politique en France, 1852–1870," *Mouvement social* (June-September, 1965), 59–85.

good reason to reject social questions as diverting attention away from politics: "In isolating political questions from social questions, some hope to isolate one class from another and reign by division."[61] He was speaking of the imperial bureaucracy, which was making gestures toward "doing something for the workers." Brisson put it bluntly: The political success of the republicans depended upon their appearing as the convincing vanguard of a popular movement. What they feared above all else was an alliance between established authority and the working class. Such an alliance could be fashioned only at the expense of the middle ranks of the bourgeoisie of country and town. They feared, proximately, their own isolation and, ultimately, a sharpened class conflict in which they would be the losers.

Quick to rush to the defense of political allies whose verbal attacks on the regime unleashed the wrath of imperial justice, republicans were notably less eager to support workers' strike action. They seemed more concerned about mobilizing workers as auxiliary troops in the mounting offensive against the regime. When republicans made rare appearances at the scene of a strike, at Le Creusot or Saint-Étienne in 1869 and 1870, they delivered stirring appeals to solidarity and to the alliance of democrats and workers while carefully skirting specific social questions. Against the mounting wave of independent workers' action they offered "the alliance of capital and labor" and "more powerful mutual aid societies."[62] They said little to distinguish their approach from that of an Edmond About, journalistic oracle of a more conservative bourgeoisie, whose contribution to the debate on the social question began and ended with a widely disseminated pamphlet with a title that speaks for itself: *Le Capital pour tous. Plus de prolétaires, 38 millions de bourgeois; l'ABC du travailleur.*[63] Small wonder, for in several places strikes were led against employers who also were local republican leaders. This was the case in the Loire region where the republican chieftain, Pierre Dorian, an important ironmaster, played a leading

61. Henri Brisson, "N'oublions la politique," *Almanach coopérateur* (1868), 121–29.
62. Fernand L'Huillier, *La Lutte ouvrière à la fin du second empire* (Paris: Colin, 1957), 53–54.
63. Cited *ibid.*, 75n.

role in mobilizing employers to smash strikes in the Saint-Étienne basin.[64] So, too, in upper Alsace and in the Nord, men in the forefront of the republicans' fight against the Second Empire struggled simultaneously against the social movement on their left. Auguste Scheurer-Kestner, in his autobiography, ignored this aspect of the *lutte politique* carried on by his uncles, cousins, and in-laws, while he celebrated their heroic battles for the Republic.[65]

In Lyon, where French militants of the First International were perhaps strongest outside Paris, the deep cleavage between republicans and socialists became most apparent. André Bastélica from Marseille and Émile Aubry from Rouen, leaders of the French section of the International, spent several days in Lyon in February, 1870. They came there to support the efforts of Albert Richard, leader of the Lyon socialists, to organize workers independently of the republicans. Their target was specifically the republican left, for the workers were attracted to men like Louis Bançel and François Raspail, whose anticlerical, radical program was devoid of social content or, rather, full of solidarity. The radicals had attempted to monopolize the workers' constituency in defense of middle-class interests. Their newspaper, the *Progrès de Lyon*, spoke for workers in bourgeois accents. Aubry sounded the warning: "Do not compromise your growing power by dupe's alliances with bourgeois radicalism." His fears were not imaginary. Imbedded in the programs of the republican candidates, Bançel and Raspail, we find these statements on the social question: "I think that the social question ought to be considered and advanced side by side with political questions" (Bançel); "*rapprochement* of all classes in society by means of common, free, and obligatory education and by the creation of associations" (Raspail).[66]

Curiously enough, Bastélica actively participated in the work of the Ligue de l'enseignement in Marseille.[67] The league, true to its origins

64. See Chapter II, herein.
65. Scheurer-Kestner, "Souvenir d'un républicain alsacien," I, *passim*, in 12706, BN NAFr.
66. S. Maritch, *Histoire du mouvement social sous le second empire à Lyon* (Paris: n.p., 1930), 231–34, 202–203.
67. Georges Duveau, *La Pensée ouvrière sur l'éducation pendant la seconde république et le second empire* (Paris: Editions Domat Montchrestien, 1946), 41.

in Alsace, was subsidized by the local bourgeoisie, the same people whom Bastélica had accused of "liberal doubletalk" when they spoke of democracy.[68] In Lyon itself, one of the original founders of the Ligue de l'enseignement, Charles Gaumont, supervised the establishment of a privately financed course in vocational training for workers. The money came from François Arlès-Dufour, Eugène Flotard, and Henri Germain, all pillars of the Lyon *haute bourgeoisie*.[69] One of the "bourgeois radicals" of whom Aubry had warned, Jean Le Royer, joined hands with the Lyon elite in their educational projects. Bastélica's association with such an enterprise suggests that republican egalitarianism, when translated into serious reform, was not mere posing.[70]

Republican social policy included nothing for the workers as a class apart. There was no reason that it should, for sporadic pressures from below did not add up to a class movement of workers in opposition to the republicans' national economic and social program. Many among the dispersed working class found radical democracy attractive. Others saw in Napoleon III's social projects equal promise for the future. Only in the context of the Revolutionary Commune do we find a clear denial of the social consensus which held together the republican coalition. Indeed, it may be argued that the making of republican democracy, in which a national bourgeoisie used radical politics to pursue bourgeois social order, contributed to the isolation of the Commune, and facilitated its defeat by an army of the Republic.

The Politics of Defense

The surrender of the imperial army at Sedan and the dethronement of Napoleon III opened up great opportunities and carried grave risks for the Empire's republican successors. They had worked for a political

68. Report of the prefect of the Bouches-du-Rhône on the Ligue de l'enseignement in 1869, in F(17) 12527, AN. The Marseille chapter originated with Freemasons and engaged in direct political propaganda. Its moving spirit was Alphonse Esquiros, who appeared alongside Gambetta in the previous elections. His politics were certainly "radical," but not "social," at least no more so than those of Bançel and Raspail, whom Bastélica and Aubry had denounced.

69. Maritch, *Histoire du mouvement social*, 179–80.

70. Jean de Moussac, *La Ligue de l'enseignement* (Paris: Librairie de la Société bibliographique, 1880), 28–29.

revolution to overthrow the Empire. Now the revolution lay in their hands and in turn raised challenges to their efforts to turn an opposition faction into a party of government and order. During the interregnum of 1870–1871, the republicans moved to consolidate their position. Almost every political action taken by the Government of National Defense, particularly from its provincial headquarters dominated by Léon Gambetta, aimed to consolidate republican power against independent social movements.

The installation of known men of order in the prefectures whenever possible testifies to the determination by leading politicians of republicanism to reinforce their fragile structure against the shocks of disorder. True, the provisional government had a war on its hands and could not afford factional squabbling; but, in fact, the government risked division more than once by its choices in local administration. The implications for future politics were unmistakable. To take two examples:

In the department of the Saône-et-Loire, strikes had disrupted the company town of Le Creusot since 1868. Ten thousand of the town's forty thousand inhabitants worked in the Schneiders' gigantic forges and foundries. Immediately following the fourth of September the republican municipal council came under attack from workers' delegates demanding a share in the town's government. From the neighboring department of the Côte-d'Or, Prefect Frédéric Morin raised the danger of insurrection. His telegraph message ludicrously understated his own estimation of the seriousness of the situation: "I think that a social question is going to be raised and that the danger is serious." He urged measures to keep the workers "making guns and not politics" and "to preserve the material order." The republican government of the town, despite its isolation, held firm against the workers. In the midst of the troubles, the subprefect of Autun, under whose jurisdiction Le Creusot fell, made an observation that explained the provisional government's pressure to keep the town under control and specifically its pressure against independent workers' action: "Le Creusot is like Paris or Lyon without a middle class."[71]

71. *Annales de l'Assemblée nationale, 1871–1876*, Vol. XXV, Annexe No. 1416,

At about the same time, Charles de Freycinet took over the prefecture at Montauban in the Tarn-et-Garonne. His mission was to suppress a nascent revolutionary commune in the name of the government of the Republic. He arrived with a well-deserved reputation as a man of order and immediately set about to establish good relations with conservative elements in the city. He did his job too well. After two weeks in office, popular disorders drove him out. Rather than capitulate to the insurrectionaries, the provisional government appointed in his place an unknown local figure with solid bourgeois credentials.[72]

Others, equally committed to republican order, defended that order with more success and, in common effort, became links in the chain of provincial republican notables which was forged at this juncture: Paul Bert in the Nord; Bert's fellow Auxerrois, Hippolyte Ribière, in the Yonne; César Bertholon in the Loire, where he directed the smashing of the Saint-Étienne commune; Alexandre Labadié, a pillar of the mercantile establishment of Marseille, in the Bouches-du-Rhône; Allain-Targé in the Maine-et-Loire; his son-in-law, Antonin Proust, in the Deux-Sèvres; and in the Alpes-Maritimes, Marc Dufraisse, self-styled defender of the "social status quo."[73] Out of the opposition of the pre-1870 days a government emerged and remained. Forty-six of the Government of National Defense's eighty-eight prefects became republican deputies, generally in their home locales. Francisque Ordinaire, who sat on the republican left in the Legislative Body for the Doubs, returned to the prefecture in Besançon. Georges Périn, whose *Libéral*

---

pp. 933, 1324, hereinafter cited as *Annales*. Morin originally dealt with the relations of labor and capital within a Christian democratic framework—particularly the variety preached by Philippe Buchez. By the mid-1860s, however, he had moved away from the church, abandoned any Christian solution to social problems, and embraced the teachings of Proudhon, whose message of social reconciliation he understood very well. "Il [Proudhon] se propose de réconcilier les classes bourgeoises et les classes ouvrières." Quoted in Jean-Baptiste Duroselle, *Les Débuts du catholicisme social en France* (Paris: Presses universitaires de France, 1951), 658–60.

72. Dispatches from Freycinet to Gambetta, September 7, 8, and 14, 1870, in Freycinet Papers, Bibliothèque de l'École polytechnique.

73. For the prefects see *Almanach national, 1871* (Paris: Imprimerie nationale, 1872) and Pierre Henry, *Histoire des préfets* (Paris: Nouvelles editions latines, 1950); for Bertholon, see dossiers individuels des préfets, in F(1b) I 156(19), AN; Labadié appears in Alphonse Esquiros, "Marseille et la Ligue du Midi," *Nouvelle revue* (February 1, 1883), 505; the quotation from Marc Dufraisse appeared in the *Bulletin de la république française*, October 30, 1870.

du Centre had proclaimed its nonrecognition of classes in 1869, became prefect in Limoges.[74]

The administrative upheaval in the Gard provides a detailed example of the process by which republicans parlayed their brief moment of power into something more permanent. Jean-Louis Laget became prefect in Nîmes on September 6. In 1848 he had been subprefect of the arrondissement of Uzès in the same department. He had also represented Nîmes on the departmental council since 1865 and subsequently became president of that body in October, 1871. Joseph Cazot shared with Laget the local republican leadership in Nîmes, where they both practiced law. Cazot ran unsuccessfully for the Legislative Body in 1869 and next turned up in Tours as secretary-general for the Ministry of the Interior. In July, 1871, he was elected to the National Assembly. Laget's subordinates, Ducamp, Adolphe Bosc, and Adolphe Bousquet, the subprefects of Alais, Uzès, and Le Vigan, were all local men who went on to represent the districts they had administered in the general council of the Gard.[75]

The republican leaders of the Government of National Defense labored earnestly to build up strong ideological and political ties with a broad middle sector of the population. Clément Laurier, director of personnel under Gambetta, laid down a general line to the prefects in late September. He urged them to agitate among the peasantry, which he considered to be Bonapartist, and to demonstrate by moderate conduct that the Republic stood for a flexible system to embrace all schools of opinion.[76] Peasant Bonapartism did not disturb him, for it represented only a stubborn attachment to the soil, which the republicans had no difficulty honoring. Laurier, in his testimony before a parliamentary committee investigating the policies of the Government of National Defense, explained that the choice of prefects generally fell

74. Henry, *Histoire des préfets*, 196–99; *Libéral du centre*, February 14, 1869.
75. *Almanach national, 1871*, xxviii, 615; A. Clerc, *Nos députés à l'Assemblée nationale: Leurs biographies et leurs votes* (Paris: Chevalier, 1872), 46–47; A. Robert et al., *Dictionnaire des parlementaires* (5 vols.; Paris: Presses universitaires de France, 1889), II, 5–6; A. Joanne, *Géographie du département du Gard* (7th ed.; Paris: Hachette, 1901), 36–39.
76. Clipping from the *Moniteur national*, September 24, 1878, on the occasion of Laurier's death, in B/a 1142, APP.

on men acceptable to moderate points of view. He had told Gambetta "that choices should be made not only with a view towards strengthening the republican party but also should take into consideration the necessity of promoting a favorable attitude towards the Republic among the middle classes."[77] The subprefect of Bar-sur-Aube confirmed with frank self-admiration the implementation of the line. "The Republic that I defend is not a predatory creature; it does not prey on anyone; it burns nothing. Under my care it is a good fellow, honest, loyal, serious of course, but brotherly. It enlightens; it ennobles; it purifies."[78]

Questions of national defense became bound up with questions of social defense. The story of the Ligue du Midi is a case in point.[79] Amid the chaos of September–October, 1870, delegates of seventeen southern departments gathered in Marseille to form a regional defense league. Alphonse Esquiros, Gambetta's own appointee as political commissar for the area, headed its central committee. Esquiros led the radical wing of the republican group in Marseille. This provided him with acceptable credentials among workers and socialists in the city, at least to the extent that they considered him an ally against the republican bourgeois establishment, represented by Labadié and Maurice Rouvier. But Esquiros' political radicalism, manifested chiefly by a fanatic anticlericalism and a disdain for "aristocrats," did not extend to a radical social program—or any social program at all. As he later said, the revolution in Marseille "was made" by the fifth of September —that is, when he and his fellow radicals proclaimed the Republic.[80] The Ligue du Midi, in his hands, operated to give the Marseille radicals leverage against their moderate republican competitors and, at the same time, to direct working-class energies into easily contained chan-

77. Assemblée nationale, *Enquête parlementaire sur les actes du gouvernement de la défense nationale* (Paris: Wittersheim, 1872), II, 12–13, "déposition de M. Laurier."
78. *Ibid.*, II, 40, report of the subprefect of Bar-sur-Aube to the minister of the interior, November 17, 1870.
79. For the Ligue du Midi and the events in Marseille, see Esquiros, "Marseille et la Ligue du Midi"; Alexandre Glais-Bizoin, *Cinq mois de dictature* (Paris: n.p., 1875); *Réveil de l'Ardèche*, October 20, 1870; Antoine Olivesi, *La Commune de 1871 à Marseille et ses origines* (Paris: Rivière, 1950); Assemblée nationale, *Enquête parlementaire*, II.
80. Esquiros, "Marseille et la Ligue du Midi," 503.

nels. For this purpose, they encouraged the formation of a proletarian *garde civique* to supersede the *garde nationale*: "Our duty at the time was to divert the attention of hot-heads from utopian aims [read: social revolution] by getting them involved in national defense."[81] The Ligue du Midi, however, never materialized as an effective regional fighting force. It did become a rally point for Communards-in-the-making in Marseille, hardly the "diversion" Esquiros had intended. From its headquarters in Tours, the Government of National Defense hurled anathemas at the Ligue du Midi and at Esquiros, accusing them of "secession," "anarchy," and "disorder." Gambetta later said that he feared for the "unity of France." Clément Laurier, Gambetta's *chef de cabinet*, put the matter more directly when he voiced his fears for the social order.[82] Isolated, repudiated by the government, unable to control the situation, Esquiros abandoned the revolution as it left the path of legality. A revolutionary commune was proclaimed in Marseille. Esquiros and his republican allies took no part in it. By their silence they assented to its suppression in April, 1871. Antoine Olivesi has summed up the meaning of the affair: "Disagreements between radical republicans [*républicains avancés*] and socialists paralyzed the revolutionary movement."[83]

In Paris itself a significant drama was being played out in the midst of war preparations. During much of April and early May, 1871, a group of republicans representing the commercial and manufacturing entrepreneurs of central Paris attempted to mediate between Paris and Versailles. This Ligue d'union républicaine des droits de Paris numbered among its members men who would be placed on the left wing of the republican movement: Georges Clemenceau, Charles Floquet, Édouard Lockroy, Frédéric Morin, Allain-Targé. The league had uneasy relations with the Commune. Although it supported the principle of municipal independence (partly as leverage against the government of Adolphe Thiers), it feared the social movement embodied in the Commune. Charles Floquet voiced the fear that civil war would play

81. *Ibid.*, 489.
82. Assemblée nationale, *Enquête parlementaire*, I, 548.
83. Olivesi, *La Commune de 1871 à Marseille*, 100.

into the hands of monarchists and Bonapartists. "The Republic itself
is at stake," he said. "All right then, we must not only develop a program for conciliation, but we must carry our message to the provinces."[84] However, no conciliation was possible. The provinces had
already spoken with the voices of the republicans who had exercised
power under the Government of National Defense. Some of the men
in the league, like Allain-Targé and Morin, came to Paris fresh from
participation in that government's work in national as well as social
defense. Whatever their private agonies, they could not live with the
ouvriériste orientation of the Commune. Thus their efforts at conciliation, a kind of practical exercise in solidarity, came to grief. Once
again, Jeanne Gaillard: "For it [the league], there was no question of
making a revolution, the revolution had been made; the problem for
bourgeois politicians was to shepherd the urban populace down the
path of republican legality."[85]

Throughout its tenure the republican Government of National
Defense published the *Bulletin de la république française* thrice weekly. A four-page tabloid printed only on the first and fourth pages so
that it could be posted on the walls of buildings, the *Bulletin* presented
a concentrated distillation of republican ideological slogans. The scores
of articles, read as one, possessed a central theme, stated bluntly in
uppercase letters at the head of the second issue: "THE REPUBLIC
MEANS ORDER!"[86] Its single purpose, defined by Gambetta himself,
was to present "the ideas of justice . . . patriotism, and civic virtue." It
hewed to a line set by fidelity to "moral principles."[87] The editor of the
Bulletin, Jules Barni, had followed a career as a radical intellectual for
thirty years. He had been a professor of history and philosophy at various *lycées*, a noted Kant scholar, and a dabbler in European radical

84. Floquet Papers, in 49 AP 1, AN.
85. Jeanne Gaillard, "La Ligue de l'union républicaine des droits de Paris,"
Bulletin de la Société d'histoire moderne, Ser. 13, No. 5, pp. 8–13. Gaillard also states
that this "radicalisme première manière montre que les radicaux de 1871 sont proches
de la Commune." I do not think that her own arguments and the evidence of the Floquet
Papers, which she and I both have consulted, support that conclusion.
86. *Bulletin de la république française*, October 16, 1870; *Temps*, December 6,
1870, for a description of the dissemination of the *Bulletin*.
87. Circular from Gambetta to all prefects, *Temps*, December 6, 1870.

politics. While in exile in Geneva during the Second Empire he had participated in the founding of the Ligue internationale de la paix et de la liberté.[88] Barni did not qualify to be in the inner circle of retainers of the republican bourgeoisie. Gambetta, echoing a common belief, dismissed the league for its "cosmopolitanism" and its harmful impact on "love of country" and "the duties of civic responsibility."[89]

Barni, however, did his job well. He wrote of the problems of small farmers—good listening for those peasants who gathered each Sunday in village marketplaces where the local schoolmaster read aloud from the *Bulletin*'s weekly fare. He argued that the good years for agriculture under Napoleon III did not result from any conscious state policy, but merely followed the general prosperity produced by the extension of the railroad network. He wondered whether France contained too many uneconomical small farms and suggested that farmers develop cooperatives. He even suggested the consolidation of small holdings into large centralized units. But this was foolish speculation, as Barni himself admitted, since "neither the temperament nor the habits" of the French peasant inclined him toward such projects. The Republic would have to get along with and absorb, politically and ideologically, the continued fractionalization of rural property.[90]

The *Bulletin*'s use as an instrument of ideological struggle comes across best in a series of six articles written on the history of the French Revolution. They previewed, with remarkable accuracy, the patriotic political histories written in the late nineteenth century by historians such as Alphonse Aulard. As history, the articles hardly went beyond a vulgar popularization that nonetheless eminently suited their purpose. The Revolution culminated the struggle of liberty against tyranny and put an end to social inequalities. Social inequality meant unjust taxes, an arrogant and privileged aristocracy, and barriers to mobility. The guild structure came in for special mention because it prevented workingmen from becoming entrepreneurs and hindered economic

88. Robert *et al.*, *Dictionnaire*, I, 171–72; A. Bitard, *Dictionnaire de biographie contemporaine française et étrangère* (Paris: Dreyfous, 1880), 83.
89. Daniel Halévy and Émile Pillias (eds.), *Lettres de Gambetta, 1868–1882* (Paris: Grasset, 1938), letter 127.
90. *Bulletin de la république française*, January 11 and 25, 1871.

liberty. Finally, not surprisingly, Barni had high praise for Robert Turgot and for Jacques Necker who struggled in vain for the free marketplace.[91]

Barni edited a column, to which several leading republican politicians contributed, entitled "Manual for a Republican." These articles discussed the tactics of political and ideological penetration. Two or three key themes repeated themselves: bury the class struggle in national solidarity, appeal to the conservatism of peasants, and revive local government.[92] Barni's work on the *Bulletin* propelled his career forward. He graduated from its editorship to the position of inspector-general of public instruction at the end of January, 1871.[93] However, his new career flickered briefly. Once the armistice with Prussia had been concluded, the Government of National Defense writ no longer ran in France.

Thirty-four years after these events, Léon Bourgeois addressed the Congress of the Radical-Socialist Party: "The class struggle, unhappily, exists in our midst. I do not believe that by prolonging that conflict will we be brought closer to the solution of social problems. I do believe that the solution lies in suppressing class antagonisms and making all men partners in the same great work."[94] Léon Bourgeois was a direct descendant of the men who made the republican revolution. They accomplished their purpose, but we are permitted to doubt that the revolution they made was a revolution at all.

91. *Ibid.*, January 6, 8, 11, 13, and 19, 1871.
92. *Ibid., passim.*
93. Joseph Reinach Papers, Ser. 2, XI, 199, in 24910, BN NAFr.
94. *Temps*, July 20, 1905.

II Making the National Party

THE INTRODUCTION has already suggested that the decisive steps toward consolidation of the Republic took place in the provinces. Chapter I has explored several regions in connection with the campaign of 1869 and the politics of national defense. In this chapter we will study several by-election campaigns and explore the politics of two departments in some depth. I will cite some voting results, but make no claim to statistical sophistication. The numbers provide illustrations, not the raw material for electoral sociological analysis. The purpose of surveying these campaigns is to discover how the republican bourgeoisie mobilized petty producers under their leadership, forged an ideological consensus, fortified republican ramparts against assaults from the right and from the left, and, of primary importance, created the political base that made possible bourgeois class rule within a democratic and egalitarian framework.

First of all, however, let us listen to the voice of Gambetta. The leading role played by the "tribune of the people" has, perhaps, been overemphasized. This may be accounted for by his exceptional oratorical abilities and the genuine courage and talent for organization he displayed during the bleak months following Sedan. Gambetta's fall from power in January, 1882, was as precipitous and sudden as his emergence as the hero of national defense in 1870. Nevertheless, he made significant contributions to the mobilization of republican ideological and political forces. His approach, apparently, took its inspiration from the largely unarticulated aspirations of the *nouvelles couches sociales*, the small producers of France. I say "apparently" because he manipulated those aspirations to accept and defend the distinctive bourgeois social message: the denial of class and the promotion of the socially integrative concept of *solidarité*. His message did not spring from below and carry upward into bourgeois ranks, but flowed in the very opposite direction.

Bourgeois and *Nouvelles Couches*: A Question of Class

On September 26, 1872, at Grenoble, Léon Gambetta announced the arrival of a "new social stratum" (*couche sociale nouvelle*) on the national scene. His statement was interpreted as either a declaration of class war or the first trumpet call of opportunism.[1] Auguste Scheurer-Kestner reported that the initial effect of the statement resounded like a "clap of thunder." The leaders of the right trembled as they scanned the transcript of the speech. Soberer minds found nothing unusual in the speech and refused to be panicked into violent rebuttal.[2] The *Journal des débats*, the most prestigious of the newspapers representing the enlightened bourgeoisie, considered Gambetta's statement a "new departure."[3] In point of fact, the speech captured the essence of the republican position and said nothing that had not been stated or implied previously. Gambetta had only called attention to the clear truth that the republican bourgeoisie had taken the first decisive step toward political power at the head of a popular coalition. To maintain that coalition it had to deliver a series of hard ideological blows against social division, and the most formidable weapon in its hands proved to be the denial that such divisions even existed. As Gambetta put it to the bourgeoisie of Lille (the perfect

1. Joseph Reinach (ed.), *Discours et plaidoyers politiques de Gambetta* (11 vols.; Paris: n.p., 1881–85), III, 89–118; Jacques Kayser, in *Les Grandes batailles du radicalisme* (Paris: Rivière, 1961), 59–64, discusses various reactions.
2. Auguste Scheurer-Kestner, "Souvenir d'un républicain alsacien," I, 68, in 12706, Bibliothèque nationale, nouvelles acquisitions françaises, hereinafter cited as BN NAFr; Report of September 30, 1872, in B/a 917, Archives de la préfecture de police de la Seine, hereinafter cited as APP.
3. Quoted in *Siècle*, October 1, 1872.

audience before which to deliver pronouncements on the social question): Republicans must ruthlessly exclude "utopians and dreamers,
showering the masses with unrealizable promises, incoherent and illogical programs, aiming at the division of classes, fomenting discord
between one and the other."[4]

In 1874, Gambetta struck a harmonious chord among republicans
in the Yonne when he reminded them of their responsibilities to integrate petty producers into the republican system. "All these elements
have attained a degree of prosperity and they comprise the *nouvelles
couches sociales* of which I have spoken before. Remember, gentlemen, I said *couches*, not *classes*: that is a distasteful word I never use."
In Le Havre, two years earlier, surrounded by the big bourgeoisie of
the city, including Armand Guillemaud, its mayor, Félix Faure, and
Jules Siegfried, Gambetta laid the republican politicians' claim to
effectively manage their affairs. He denounced "brutal revolutionary
action" and the legacy of "horrible social wars." The national republican party had established itself as an antirevolutionary party, "a conservative party . . . which assures the peaceful and legal working out
of the legitimate consequences of the French Revolution."[5]

Following the proclamation of the Empire in 1852, Louis Napoleon chose to deliver his message of reassurance to the provincial bourgeoisie (*L'Empire, c'est la paix*) in Bordeaux. Was it coincidental that
the nation's most celebrated republican politician, Léon Gambetta,
went to the same city for the same purpose in June, 1871? His close
friend and collaborator, Eugène Spuller, suggested an approach to
republican political agitation that pointed in that direction. The first
order of business was to mobilize the "scattered forces of the republican party today so deeply wounded, to discipline the spirit, to rekindle
hope, to calm anxieties, to console the defeated, to calm restlessness,
and above all to reconcile the two Frances which are locked in struggle."[6] Spuller urged Gambetta to lead election campaigns in this spirit

---

4. *République française*, February 9, 1876.
5. Reinach (ed.), *Discours*, IV, 156, II, 258–63.
6. Spuller to Gambetta, June 13, 1871, reprinted in the *Revue de Paris* (June,
1900), 450–80.

and to issue a strong statement against the Commune, which he called the work of "irresponsible idiots."[7] Showing incredible callousness toward victims of the repression and an admirable singlemindedness of purpose, Spuller dismissed the notion that anyone "would dare to doubt [our] loyalty. Who will seriously believe that your conservatism compromises republican principles? . . . All of us must give evidence of our political intent and governmental ability if we are to capture the Republic."[8] What better starting point down that road than among the bourgeoisie of Bordeaux?

Gambetta arrived in Bordeaux on June 26. To a cheering crowd he outlined the policy that the republicans were to follow without deviation for the next four years. He began, in a conventional way, by declaring his faith in the ability of the republican party to "regenerate the nation and found a free government." Universal suffrage was the key to political power and the perpetuation of a stable social order, as Napoleon III had demonstrated. With Bonapartism dead, the republicans would inherit political power. In almost word-for-word recapitulation of Spuller's advice, Gambetta went on to claim for the republicans (the word *radical* is conspicuously absent) the role of the "party capable of directing the orderly business of government." As proof of the party's plans, he stated his determination not to oppose the present government outside the legal limitations. The National Assembly had the right to pass laws. He thus contradicted those, including himself, who earlier had refused to recognize the Assembly's mandate beyond the issue of peace or war. There was a difference between opposition to the Empire and opposition under these changed circumstances. Opposition under the Republic "should prod action and aim to grasp the reins, and not seek destruction. I affirm that we will respect your authority, recognize the legality of your position, and not subvert your administration, but we will not abandon the right to criticize and press for reform; and we will allow the whole people

7. "The enemies of our great conservative party have laid at our feet the crimes of a few thousand miserable creatures." *Gard républicain*, June 20, 1871; "Many are trying to identify the republican cause with the Commune." *Progrès de l'Est* (Besançon), May 31, 1871.
8. Spuller to Gambetta, June 11, 1871, reprinted in the *Revue de Paris*, 450–80.

through universal suffrage to decide between those who despise us and those who fight for the Republic and liberty."[9] Gladstone could have said as much when he handed to Disraeli the emblems of government.

Gambetta then turned to outline a plan of action. He urged his bourgeois audience to finance and undertake political education and propaganda. He reminded them of "force in numbers." The peasants demanded constant attention and work. Since their revolution ended in 1789, making the land theirs, they had ceased to play an active political role and remained an inert mass whose weight constituted power in the hands of ambitious men. "What we want is a rural Assembly in the broadest and truest sense of the word, for a true rural Assembly is not a collection of backward country gentry, but a body composed of free and enlightened peasants." He ended on a strident patriotic note. "I do not want the new Frenchman only to be able to think, read, and reason; I want him to act and to fight. At the side of the teacher the physical instructor and the soldier must stand; so that our children, who will be our soldiers as well as our future citizens, can handle a sword, shoot a rifle, carry out long marches, sleep under the stars, endure bravely all conceivable hardships for the fatherland."[10] National regeneration meant the Republic of the healthy marketplace. The republican program, which Gambetta called "both radical and conservative," moved toward the twin goals of national power and social peace. It was radical only insofar as new political circumstances demanded a radical departure from past practices. It was conservative in its emphasis on completing the Revolution, not beginning a new one.

We can retrace these steps further. "My program," Gambetta said on the morrow of Sedan, "is at once republican and conservative." He did not idly indulge in the construction of paradoxes. Social reconciliation was imperative to the founding of a democratic and egalitarian capitalist order.

France cannot be governed in opposition to the bourgeoisie; at the same time their interests cannot be allowed to predominate to the total exclusion

9. Reinach (ed.), *Discours*, II, 17, 18–19.
10. *Ibid.*, 11, 21–23, 23–24.

of laboring people. Only the Republic can effect the harmonious reconciliation between the legitimate demands of workers and the respect for the
sacred rights of property. . . . To attain this goal, two things are necessary:
to dissolve the fears of one and to calm the passions of the other; to teach
the bourgeoisie to cherish democratic government and to teach the people to
have confidence in their elder brothers.[11]

Without the addition of a powerful reagent (the ideological leadership of the republican bourgeoisie), French society was a potentially
unstable mixture. Unless those "fears" (of revolution and class conflict) were dissolved, order and social peace would arrive only at the
price of tyranny. Republican democracy, with its solidarist ideological
core and its opening to entrepreneurial freedom, performed a catalytic
action necessary to transform stubborn elements of conflict into a
stable national society capable of withstanding any challenge to the
social order.

The stage had been set during the years of the "republican revolution." The task for the immediate future was to extend the political
leadership of the republican bourgeoisie to the remote corners of the
nation. Armed with a coherent ideological message, the representatives of industrial and agricultural capital proceeded to translate that
message into a political movement. They filled their ranks with men
drawn from the *nouvelles couches,* opened local political careers to
talent, and through them, made the Republic synonymous with the
union of all producers. The republican party became the party of the
marketplace, which gave political content to a social movement defined not by class but by solidarity—that is, the denial of class. Two
consequences followed. Petty producers could identify their own place
and the vehicle of their own ambitions in a society defined as open and
egalitarian; the ruling bourgeoisie thus mobilized allies against class-
based social movements of either "aristocrats" or workers. Secondly,
and in contradiction, the bourgeoisie found itself forced to deliver on
the promises implicit in republican ideology; whatever its inclinations,
it was effectively blocked from undertaking a thoroughgoing program
of capitalist concentration. But at the time the price paid did not appear

11. *Mémorial des Deux-Sèvres,* September 3, 1870.

too high considering the quality of the goods purchased: a stable bour-geois order supported by capitalist production on the one hand and traditional economic relations on the other.

In the following discussion these developments are traced on the political level, especially in the rural communities of France. In this connection we should recall that the republicans inherited the peasant multitudes from the imperial regime. We will find that they possessed the necessary tools to capitalize on their legacy.

Going to the Country

The great effort did not come until the eve of the National As-sembly by-elections in July, 1871, and the elections to departmental general councils later in the year. But initial starts were made. Frédéric Morin captured the mood:

The democratic party . . . sometimes called the radical party . . . must initiate or rejuvenate the scattered republican cadres. From district to district, indeed from village to village, the republicans have become con-scious of themselves and others around them. Let us follow this up by creating new newspapers, people's libraries, meetings. . . . Politics must cease to be merely an intermittent fever among us and become a central part of our lives. . . . If we inculcate the spirit of solidarity in all these organizations and avoid internecine struggles, if it becomes apparent that we can form a stable government and a truly progressive administration— then the Republic will be welcomed even more widely than it is today, for it will have demonstrated its primary concern for the national interest.[12]

Local organizations played a key role in radical planning. They served effectively to generate interest in politics in a generally apathetic population. Imperial rule had brought many benefits to France, but it did not leave a politically mature population. There was good evidence that most Frenchmen had still not gotten over twenty years of political torpor. The attorney general of the Rennes district, in a periodic report to Versailles, noted the apathy of the population outside the great towns. Three notes from the subprefect of Nyons in the Drôme indi-

12. *Rappel* (Paris), November 2, 1871.

cated similar apathy. He stated that the people welcomed the Republic unenthusiastically and had little interest in active political participation.[13] Thus, republicans concentrated on promoting direct popular political action at the lowest level, in villages and towns. The diversity of names under which local groups organized, some called republican societies, others simply committees, masked the essential common aim, which was, in the words of Armand Duportal of Toulouse, "to prepare the ground for the future and render impossible any attempt at monarchical restoration." Duportal worried about the revival of aristocratic rule. This led him to a brief involvement with a commune-style uprising in Toulouse when it appeared that the forces of reaction had conquered the nation. He later spent considerable energy living down that experience, reserving his bitterest polemical denunciations for the "exploiters of the basest instincts of the mob . . . [who] specialize in promoting for themselves a shabby popularity by pandering to the hatred of the rich by the poor. . . . The Republic wants nothing of these false benefactors, these Jesuits in trousers, these chanters of Communard and red paternosters."[14]

From Troyes came word of the formation of the committee, Aube union républicaine. A few members of the Troyes municipal council constituted the core of the committee. Its plans and aspirations were vast in comparison with its small numerical strength. The prospectus underlined the necessity of educating the voter through the distribution of information and the holding of public discussions. The vote, both legal and powerful, brought overwhelming force in support of the Republic. It was sufficient, according to the founders of the committee, to organize ad hoc associations only at election time. For the essentially frantic and aggressive conditions then prevalent produced hostility and suspicion in a population that had to be approached slowly and carefully. The association aimed not only to disseminate electoral propa-

13. Attorney general of Rennes to the minister of justice, March 23, 1871, in BB (30) 390, Archives nationales, hereinafter cited as AN; subprefect of Nyons to the prefect of the Drôme, October 28, November 23, and December 25, 1870, in M 1298, Archives départementales, Drôme, hereinafter cited as AD, appropriate department.
14. *Emancipation* (Toulouse), January 15, 1871; *Emancipateur* (Toulouse), July 21, 1872.

ganda, but also to maintain a steady flow of printed material through public libraries and public meetings.[15] Municipal elections in April brought out more of the same developments and provided solid evidence that the momentum of the previous year had not been totally dissipated. In the department of the Ain, for example, the republicans elected twenty of twenty-seven municipal councilors for Bourg-en-Bresse, the departmental capital. Self-styled "men of order," hangovers from the defunct regime, campaigned vigorously but in vain. The republican list included the flower of the town's *petite bourgeoisie*: a carpenter, weaver, printer, watchmaker, pharmacist, goldsmith, grocer, wine merchant, and tailor. Members of the liberal professions also appeared: two physicians, a retired magistrate, and a solicitor. The republicans did not concentrate their forces entirely in Bourg, but scattered among the small towns and villages, where they succeeded in displacing the influence and control of local landed proprietors.[16] Other departments produced similar results. The popular movement appeared to be making great strides.

One of the more striking republican electoral successes occurred in the Orne. During the Second Empire, this department had been safe for official candidates of the regime. By the elections of 1869, however, the imperial stranglehold was broken; liberal candidates substantially increased their share of the vote. No "democrats" appeared on the ballot. In February, 1871, the victorious candidates were evenly divided. Among old established notables the Duc Edme d'Audiffret-Pasquier and Albert Christophle headed the Orne deputation. While the rich manufacturer Christophle enjoyed an immense local influence, Audiffret, an Orleanist, saw his local influence on the wane.[17]

Before the summer of 1871 no avowed republican had ever won an election in the Orne. The success of the republican Charles Lherminier over three opponents is thus worth some attention as an example of

15. *Comité national de l'Aube* (Troyes, 1871).
16. *Courrier de l'Ain*, April 27, May 2, 1871; *Progrès de l'Ain*, April 29, April 20, 1871.
17. Attorney general of Caen to the minister of justice, May 10, 1872, in BB (30) 390, AN.

what was accomplished in hostile territory. Lherminier showed surprising strength in rural areas, although not uniformly so, and fared worse in the cities, which historians have always assured us were the centers of republican strength.

Lherminier was a native son who had been subcommissar of the provisional government of the Orne in 1848. We have no information as to the relative success of his mission, but it would appear to have left a residue of favorable memories. The reshuffling of the departmental administration after the fourth of September did not include Lherminier. Gambetta appointed Christophle to the prefecture, thereby maintaining his bridges to the big bourgeoisie.[18]

Lherminier styled himself a conservative republican. He did not publish a detailed platform, but the local republican newspaper, the *Progrès de l'Orne*, devoted a good deal of space to the campaign. Its main theme was the true conservatism of Lherminier in contrast with the fraudulent conservatism of his monarchist opponents. In staying away completely from the issue of the Republic and republican principles and concentrating on Lherminier's solid conservatism, the *Progrès de l'Orne* closely followed the republican pattern of presenting candidates as mature men of government and solid citizens. The newspaper devoted serious attention to the peasant vote, which it correctly considered to be the key to victory. The *Progrès* published a painfully simplified explanation of the bounties that the Republic had brought to the peasants. The Republic had liberated the peasants and had given them dignity. Before 1789, the writer explained, the peasantry had been chattels, pieces of property like horses and furniture to be bought and sold at will by the privileged class. But since then peasants "were no longer a LEASEABLE OR SALABLE object, [they] belong to [themselves] alone. [They] are today SOMETHING, before [they] were NOTHING."[19]

Of the four arrondissements in the Orne—Alençon, Argentan, Domfront, and Mortagne—Lherminier received the largest plurality

18. *Almanach national, 1871–1872* (Paris: Imprimerie nationale, 1873), xxxiii; "Albert Christophle," *Album mariani* (Paris: n.p., 1896).
19. *Progrès de l'Orne*, July 1, June 29, 1871.

in the last. Mortagne was the second largest arrondissement according to the number of registered voters, Alençon being the smallest and Domfront the largest. In Mortagne outside the chief town, Lherminier amassed twice as many votes as the combined total of his three opponents. Most of the communes in Mortagne were very small, averaging fifty to three hundred voters, and Lherminier's strength was greatest in the small communes. Even taking into account the slight difference in size between the smallest and the largest commune, we can differentiate between the chief towns of the cantons and the villages. The chief towns had a larger permanent urban population, generally more sophisticated, and included most members of the liberal professions and the most prosperous merchants. Their composition made them natural centers of political activity from which republican stalwarts radiated outward.[20]

The town of Mortagne dominated the canton of the same name. In 1869 the liberal opposition had done poorly in that canton. Lherminier in 1871 received 1,400 votes in the canton to the combined total of 1,150 for his opponents; in the town of Mortagne, with 1,394 registered voters, he lost by a few votes. In three small communes, each with about 250 voters, he won decisive victories. Turning to the canton of Bellême in the same arrondissement, we find a similar result. Lherminier showed great strength in the rural areas, and this time he also carried the chief town, with 820 voters, and the next largest town, with 810 voters, by a five to one ratio. In three typical small communes, with 183, 128, and 80 voters, he won five to one, two to one, and five to one, respectively. This canton had given more votes to the liberals in 1869 than had Mortagne, but nowhere near a majority. The only three cantons in this arrondissement to give the liberals a majority in 1869 were Laigle, Moulins-la-Marche, and Pervenchères. Lherminier carried the first two, heavily in the case of Laigle, barely in Moulins. However, in Pervenchères he was defeated two to one. Even there he performed best in the small communes. In an adjoining canton of almost the same size, Nocé, Lherminier won the medium-sized com-

20. All figures thus far given and subsequently cited are from Assemblée nationale, 1871–1876, élections partielles, Orne, July 2, 1871, in C 3453, AN.

munes, of about 350 voters, while holding his own in the chief town and the small communes. In the smallest commune, with 64 voters, he won six to one. For the arrondissement of Mortagne, at any rate, the republicans' emphasis on the peasantry paid bountiful rewards as they transcended the traditional limitations of their strength.

Lherminier's strong rural appeal did not carry throughout the department. In the arrondissement of Argentan his urban strength was striking. In the two cantons in which he suffered the sharpest defeats, Lherminier salvaged only a few votes in the chief towns, neither of them very much bigger than the other communes of 150 to 300 voters. Only in the town of Argentan did he acquit himself at all well; he had the most votes of any one candidate, but the combined votes of the other three totaled twice his. Finally, the arrondissement of Alençon provided mixed results. Lherminier polled more votes there than any of the individual opponents, but their total was better than twice his. In the canton of West Alençon, his strength in town extended somewhat to the outlying districts. But just across the city, in East Alençon, Lherminier failed completely to capture the suburbs. Strangely enough, he was elected general councilor in East Alençon just three months later. Considering that the Orne was high on the republican list of retrograde departments, Lherminier's modest victory provided a cause for great rejoicing. His successful campaign provided solid evidence for the republicans that their conscious decision to adopt a conservative posture would best serve their interests.

Like the Orne, the Hérault, on the eve of July elections, appeared to be unpropitious territory for the republicans. The February elections had returned right-wingers to all seats, thus confirming the proposition that in the absence of political groups and administrative pressure the local notables invariably win.[21] But the Hérault contained the seeds of republican growth: in 1869 democratic candidates had scored some small successes in the urban areas—Montpellier, Béziers, and Lodève. The reason for the republican defeat in February lay in the successful

21. Jacques Gouault, *Comment la France est devenue républicaine* (Paris: Colin, 1957), 211.

effort of the old local rulers to identify the republicans with the war party. In July the "liberal conservatives," as they called themselves, played the same theme with slight variations, referring to the republicans as "socialists" and themselves as "moderates."[22] By July, 1871, the republicans suddenly emerged as the majority party.

The republican candidates, Eugène Arrazat and Albert Castelnau, designed their electoral platform to reach the widest possible audience. Castelnau had been relatively unknown in the department, but Arrazat was a popular young lawyer in Lodève, where he was mayor.[23] They had the support of the unified Hérault journalistic network, the liberal *Liberté de l'Hérault* and radical *Droits de l'homme*. Heading their platform was a clear statement of their respect for property, the family, and religion. The program promised to open jobs at all levels of the administration to talented persons, to reduce government expenses as well as abolish state religious activity, to bring about administrative decentralization, and to equitably distribute the tax burden. Editorial comment on the program further emphasized their essential conservatism while not dissimulating their hostility to Thiers' government, which Arrazat and Castelnau asserted was no government at all, but merely a temporary arrangement. There is no evidence of administrative interference in the campaign.[24] If anything, the local officials, predominantly republican in sympathy, managed to pin the monarchist label on the conservative candidates, which admittedly hurt them. The conservatives themselves avoided the monarchist issue entirely.[25]

The final result did not produce an overwhelming republican victory. The figures were 51,683, to 39,766.[26] But republicans had

22. Assemblée nationale, élections générales, February 7, 1871, prefect of the Hérault to Jules Simon, February 9, 1871, Assemblée nationale, 1871–1876, élections partielles, Hérault, July 2, 1871, electoral poster of the Comité conservateur libéral, all in C 3451, AN.

23. A. Clerc, *Nos députés à l'Assemblée nationale: Leurs biographies et leurs votes* (Paris: Chevalier, 1872), 54.

24. *Temps*, July 1, 1871; *Liberté de l'Hérault*, July 2, 1871; *Gard républicain*, July 17, 1871; *Impartial du Finistère*, July 9, 1871.

25. In C 3451, AN; minister of the interior to the prefect of the Hérault, October 31, 1871, in 4M 179, AD, Hérault.

26. These and all succeeding figures in this section are from Assemblée nationale, élections partielles, Hérault, July 2, 1871, in C 3451, AN.

widened their electorate to include the rural areas that had voted Bonapartist in 1869. In the canton of Montpellier, Arrazat and Castelnau
had no difficulty attaining a plurality of 67 percent. In the canton of
Lunel they barely carried the cantonal capital while showing surprising
strength in the smaller towns and villages.

The arrondissement of Béziers was an old republican stronghold,
based largely on the city of Béziers. Arrazat's and Castelnau's three to
one victory in that city came as no surprise. But they also gathered large
majorities in small towns and villages, especially in the canton of
Agde, where the rural vote offset a severe defeat in the chief town.
The pattern held in the arrondissement of Lodève, where they combined traditional strength in the capital with substantial gains in the
country.

Clearly, the results of the February election had presented a dis-
torted image of the real mood of the population in the Hérault. There
was a progressive development of republican strength from 1869 to
1871, and the most dramatic change appeared in the rural areas. In the
Hérault the republicans were no longer exclusively the party of the
cities; they had become the political masters of the entire department.

The Gard was another department where democratic strength had
been evident in 1869 but which had fallen to the conservatives in
February. The July election was a close contest. The victorious republican candidates, Jean-Louis Laget and Joseph Cazot, owed their
success to the rural vote. The republicans pressed heavily on the
monarchist issue. "The battle," wrote the *Gard républicain*, "is joined
between republicans and legitimists, between the sovereignty of the
people and the sovereignty of a prince." Cazot and Laget committed
themselves to restore the economy and defend the status quo against
the irresponsible attacks of monarchist revolutionaries. Their opponents offered nothing to match their strength, which had been
fortified by the solid local position they had built during the war. The
Courrier du Gard, the organ of respectable Nîmes society, divined the
trend and warmly supported Cazot and Laget.[27]

Yet another indication of the republican infiltration into territory

27. *Gard républicain*, June 22, 25, 1871; *Temps*, July 1, 1871.

previously in enemy hands was the number of established notables, many with national reputations, who were defeated in their own bailiwicks in general council elections in October. Among them we recognize several imperial officials: Justin Chasseloup-Laubat in the Charente-Inférieure, Comte Pierre Daru in the Manche, Charles Abbatucci in Corsica, and Louis Buffet in the Vosges. Various legitimists, Orleanists, and liberals also did not escape: Nathaniel Johnson in the Gironde, Léonce de Vogüé in the Cher, Ernest de Cissey in the Ille-et-Vilaine, Duc Edme d'Audiffret-Pasquier in the Orne, Léon de Jouvenel in the Corrèze, Lambert de Saint-Croix in the Aude, Duc Charles de la Rochefoucauld-Bisaccia in the Sarthe, and Baron Charles Décazes in the Tarn.[28] The political demise of these gentlemen not only marked the rising tide of republicanism, but drew attention to the vigor of the bourgeois–*nouvelles couches* alliance.

Republican hegemony in departmental councils constituted a significant breakthrough. It was on that level that the bonds between the high republican politicians and the local bourgeoisie were forged. Gambetta outlined the process in detail in a public letter addressed to Albert Cornil, president of the Allier general council. Cornil had some experience with taking hard blows in defense of republican solidarity. He had been appointed prefect in the Allier after the fourth of September. His tenure lasted until late that month, when he was driven from the prefecture by the working-class leader, Félix Mathé, with accusations of "shallow intriguer" and "reactionary." But the following summer Cornil and his band returned in force to wreak their vengeance. Elected president of the Allier general council, Cornil and his associates rolled to victory under the banner, "the republican principle is the conservative principle par excellence."[29]

The republican victories, Gambetta began, marked a veritable revolution in French politics. Although national issues were not at stake in the campaign, the results clearly indicated the will of the people to confide their most basic interests to the republicans' care.

28. *République française*, December 5, 1871.
29. J. Cornillon, *Le Bourbonnais à la fin de l'empire et sous le gouvernement de la défense nationale* (Moulins: Bougarel, 1924), 102–12; *Circulaire du comité provisoire pour la fondation d'un journal républicain dans l'Allier* (Moulins, 1871).

"We can conclude," Gambetta said, "that the elections have deep political significance and that they are decidedly republican." For the first time in French history, he maintained, decentralization furthered democratic government (republican rule) instead of concentrating power in the hands of the reactionary elements who had made of the local assemblies schools of monarchism. "The *petite bourgeoisie*, workers and peasants" had assumed an active role under the republican leadership. This made up the essence of the Republic.[30]

Turning to the tasks facing the republicans sitting in the local assemblies, Gambetta advised "complete avoidance of national political issues." The republicans' business was to prove their abilities as efficient and impartial managers of local affairs. Sterile debates about issues over which they had no power of decision and useless badgering of the prefects would only reinforce the still prevalent notion that republicans were only noisy partisan politicians unable and unwilling to perform useful functions in government. He urged exclusive concentration on matters of local concern: public health, education, roads, canals, taxes, agricultural and industrial conditions. This did not add up to very exciting work, Gambetta admitted, and it brought little immediate glory to ambitious men. However, in the long run the investment of hard work would be rewarded with handsome political dividends. "The ambition of this party is to prove itself . . . in all phases of political and social life the defender of every legitimate interest . . . that it conceives politics as a means to protect, develop, and secure the rights of the . . . bourgeoisie and proletariat who form the core of French democracy."[31]

The republican sweep through the provinces continued with the results of two by-elections, in the Somme and in the Yonne. Political life in the Somme before 1870 was dominated by a few great landowners and wealthy industrialists. Bonapartism was securely entrenched. In 1869 the official candidates to the Legislative Body won heavy majorities in all parts of the department except the capital,

30. Reinach (ed.), *Discours*, II, 474–76.
31. *Ibid.*, II, 477–81.

Amiens, the single democratic stronghold. A substantial population of independent peasant proprietors voted Bonapartist. However, by 1872, a politically conscious middle class challenged the monopoly of the dominant oligarchy. After the Franco-Prussian War, which these people knew firsthand, the political influence of the middle classes and peasants waxed as the Bonapartist notables were discredited. Republicanism in the Somme underwent a transformation from "radical revolution" to "social conservatism" as middle-class and peasant participation increased.[32]

Both republicans and conservatives were unprepared for the election held on January 7. Jules Barni hurried from Paris after the new year to announce his candidacy and to organize the electoral machinery. Barni was widely admired among the Amiens democrats for his literary exploits as editor of the *Bulletin de la république française.* In the countryside he was either unknown or distrusted for his socialist antecedents.

Consequently, Barni devoted the few campaigning days available to speeches in the villages. He spoke "with respect of Divine Right, of the ancient French monarchy," but gently convinced the assembled farmers of the incompatibility of that hallowed institution with modern conditions. He recalled that the First Republic had introduced universal education, for which many of the yeomen of Picardy had cause to be grateful. Barni rudely rebuffed efforts to link him with the dissident radicals, pointing to his "honest and moderate program" in contrast to the wildly passionate declamations of Victor Hugo and Louis Blanc.[33]

The day before the election Barni had no announced opposition. The notables of Amiens and Abbeville, in a desperate effort to prevent Barni's election by default, placed on the ballot the name of Albert Dauphin, without the latter's consent. Dauphin was mayor of Amiens, general councilor for that city, Imperial Knight of the Legion of Honor,

32. G. Lenormand, "Le Mouvement républicain dans la Somme au début de la troisième république, 1870–1877," *Revue historique,* CXCVI (1946), 2–6, 13–17.
33. *Somme,* January 2, 5, 1872, quoting the *Mémorial d'Amiens; Journal du Havre,* January 3, 1872.

and had served as interim prefect after the resignation of the Government of National Defense. Dauphin was a political power in the Somme, but he was as yet decidedly uncommitted and more than a little wary of notables. When he discovered to his utter amazement that his name appeared on the ballot in opposition to Barni's, he firmly disassociated himself from his erstwhile patrons.[34] However, the device worked, for Dauphin defeated Barni by eight thousand votes. Dauphin, unwilling to enter the Assembly under these terms, resigned immediately. This constituted a tacit endorsement of Barni in the new election scheduled for June.

The republican organization in the Somme began the second campaign fully three weeks before election day. Barni had no automatic votes in a department that still bent to the will of the notables. He had even been unable to carry Amiens. But he did have one overriding advantage shared by all radical republicans: a firm grasp of the new style of democratic politics and a willingness to direct his appeal to the broadest spectrum of the population. He also had an energetic and dedicated newspaper and propaganda network, which the notables could not match.

Barni enlisted the aid of René Goblet. Goblet was native to the region, a successful Amiens lawyer, attorney general for the district court after the fourth of September, a successful candidate in the July elections, and one of the founders of the *Progrès de la Somme*—in a word, the most formidable republican politician of the area.[35] Goblet, appearing on platforms with Barni, mocked the prevalent contention that he and Barni were "radicals" or "dangerous" men. "We are," he insisted, "purely and simply republicans." He could vouch for Barni's conservatism and his complete support for the Thiers government. The closest thing to a formal platform presented to the voters was a general statement of purpose printed by the *Progrès* at the outset of the campaign. The journal stated its intention to be "the organ, not of

34. *Somme*, January 6, 1872; Assemblée nationale, 1871–1876, élections partielles, Somme, January 7, 1872, in C 3456, AN.
35. A. Robert *et al.*, *Dictionnaire des parlementaires* (5 vols.; Paris: Presses universitaires de France, 1889), III, 196–97; Clerc, *Nos députés*, 148.

... a faction or an impotent minority, but of a disciplined and powerful party; it represents not a turbulent and radical opposition, but a governing party." It invited all those willing to defend "liberty and property" to engage in a department-wide propaganda campaign to educate the masses.[36]

A great many pamphlets called *Popular Publications*, printed by the Union républicaine de la Somme, were distributed in bulk for local circulation to men scattered throughout the department. Excerpts from Barni's own writings appeared in the press. The widely distributed propaganda literature had substantial effects in the countryside, where public meetings devoted to discussions of the issues and the candidates attracted large and friendly crowds. Barni himself visited every canton in the department at least once, something he had not been able to do in January. Fortunately for Barni the opposition was split between Cornuau, the candidate of the great bourgeoisie and the landowners, and Lejeune, whose personal position remained vague but whose sponsoring group, the Union patriotique, bore close resemblance to a defunct Bonapartist committee.[37]

Barni owed his victory to a substantially larger vote in June than in January. We have no way of knowing whether the republican machine or the weather was responsible—probably a little of both. The canton of Roisel in the arrondissement of Péronne provides an especially dramatic example. Out of 5,362 registered voters only 2,800 voted in January, giving to Barni and Dauphin, respectively, 1,645 and 1,213 votes. In June 3,400 voters gave Barni nearly 2,600 votes to the combined total of 800 for his opponents. Barni's strength was evident in every commune of this primarily agricultural canton, a canton where government candidates under the Empire had never faced a serious challenge.[38] The pattern repeated itself in other cantons of that arrondissement. Barni always benefited by the increased vote. In the case of

36. *Progrès de la Somme*, May 20 and 26, June 8, 1872.
37. *Progrès de la Somme*, May 23, 27, and 28, June 8, 1872; *Mémorial d'Amiens*, June 2, 1872.
38. These and succeeding figures taken from Assemblée nationale, élections partielles, Somme, June 9, 1872, in C 3456, AN.

the canton of Albert, where the democratic candidate had not received a single vote in 1869, he gathered a large bloc of votes in both the chief town and the villages. In January Barni had been heavily defeated by Dauphin there. The second time around he enjoyed a comfortable margin over the combined totals of his opponents.

The June republican electoral effort in the Somme proved least successful in the arrondissement of Amiens in comparison with the January totals. Dauphin defeated Barni 19,000 to 13,400 votes in January. In June 8,000 more voters went to the polls. Barni's total increased to nearly 19,000. But the combined votes of his opponents reached 21,000. For every new vote cast for Cornuau and Lejeune, Barni received 3. However, with the exception of the city of Amiens, Barni's urban vote fell behind his rural totals. The canton of Corbie, within the sphere of influence of Amiens, had been one of only two cantons to vote more than 10 percent for the democrat in 1869. That pattern was maintained: Barni drew 2,500 votes compared with 2,000 for his opponents.

Unlike Jules Barni, Paul Bert, the republican candidate in the Yonne, was a newcomer to politics who had served his maiden tour of public office as prefect of the Nord under Gambetta. He was well known in his birthplace of Auxerre as a local boy who had gone to Paris and established a distinguished academic career as a biologist. Financial obstacles never hindered the progress of his scholarly career. Reportedly the Bert family enjoyed an income from 40,000 francs of *rente*. His family's local stature did not suffer during the Second Empire and his enemies went so far as to imply that Bert's father had accepted favors from the local imperial officials.[39]

The republican leaders of the Yonne, casting about for an attractive candidate for the June, 1872, by-election, found in Bert, with his Paris connections, local prestige, and personable physical attributes, an eminently suitable choice. When approached, Bert accepted on the condition that he be formally selected by a democratically chosen conference of departmental committees. This procedure would insure

39. Report of police agent, June 10, 1872, in B/a 870, APP.

republican discipline and bring into the electoral process the rural communes. The committees formed were strictly representative of departmental opinion and continued to serve as a medium for electoral propaganda throughout the campaign.[40]

Bert's program was purposely vague. He believed in the "democratic and laic republic" and also in "social peace and decentralization."[41] The congenial intellectual climate of the Yonne allowed Bert to emphasize heavily the anticlerical position. In the Middle Ages the Yonne had been ultra Catholic. During the Wars of Religion it had remained solidly behind the League. Henry IV punished the region by stripping the towns of their municipal franchises and thus forever turned the Yonne bourgeoisie against the Bourbon monarchy. The Yonne did not escape the strange religious mutations of the seventeenth century. Jansenism became exceedingly popular, probably as an expression of defiance against the monarchy and the Gallican church. The events of the Revolution sealed the Yonne's religious configuration. One could find orthodox Catholics in the cities, fewer in the villages. Priests were welcome nowhere.[42]

Bert found large and enthusiastic crowds wherever he spoke. The committees did their job well. An appearance in Tonnerre, home of his second opponent Comte Stanislas de Clermont-Tonnerre, attracted persons from eighty-two surrounding communes—the faithful, the sympathetic, and the curious. They were mobilized by republican shock troops consisting of sixty mayors and twenty former mayors. In keeping with the diversity of his listeners, Bert always presented himself as a moderate: "What will be my position in the Chamber? . . . I will join the great conservative republican party of which Thiers is the soul; I will take my place beside him and Gambetta, that great and patriotic citizen." These two were his heroes. Thiers, because he made it possible for "timid souls" to rally to the Republic; Gambetta for his "political ability and the immense services he has rendered to

40. *Yonne,* June 4, 1872; *Liberté* (Auxerre), May 15, 20, and 24, 1872.
41. *Yonne,* June 1 and 4, 1872.
42. Pierre de Pressac, *Les Forces historiques de la France: La Tradition dans l'orientation politique des provinces* (Paris: Hachette, 1928), 79–83.

the Republic by quieting the impatient and damping dangerous passions." Bert's Republic, the "democratic republic," was the government of the people, promised liberty to all, and threatened violence to none.[43]

The majority of Bert's votes came from the three leading cities of the department—Auxerre, Avallon, and Tonnerre—and from small towns of 300 to 500 electors. In each of the cities his margin was better than two to one over the combined totals of his two opponents, Alexandre Javal and Clermont-Tonnerre.[44] In the canton of Toucy (arrondissement of Auxerre) Bert not only won the chief town by a vote of 365 to 181, but he swept the small towns and villages. There were some deviations from this pattern. In the cantons of Courson and Coulanges-sur-Yonne (Auxerre) Bert held his own in the villages, scored decisive victories in the small towns, and lost by narrow margins the chief towns of both cantons. Those cantons that had no single dominant town, such as Guillon (arrondissement of Avallon), delivered urban and rural votes for Bert in equal numbers. The same analysis can be made for the cantons of the arrondissement of Tonnerre. Linking himself with Gambetta and Thiers, pronouncing in favor of the social status quo—that is, against the "social question"—Bert nevertheless maintained a strong commitment to egalitarian democracy, thereby taking his place among the many men of movement and order.

Republicans, we have seen, rose to the challenge of extending their hegemony to rural France. Most of the small farmers to whom they addressed themselves did not participate in the national market. For them, the state entered their lives only intermittently to collect taxes. But, if the bourgeois spirit includes a grasping attachment to property, farmers were as thoroughly bourgeois as the most successful industrial entrepreneur. They too, on the most basic level of exchange, participated in the capitalist economic order. Farmers, as petty producers, also showed deep strains of rural populism. The republicans set out to demonstrate how the bourgeois order, with its egalitarianism and

43. *Liberté* (Auxerre), June 3 and 5, 1872; *Yonne*, May 28, 1872.
44. These and all succeeding figures from Assemblée nationale, élections partielles, Yonne, June 9, 1872, in C 3457, AN.

its attachment to property, served the interests of farmers. A substantial part of that effort grew out of the campaign against monarchism and Bonapartism.

The Lilies and the Eagle

The real possibility of a restoration did not exist except in the fantasies of the few followers of the Comte de Chambord. But the republicans grasped at the issue and magnified it for use as a propaganda vehicle. Monarchism represented a threat to the economic and social status quo in rural France. The republicans turned this fact to their advantage by representing themselves as defenders of the established order. Bonapartism provided a more serious challenge on the level of entrenched monopolies. As for the power of the imperial political machine, which had rested on the peasant masses, it fell intact into republican hands.

Historians have perpetuated the legend of the real possibility of a restoration. That it did not come off has been variously explained. Certain moneyed interests, it is alleged, sabotaged the great event just before its consummation. Or, the "monarchists" were not monarchists at all, but self-seeking politicians who used the issue as a lure to tie up a few dozen votes.[45] Even as experienced a politician as Jules Simon seemed genuinely agitated by the prospects of a restoration, judging from the soothing letters he received from his friends in the autumn of 1873. Simon would have done well to heed the words of Alfred André, deputy from the Seine and a regent of the Bank of France: "The restoration seems to me absolutely contrary to the interests of our country. . . . What madness to create a regime distrusted by the middle classes and hated by the masses. . . . As far as I can see, the monarchy could neither guarantee liberty nor preserve order and social stability."[46] André's perception of political realities was, of course, highly accurate. Yet, in terms of sheer quantity, the monarchist issue dominated the literature of the time. The clue to the resolution of this

---

45. E. Beau de Loménie, *La Restauration manquée* (Paris: Editions des portiques, 1932); Arthur Loth, *L'Echèc de la restauration monarchique* (Paris: Perrin, 1910).
46. Jules Simon Papers, in 87 AP 3, 4, 5, AN; *République de la Nièvre*, October 23, 1873.

paradox lies in locating the debate between monarchy and republic and exploring its rationale.

It turns out that only in republican circles was the issue persistently raised. The reasons will become immediately clear. The validity of the republican claim to national stature rested on the broad appeal of egalitarian democracy. In this scheme the peasant vote counted heavily. Rural votes, in the words of Henri Martin, were "absolutely essential."[47] Monarchism was the one issue against which the largest number were united. It was ideally suited to republican publicists who delighted in the florid descriptions of the past sins of kings and the horrors which a restoration would bring. One example suffices:

THE BALANCE SHEET OF THE MONARCHY

ONLY THE PEOPLE PAY TAXES
Nobles and priests, WHO OWNED TWO-THIRDS OF THE LAND, pay nothing.
DIME
CORVEE
MOUTURE
TAILLE
DÉFENSE DE TUER LE GIBIER
AGRIER, AIDE, BANVIN, BICHENAGE, BOUTEILLAGE, CENS, CHAMPART, CHIENNAGE, CAPONNAGE, ENCENSOIR, MAINMORT[48]

The press fought 1789 all over again and exploited every opportunity to revive that dead world. The device became a habit; even after Chambord's final farewell to his subjects, the provincial press returned, in dull moments, to the theme. Jean Turigny of Nevers could in apparent seriousness report to his constituents in 1874 that he was successfully holding the republican fortress against royalist advances. A journalist in the Corrèze still insisted in 1875, after the constitutional laws had taken effect, that the single political issue remained republic versus monarchy. He warned his readers to gird themselves for another Bourbon assault upon Marianne's virtue.[49]

47. Letter from Henri Martin, May 5, 1872, Jules Simon Papers, in 87 AP 5, AN.
48. *Républicain de l'Allier*, October 4–5, 1874.
49. *République de la Nièvre*, January 27, 1874; *République de la Corrèze*, April 19, 1875.

It is difficult to take all of this seriously when confronted with the private thoughts of the high republican politicians, all of whom saw in the fiasco of the two flags a splendid opportunity to make political capital. Gambetta encouraged his correspondents in the provinces to drum up popular demonstrations against the monarchy and to circulate protest petitions for delivery to Thiers and MacMahon.[50] The commotion served two useful purposes. In the first place, the agitation against the monarchy kept the republicans in the public eye and associated them with a popular cause. Secondly, a massive demonstration showed the depth and extent of republican support in the provinces. Louis Latrade wrote to Simon that every advantage ought to be taken of present conditions to whip up enthusiasm for the Republic. "You cannot imagine," he said with amusement, "what horrors our peasants in the Corrèze identify with ... Henry V." Every new royalist manifesto announcing the imminent return of Chambord produced a closing of the ranks on the left. The louder the regal trumpets blared, the more the simple and decent citizens embraced the Republic if only to save themselves from an unthinkable alternative.[51]

Republican propaganda, in making the fullest use of the anti-monarchist theme, concurrently extended their program of social conservation. For this purpose, they mobilized the forces of specialized journalism: the cheap pamphlet written for a mass rural audience. Among the publicists writing exclusively for a rural audience, Pierre Joigneaux stands out with his *Feuille du village, Nouvelles lettres aux paysans,* and *La Politique du village.* Joigneaux addressed himself primarily to economic matters. The Republic, he proposed to demonstrate, guaranteed property against the conspiracies of its enemies, whose aims were to restore the social abuses of the *ancien régime,* repudiate the economic settlement of the fourth of August, and replace with authoritarian government the individualism and economic freedom cherished by the independent farmer. Joigneaux expanded the idea of solidarity in its application to the French peasantry. He asserted

50. Daniel Halévy and Émile Pillias (eds.), *Lettres de Gambetta, 1868–1882* (Paris: Grasset, 1938), letter to an unidentified recipient, October 20, 1873.
51. Latrade to Simon, September 26 and October 4, 1873, Jules Simon Papers, in 87 AP 4, AN.

that the union of the bourgeoisie and the peasants, both social conservatives, both hostile to big government, both faithful worshipers of laissez faire, was a natural union combining the most democratic elements of society: merchant, artisan, and farmer. Joigneaux's example was taken up and imitated by other writers like Dionys Ordinaire, whose syndicated column, "Aux Paysans," appeared on the front page of a dozen provincial newspapers. Ordinaire argued that the Republic had brought economic freedom to the peasant and that only the Republic guaranteed the preservation of that freedom.[52]

Newspapers published imaginary dialogues between farmers as they reflected on the current state of politics during their weekly encounters in the cafés on market day. A favorite literary device was the invention of a pillar of the community who preached to his neighbors. In one example, the curé, a progressive fellow, addressed peasant proprietors and agricultural laborers in the following terms:

> Everywhere there is tranquillity. The economy is regaining its strength. The markets are stocked with goods. You can sell your entire crop at a good price. You have no worries about disorder which, in the past, has ruined you. There is no shortage of work. You are well paid. You can save a little. You are able to buy some more land. Your social status has improved. You find excellent mates for your children. You have a little put aside for the declining years. If the assembly of monarchists, elected out of *fear of the Prussians*, is replaced by republicans . . . your well-being will be secure for all time.

Other articles in this same series dwelt in the most general terms on the differences between republicans and monarchists, painting the most grotesque pictures of what France would become should the "conservative" republicans fall before the "revolutionary" monarchists.[53]

A short pamphlet by G. Maze on the history of French revolutions pointed to the events of 1789 as proof that the original revolutionaries were true conservatives who aimed only to revitalize the moribund monarchy and were driven to unplanned excesses by a royalist con-

---

52. Pierre Joigneaux, *Nouvelles lettres aux paysans* (Paris: Chevalier, 1871); *Peuple souverain* (Paris), August 8, 1871; *Progrès de Lyon*, January 14, 1874; *Petit marseillais*, January 7, 1872; *Avenir de Gers* (Agen), May 27, 1871.
53. *Emancipateur* (Toulouse), September 1, 15, and 22, 1872.

spiracy. Monarchies, he continued, have always fallen of their own dead weight (1792, 1830, 1848); republics are always overthrown (1799 and 1851). Thus republicans need never resort to violence to achieve their ends; monarchists must always do so. Republicans do not oppose religion, which they respect in all its forms, and they stand fully behind the sacred institutions of family and property. Jules Barni, in another pamphlet, developed at laborious length five personal characteristics that dignified citizens of the Republic: personal dignity, which included sobriety, independence, and honest labor; devotion to the family and the traditional virtues of the good father and the constant husband; liberty without license and the untrammeled expression of the individual spirit; equality of opportunity without "brutal leveling"; and humanity toward the ill fortune of others and toleration of diverse opinions.[54]

Yet another pamphlet in the same series recounted an imaginary conversation between a rural mayor and his constituents. They examined the economic ideas of four hypothetical candidates to the National Assembly. The legitimist, a local feudal lord; the Orleanist, a banker and manufacturer; and the Bonapartist, a retired general of humble stock, all ignored the requirements of thrift as they spoke approvingly of large government budgets, in violation of the basic rules for running a farm. They lost their audience, since these folk knew that "France is simply a large farm," whose operating principles were directly analogous to those of the five-hectare field. The republican, on the other hand, a local boy with a "clear eye," promised to do ceaseless battle for a reduction of the debt, cutbacks in the public works budget, a reexamination of the railroad conventions, and a revision of the tax structure to remove the unequal pressure from the small landowner and merchant. "It is clear," the mayor and his friends concluded, "who has in his heart the best interests of the country."[55]

The republicans of the Oise founded a newspaper called the

54. G. Maze, "Fin des révolutions," *Société de l'instruction républicaine* (Paris: Chevalier, 1872); Jules Barni, "Moeurs républicains," *Société de l'instruction républicaine* (Paris: Chevalier, 1872).

55. P. Hubbard, "Le Budget des trois monarchies et le budget de la république," *Société de l'instruction républicaine* (Paris: Chevalier, 1873).

Gazette des paysans, whose readership is indicated by its title. Published thrice weekly, the newspaper served as the official organ of the radical republicans in that department. Public meetings, organized through the newspaper, were held often and were well attended. The influence of the "dukes, marquis, counts, viscounts, barons, and curés" waned as the committees of Compiègne, Ribécourt, Senlis, and Noailles blanketed the department.[56]

Town bourgeois formed special committees to finance and direct the dissemination of propaganda materials in the countryside. One such group was the Société d'enseignement politique de Bordeaux, which organized public meetings in market towns and published and distributed printed materials. Republican electoral committees, usually operating from the larger towns, took care to leave open places on their lists for candidates chosen in the rural communes. The most honored and valuable men on the committees were not the few famous names but the anonymous organizers, who worked at the grass roots disregarding their personal comfort and physical well-being.[57]

In electoral campaigns the monarchy-versus-republic issue came in for heavy use. Georges Périn, successful candidate in a May, 1873, by-election in the Haute-Vienne, spoke of nothing else in his campaign: "The monarchist candidacy means: a return to the past, restoration of privilege, the dominance of the nobility and clergy, the eradication of your rights, destruction of universal suffrage. Georges Périn's candidacy means: the Republic, which symbolizes peaceful progress, universal education, cheap government, in a word, order, justice, and liberty."[58] Even Jean Turigny, a stubborn radical of ancient vintage and founder of the intransigent *Tribune nivernaise*, did not hesitate to wage a conservative campaign in the Nièvre where the rural vote was of decisive importance. Those speaking on his behalf recalled his contributions to the literature of rural pamphletry, specifically *Le Roman du village* and *André le paysan*. Cyprien Girerd, a deputy from

56. *Gazette des paysans* (Beauvais), June 2 and 23, 1872.
57. Clipping from the *Journal de Die*, February 12, 1871, in 9M 10, AD, Drôme; *Constitution*, September 29, 1871; "Nécrologie de M. Auriol," *République de la Nièvre*, July 3, 1873.
58. *Progressif de la Haute-Vienne*, May 4, 1873.

the Nièvre, campaigned for Turigny on a republic-versus-monarchy platform. And nineteen prosperous merchants from Nevers signed a manifesto backing Turigny in the name of the republican defense of the social order. François Gaudy followed the same pattern in his successful campaign in January, 1872, for an Assembly seat from the Doubs. Olivier Ordinaire (the name is endemic in the Franche-Comté), writing in Gaudy's newspaper, declared that the election of republicans such as Gaudy guaranteed the rights of the peasant proprietor against the revolutionary ambitions of the agents of kings and emperors.[59]

Local History: The Loire and the Nord

The foregoing discussion has concentrated on the republican bourgeoisie's work in mobilizing troops for its political forces among petty producers and peasants. We began with a consideration of the republicans' position on the class question, and correctly so, for in that particular context the evolution of the republican movement with its particular social ideology takes on sharp definition. Let us consider in greater depth two departments, the Loire and the Nord, where republicans confronted the class question directly and dealt with it in a manner consistent with their social outlook. Both departments contained an assortment of industrial enterprises in textiles, mining, and metallurgy. A solidly entrenched bourgeoisie grasped the leadership of both departments' political affairs and emerged to head a triumphant republican coalition.

The industrial revolution had not fully transformed the economy of the Loire. Modern capitalist enterprises stood side by side with "archaic workshops." Heavy industry was concentrated in the immediate region of Saint-Étienne and Rive-de-Gier. Apart from such gigantic metallurgical complexes as Petin-Gaudet and Terrenoire, small metals and textile plants were scattered throughout the department.

59. Biographical note on Jean Turigny, in B/a 948, APP; *Impartial du centre* (Limoges), July 27, 1870; *République de la Nièvre*, October 9 and 11, 1873; *Républicain de l'Est*, January 6, 1872.

Extensive survivals of the domestic system meant that much industry was closely woven into the fabric of small-town and rural life. The small independent peasant proprietor dominated the agricultural scene. More than 80 percent of all farms were owner cultivated, and the great majority were less than sixty acres in extent.[60]

Until 1860, this placid scene of a comfortable provincial economy run by local bourgeois had been disturbed only sporadically. The sudden intrusion of modernization, which brought in its wake depression, outside capital, and working-class militancy, came as a severe shock. Since mid-century the Saint-Étienne coalfields had seen their share of the total coal output in France decline compared with the production of the Nord–Pas-de-Calais basin. The economy became unbalanced. On the one hand, Terrenoire increased production tenfold between 1866 and 1868, partly because of military contracts, whereas textile production, particularly in Roanne, languished. Not surprisingly, the owner of Terrenoire, Alexandre Jullien, was a Bonapartist, whereas the employers in Roanne embraced republicanism. Because of the dominant role textiles played in the Loire economy, the recession had a snowballing effect on the prosperity of the entire population.[61]

The employers blamed the 1860 commercial treaty with England for their trouble. Importations of cloth across the Channel had increased five times since the treaty was signed. What Claude Fohlen calls "a curious spectacle" appeared: "workers and employers denouncing with one voice what they believed to be the cause of their common troubles, the commercial treaties concluded since 1860, and together demanding a dramatic change in economic policy."[62] A radical reorientation of economic policy appeared unlikely without a change of regime. The spectacle of employers and workers chanting in unison

60. J. Merley, "Les Elections de 1869 dans la Loire," *Cahiers d'histoire*, VI (1961), 59, 70–71; Max Perrin, *Saint-Étienne et sa région économique: Un Type de vie industrielle en France* (Tours: Arrault, 1937), 435–39.

61. Pierre Léon, "La Région lyonnaise dans l'histoire économique et sociale de la France: Une Esquisse," *Revue historique*, CCXXXVII (1967), 46; Merley, "Les Elections de 1869," 64, 82–83; Émile Levasseur, *Histoire des classes ouvrières et de l'industrie en France de 1789 à 1870* (Paris: Rousseau, 1904), 608.

62. Claude Fohlen, *L'Industrie textile au temps du second empire* (Paris: Plon, 1956), 410.

was indeed curious; 1869 became the year of strikes in the Loire[63] and spurred the republicans to intensify their political action against the Empire in the hope of maintaining their solidarity with the workers under cover of appeals to democracy.

As the government prepared for the elections of 1869, evidence accumulated to signal the erosion of the Empire's electoral base. Surveying the gloomy scene, Eugène Rouher found that even among the peasants, loyalty to the Empire could no longer be assured. All that remained was a scattering of notables who had nothing to recommend them except their distinguished ancestry.[64] What had happened was not so much a mechanical breakdown of electoral machinery as the alienation of the middle classes, who had given up their allegiance to the established order.

The republican alliance of urban and rural bourgeois in the Loire fought the campaign of 1869 on two fronts: against the Empire and its authoritarian political and economic structure and against independent workers' action. Their forces, initially concentrated against the regime, shifted as local conditions demanded more effort along the second front. The election provided an opportunity to suppress the antagonism of capital and labor under a cloud of republican slogans. In this manner, Jules Favre, in his campaign in Roanne, urged the solidarity of the propertied and the propertyless against a common foe.[65] In Saint-Étienne, where Pierre Dorian held court, the republicans most successfully turned to their own advantage the Empire's unpopularity.

Pierre Dorian emerged in the 1860s as the dominant figure among republicans in the Loire. An established businessman, he enjoyed the prestige, respectability, financial position, and wide circle of acquaintances that qualified him for the republican leadership. The separate threads of enlightened capitalism, the Protestant ethic, and a Saint-Simonian faith in the historic mission of the industrial bour-

63. Fernand L'Huillier, *La Lutte ouvrière à la fin du second empire* (Paris: Colin, 1957), 29.

64. Letters from Raoul Duval, from the mayor of Pau, from an unidentified correspondent, May 8, 21, and June 3, 1869, and various other letters received during the spring of 1869 from prefects, justices of the peace, and tax officials, Rouher Papers, in 45 AP 3, AN.

65. *Avenir national* (Paris), June 9, 1869.

geoisie merged in his career. A pioneer in paternalism, Dorian organized model company towns around his metallurgical plants in the Loire and the Haute-Loire. But his fundamental commitment was unmistakable. When his workers attempted to establish a mutual benefit society independently of the company, Dorian refused to recognize it. In 1869, during the strikes in the Saint-Étienne basin, he coordinated the employers' antistrike action.[66]

Dorian's republicans faced only one obstacle on their road to power. The workers, hardly comfortable within the established republican opposition, found their spokesmen in the Comité d'union démocratique, led by two lawyers from Saint-Étienne, Aristide Martin and Victor Duchampt, who presented a serious danger to the republicans. Martin and Duchampt led troops drawn exclusively from the proletariat. They deliberately avoided all political collaboration with the republicans and, because they claimed for themselves the republican label, blackened the image of republican respectability that Dorian's organization had managed to create. The more Martin's campaign speeches inflamed class hatred and the more frequently he recalled Dorian's role as strikebreaker, the greater was the threat he posed. Dorian had originally intended for one of his lieutenants, Martin Bernard, to contest Saint-Étienne's seat for the Legislative Body. But rather than run the risk of a weak candidate being eclipsed by a socialist, Dorian himself stood for election. Heavily financed and backed by a well-organized propaganda network, he easily defeated Aristide Martin.[67]

In his campaign, Dorian made little effort to turn the socialists' flank by direct appeals to solidarity. He did not need to. His position of overwhelming strength, the solid phalanx of employers behind him, the tradition of a popular alliance against the Empire, and the political weakness and immaturity of the workers allowed him to campaign without embarrassment on the most obvious slogans. César Bertholon, Dorian's propaganda chief and editor of the *Eclaireur* of Saint-Étienne,

66. Georges Duveau, *La Vie ouvrière en France sous le second empire* (Paris: Gallimard, 1946), 440–41; L'Huillier, *La Lutte ouvrière*, 29.
67. Merley, "Les Elections de 1869," 75–86.

concentrated on "verbal broadsides directed against the Empire" and "the repetition of the most ancient slogans of political democracy."[68] Some years later, Étienne Lamy, a Catholic traditionalist with a social conscience, noted:

The only thing that interested the workers was the social revolution. But that was precisely what the bourgeoisie . . . intended to avoid. Dorian, as a leading figure in the metallurgical industry, remained committed to traditional property arrangements, while as an aspiring politician he had to present the impression of being a passionate reformer. Under the Empire, his newspaper, the *Eclaireur*, distracted the workers from their true interests with red herrings, focused their hatred on the soldier and priest, rather than the employer.[69]

Lamy took advantage of thirty years of hindsight and underestimated the democratic ideology. Following the story for the next four years, we can retrace the steps that led to the formation of a solid republican bloc, increasingly conservative in its social orientation, and, of necessity, increasingly hostile to working-class aspirations.

Had they the choice, the republicans in the Loire would have preferred a peaceful and orderly transition from Empire to Republic. The reforms associated with the liberal Empire pointed to a weakening of Napoleon's authoritarian will. As it was, the abrupt collapse of Napoleon's regime threw everyone in France into a state of temporary confusion. At no time during the autumn and winter of 1870 did the Government of National Defense possess the means to impose its unchallenged authority throughout unoccupied France. That government, hastily assembled and often paralyzed by the disruption of communications, depended upon local officials to maintain order.

César Bertholon, Gambetta's prefect in Saint-Étienne, found that he would have no trouble maintaining order and putting his own people in office if he had to deal only with local Bonapartists. It was from the left that the danger to his authority appeared. Trapped between what he called "the two extremes," Bertholon struggled against

68. *Ibid.*, 79.
69. Étienne Lamy, "Le Gouvernement de la défense nationale," *Revue des deux mondes*, XXII (July-September, 1904), 797.

"a group of his old friends." He recognized members of the 1869 workers' opposition among his adversaries.[70]

The Government of National Defense put the highest priority on its commitment to prevent revolutionary violence. It sought to establish itself as the legitimate government of the Republic (a Republic whose legal existence was not universally recognized in France) and to give daily testimony to the fact that "the Republic is from now on the only form of government which can reestablish the greatness, the wealth, and the moral health of the nation." This required that the government and its local representatives adopt a conservative stance emphasizing material security and moral order. "Speak of nothing else," instructed Clément Laurier, Gambetta's *chef de cabinet*, "but that our Republic is a government of order . . . and the only possible expression . . . of civilization."[71]

Republicans in the Loire eagerly set out to apply Laurier's advice. They proved their effectiveness by suppressing the mounting agitation of the extreme left, which burst forth in Saint-Étienne on October 31, the same day a similar uprising occurred in Paris. Bertholon, with help from Dorian and government agents dispatched by Alphonse Gent from Marseille, quickly put down the revolt. As much as the violence on the left threatened order in the Loire, the justification for its suppression strengthened the position of the republican establishment. For they could continue to oppose independent workers' action as a necessary element of patriotic defense and republican solidarity and yet defend the propriety of their position by referring to the strictures sent down from Tours "to stand firm and unyielding against the demands and pressures of extremists."[72]

With the resignation of the Government of National Defense, César Bertholon surrendered the prefecture in Saint-Étienne to the new administrators, all of whom were wealthy veterans of the Em-

70. Dossiers individuels des préfets, Bertholon to Arago, February 11, 1871, in F(1b) I 156(19), AN.

71. "Enquête parlementaire sur les actes du gouvernement de la défense nationale," circular dispatch from Clément Laurier to all prefects, September 23, 1870, *Annales de l'Assemblée nationale, 1871–1876*, XXV, 595–96, hereinafter cited as *Annales*.

72. *Ibid.*, XXI, 512–19, XXV, 595. Gent was "superprefect" for the Midi and the Rhône valley.

pire.[73] Bertholon took up where he had left off in 1869, resuming his journalistic and organizational labors for the republican party. He, Dorian, and their collaborators founded two newspapers, the *République de la Loire* and the *République des paysans*. They also launched the Alliance républicaine, whose curious fate at the hands of its original sponsors marked one further step in the consolidation of republican order.

The financial, political, and editorial character of the *République de la Loire* reflected the social orientation of the embryonic party. It was financed by a small group of middle-class and professional republicans. The initial stock issue was capitalized at 35,000 francs divided into 700 equal shares of 50 francs. Pierre Dorian was the largest stockholder with 104 shares, symbolizing his continued preeminent position in the department and the generosity of his purse.[74] César Bertholon was a modest stockholder, but his importance for the republicans of the Loire exceeded his financial stake in the newspaper. Bertholon's reputation was spreading throughout the southeast. The republicans of the neighboring department of the Isère placed his name on their electoral list for the national elections of 1871. Among the other stockholders were Jean Audiffret, former subprefect in Roanne under Bertholon and a republican activist of long standing; Jean Baptiste Chevassieux, mayor of Montbrison and unsuccessful candidate for the National Assembly on the republican list; and Valentin, a prosperous merchant of Saint-Étienne.[75] Four of the stockholders were elected to the department's general council later in 1871. Among the single-share subscribers predominantly modest bourgeois stand out.[76]

73. Dossiers on prefects, subprefects, and other administrative officials, in 1M 6, AD, Loire.

74. Dorian's solid position in the department accounted for the fact that he alone among all republican candidates for the National Assembly in February, 1871, was elected. His name had appeared on the "conservative" list as well. 10M 74, 3M 12, AD, Loire; *Réveil de l'Ardèche,* January 8, 1871. Dorian had something of a national reputation as a pamphleteer, and he contributed to the *Bibliothèque démocratique. Impartial du centre* (Limoges), July 22, 1870.

75. Election lists, in 8M 17, AD, Isère; 10M 74, AD, Loire; *Réveil de l'Ardèche,* February 8, 1871; *Rappel* (Paris), September 24, 1872.

76. Prefect of the Haute-Loire to the prefect of the Loire, February 21, 1873, in 10M 74, AD, Loire. According to this report, the editor of the *République de la Loire,* Henri Lefort, had made the acquaintance of Pierre Dorian while the former was Gam-

The *République de la Loire* circulated as a general interest newspaper for businessmen and professionals. Popular entertainment and the most obvious propaganda were handled by two local newspapers: the *Eclaireur*, which covered Saint-Étienne and which Bertholon continued to run, and the *Courrier de Roanne*, edited by Audiffret and another ex-subprefect, Brison.[77] Few departments, at this early date, possessed so complete a republican network.

But the story does not end there. No republican party with a commitment to order and property could expect to attain power without considerable support in the countryside. As the alliance with the workers weakened under the pressure of a new political situation, the republicans sought to enlist the peasantry in their cause. Unlike in 1848, the specter of popular democracy no longer struck terror in the countryside, where twenty years of imperial rule had left a population anxious for political liberty.

Bertholon, displaying amazing energy, appeared at the helm of yet another newspaper in early 1872. The *République des paysans* was a unique project. Published in Saint-Étienne in tabloid form every Tuesday, it exclusively served a village readership that could neither afford nor take the time to follow the daily press. Eighteen months after it first appeared, the newspaper had made enough of an impact to attract the attention of Marshal MacMahon's government, which considered its influence dangerous to the stability and popularity of the Government of Moral Order. It enjoyed a far wider circulation than the government press, was frequently distributed free to farmers, and clearly appealed to the very people on whom every frankly reactionary French government counted.[78]

The *République des paysans* was filled with the endless trivia and

---

betta's prefect in the Haute-Loire. Dorian was a sharp judge of talent and put Lefort to work for the republican cause. Lefort was, his file said, less a committed republican than a bright and ambitious seeker of well-paid steady employment. Apparently he had his price. "I look upon him," wrote the prefect of the Haute-Loire, "as one of those men thrown about by revolutions, but who are worth more than the low stature to which these circumstances have brought them."

77. *Peuple souverain* (Paris), October 13, 1871; subprefect of Roanne to the prefect of the Loire, June 2, August 26, 1871, in 10M 72, AD, Loire.

78. Prefect of the Loire to the minister of the interior, October 30, 1873, in 10M 74, AD, Loire.

stylized polemic characteristic of all local newspapers that systematically reprinted articles from the big Paris dailies. However, its reporting of the local politics most directly affecting the interests of the peasantry matched the best offered anywhere. Bertholon's editorials attacked the government and called attention to the thin margin of prosperity under a regime that seemed not to take seriously its mandate to establish a constitutional Republic. Continued refusal to found the Republic on a legal basis, he warned, would produce a swift and devastating depression. He pointed to some of the achievements of the National Assembly that illustrated its reactionary inclinations: higher taxes on consumer goods and taxes on short-haul transport, all of which fell most heavily on the *petit proprietaire*.[79]

Bertholon sketched a picture of the Republic that harmonized with the modest aspirations of his rural audience. Not only did he raise the moral imperative of government by the people, but he linked the survival of the independent producer to the vitality of popular government. The people had expelled from positions of local power privileged notables and replaced them with new men whose modest origins marked them as men of the people. (We must assume that even Pierre Dorian fit the description of a "new man.") The message to the old ruling oligarchy, "whether they be nobles, priests, or big capitalists," was unambiguous: "They no longer may treat us as children whom they lead by the nose." Under the Republic, the small farmer and entrepreneur could look forward to more participation in public affairs in contrast to past "empires and kingdoms who have made the farmer's bed . . . and sown and harvested the political and administrative fields . . . and controlled all privileges, favors, sinecures."[80]

Bertholon knew his clientele and understood that the legitimate aspiration of the people for democratic institutions was tempered by an instinctive regard for material interests. In precisely this context the Republic offered the most and threatened the least: "The proverb says: who moves carefully, moves surely, and it is for that reason above all

79. *République des paysans,* January 2, 1873, October 19, 1872. Mention of the railroad tax was an inspired touch, recalling the inequities of the Empire.
80. *Ibid.,* February 4, 1872, December 4, 1873, February 4, 1874.

that I want to see the Republic securely established, so that we can get on with the business of reform in a practical and sensible manner and *face without danger social questions. It is no longer a question of over-throwing the existing order*, but of modifying it as we feel the need. . . . Universal suffrage makes possible the representation of all interests, all opinions, all aims. No one is isolated. . . . Neither oppression nor exploitation is possible."[81] In this excerpt from an almost unknown newspaper in a corner of France we can see summarized with clarity and precision the progressive yet conservative social ideology of the new republicanism. Viewed within the context of the times and particularly against the background of the struggle for power in the Loire, these words communicate a significant message. Just as the regimes of the past had appeared to represent the interests of a tightly knit privileged class, reflected in the dominance of Parisian capital and big landed property, the new republican institutions were to express the self-consciousness and determination of the middle classes to defend their liberty and property. Thus was the alliance between town and country forged, an imposing combination of diverse elements of the population eager to establish popular government and deeply antagonistic to any deviation from the path of orderly progress, whether under pressure from the right or, especially, from the left.

The republicans in the Loire constituted less of a political party, except in the most informal sense, than one of many nexuses of social and personal relationships, which combined to steer a course through turbulent political waters. The brief and dramatic life of the Alliance républicaine of Saint-Étienne and Roanne exposes the strong undercurrent of social conflict beneath the surface of republican politics. The Alliance républicaine was founded during the Franco-Prussian War under the patronage of César Bertholon and Jean Audiffret, who turned their official positions to effective political use. Both men played an active role in the organization and exercised close control over its activities. Shortly after its formation, the alliance had secured a beachhead in the Loire from which republicans launched propaganda and organizational efforts throughout the department. Its organizational

81. *Ibid.*, May 16, 1872, italics added.

structure was simple, but it provided a setting in which four hundred of the most politically active bourgeois of the Loire managed the political affairs of the department. After the resignation of the Government of National Defense, the alliance continued to hold regular weekly meetings on Saturdays in order to prepare for the coming local elections.[82]

During the Commune, Roanne and Saint-Étienne had experienced disturbances common to all large French cities. Thiers' government, on the edge of panic, accused the alliance of attempting to organize revolutionary communes in the two towns. Nothing was further from the truth. Bertholon had fought Communard influences in the Loire. The alliance acted as his auxiliary and continued to play that role after Bertholon left power. Of its devotion to order there could be no question.[83] To be sure, its commitment to order stopped far short of contemplating an alliance with liberal monarchists or rightist Bonapartists, for whom the republicans appeared to be dangerous radicals.

The general council elections in Roanne in the autumn of 1871 were especially tumultuous because of depressed conditions in the textile industry. Workers threatened strikes and denounced the employers for callousness in the face of hardship. The leader of the employers, Raffin, president of the alliance and mayor of Roanne, held off the rebellion of the workers by promising reforms while he planned to use the elections to consolidate his power and that of his collaborators. Raffin personally visited most of the cantons in the arrondissement of Roanne; he supervised the distribution of pamphlets printed by the alliance; and, it was alleged, he bought votes for his fellow manufacturer Charles Cherpin in the town of Saint-Albans. In this campaign, as in 1869, the republican leadership claimed for itself exclusive leadership of all popular forces, exclusion of independent workers' action, and unity behind a sweeping democratic program.[84]

What was this program? It emphasized general principles: repre-

---

82. Report of the police commissioner of Saint-Étienne, October 9, 1871, report of the prefect of the Loire, August, 1871, undated memorandum, all in 10M 70, AD, Loire; *Rappel* (Paris), September 21 and 23, 1872.
83. Circular of the Alliance républicaine, in 10M 70, AD, Loire.
84. Subprefect of Roanne to the prefect of the Loire, October 20, 1871, *ibid.*

sentative government, freedom of the press, assembly, and association, popular participation in government, equitable economic policies, and separation of the church and state. Most of the alliance's program closely resembled the platform of the Paris Alliance républicaine, founded by Alexandre Ledru-Rollin, Henri Brisson, Charles Floquet, and Tony Révillon, to oppose socialist influence in Paris.[85]

No formal connection existed between the two groups; the similarity of program can be accounted for easily by the ideals common to all republicans. However, the final statement of the Parisian program was reproduced by the republicans of the Loire, for it reflected their special attitude toward the social question: " 'The Republic is one and indivisible—Republic, not of classes, but a fusion of all classes; not only of form, but of substance, whose roots strike deeply into the depths of society—Republic, determined to harmonize, by the application of science and common sense and without violent shocks, the most superficially antagonistic interests.' "[86] This statement expressed not only the dream of a new world in which men believed with the utmost sincerity, but also articulated a democratic ideology that grew out of the social and cultural aspirations of a great many Frenchmen, urban and rural. Yet this ideology—which rested on the conviction that political liberty provided a sufficient framework within which decent, honest, and hardworking men could make their way in the world— did not correspond to the emerging realities of life in working-class communities.

In these terms, the alliance acted as a double-edged weapon to consolidate republican power in the Loire while isolating the workers' groups. But the alliance was not sufficiently disciplined to prevent some use of the organization on behalf of the workers. Rolland, a former staff member of the *Eclaireur* under Bertholon, placed himself at the head of a burgeoning strike movement in Roanne in October, 1871. He printed pamphlets supporting textile workers who were demonstrating against extensive layoffs. Rolland claimed to be acting under

85. *Alliance républicaine de la Loire: Programme, ibid.; Avenir de Gers* (Agen), January 17, 1871.
86. Kayser, *Les Grandes batailles du radicalisme,* 55, 322.

orders of the alliance, transmitted by César Bertholon himself.[87] In the light of Bertholon's past activities and his current job as republican propaganda chief under Dorian, it seems unlikely that such instructions existed. But the episode underlined the danger of using weapons sharpened on both sides. Scattered socialists infiltrating the alliance turned it from an asset into a liability for the republican leadership. After the elections to the general council, the alliance no longer was indispensable. Rather than abolish the alliance on their own initiative, which would have been embarrassing, the republicans took advantage of a general government crackdown on political associations. In late October, the police raided a meeting of the alliance and closed its offices. The following year, a handful of members were brought to trial on charges of fomenting rebellion against the state. According to Amiel Dabeaux, the subprefect of Roanne who planned the raid, none other than Charles Cherpin and Jean Audiffret informed the police as to the time and location of the meeting to be raided. Cherpin appeared at the trial as counsel for the accused; Dorian helped to underwrite the costs of the defense.[88]

At their trial, the defendants insisted that the alliance's membership included only "the most devoted adherents of order," that its supposed radicalism was the work of a few provocators, that they worked only to enlighten and stimulate the population, that their society was not secret, and that they had no sympathy for Communards. The prosecution attempted in vain to establish a clear connection between the alliance and the First International. The accused stubbornly maintained that their ideas were those of "conservative republicans."[89]

As a result of the trial, a few republicans were fined and the Alliance républicaine liquidated. It was a cheap price for the "devoted adherents of order" to pay to enable them to remain steadily on the moderate course, demonstrate that militant republicanism stood for social conservation as well as social reform, and thus escape the di-

87. Report of the prefect, October 22, 1871, in 10M 70, report of the Sureté générale, October 8, 1871, in 10M 72, AD, Loire.

88. *Avenir du Var* (Toulon), September 25, 1872; subprefect of Roanne to the prefect of the Loire, October 30, 1871, in 10M 70, AD, Loire.

89. *Rappel* (Paris), September 22 and 23, 1872.

saster of alienating the middle classes and the peasants from the Republic.

The swing away from radicalism was confirmed in 1873 with the choice of a republican candidate to succeed Pierre Dorian in the National Assembly. With Dorian's death, Charles Cherpin became the senior republican deputy and in that capacity guided the selection of the candidate. Cherpin's first impulse was to favor Bertholon, the most experienced and widely known politician in the department. However, Bertholon had made many enemies as prefect, and Cherpin feared that his record of radicalism in 1848 would make him vulnerable to the kind of character assassination that supporters of MacMahon's regime specialized in. Better, Cherpin concluded, to find someone noncontroversial, a known moderate, appropriate to a situation in which "moderation is not a crime but, on the contrary, an essential quality."[90]

The choice fell to Francisque Reymond, who had made his fortune in the building business with the help of substantial government contracts under the Empire. He had since retired to a large estate near Montbrison, where he cultivated various crops and the life-style appropriate to a country gentleman. Reymond had not shown the slightest interest in politics before 1870. Like any successful businessman after Sedan, he rallied to the Republic because he saw it as a barrier to extremism of the right and the left. In 1871, Reymond ran successfully for the general council with the patronage of the Alliance républicaine. He performed well as a public servant, having roads and canals repaired and bringing into Saint-Étienne direct telegraph service from Lyon. He sat on the left in council meetings, nominally a "radical," but in reality a conservative devoted to order. Men such as Reymond, Dorian, and Cherpin, who combined a fervent belief in democracy with an abhorrence of social disorder, most faithfully reflected the spirit of republicanism. Reymond's candidacy was opposed by only a few irreconcilables, presumably the same people who had infiltrated the Alliance républicaine. His electoral platform included defense of the

90. Letters from Cherpin to Simon, September 15 and 16, 1873, Jules Simon Papers, in 87 AP 2, AN. Permission to use these papers granted by Madame Delorme-Jules-Simon to whom I give thanks.

Republic, praise for universal suffrage, and the exclusion of any member of a French royal house from the presidency of the Republic.[91]

Reymond had made Montbrison his own political fief. He was ideally situated to carry this decidedly rural area, which, added to traditional republican strength in the towns, would guarantee victory over the government's candidate. The employers of the area, mainly in small industry, were frequently former workers themselves who had moved one rung up the social ladder. They therefore had good reason to be attracted to the candidate of middle-class democracy. The farmers, though independent smallholders, might have wavered, but their suspicion of curés and aristocrats drove them into the republican camp. For this reason Reymond exploited to maximum effect the scare of a monarchical restoration associated with the *affaire du drapeau blanc*. "The agents of the republican candidate," the subprefect complained, "are eager . . . to raise the alarm among the rural people, announcing that the restoration of the monarchy . . . will necessarily mean the resurrection of the *ancien régime* complete with clerical rule."[92]

The election returns showed that Reymond's margin of victory in the arrondissement of Montbrison was greater than in Roanne. He won overwhelming victories in its rural cantons. For example, in the canton of Saint-Germain-Laval, isolated from any urban center, where the democratic candidate in 1869 had won just 5 percent of the vote and where Cherpin had won 50 percent in July, 1871, Reymond won 67 percent.[93] This may be partially ascribed to his position as a local landowner; more likely, however, this success was the fruit of César Bertholon's labors among the farms and villages of the department.

Reymond's relatively weak showing in the city of Roanne compared with his strength in isolated rural areas suggests two related conclusions that transcend the narrow confines of one department.

91. Report of the prefect of the Loire to the minister of the interior, September 30, 1873, report of the subprefect of Montbrison to the prefect of the Loire, October 25, 1873, in 3M 13, AD, Loire; *République des paysans,* October 9, 1873.

92. Report of the subprefect of Montbrison to the prefect of the Loire, October 25, 1873, in 3M 13, AD, Loire.

93. Election partielle à l'Assemblée nationale, October 20, 1873, *ibid.*

First, the campaign provided a dramatic demonstration of the effectiveness of the alliance that the republican bourgeoisie had forged with petty producers. Second, the refusal by large numbers of workers to vote for a republican, even when the alternative represented an old paternalist order, suggests that the republicans' position on the social question reflected a distinct class outlook that workers recognized as alien to themselves. None of this happened by accident. On the contrary, what happened in the Loire between 1869 and 1873 shows in detail the conscious choices made by local bourgeois in putting together a ruling coalition within which they reserved for themselves a dominant position.

Whereas the Loire embraced an area of declining production, the troubles in the Nord derived from a different set of circumstances. Its entrepreneurs fell victim to the stresses produced by industrial concentration, which were tightened by the crisis in production of 1867–1868. Linen and wool industries received a momentary boost as a result of the cotton shortage brought on by the American Civil War. Many plants enjoyed a brief Indian summer of prosperity only to be left in the lurch after the Confederate surrender reopened the southern ports. Cotton substitutes found no market. The cotton industry itself, which had benefited from a massive infusion of capital provided by several local banks, could not compete with the sudden irruption of Lancashire goods. Depending on future profits to amortize the loans, the crisis drove them to the wall. Dozens of business failures followed. Large and established firms were not immune to the infection but, on the whole, they sustained the stresses with less misery. Unemployment skyrocketed in 1866 and 1867 and with it came the demand by workers for jobs, the *petite bourgeoisie* for customers, and manufacturers for markets. If this conjuncture were not enough to turn the capitalists of the Nord against the regime, the prospect of labor agitation decided the issue.[94]

The republican movement in the Nord included the usual complement of businessmen, journalists, and lawyers. With the stock of

94. Claude Fohlen, "Crises textiles et troubles sociaux: Le Nord à la fin du second empire," *Revue du Nord,* XXXV (1953), 107–23.

the regime collapsing, their ranks grew rapidly. They quickly injected their distinctive class outlook into their politics. Republicans in Lille blamed the regime for the disruption of the social order accompanying hard times and industrial violence. To them, it appeared that the imperial author of *L'Extinction du pauperisme* might act on the utopian sentiments of his youth at their expense. Gustave Masure, editor of the republican *Progrès du Nord*, summoned the bourgeoisie to its responsibilities: "Any indifference at this juncture is doubly dangerous in this manufacturing region where all citizens, the bosses even more so than the workers, should follow closely every turn in the path of social change and should seek to forge links among all interests through the careful application of economic science."[95] Some workers remained unmoved by this old-fashioned paternalism cloaked in democratic garb and sent forth with the benediction of science. In one area of the industrial north torn by recession, layoffs, and unrest, the coalfields of the Pas-de-Calais, workers delivered their votes, as usual, to the emperor.[96]

In the wake of Sedan and the Commune, the republican bourgeoisie of the Nord girded itself for the task of defending order within the republican revolution. Once again, Gustave Masure led the assault on class divisions: "The Republic cannot be defined as a particular kind of social formation; it is simply a form of government whose special function is the suppression of narrow interests which, in monarchies, throw up obstacles to the realization of the republican ideal. . . . All that the government owes to society is liberty, that is, equality of rights and duties."[97] Associations similar to the Alliance républicaine appeared. The demanding organizational tasks expected of all members of such associations effectively excluded workingmen who could not spare time away from the job. In Roubaix, where workers could not be frozen out entirely, their independent organizations were absorbed

95. *Progrès du Nord*, September 13, 1866, quoted in Pierre Pierrard, *La Vie ouvrière à Lille sous le second empire* (Paris: Bloud and Gay, 1965), 477.

96. In the plebiscite of 1870. A. Fortin, "Les Conflits sociaux dans les houillières du Pas-de-Calais sous le second empire," *Revue du Nord*, XLIII (1961), 354–55.

97. *Progrès du Nord*, March 17 and 18, 1871, quoted in Robert Vandenbussche, "Aspects de l'histoire politique du radicalisme dans le département du Nord (1870–1905)," *Revue du Nord*, XLVII (1965), 255.

into bourgeois republican committees. Workers received token representation on the steering committee.[98] The key figure behind this operation was Jules Deregnaucourt, whose role in Roubaisian politics paralleled that of Pierre Dorian of Saint-Étienne.

Deregnaucourt had survived the change of regime smoothly. His position as a major sugar beet producer and machinery manufacturer made him a familiar and trusted figure in business and agricultural circles. He also had some interests in textiles and in coal mining, which did not hurt him in a territory dominated by the Anzin Coal Company. In February, 1871, Deregnaucourt, always a man of order, took himself to Lille to protest to Prefect Paul Bert the dismissal of the mayor of Roubaix, an imperial appointee. Apparently, he and Bert struck a compromise, for Deregnaucourt himself returned to Roubaix with the seals of mayoral office. From that position Deregnaucourt launched his political career, which rested upon the solid foundations of the Roubaisian *patronat.* As its leader, he fought the influence of the local workers' movement and, in an effort befitting a conservative republican capitalist, organized a company-controlled Conseil des prud'hommes, which masqueraded as a workers' committee. High republican politicians, like Gambetta, praised his work, which, it was said, avoided violence and protected private property.[99]

Economic conditions in Roubaix in the early 1870s created a climate most favorable to the continued political ascent of a man of Deregnaucourt's character. The city had weathered the storms of 1867–1869 with a renewed burst of productive energy. Wool production emerged as the city's first enterprise, and mechanical processes in spinning, carding, and fulling replaced traditional handicrafts. Roubaix's capitalists fattened on a significant expansion of the domestic market and an even more spectacular export trade. By 1875 she stood second only to Lyon in exports.[100] Coal production in the

98. Association électorale républicaine de Roubaix, *Règlements* (Roubaix, 1871).
99. Clipping from *Gaulois,* September 17, 1872, in B/a 1013, APP; *République française,* November 23, 1871.
100. Report of the general council of the Nord, April, 1883, in F(12) 4841, AN; Claude Fohlen, "Esquisse d'une évolution industrielle: Roubaix au dix-neuvième siècle,"

eastern part of the department experienced an equivalent upsurge. Recovery from the war was accomplished without effort. When a shortage of workers drove the price of labor up and reduced profits, the coal entrepreneurs imported large numbers of foreign workers, chiefly from Belgium.[101] The capitalists of the Nord experienced first-hand the benefits of republican order and would defend their fortress against attacks from either the right or the left.

Deregnaucourt successfully contested a seat in the National Assembly in June, 1872, which had fallen vacant when General Louis Faidherbe resigned in protest against the Treaty of Frankfurt. Republicans in the Nord were deeply stung by the loss of a proved republican general, especially one who had demonstrated a sharp eye for business prospects during his proconsulship in Senegal.[102] However, Deregnaucourt made up for the loss with his steadfast position on order and solidarity. To the "merchants and industrialists of the Nord" he promised to serve the "economic interest" and satisfy "the economic needs" of the region. He urged those "gentlemen privileged by birth, fortune, and power" to rally behind popular government without fear of compromising their ruling-class position. Indeed, they had nothing to fear from Deregnaucourt, who in one breath assured workers and petty producers that republican democracy carried the promise of social reform and social peace.[103]

Deregnaucourt deliberately sidestepped all concrete issues. He made only the vaguest reference to tax reform: "Taxes ought to be paid by those who have the means . . . the expenses of the state ought not to fall on industry, commerce, and agriculture."[104] Businessmen

---

Revue du Nord, XXXIII (1951); France, Bureau de la statistique générale, *Annuaire statistique* (Paris: Imprimerie nationale, 1894), partie rétrospective, 535.

101. A. Lequeux, "Les Mines de houille du Nord et du Pas-de-Calais et la crise de 1872–1873," *Bulletin de la société géographique de Lille* (1933), 167–70.

102. Halévy and Pillias (eds.), *Lettres de Gambetta,* letter from Gambetta to Faidherbe, September 27, 1871; Louis Faidherbe, "L'Avenir du Sahara et du Soudan," *Revue maritime et coloniale,* XXXI (1863), 221–48.

103. *Libéral du Nord,* June 2, 1872; *Manifeste des conservateurs républicains* (Lille, 1872); *Adresse des ouvriers de l'arrondissement de Lille, à tous les travailleurs du Nord* (Douai, 1872).

104. *Peuple souverain* (Paris), May 26, 1872; *République française,* May 24, 1872.

could not quarrel with that. Deregnaucourt's electoral poster reflected in the starkest terms the republican message. The words *solidarity, order, the principles of 1789* all appeared boldly emblazoned in black letters on a yellow background:

> WORKERS   EMPLOYERS   TRADESMEN   BOURGEOIS
>   CRAFTSMEN   FARMERS
>
> All of you, self-made men, liberated by the immortal Revolution of 1789, all of you who were NOTHING under the former regime and who are EVERYTHING today, do you want to plunge back into the past?
>
> You are being invited to commit moral and political suicide by those who propose to withdraw to an earlier century in order to refasten the chains about your necks. . . .
>
> Thiers asks your support against the wild WHITE REVOLUTIONARIES
>
> VOTE FOR THE FRIEND OF FAIDHERBE AND THIERS[105]

The republican bourgeoisie of the Nord had found their man.

These examples provide further illustration of how the Republic developed within the Empire and came into its own after the "republican revolution" of 1870. They also describe the social and ideological limits within which the Republic evolved. In these first years of the Republic, provincial bourgeois had moved quickly to occupy positions of local power, took the first steps toward establishing their ideological hegemony, and temporarily neutralized and absorbed the first thrust of independent working-class action.

Transition

Thus far we have explored the shaping of a distinctive ideology that derived from the class interests and perceptions of the industrial and agrarian fractions of the French bourgeoisie. We also have witnessed how that ideology was formulated to embrace a larger community, the world of petty production. Jules Ferry's dictum that a stable bourgeois order could not survive without the support and the collaboration of rural France echoed frequently during the years of preparation. Gam-

---

105. Elections à l'Assemblée nationale, élections partielles, January 7, 1872, Nord, in C 3453, AN.

betta's appeal for a "rural National Assembly" and Henri Martin's invocation of "rural democracy" constituted both self-serving rationalizations and hard, realistic judgments—rationalizations because such a view justified, indeed sanctified, evading the harsher realities of the social question; realistic judgments because experience consistently proved Ferry right.

What follows recreates the forging of a socioeconomic program that was designed to serve primarily bourgeois interests while not appearing to swindle petty producers. This accounts for the repeated statements about "national" production, "national" education, and the "national" market that we will encounter in subsequent chapters. The program itself included a variety of constituent elements: reform and extension of the railroad system, educational reform, and the outlines of nationalist economic policy. The promotion and implementation of these programs followed closely the ideological formulations and the character of the republican alliance described in the first two chapters.

Much of the politics of the late 1870s and the early 1880s, which appear confusing and contradictory on the surface, take on coherence when we focus on the efforts of the republican bourgeoisie to reconcile diverse and opposing interests while working simultaneously to reinforce its own primacy. Battles waged against "clericals" and "aristocrats" in the name of democracy, even more so radical democracy, although not staged maneuvers and taken seriously by all engaged, were fought in defense of the bourgeois Republic and enabled the republican bourgeoisie to establish itself as the party of progress and order.

The Republic required, among other things, a national transportation system consistent with the interests of industrial and agrarian capitalists. At the heart of the matter lay the question of completing the railway network. The railroad question did not involve merely the resolution of technical and financial problems. How and under what conditions the third rail network was to be built immediately became explosive political issues that exposed the strengths as well as the weaknesses of the republican coalition, underlined its essential class foundations, and provoked a frontal assault against the bastions of *haute finance.* The struggle came to a head in the famous *seize mai* crisis, which was not simply a right-wing coup preparatory to a royalist restoration, as it has habitually been interpreted. The crisis occurred in the larger context of the struggle over railroads, and its resolution made possible the Freycinet national transportation plan.

Chapter III

[Rails for the Republic

MARCEL BLANCHARD has reminded us that the construction of the trunk line railways during the Second Empire marked the effective beginning of a French industrial revolution. He emphasized forcefully the close "link between the extension of the railway network and the industrialization of France."[1] Neither provincial industrialists nor Paris bankers overlooked the significance of this relationship. Nor did either of the contending fractions of the French bourgeoisie miss the fact that control and ownership of the railroads would prove to be decisive for the economic configuration of the nation and for the distribution of political power. Hence, by throwing the spotlight on railroads, we can illuminate the steps by which the republican bourgeoisie forged a national industrial policy consistent with its material interests and ideological perspective. This process involved nothing less than gaining mastery over the destiny of the French political economy. To do so republican bourgeois committed themselves to battle against financial capital. They could truthfully claim that the bankers denied the nation economic progress, extended markets, entrepreneurial freedom, and social peace. Those goals had defined the republican program since the movement took initial shape in the late 1860s. The Republic thus stood in diametrical opposition to "oligarchy" and to the "new feudalism," which, under various masks, prevented industri-

1. M. Blanchard, "La Politique ferroviaire du second empire," *Annales d'histoire économique et sociale,* VI (1939), 529.

ous entrepreneurs from enjoying the full fruit of their labors. This was an egalitarian perspective, to be sure, but one circumscribed within a perimeter of capitalist social values.

Early Railroad Development

Not many years after the birth of railroad technology in the early 1830s French capitalists began to debate the question of private versus state ownership of railways. From the very beginning, this issue was bound up with questions of political economy, social policy, and the nature of successive regimes. The arguments that were advanced on the side of state ownership rested on national industrial requirements. But in the early years such arguments carried no force, for the national market, a product of the railroads themselves, did not exist. Consequently, a provincial bourgeoisie of sufficient numbers and local power also did not exist. Thus the demands of Alphonse de Lamartine, in 1838, that the railroads be built under a state monopoly fell on barren soil.[2] By the time the first railroad bill became law in 1842, some took note of the handwriting on the wall. Anselme Pelestier, writing in the democratic *Revue indépendente*, foresaw a time in the near future when a "barony of bankers" would exert a stranglehold on all production dependent upon rail transport.[3]

Garnier-Pagès, who generally made more sense than Lamartine, also supported railroad nationalization: "The existence of financial companies, cast in the mold of monarchical, aristocratic, federal government, is totally incompatible with the principle of democratic, republican, unitary government."[4] Garnier did not indulge in abstract constitutional theory. He dealt in harder currency. He spoke directly to the interests of a growing number of industrial and agrarian bour-

2. R. Matagrin, "Le Rachat des chemins de fer en 1848," *Revue socialiste* (1904), 419.

3. *Revue indépendente*, XIII (1844), quoted *ibid.*, 423–24. "Partout on reconnaît les éléments . . . d'une aristocratie se soutenant par mille alliances interlacées, gouvernant à leur gré toutes les branches de la production et de la consommation, et ne laissant aucune industrie passer un écu sans relever sur lui une prime presque discrétionnaire."

4. *Ibid.*, 440.

geois. While their general class position was identical to that of big capital, their specific interests as a class of industrial entrepreneurs were in opposition to those of big capital. The bourgeois had become concerned with the state of the national market under the conditions of financial speculation (carried on frequently at their expense) characteristic of the July Monarchy. Quite naturally, they expressed their own political ambitions in national unitary terms against the alleged "federalism" of the Orleanist notables. Bourgeois agitation, however, came prematurely, and the principle that building the national market could be incompatible with the perpetuation of private monopolies did not necessarily follow. A fusion of the state bureaucracy with the companies would produce the desired result. In effect, the practical argument for nationalization led with equal force and logic to its opposite: state subsidy for private investment. This fact continued to muddy the waters of the argument.

National industrial requirements versus the narrow interests of a fraction of the bourgeoisie returned the focus to railroads during the Revolution of 1848. The Revolution brought a mixed bag of politicians to power, but its dominant mood was a determination to liberate France from the grip of the bankers who had operated under the July Monarchy. This control by banking interests was most visible in the railroads.

Various projects for state *rachat* (return to state ownership) appeared, but none became law.[5] *Rachat* entailed difficult and, at the time, insurmountable problems. For how would the business be financed? The general view held that railroad shareholders should be compensated with shares in the 5 percent *rente*. But at what level of value? Both the price of railroad shares and *rente* fell precipitously on the Bourse during the first half of 1848. And large-scale distribution of more shares of *rente* might easily drive its price down further. The price of shares, however, did not accurately reflect the actual financial

5. One exception should be noted: the temporary nationalization of the Paris-Lyon Railway *pari passu* with its construction. Frederick de Luna, *The French Republic under Cavaignac* (Princeton: Princeton University Press, 1969), 239, argues that this step was "important," citing Louis Girard as his authority. But why so important, unless it was to underscore the point that the republican bourgeoisie of 1848 acted consistently with bourgeois interests as perceived at the time.

condition of the railroad companies, which was sound and held great promise for the future.[6] Evidently, speculators (unleashed perhaps by the railroad owners) deliberately drove the price down to blackmail the Provisional Government into abandoning a general *rachat*. While denunciations of the "barony of bankers" filled the air, the Republic quietly permitted the continuation of business as usual. The railroads held a dagger at the throat of the Provisional Government. Their managers threatened to lay off thousands of workers if public confidence in the future of the lines were not reasserted; in effect they demanded that all talk of *rachat* cease. A new influx of unemployed into Paris, already swollen with refugees from the *tour de France*, promised grist for the mill of left-wingers.[7] Popular passion against the railroads reached its peak at the same time, expressed in the "destruction . . . of a large number of stations on the northern line, at Saint-Germain and at Rouen; the burning of several railroad bridges: those of Asnières, Bezons, and Rouen-au-Havre."[8] The government of the Second Republic, whatever its radical tone, did not forget its links to provincial producers who could not be expected to have any patience with Luddism. They did, however, want more railroads. Louis Napoleon, with the bankers in his pocket (or he in theirs), delivered where the Republic could not.[9]

The second network, comprised of the main trunk lines and their principal tributaries, was completed during the prosperous 1850s and early 1860s. This achievement established the future pattern of railroad development and, over the short run, confirmed the monopolies of the six great companies in the Conventions of 1859.[10] Rationaliza-

6. The prices of shares in the Orléans, Paris-Rouen, Avignon-Marseille, and Nord railways all fell to roughly one-third their January value by April. The price of the 5 percent *rente* fell to fifty francs per share from its high in the eighties. E. Théry, *Histoire des grandes compagnies françaises de chemins de fer dans leur rapport financier avec l'état* (Paris: L'Economiste européen, 1894), 30, 23.

7. Matagrin, "Le Rachat des chemins de fer," 438–40. The *tour de France* was the movement of artisans and journeymen from town to town to ply their crafts. Paris was customarily the last stop.

8. Théry, *Histoire des grandes compagnies*, 30.

9. Here the reader is well advised to go to Emmanuel Beau de Loménie, *Les Responsabilités des dynasties bourgeoises* (4 vols.; Paris: Denoël, 1946–63), I, chapter on the Second Empire, to see how it was done.

10. The six companies were the Nord, the Est, the Ouest, the Paris-Orléans, the Paris-Lyon-Mediterranean, and the Midi.

tion of the railroad network, after years of chaos and ruinous competition, was achieved at the price of a one-dimensional and lopsided development of transportation, whose effects fell most heavily on small and marginal enterprises. For monopoly carried with it nearly total discretion as to the rates and terms of carrying traffic. Jeanne Gaillard has recorded the effects of this situation and suggested a link between renewed opposition to the railroad monopolies and general political opposition to the Empire: "The companies have ruined overland traffic and diverted water transport; they remained unmoved by the complaints of merchants forced to use their railways. Besides, the companies were assured of the collaboration of the state to the point where small and medium-sized commerce no longer could doubt their ultimate fate."[11]

Napoleon III's government attempted to turn the flank of opposition in 1865 by providing for the construction of local rail lines to serve restricted markets. The measure purported to respond to numerous demands, especially from the southwestern and central parts of France, to build new lines into areas excluded from outside markets. Each person naturally wanted trunk lines to pass through his own town, hoping a backwater could be transformed into a brilliant metropolis. The general council of the Corrèze urged the minister of public works to arrange for the projected Lyon-Bordeaux railroad to pass through Clermont-Ferrand and Tulle. Receiving no satisfaction, the notables of the Corrèze asked the prefect to intercede with the railroad owners themselves; they further requested that he approach the Paris-Orléans (P-O) Railroad Company to extend to Tulle its line terminating in Limoges. This exchange occurred in 1865. In 1874, their requests still remained unheeded.[12] Ultimately, as these events suggest, the power of decision lay with the companies themselves and not with the government. What is more, the government appeared to prefer it that way, confirming the suspicions of anxious and frustrated provincial entrepreneurs that the Bonapartist regime reserved the choicest

11. Jeanne Gaillard, "Notes sur l'opposition au monopole des compagnies de chemins de fer entre 1850 et 1860," *1848*, XLIV (December, 1950), 237.
12. Conseil général de la Corrèze, *Procès-verbaux des délibérations, 1865, 1874* (Tulle, 1866, 1875).

cuts of the fatted calf for its favored friends. By 1881, the Clermont-Tulle line had been built as part of the newly created state railway system. Four leading republican politicians dominated its board: Joseph Calmon, Jean Lebaudy, Jules Lesguillier, and Louis Latrade, republican leader of the Corrèze.[13]

André Lavertujon, a republican liberal from Bordeaux, pointed out that at the moment when the law of 1865 was passed, the time was ripe to force the big companies to lower rates and submit to stricter state control.[14] But the terms of the law itself denied that possibility. Neither the communes nor the departments, into whose hands the initiative for developing local lines was placed, possessed the necessary fiscal resources to do what the government said they were supposed to do. Only the big companies, in coalition with local notables, mainly big landowners, were in a position to spark the development of local lines, and they would do so only at the price of their continued monopoly. Even as conservative a businessman as the Le Havre shipper Jules Siegfried understood the deception inherent in the 1865 law. Departmental councils established priorities for local lines, but the State, "perhaps under the influence of the big companies, exploited its power to declare certain lines 'in the public interest' to hold up or even prevent the building of these lines, thus reserving to the big companies the most profitable of them."[15] Thus a measure allegedly designed to promote competition within the transportation system in reality provided a cover for the perpetuation of monopoly.[16]

Writing at the height of the railroad controversy in the late 1870s, Alphonse Chérot, *polytechnicien* and former railroad official, lamented the failure to implement the 1865 law for the sake of internal development. He explained the failure on the recognition by the imperial government that the law was "essentially republican"; that is, it would have shifted economic initiative from Paris to local governmental bodies. This amounted to decentralization of economic authority en-

13. *République de la Corrèze*, August 11, 1881.
14. *Tribune française*, June 21, 1868.
15. Jules Siegfried, *Quelques mots sur la question des chemins de fer en France* (Le Havre: Brindeau, 1875), 18.
16. Louis Girard, *La Politique des travaux publics du second empire* (Paris: Colin, 1951), 296; *Rappel* (Paris), April 21, 1878.

tirely incompatible with the imperial system. Decentralization was not to be valued for its own sake as a barren institutional arrangement, but for its contribution to the viability of the national industrial order. Railroad monopolies, in Chérot's view, violated the basic principles of political economy, "the division of labor and free competition." What was worse, the free development of production in the provinces stood still while the railroad companies remained the "absolute masters of all commercial activity . . . [and] regulators of all agricultural and industrial production."[17]

The railroad monopolies survived the Second Empire with their dominant position intact. However, their cartel, the first in Europe if we except the Prussian State Railway Administration, rested on shaky foundations. Cartels at this juncture could not be legitimized by appeals to economic rationality as they were to be at the end of the century.[18] Cartel formation preceded the construction of a complete transportation network and, as a result, impeded its consummation. Small wonder, then, that a growing number of industrialists, farmers, and commercial men, whom the railroads brought into the market, looked upon themselves as victims of the railroad monopolies. Inasmuch as the cartels were brought into being and sustained through the will of the state, these men looked to the state for restitution, but the nature of the Bonapartist state had precluded this restitution. Thus, the railroad question became a political question of the first magnitude, a question to be resolved under the Republic according to the terms set by Bonaparte's republican successors.

Railroads and the National Market

The railroad issue was not taken up again in earnest until 1874, when it became central to the political struggle between the republicans and the Government of Moral Order. A brief flurry of activity occurred two years earlier, itself of no consequence but an indication

17. A. Chérot, *Les Grandes compagnies des chemins de fer en 1877: Dangers politiques et économiques de leur extension* (Paris: Guillaumin, 1877), 5–16.
18. Charles Assolant, *De la nécessité et des avantages du rachat des chemins de fer* (Paris: Jeanmaire, 1881), 7.

of the direction in which the republicans were moving. During the debate on the budget of 1872, Clément Laurier, Gambetta's one-time colleague in Adolphe Crémieux's law offices and his *chef de cabinet* in 1870, introduced a measure requiring the state to exercise its option to repurchase the railroads, as provided for in Article 37 of the Conventions of 1859. The railroads, he said, would then stand as collateral for the three-billion-franc loan floated to pay the second installment on the German indemnity. He argued that such solid security would allow the government to borrow at a favorable rate of interest. Stockholders in the railroads, he went on, would lose nothing; in fact, they would gain with the establishment of the state as creditor. A more far-reaching motive lay behind Laurier's bill. As explained in the *République française*, "the best feature of the bill . . . is that it returns to the state property which rightfully belongs to it and which it is in the interest of everyone that it possess. . . . [The state must possess] the power to assure to industry and commerce regular transport services."[19] Laurier's bill disappeared, never to reach the floor of the National Assembly.

The beginning of the great depression passed unnoticed in the offices where the railroad companies counted their receipts. Except for the Paris-Orléans, all the companies showed an ascending rate of gross revenues. Elsewhere in the economy, certain ominous signs appeared, which focused attention on an unhealthy political climate for business and the lack of a national transportation infrastructure.

The first indications of severe depression appeared in the slump of 1873–1874. Up to one-quarter of the silk factories in the Rhône River valley closed down between the summer of 1873 and the following spring, throwing hundreds out of work. The effect on a major industry was contagious. Small workshops producing mainly soft consumer goods closed because of a lack of buyers.[20] Silk production suffered in the east as well. Of four large plants in Nantua in the Ain employing 3,500 workers in 1872, three survived until 1874 with a

19. *République française,* February 4 and 5, 1872.
20. Drôme: situation industrielle, troisième et quatrième trimestres, 1873, deuxième et troisième trimestres, 1874, in F (12) 4499, Archives nationales, hereinafter cited as AN.

total work force of only 1,946. Other textiles in the same region suffered equally, and the drop in total wages paid adversely affected general business conditions.[21] Beginning in 1874, reports indicated that the once-flourishing Fourchambault blast furnaces were operating at substantially less than capacity. Half the workers had been laid off and the rest were working abbreviated shifts. The consequent drop in consumer demand raised a general complaint among the merchants against the government's economic policy or, more precisely, its lack of policy.[22]

A revived spirit of economic Bonapartism precipitated events that seemed to confirm the darkest predictions. The Duc de Broglie, vice-president of the Council of Ministers under MacMahon, filled his cabinet with old Bonapartist notables and representatives of *haute finance* and big business. His majority in the Assembly, in fact, depended on the votes of the small Bonapartist contingent, and the government made extraordinary efforts to elect more Bonapartist candidates.

Broglie appeared to go out of his way to sabotage France's orderly recovery from the war. He used the full power of the state administration to try to break republican power in local government, the strongest link in its political chain. His stated policy was to remove all mayors who had the slightest connection with radical or republican organizations. In doing so, he threatened a wholesale disruption of local government, for there were few elected officials who had not obtained office on a republican ticket.[23] Broglie's prefects, most of whom had served in similar positions under the Empire,[24] went about their tasks with enthusiasm, but their expectations of a smooth operation received a severe jolt. Many prefects reported that they were unable to find candidates to fill the evacuated *mairies*. New municipal elections were scheduled for autumn, 1874, and the government had been un-

21. Ain: situation industrielle, 1872–1874, in F (12) 4479a, *ibid.*
22. Nièvre: situation industrielle, première trimestre, 1874, in F(12) 4522, *ibid.*
23. Report from the canton of Maugio, in F(1b) II, Hérault 8, prefect of the Gard to the minister of the interior, January 20, 1874, in F (1b) II, Gard 6, *ibid.*; *Gironde,* March 3, 1874; *Siècle,* February 14, 1874.
24. Thirty-nine of his appointees, to be exact. *Avenir de la Haute-Saône,* June 28, 1874.

able to provide solid evidence of its ability to guarantee a favorable outcome. The republican machine seemed too formidable even for the massive coercive power of the administration. Prospects of a short tenure turned away all but the most zealous defenders of the "moral order." The prefects and their local collaborators often found themselves isolated from public opinion and were not equipped to give new appointees, when they could find them, sufficient authority. The result was widespread administrative anarchy.[25] The government mistakenly expected that local landowners appointed as mayors would encounter no opposition, for it was generally believed that a flabby political spirit among the peasants would cause them to submit to their new masters who, in other times, carried great weight with the rural population. Broglie had not added to his calculations an entirely new factor—republican penetration of the villages.[26]

Against this background, it is not difficult to understand a mood of quiet panic as the Broglie-Bonapartist faction stumbled from one unpopular policy to another. Nagging doubts were raised about the aims of the government in the conservative press. Certainly, the sudden evaporation of a healthy business outlook was not to be taken lightly. "Merchants, manufacturers and farmers [were] unanimous in their complaints" about the serious consequences of the government's reckless tampering with good order.[27] Republicans took maximum advantage of the opening to parade their commitment to a sound, stable, unadventurous economy. They pointed to the sound state of finances up to this time (to which, truthfully, they had contributed nothing), gains in the value of foreign trade, increased coal production, and a boom on the Bourse, especially in the quotations of the 3 percent and 5 percent *rentes*.[28] What did the government offer to the

25. Prefect of the Haute-Garonne to the minister of the interior, January 25, 1874, in F(1b) II, Haute-Garonne 9, prefect of the Hérault to the minister of the interior, February 9, 1874, in F(1b) II, Hérault 8, AN.

26. Prefect of the Hérault to the minister of the interior, February 18, 1874, in F(1b) II, Hérault 8, *ibid.;* police commissioner of Courtezois to the prefect of the Vaucluse, February 3, 1874, in M 108, Archives départementales, Vaucluse, hereinafter cited as AD, appropriate department.

27. *Journal de Paris*, quoted in *Tribune française*, September 14, 1873.

28. A. Laserve, "La République et les affaires," *Société de l'instruction républicaine*, n.s., No. 17 (Paris: Chevalier, 1875).

classes moyennes who awaited evidence of its good faith? The government presented them with a new tax on short-haul railroad rates (short-haul lines directly served the independent farmer and the manufacturer dependent upon the local and regional market).[29]

Once again, railroads became the center of attention. A comprehensive investigation of rate policy was conducted by a parliamentary committee of inquiry headed by Charles Dietz-Monin in 1873 and 1874. Its investigations elicited written responses to a questionnaire circulated among chambers of commerce, mayors, general councilors, and commercial courts which revealed the depth of dissatisfaction with the existing structure.[30]

The testimony of provincial businessmen included none of the strident rhetoric characteristic of politicians' declamations: no denunciations of the"barony of bankers," no demands for a general *rachat* of all railroads, no pressure to nationalize the railroads, no reduction of the subtle complexities of entrepreneurial life to the simplistic tableau of plot and counterplot painted in stark primary colors. They spoke of hard times and the railroads' responsibility for their condition. Frequently, freight traveled in a roundabout fashion, resulting in swollen costs, simply because one company refused to use the lines of a competitor. The Société pour la défense des intérêts commerciaux du Havre noted a drop in port loadings as a result of this abuse. The manufacturers of Cholet "pay for the transport of coal from Saint-Nazaire according to the distance covered, 177 kilometers, while the actual distance is only 128 kilometers." Wine wholesalers in Beaune, traditionally the middlemen for the producers of the Mâconnais, feared bankruptcy because the Paris-Lyon-Mediterranean (P-L-M) Railroad added a surcharge to its rates to Paris if freight originating in Mâcon stopped at Beaune, even though the latter was on the direct line. Unequal rates favored some regions over others.[31]

Unanimity prevailed that a uniform rate system be established

29. *Union républicaine de l'Eure*, March 13, 1874.
30. A. Picard, *Les Chemins de fer français* (3 vols.; Paris: Rothschild, 1884), III, 154–59.
31. *Annales de l'Assemblée nationale, 1871–1876*, Vol. XXXI, Annèxe 2291, pp. 523–25, 526–27.

throughout the country. No one suggested the apparently logical step of creating state railways out of the private companies.[32] Finally, a curious mutation of public officials into servants of private interests appeared to be taking place. The chamber of commerce of Orléans noticed this as it watched the *commissaires de surveillance administrative*, who "go through the motions of defending the public interest by appearing to enforce a strict observance of the rules and rates for rail traffic, thus demonstrating their independence of the big companies. Unhappily, for whatever reason, this is not the case; and public opinion regards them as employees of the companies fulfilling their duties with the deference of subordinates."[33] The companies extended their influence far beyond the major trunk lines. Interlocking directorates and special financial and rolling stock arrangements brought regional lines under their control. Several lines exploited by the Orléans-Chalons company (in turn linked to the Paris-Orléans) operated under the direction of major figures in the banking-railroad complex: Charles de la Rochefoucauld, Benjamin Delessert, Charles Hottinguer, Auguste de Talhouet, among others. Hottinguer ran coal mines in Épinac (Saône-et-Loire), which shipped coal out on a special railroad running to Vélars. The Épinac-Vélars company was administered by a triumvirate of directors: Hottinguer, Delessert, and Charles Mallet. With that kind of muscle, no other local line could hope to compete with the Épinac-Vélars.[34]

The Dietz-Monin committee scheduled open hearings for early 1875. They never occurred. The republicans charged that pressure from the great companies forced the government to suppress the committee before it could fulfill its mandate.[35] The tradition of the Empire remained unchallenged: cheap subsidized credit was provided for the big companies while the small, independent lines went begging for credit at ruinously high interest rates. The government remained unmoved. Pierre Magne, minister of finance, attempted unsuccessfully to push through the Assembly's budget committee a 5 percent increase

32. *Ibid.*, 543–49.
33. *Ibid.*, 568.
34. *Annuaire des chemins de fer* (Paris: n.p., 1877).
35. Picard, *Les Chemins de fer*, III, 159.

in all indirect taxes on consumption commodities. This topped a whole series of taxes on business introduced the previous year. What could be expected, the republicans charged, from an ex-Bonapartist whose unique concern was "to continue the Empire's policy of distributing handouts to the companies while crushing the people under new taxes." Magne dramatically demonstrated how one faction could ignore the general interests of producing classes, whose concern for popular welfare, the high price of the "ordinary laborers' simple glass of wine," expressed not the anxieties of a social conscience but the reflexes of an industrial bourgeoisie reaching out for consumers and markets.[36]

The debate in 1875 over proposed new concessions to the P-L-M took the issue one step further without resolving it. Under the law of 1865, these new lines had been marked for development by independent companies. The minister of public works, Eugène Caillaux, ignored the previous arrangement to award the rights to the P-L-M. Soon afterward he reaped his reward with a seat on the board of directors of this same company.[37] Caillaux had followed a career reproduced frequently in modern French political life. He trained in engineering at the École polytechnique, joined the Corps des ponts-et-chaussées, and ran the Le Mans office of the Ouest Railroad Company until 1862, when he became engineer-in-chief of the entire network. From that position he moved rapidly to political eminence: the railroads' man in the cabinets of 1874, 1875, and 1877.[38]

Jean Baptiste Krantz, a banker and deputy holding orthodox financial views, deplored the long-term implications of this latest administrative stroke. Monopoly, he warned, "will turn out to be, without a doubt, the direct cause of the collapse of our economic system." Not only did concentration undermine the free marketplace, Krantz's principal concern, but it stunted the equitable expansion and open character of the marketplace.[39] He was wrong; the "economic system" itself gave birth to the monopolies. Krantz's misjudgment draws

36. *République française*, April 17, June 29, 1874.
37. *Annuaire des chemins de fer.*
38. G. Vapereau, *Dictionnaire des contemporaines* (Paris: Hachette, 1880), 342.
39. Quoted in Charles Baïhaut, *Rapport de la commission du troisième réseau: Convention pour rachat d'une partie de la compagnie Paris à Orléans* (Paris: Quantin, 1880), 16.

attention to the special quality of the French experience. Capitalist industry in France arose under the shadow cast by finance capital. Thus, while it struggled to throw off the fetters imposed upon it, industry remained beholden to finance capital to the extent that the latter retained its command of the transportation system. Perhaps what Krantz feared, but dared not utter, was a reaction against a political system that allowed such abuses to accumulate unchallenged. If republican democracy failed to contain the power of high finance, some other political arrangement might succeed.

Arguing from a less doctrinaire position and thus more in tune with the aspirations of provincial producers, Henri Tolain complained that Caillaux's decision would subvert the efforts of small companies to secure a foothold in the railroad business and mortgage an increasing portion of France's economic future to "a small number of big capitalists." The former socialist had assimilated the ideological assumption of the marketplace with a vengeance. Alexandre Clapier, following Tolain, "unmasked the shady tactics which the companies, with the collaboration of the public works bureaucracy, used . . . to negate the effects of the laws of 1865 and of 1871."[40] The day following the foregoing debate in the National Assembly, Spuller pointed out that the issue was not the companies' power in the abstract, but the misuse they made of such power to deny the national economy its necessary connective tissue. He cited the two-year-old proposal to build a Calais-Marseille line aimed at rerouting Near Eastern traffic through the French ports. None of the companies showed the slightest interest in building that link. This was reason enough to create new companies: "What we are talking about is not a revolutionary act, but a prudent act; we must direct ourselves to the task of making up for lost time and regaining for France the high world position which she always ought to occupy."[41]

Henri Germain argued in much the same terms during the debate in 1875 over granting new concessions to the P-L-M. *Grand bourgeois*, international banker, and republican, Germain had represented the

40. Picard, *Les Chemins de fer*, III, 188; *République française*, May 26, 1875.
41. *République française*, May 27, 1875.

department of the Ain, his country seat, since 1871. He also presided over its general council.[42] Germain had more than merely a weekend farmer's attachment to the region. The Ain produced large quantities of silk cloth in workshops owned by Lyon merchants and moved within that city's industrial orbit. Germain's Crédit lyonnais drew part of its financial resources from Lyon silk. He would thus be particularly sensitive to that industry's fortune, particularly as it was undergoing crisis. In successive elections to the Chamber of Deputies in 1876, 1877, and 1881, Germain easily retained his seat for the arrondissement of Trévoux. Its republican committee, dominated by the local *petite bourgeoisie*, regularly cranked out election statements for him that were "radical" by any standard.[43] Germain coexisted easily with such radicalism inasmuch as its spokesmen were, after all, republicans and men of order like himself: impatient with aristocratic hangovers and eager to get on with the consolidation of the middle-class Republic. And they could envision great benefits from being represented by one of France's leading bankers.[44] Germain's own statements for 1881 bear looking at, because they show how a *grand bourgeois* republican managed to occupy an ideological terrain broad enough to accommodate his petty producer constituents.

Germain began by recalling the heroic days of the early 1870s, when all popular forces mobilized their solidarity against the monarchical threat. Now was the time to consolidate.

Property today is accessible to nearly everyone who is hard working and thrifty. . . . [We must move] to abolish the salt tax. . . . The state must undertake larger subsidies to the departments and to the communes. While in politics triumphant democracy prevailed over wealth and conquered the government, civil society was struggling against a tough adversary. . . .

42. *Almanach national* (Paris: Imprimerie nationale, 1872–76).

43. *Progrès de l'Ain*, August 9 and 16, 1881. One item in the 1881 platform called for accelerated railroad construction, but said nothing about state ownership.

44. Germain at the April, 1875, session of the general council of the Ain: "Les républicains de la veille n'oublieront pas les mécomptes du passé; ils imiteront la sagesse de leurs chefs votant naguère les lois constitutionnelles; comme eux, ils comprendront qu'ils doivent être aujourd'hui les plus ardents conservateurs et, en agissant ainsi, ils ne tardèrent pas à voir disparaître de l'administration ceux qui en trop grand nombre, sont encore les adversaires de l'ordre de choses établi le 25 février." Clipping from the *National*, April 14, 1875, in B/a 1093, Archives de la préfecture de police de la Seine, hereinafter cited as APP.

it is time that the state take back into hands public education. . . . the clergy will be forced to cease its meddling in the administration. . . . French democracy today needs only order and peace. . . . *Who today would dare advocate the division of property? Who would deny the right of the most humble citizen to seek after the highest offices in the state?*[45]

Democracy delivers its material bounty; its soil nourishes healthy ambition; business enterprise flourishes. We are back with the railroads.

Viewed from this angle, Germain's intervention in 1875 in the P-L-M debate made political sense. He deplored the high-handed manner by which Caillaux, the minister of public works, dismissed the needs and aspirations of small capitalists and entrepreneurs struggling to become capitalists. What sense did the Republic make under such conditions? Then the banker spoke. One serious consequence of limiting railroad development to the six big companies was the narrowing of the capital base, which denied to tens of thousands of Frenchmen the opportunity to participate in this great adventure. Germain professed concern for the apparent lack of internal outlets for accumulated capital. As a result, "French capital, to the detriment of the nation's wealth, crosses the frontier and finds investments in foreign lands." Not only did he want to see independent companies win concessions, but he insisted that the state guarantee their viability. It had a "moral" obligation to do so. Common agreement held that the big companies had attained their preeminent financial position due to state support. "When the companies bent under the weight of their commitments, the state told them: you have earned what you possess, you have acted honorably, you are a potent instrument in national production; I'm going to help you and, in doing so, I am acting loyally in the national interest."[46] Independent lines, he concluded, deserved equal consideration, or perhaps more, since their power did not threaten the public welfare. These are certainly the words of a parvenu banker who resented being excluded from the cartel. Their significance, however, lies in his moving from a narrow-interest argument to a sweeping declaration of republican principles.

45. Elections générales de 1881, Ain, in C 3502, AN. Italics added.
46. *Discours parlementaires de M. Henri Germain sur les finances* (Paris: Lahure, n.d.), I, 325, 328, speech delivered May 27, 1875.

Jules Siegfried, never given to the hysterical outbursts that drama-tized some of the antimonopoly polemics, nevertheless placed himself firmly on the side of revision of the railroad conventions. As a leading member of Le Havre's municipal council and president of its chamber of commerce, his voice carried considerable authority. He had also become one of the stalwarts of the conservative Republic in Nor-mandy. Not surprisingly, Siegfried expressed a single-minded concern for the state of French trade, whose situation he found disturbing. He produced figures for 1875 to demonstrate that Le Havre consistently fell behind foreign ports like Antwerp and Hamburg in the quantity of goods handled. This was especially true for cotton, his particular specialty. Why had this happened? Siegfried found the answer in an examination of the rates (calculated by ton per kilometer) prevailing on the railroads that served those ports. In every case, French rates were higher. At this juncture of depression and falling prices, "more ener-getic competition" resulted, "and in business we know very well that the aim of merchants and manufacturers is not to maximize profit on a small volume, but to make a small profit on each unit of increasingly expanded volume." (This man, at least, would have been dumb-founded to learn that French entrepreneurs were "backward.") Sieg-fried cared nothing for the witch hunt, carried on by some politicians, against "clerico-monarcho-bonaparto-monopolists," as they were some-times picturesquely known. Like the hardheaded, immensely success-ful businessman that he was, Siegfried merely followed his calculations to their logical and devastating conclusion. The railroad monopolies were pillaging the country and standing in the way of industrial development. They had infiltrated the bureaucracy and had been "clev-er enough to choose their administrators, engineers, and directors from among powerful politicians . . . naturally, the only action of the state appears to consist of confirming the acts of the companies and prevent-ing any tampering with their sacrosanct monopoly!" This is tough language and precisely the kind that should instruct us to take seriously the railroad question as a major political issue.[47]

The formal establishment of the Republic, which coincided with

47. Siegfried, *Quelques mots sur la question des chemins de fer,* 8–22.

a brief business recovery, appeared to promise for bourgeois and small producers alike a new dispensation of prosperity and social consolidation. Whether or not short-term swings of the business cycle can be attributed to political events (and they frequently can) is a question we may bypass here, for the uncertainty reflecting constricted markets and forced unemployment gave way to a distinct mood of optimism as provincial producers contemplated the realization of material and social benefits under the Republic. The quarterly reports of the prefects on industrial conditions suggest as much. A large weapons and ordnance plant in Tulle in the Corrèze, operating for the most part under state contracts, saw its work force increase by nearly three hundred from the spring of 1875 to the late summer of 1876. The principal industry of the Somme, beet-sugar production, enjoyed high levels of production and prices in spite of reported German competition.[48] In the case of the woolen industry of the Maine-et-Loire, both small producers and large establishments shared in the good business conditions. As in all textiles, the large producers dominated the spinning industry, whereas the small characterized weaving.[49] Significantly, agricultural demand for consumer goods and machinery strengthened the links between the industrial bourgeoisie of the towns and peasant farmers of the country.[50] French producers worried about the state of the rural market and for good reason, for that market accounted for a large percentage of their sales while never reaching mass-demand proportions. As that market waxed and waned, so did industrial pros-

48. Situation industrielle des départements, for the Aude, the Corrèze, the Eure, the Gers, the Loir-et-Cher, the Maine-et-Loire, the Orne, and the Yonne, in F(12) 4479a to 4550, Corrèze: situation industrielle, deuxième trimestre, 1875, troisième trimestre, 1876, in F(12) 4498, Somme: situation industrielle, troisième trimestre, 1877, in F(12) 4541, AN.
49. Maine-et-Loire: situation industrielle, quatrième trimestre, 1875, in F(12) 4518, ibid. Wool spinning was organized in seven establishments employing a total of 2,821 workers. Weaving counted 11,000 "patrons" and 16,000 workers. In the latter case, distinctions between employers and workers are deceptive; evidently, many of the 11,000 were small craftsmen who might have employed one or two workers on a seasonal basis. We have no way of knowing whether they owned their own tools or were a rural-based proletariat. This is of less significance if we remember that the large spinning establishments controlled the market so that cottagers existed in a mesh of social relations combining features of independent petty production and direct exploitation.
50. Figures for machinery production and sales in the Loir-et-Cher: situation industrielle, troisième trimestre, 1875, in F(12) 4510, ibid.

perity. Therefore, industrialists, especially the smaller ones, had to be less than enthusiastic about a public works policy that excluded them from those markets while favoring big producers, railway monopolies, and the export business. For better or worse, French production organized in small units survived or perished with the fluctuations of the internal market.

1876: Business Above All

Electioneering in 1876 brought to life these preoccupations with a socioeconomic order consistent with industrial and market requirements. Sweeping ideological issues were notably absent. Candidates in every part of the country offered their constituents the crudest and most blatant material inducements. Republicans radiated enormous self-confidence in their mission to lead the nation to new heights of industrial prosperity. Their words, which they soon expected to translate into deeds, leave no doubt as to their social outlook and cultural formation. They spearheaded a coalition combining the industrial bourgeoisie with urban and rural petty producers. Their appeals to solidarity and equality smothered the tension in that sort of alliance; and to that extent they were prisoners of it.

The Orne was for years a stronghold of peasant conservatism. Its bourgeois, outnumbered and isolated, had emerged recently to occupy positions of local social standing, their achievement made easier since they too were "men of the people" recently blessed with entrepreneurial success. Abadie, from the arrondissement of Bellême, promised to lead his people down the road to prosperity, counting off the milestones: "work, order, thrift, and political wisdom." His special message for farmers promised them endless horizons, in the "rational quest for agricultural improvement, the only solid basis for foreign trade, by the construction of railroads and canals." An engineer by profession, Abadie had made his fortune in manufacturing and had taken his place, so his friends claimed, among "the new and only true nobility, that which mobilizes intellectual and material forces."[51]

51. Elections générales, 1876, Orne, in C 3468, *ibid.; Bien public* (Alençon), February 10 and 13, 1876.

Sadi Carnot, a leading advocate of extended railways, struck a theme that was to repeat itself in many variations: "Republican France works; it saves; it accumulates wealth; it pays off the debts of fallen regimes." His collaborators in the Côte-d'Or, Leroy and Louis Hugot, both substantial merchants, drew the conclusions that the propertied classes expected, pointing to the Republic as the regime existing "to secure a material order threatened by the most hateful and the most criminal of insurrections."[52] They knew better. No one expected a renewal of class warfare, and no one believed that established society trembled under the gun of the mobilized proletariat. Linking the internal improvements to a defense of order justified the fiscal robbery necessary to translate the savings of petty producers into massive public works projects, from which those same producers would receive dubious benefits. Also, it should be obvious that raising the red specter balanced off equally harsh attacks on "aristocrats," "oligarchies," and monopolies of finance capitalism. Always careful to cover their left flank, the leading politicians of the Republic took these ideological gymnastics in stride, keeping a keen eye on the main chance: a popular coalition under bourgeois patronage or, the variants are endless, "*Moderation, Conciliation, Alliance* forever and indissoluble between the people and the bourgeoisie."[53]

A similar message came from Joseph Sentenac in the Ariège. Like so many other local republican leaders, Sentenac was a lawyer who had made his political debut as an official of the Government of National Defense under Gambetta, in this case, as subprefect of the arrondissement of Saint-Girons in the Ariège.[54] Sentenac plunged into the campaign, proudly displaying his republicanism, "henceforth the name by which are known the true conservatives . . . concerned with upholding the principles of social conservation." He spoke directly to industrial and commercial interests about "credit, employment, confidence." The accent was repeatedly on the hard business of business.[55]

52. *Progrès de la Côte-d'Or*, February 17 and 10, 1876.
53. Docteur Mallet, aspiring deputy from the Gard. *Midi* (Nîmes), February 13, 1876.
54. A. Robert *et al., Dictionnaire des parlementaires* (5 vols.; Paris: Presses Universitaires de France, 1889), V, 302.
55. Elections générales, 1876, Ariège, in C 3459, AN; electoral brochure.

Louis Latrade and Auguste Lecherbonnier, two republican stalwarts in the Corrèze, where railroads had penetrated only marginally, claimed their rights to reelection on the basis of their "aptitudes for understanding and dealing with innumerable questions of administration, taxes, and political economy." Philippe Devoucoux, president of the general council of the Cher and mayor of Bourges, boasted of his experience as a "businessman." Our imagination must fill in the tantalizing details of the "host of discreet and private services" he expected to deliver. In another district in the same department, the candidate Boulard brought the talents of a "serious man, former magistrate, with solid convictions," in a word, "an excellent deputy to represent business interests in the department." Girault, unsuccessful candidate in the district of Saint-Amand in the Cher, identified himself with "two great interests," capital and labor, in whose union he found the bedrock of national strength and prosperity.[56]

Up to a point, the rhetoric may be written off as standard electioneering, no different from what had gone before and what would come after. But we need not then conclude that the foregoing rhetoric remains valueless for the historian of ideology and *mentalité*—or even railroads. The evidence leaves little room for doubt that such republican deputies were sent to Paris by their neighbors to deliver the material goods. The absence of such burning issues as clericalism and monarchism suggests that most people did not take the old slogans seriously, unless and until they masked threats against the Republic of Equality, Property, and Solidarity. Then the people took these issues very seriously indeed.[57]

The Nation Against Monopolies

The storm over railroads broke in the early spring of 1877. The precipitating issue itself gave no warning of the magnitude of the

56. *République de la Corrèze*, February 10, 1876; *Union républicaine du Cher*, February 15 and 10, 1876.

57. "What struck me as extraordinary, my dear Watson, was not that the dog barked, but that he *did not* bark." A. Conan Doyle, *The Hound of the Baskervilles* (New York and London, many editions).

struggle. At stake was the disposition of some small, debt-ridden companies in the west. All of the companies, but especially the Company of the Charentes, held the investments of many local producers, who expected their money to finance new links to both the regional market and the national transportation system.[58] They were bitterly disappointed. The autonomy of the Company of the Charentes, that is, its independence of the financial and operational control of the powerful Paris-Orléans company, proved illusory. According to the testimony of a stockholder of the Company of the Charentes, the government "which had *planned* and *proposed* the Charente line . . . has permitted it to stagnate, to remain sealed off and deprived of direct outlets to the big commercial centers by the big companies." Consequently, the company went into bankruptcy.[59] The official solution, first proposed in late 1876 by the minister of public works, Albert Christophle, was to authorize the P-O to take over all the independent western lines at a price below current values. Thus, at one stroke, businessmen in the west found themselves deprived of what they considered to be a legitimate return on their modest investment and abandoned to the mercies of the banking barons in control of the P-O.

The question of the fate of the western lines triggered a debate on general railroad policy. Christophle had argued that those small lines had collapsed because they carried insufficient traffic. Since they were uneconomical to run according to the logic of this analysis, the P-O could maintain them in service only with a substantial subsidy. But Christophle's self-advertised disinterest in the matter came under suspicion. "We never thought we would see the day," wrote Spuller, "when a minister in a republican government would conclude an agreement so obviously rigged to the advantage of the finance aristocracy." Spuller's judgment was that Christophle, like Louis de Franqueville, Eugène Rouher, Eugène Caillaux, and Léon Say, "was the big companies' man."[60] Why did Spuller express outrage that a "republican" sold out

58. The number of outstanding shares was divided roughly equally between stockholders living in Paris and those with local addresses. Petition of the stockholders in the Company of the Charentes to the Chamber of Deputies, November 11, 1877, in C 3180, AN.

59. *Ibid.*

60. *République française*, March 22, 1877.

to high finance? Why did he focus on the contradiction between being a republican and being a partisan of high finance? He was asserting implicitly that opposition to high finance defined one essential attribute of republicanism to the extent that the republican party had originated as the economic and social movement of the industrial and agrarian bourgeoisie. Spuller placed a question of class interest at the center of the political dispute. This explains why the struggle over railroad policy took on the aspect of a general confrontation between fractions of the French bourgeoisie and, conversely, why the subsequent "crisis" over the regime dissipated without a blow being struck. Given the ideological framework characteristic of republican bourgeois—nationalist, egalitarian, secular positivist—we can appreciate the force of their antagonism toward "aristocrats," "clericals," and "financial oligarchs," whom they identified as one. Given also their concern for the life of business, industrial fecundity, and markets—as much a part of them as their anticlerical egalitarian nationalism and indeed the companion of these loftier sentiments—we can know that somehow a resolution of the railroad question would be found on the basis of mutual accommodation and higher class solidarity.

More specific criticism came from Richard Waddington of the Rouen textile family, who headed a parliamentary committee assigned to examine the P-O convention. Waddington disputed Christophle's claim. According to local businessmen in the west, he reported, the P-O deliberately diverted traffic from the secondary lines and refused the petitions from the businessmen to develop links with the Midi and P-L-M railroads. Waddington went on to describe the proposed convention as a gross inflation of the power and position of an already gigantic concern. "The people have spoken, and they earnestly insist that new lines be built, that their autonomy be respected, and that the schedules of freight rates be reformed."[61]

Waddington and his colleagues Jules LeCesne (Le Havre shipping), Daniel Wilson (Paris commercial interests), and Paul Bethmont (sometime railroad lawyer) proposed an amendment to the

61. *Journal officiel de la république française: Chambre des députés, compte-rendu sténographique,* February 28, March 1, 1877, Annexe No. 756, hereinafter cited as *JOC.*

convention, which (1) called for an inquiry into the feasibility of a state take-over of all railroads and (2) urged that the state get on with railroad building through the enfranchisement of *compagnies fermières*. The second proposal was conceived as a stopgap but easily could have become the rule for future construction. The amendment did not specify the method of finance. In support of the proposal, Laroche-Joubert raised the familiar argument about consolidating the national market, and although he professed no enthusiasm for an expanded bureaucracy, he insisted that the "railroads ought to be built and exploited by everyone . . . in the interests of everyone, and not built in the interests of a small number of big capitalists." Bethmont defined the issue as one of widening the capitalist marketplace; the question, he said, was progress through public works versus "the crushing of all initiative by maintaining the monopoly of the six powerful companies."[62]

Henri Allain-Targé injected an economic nationalist note. He rejected the notion that the state's business was to support competition within the railroad network. He considered the prevailing faith in the "power of competition" and in the "force of individual initiative" to be an "illusion." That railroads constituted natural monopolies could not be denied. In the interests of "our greatness" and of "French business" the small companies had to be bailed out and integrated into a coherent network. At this juncture, then, he invoked the state, not as the guarantor of redundant competitive lines, but as the agent of the nation's "superior interests." This, he insisted, was in the "republican tradition," which historically yoked together the national interest and the interest of business.[63] Allain-Targé proposed that all lines in the same area be concentrated under one management "so as not to establish, at state expense, competition among lines subsidized by that state which would be ruinous for the public treasury, the companies, and the people." He coupled this proposal with one to authorize the state to acquire the bankrupt western lines. Taken together, the two elements of his measure cleared the way for the absorption of

62. *Ibid.*, March 23 and 20, 1877.
63. *Ibid.*, March 14, 1877.

small lines into the P-O network under state supervision of rates and traffic distribution.[64]

Allain-Targé walked a thin line between two contradictory positions. On the one hand, he accepted the myth of the democratic marketplace, which he had had a hand in formulating, and at the same time recognized that the absence of an aggressive republican economic policy left the field to the continued domination of *haute finance* through its control of lending capital. And that, in turn, meant more of the same: the milking of railroads for bankers' profits, the outward flow of capital, the stifling of the internal market, and the disintegration of the republican alliance of industrial and agricultural producers, everything the republicans had fought against for ten years. On the other hand, he had to balance contradictory facts: the state did not command the resources to finance the railroads on its own, and total state ownership would sacrifice the financial stability so precious to the industrial bourgeoisie. In other words, he was forced to confront the consequences of the consolidation of the national market, which required concessions to the bankers and their railroad companies. Thus, from the radical critique of existing financial-economic arrangements came the compromise that took its final form in the Freycinet Plan and the Conventions of 1883.[65]

Several voices were raised in protest against what appeared to be Allain-Targé's deliberate attempt to sidetrack the move to authorize state purchase of the western lines. Charles Laisant, the radical engineer from Nantes, called for a "great integrated plan" for state repurchase, beginning with the Nord or the P-O. He wanted the state to start at the top with a money-making operation to help finance further acquisitions. Jules LeCesne, a big shipper from Le Havre, complained that Allain-Targé had demonstrated the wickedness and arrogance of the big companies and then contradicted himself by proposing to deal with precisely the same people. He, for one, did not believe that the P-O or any other company would meekly submit to state control

64. *Ibid.*, February 19, 1878, Annexe No. 416; Sadi Carnot, *Rapport: Incorporation de divers chemins de fer d'intérêt local dans le réseau d'intérêt général* (Paris: n.p., 1878).
65. *JOC*, March 14, 1877.

of rates. "Their bowing and scraping today are only a trap, a deception; tomorrow we will find them more arrogant than ever." LeCesne's principled stand happily coincided with self-interest. Léon Say pointed out that existing rate schedules favored goods arriving into France by rail from foreign ports. LeCesne hoped to put a stop to that. Trade figures for 1878 confirm his concern. Coal imports, once a large item in Le Havre's commerce, had dropped to a small fraction of its total business. On the other hand, how realistic was it to expect that rails could ever compete with the cheaper, water-borne barge traffic, which historically carried English coal up the Seine to Paris? In truth, LeCesne and other port businessmen sought local control of railroads, managed in accordance with their own preeminent positions in the provincial industrial and commercial bourgeoisie that dominated the republican party. That they echoed the populistlike, anticapitalist rhetoric of radical democrats does not alter the hardheaded capitalist calculations behind their politics.[66]

When the government of the *seize mai* handed over the western lines to the P-O on a provisional basis, advocates of state ownership blamed Allain-Targé for legitimizing the thievery before the fact. His reply showed how the chief politicians of the Republic fused their egalitarian principles to an economic nationalism that placed first the interests of industrial and agrarian production:"How can I, the defender of commercial and industrial interests and the interests of the state, possibly have the same views as members of a cabinet which includes three directors of big companies and which is totally devoted to those *international interests* and to the privileges of a financial oligarchy whose disruptive actions and feudal pretensions I fought." Allain-Targé went on to denounce the new government's alleged plans to deliver the entire French transportation and entrepôt industry into the hands of high finance—both French and foreign.[67] Allain-Targé did not like "aristocrats," especially big bankers whose loyalties to the fraternity of international finance made them enemies of the

66. *Tableau général du commerce de la France avec ses colonies et les puissances étrangères pendant l'année 1878* (Paris: Imprimerie nationale, 1879), 90.
67. Clipping from *République française*, June 7, 1877, in B/a 929, APP, italics added.

national economy. Like Spuller, Gambetta, and Ferry later on, he spoke for national production and for that class of capitalists whose factories, workshops, and farms formed its bedrock.

Republican antimonopolists clearly divided regarding the best course for future railroad development. Each side in its own way wanted to break the power of the big companies. But there unanimity stopped. Gambetta, Spuller, and their collaborators clung stubbornly to the principle that something be done to salvage the small companies and keep them operating. They chided Allain-Targé for "not having faith in the benefits of competition and private initiative." They professed no interest in a monolithic state monopoly, preferring state operation of the trunk lines and autonomous companies for the feeder networks.[68] From the self-named "radical left" came demands for a state monopoly: "and when we speak of the state, we do not mean kings and emperors; we mean the state as society, that is, ourselves."[69] Superficially, this sounds like another variation on the antimonopolist theme. Yet if the lyrics seemed similar, the music was very different. This sort of "popular" *étatisme* echoed the diffuse sentiments of the mass of small producers who, unlike the self-confident and pragmatic republican bourgeoisie, did not come together as a self-identified class of entrepreneurs. Their conception of nationalist economics had less to do with building up the industrial and agricultural market than with protecting petty production against the overwhelming tide of capitalist production. Only the state possessed the power to provide such protection.

These people could not be ignored by the leading politicians of the Republic, who remembered where their votes came from. Yet something more than crude opportunism was at work here. From the very beginning of the attack on the Empire in the late 1860s, republican leaders and ideologues committed themselves to the democratic marketplace. That they did so for their own reasons did not negate

68. *République française*, March 7 and 17, 1877.
69. *Homme libre*, March 14, 1877; also Camille Pelletan in *Rappel* (Paris), March 15, 1877: "C'est l'Etat, c'est-à-dire, vous, moi, tout le monde, qui paye, toujours les fautes des unes, et pour l'aggrandissement des autres. De là un pouvoir terrible entre les mains d'intérêts privés—c'est-à-dire, contre l'intérêt public."

its wide appeal. The government of the Republic, also known as a "government of laborers [*travailleurs*],"[70] was marked by the spirit of "savings and of carefully accumulated wealth." Republicans claimed for the state the obligation to "come to the aid of farmers by dredging canals, building local roads and railroads."[71] Only the entrenched power of the financial aristocracy stood in the way of the realization of their aspirations for a democratic political economy—or so the republicans said. All antimonopolists, therefore, stood united behind egalitarian, nationalist, antiaristocratic principles. "Private initiative," in these circumstances, meant something else besides blind adherence to the principles of entrepreneurial freedom. It meant security for small producers and the owners of local railroads against "speculation" and the "crushing despotism of monopoly and wealth."[72]

Two political figures with business connections but of different origin and background demonstrated the depth of solidarity among republicans when it came to protecting the national economy against the alleged piracy of the "big companies." They also added their voices to those of others who recognized that railroad policy constituted an important aspect of republican social policy. The breadth of class collaboration on this issue extended to an alliance that began to take form between the traditionally liberal, internationally oriented port businessmen and the conservative manufacturers of the interior. The stands taken by two apparently dissimilar figures, Jules Lesguillier and David Raynal, illustrate the point. Lesguillier graduated from the École polytechnique as a civil engineer, joined the Corps des ponts-et-chaussées, and took part in the construction of the French-financed Spanish railways.[73] From 1878 to 1881 he administered the newly organized French state railway system. Lesguillier resigned from that job with a blast at Léon Say and the big bankers and proceeded to get himself elected deputy from the wool-manufacturing department of

70. In the prevailing discourse of the time, *travailleur* meant small producers, artisans, farmers, mechanics, while *ouvrier* referred to factory hands and other wage laborers.
71. Léon Gambetta, *Discours à Romans* (Paris: n.p., 1876), 27–28.
72. *Rappel* (Paris), March 15, 1877.
73. Robert *et al.*, *Dictionnaire*, II, 130.

the Aisne.[74] Raynal came from a family of Jewish merchants in Bordeaux; he studied law to prepare himself for business and politics. A deputy from the Gironde first elected in 1879, Raynal rose rapidly in republican circles. He became minister of public works under Gambetta in 1881. Raynal's second-in-command at the ministry was Jules Lesguillier.[75]

In their own ways, both Lesguillier and Raynal served industrial enterprise. Despite his background, Lesguillier did not exert himself for the cause of state railways out of an appetite for building a bureaucratic empire. "I have declared myself publicly against the immense undertaking in the repurchase [of railways by the state]; but I would rather go down that road and surrender two billions in excess indemnities to the [six great] companies than lose six billions—which will surely follow the delivery of national industry into the hands of the *haute banque*."[76]

Both men understood that railroad development raised serious political issues that involved nothing less than the social configuration of the Republic itself. Lesguillier worried that "budgetary necessities will postpone indefinitely building lines for which the people wait impatiently. That raises the fear that, in certain departments, we will witness a turning away from the Republic."[77] Raynal stood that gloomy prognosis on its head. The railroad program, he said, "is not only a program for business, it is still more a political program. Stimulating the business of the country makes good political sense; and that is why our politics are sound politics. This program . . . will create wealth for the entire country and promote the solidarity of all interests." Raynal went on to project the broad social implications of a national railroad policy: "The Republic will press forward with public works and public education. We must enlighten the population so as to avoid its being victimized by relapses."[78] Raynal made the essential connection be-

74. Jules Lesguillier, *La Question des chemins de fer et M. Léon Say* (Château-Thierry: Imprimerie de l'Echo républicain, 1882).

75. Jean Jolly (ed.), *Dictionnaire des parlementaires français* (7 vols. to date; Paris: Presses universitaires de France, 1969–), I, 3.

76. Lesguillier, *La Question des chemins de fer*, 4–5.

77. *Ibid.*, 14.

78. *République de Nevers*, May 11, 1881.

tween the two great programs of public works, railroads and schools, and the making of the Republic. Each marked a phase in the implementation of social policies consistent with the class perspective of the republican bourgeoisie.

An article entitled "Economie et protection," appearing in the Gambettist daily, the *République française*, exposed the fundamentals that lay behind the railroad controversy and gave it significance in the shaping of the French political economy. No signature followed the article; this means that Eugène Spuller, editor-in-chief who wrote all unsigned articles, authored it. Spuller raised the preeminent question of markets, which he correctly understood to be the central preoccupation of the provincial industrial bourgeoisie. They demanded and had a claim to protection. But of what sort and under what conditions? Sidestepping a direct confrontation with the tariff question, which in the past had brought the republican coalition to grief,[79] he made protection a function of public works. Protection means, he said, "legislative acts assuring secure outlets and first-class means of transport, favorable conditions for loading, unloading, and warehousing, and reasonable rates on our railroads and canals." Spuller marked off his position in stark contrast to the free-trade position of the enemy faction; the gulf was wide and to his mind unbridgeable: "This is what we should mean when we speak of internal free trade, not that false theory which preaches the abolition of customs duties for the outside world and, for ourselves, guaranteed interest, the maintenance of the monopolies of the big companies, the Crédit foncier, and the match trust." He concluded with an urgent call for a new dispensation in railroad policy and for lower rates.[80]

Spuller's argument reopened a historic struggle in France. Repeatedly since 1789, the bourgeoisie in control of textiles, mining, and metallurgy and the myriad of small commodity producers found that their interests in a wider internal market and direct investment in making that market conflicted with the external orientation of high

79. See Tudesq's findings on the presidential election of 1848; Cavaignac carried the ports against Louis Napoleon but was swamped in the interior. André-Jean Tudesq, *Les Elections présidentielles et la presse* (Paris: Colin, 1965).
80. *République française*, March 11, 1877.

finance. That elements of the latter had made their current political alliance with "antinational" elements, *i.e.*, Rome, only sharpened the conflict.[81] Looking back at the public works program of the Empire, which had made the market that had brought them into existence, republicans purported to discover a deliberate subordination of the long-term viability of the national market to short-term political or financial advantages.[82] Apparently the industrial bourgeoisie viewed the perpetuation of the monopoly in railroads as part of a larger scheme, inaugurated under the Empire, to develop the international links of French commerce and finance at the expense of internal production. Monopolies had the necessary effect of "stifling the vital sources of production by reducing them to a condition of inferiority vis-à-vis foreign competition."[83]

More than a question of specific economic interest was at stake in this confrontation of oligarchs and bourgeois republicans. For the latter, reorganizing the railroad system combined a step necessary to national economic development with a gesture symbolic of the provincial producers' determination to fashion the general shape of the political economy according to their own class interests. Few voices spoke out for protection against foreign goods at the gates of entry to France. But it is significant that, when discussions of the future configuration of French tariff policy reached the open, representatives of industry echoed Spuller.[84] Republicans had argued consistently that the Republic embraced all producers and all property owners and justified itself in the established reality of solidarity, prosperity, and social peace. These factors were linked to the perpetuation of a vigorous national marketplace. Bourgeois oligarchs, with their gentry and

81. Joseph Reinach (ed.), *Discours et plaidoyers politiques de Gambetta* (11 vols.; Paris: n.p., 1881–85), VII, 296–303. Speech to his constituents in the twentieth arrondissement of Paris.
82. *Avenir de Gers* (Agen), January 19, 1878.
83. Chérot, *Les Grandes compagnies*, 16.
84. Commission du tarif général des douanes, *Sénat: Enquête sur les souffrances du commerce et de l'industrie et sur les moyens d'y porter remède*, session of March 25, 1878, deposition of the Comité commercial et industriel de Normandie: "M. de Freycinet . . . a pris l'initiative de projets dont la réalisation aurait d'heureuses conséquences. Nos canaux seraient améliorés et complétés; nos chemins de fer recevraient une grande extension," in AD XIX F25, AN.

clerical allies, holding to rigid doctrines of free trade, railroad monopolies, and a devil-take-the-hindmost conception of the political economy, sowed the seeds of republican decomposition and social disintegration.

As Spuller spoke for the provincial bourgeoisie, Léon Say spoke for the bankers of Paris. Grandson of the laissez-faire economist Jean Baptiste Say and bearer of his message, high official in the Rothschild bank, administrator of the Nord Railway Company, no man better epitomized the aristocracy of high finance than did Léon Say; and no man spoke with as much authority in the name of the ruling class.[85] In 1876, arguing against tax reform, Say placed himself in direct opposition to the point of view expressed by Spuller. Say welcomed efforts to increase the profits of industrial production, but he did not believe that they were to be found internally: "Since domestic customers cannot enlarge their consumption because of the high cost of living, we must search out foreign customers."[86] Imperialism was the active ingredient in Say's prescription for France's economic ills, the imperialism of free trade and capital export so distinctive of the Second Empire. The industrial bourgeoisie did not oppose empire, as we shall see, but its conception of empire differed in important respects from Say's. As for the petty producers, the *nouvelles couches* who could not be discounted as a political factor, they might escape exploitation in an internal market otherwise rigged against them, but as entrepreneurs they would only lose by the diversion of investment capital away from public works.

Although these quarrels over the shape of the economy split the bourgeoisie, ideological consensus prevailed over specific material interest. Dismantling the railroad system, throwing it into a state of anarchy, and expropriating the big companies at incalculable cost to the state made no sense at all if carried out to prop up the weakest sector of the economy. Although the republican bourgeoisie flirted with radical populism, it knew better than to continue to do so while the social structure went up in flames. Dominant preoccupations with

85. *République française*, March 22, 1877.
86. Léon Say, *Les Finances de la France sous la troisième république* (3 vols.; Paris: Guillaumin, 1889), II, 108–14.

solidarity, with social peace, with the subordination of petty producers to bourgeois hegemony determined the ultimate character of political alliances. And even if men like Say and Spuller differed, and differed violently and publicly, on how railroad and tariff policies were to be manipulated, they shared in that consensus. The stalwarts of "moral order" did not.

Thus, each faction ultimately had to compromise its position. However, first it was necessary for the republican bourgeoisie to turn back yet another assault against its position. Once this had been accomplished, in the aftermath of the *seize mai* crisis, those elements of the banking-railroad community that did not share the hardline ideological position represented by "moral order" found doing business with the republican bourgeoisie not only surprisingly painless but desirable. The latter, secure in its political power, could afford to do business with the railroads from a position of strength. Therein lay the political origins of the Freycinet Plan.

Chapter IV

The Seize Mai *and* the Freycinet Plan

THE DEBATE on railroads in 1877 ended abruptly in the political crisis of the *seize mai*. On that day, Marshal Patrice MacMahon, president of the Republic, dismissed the republican cabinet of Jules Simon on the pretext that Simon had not protested vigorously enough against extreme anticlerical statements emanating from certain republican circles. MacMahon replaced Simon with the Duc de Broglie, whose government served as a stopgap until the administration could organize new parliamentary elections in an attempt to defeat the 363 deputies who had condemned the *seize mai* coup.

The Old Order Confronts the New

Broglie's policies recapitulated those of his previous administrations of 1873 and 1874. Like the Bourbon kings his soldier ancestors once served, he learned nothing and forgot everything. Ignoring the deepening economic crisis and its attendant threat of social upheaval, he installed a regime that represented the narrowest interests of the *haut bourgeois* oligarchy. In so doing, Broglie made certain the ensuing political struggles would be remembered as an episode of bitter intraclass warfare.

Several years after the *seize mai* crisis had passed and with the ultimate resolution of the railroad question on the horizon, Alexandre Papon, republican deputy from the Eure, introduced legislation challenging that very resolution. In the course of his argument, Papon advanced some interesting opinions about the May crisis. He recalled that the parliamentary committee charged with the general task of reviewing transportation policy had leveled some harsh criticisms at the big companies. Its interim report, he asserted, had touched off the heated debate in the Chamber. The upheaval in May and the subsequent elections interrupted the committee's work, thus reducing temporarily the pressure on the monopolies while they regrouped their forces. Papon pursued his argument to its inexorable conclusion: "We must recognize that the big companies, under a shadow cast by the attitudes of the great majority of the committee . . . were not uninvolved in the enterprise of the *seize mai*."[1]

Further circumstantial evidence may be marshaled in support of Papon's assertion. We need look only at the composition of the *gouvernement de combat*, which took office after Jules Simon's dismissal. The intimacy in the relationship between its personnel and financial control of the railroads is striking. Every key member of the cabinet had personal ties to the big companies. Eugène Caillaux, minister of finance, sat on the board of the P-L-M, surrounded by the brightest stars in the banking firmament: Edouard Blount, Charles Mallet, Jacques de Rothschild, Charles Hottinguer, François Bartholony, and Alfred André. Oscar de Fourtou and his secretary of state at the Ministry of the Interior, Baron René Reille, were directors of the Paris-Orléans company. The foreign minister, Décazes, moved in the highest circles of the interlocking financial-industrial complex through his position in the Aveyron mining industry. Even the vice-president of the Council of Ministers, the Duc de Broglie, administered feeder railways from his plants to the trunk lines as chairman of the Saint-Gobain glassworks. His company, a large customer, benefited from differential freight rates that served the interests of big business.[2] Auguste Pâris, minister of public works, previously had distinguished himself in the National Assembly as a spokesman for the interests of the Nord Railway Company.[3]

1. Alexandre Papon, *Proposition de loi sur la constitution du réseau national des chemins de fer* (Paris: Schiller, 1881).
2. *Annuaire des chemins de fer* (Paris, 1877).
3. Pâris argued against granting secondary line concessions to the Flanders-Picardy

Papon had noticed that the raising of such demands, even though they had been heard before, brought a fraction of the *grande bourgeoisie* into open conflict under monarchist and Bonapartist banners. They appeared to challenge the Republic itself. Others shared his view. Jules Lesguillier found himself in accord with the conspiracy theory insofar as he suggested that the big companies anticipated the imminent collapse of the Republic: "They recall the happy days of 1852, those magnificent concessions obtained at the expense of the public purse, and for which they laid out several millions to pay the costs of the coup d'etat. They expect that a restoration will deliver into their hands, at a cheap price, new windfalls."[4] Charles Floquet suggested a less sinister configuration, the implications of which struck deep into the soil of France. At stake in the political struggle was nothing less than the security of rural property and, by extension, all property. Not for the first time, nor would it be the last, did a republican link together democratic liberty, property, and the struggle against reaction. Republicans were "the guardians of the principle of modern property, wrenched free of feudal and ecclesiastical usurpation and bequeathed to our French peasants."[5] Thus, we should not be surprised to discover that the votes against the resolution of the "363" condemning the Broglie government corresponded closely to the opposition to a measure designed to limit the extension of the big companies.[6]

But to make a case for the central importance of railroad policy in the making of the Republic on the basis of such evidence would bring us perilously close to dealing in money-interest determinism, a currency of even less value than economic determinism. We could then cheerfully leave the last word to Beau de Loménie, whose interpretations of the course of French history turn on an assumed reflexive

company in preference to the Nord Railway Company. A. Picard, *Les Chemins de fer français* (3 vols.; Paris: Rothschild, 1884), III, 229.

4. Jules Lesguillier, *La Question des chemins de fer et M. Léon Say* (Château-Thierry: Imprimerie de l'Echo républicain, 1882), 12.

5. Charles Floquet, *Discours et opinions* (2 vols.; Paris: Dervaux, 1885), I, 72–81.

6. Of the 158 who voted against the "363," 120 also voted against the railroad measure. *Journal officiel de la république française: Chambre des députés, compte-rendu sténographique*, March 22, June 20, 1877, hereinafter cited as *JOC*.

relationship between direct economic interest and politics.[7] Let us look further.

A government of whatever character does not long survive the dissipation of its moral force. Unless a regime can make some credible claim to legitimacy that is acceptable to a significant part of the nation, to a class, or at least to a ruling fraction of a class, it will fall. The government of the *seize mai* possessed no moral authority to begin with, and its efforts to manufacture such authority failed utterly. Its collapse was never in doubt. It faced a national coalition led by tough, seasoned, and exceedingly resourceful political cadres who served major class interests. In defense of those interests and of their conception of society, they would show no hesitation in delivering an opposing faction to the sacrificial altar.

The government's administrative apparatus labored heroically to defeat republican candidates. Fourtou's circular to his prefects in July directed them to "appeal to all conservatives" and to stress the prospects for "political and social upheaval" should the "radical party" triumph.[8] His office organized the distribution of government propaganda pamphlets, sent batches of reprints of newspaper articles to the provinces, sniped at the opposition press, revoked republican mayors, and diverted administrative funds to friendly candidates.[9] All to no avail. The republicans returned stronger than before. They did so because the country did not believe that men who had fought for equality and entrepreneurial freedom against monopoly and privilege threatened "social upheaval." If anything, the country believed the opposite.[10] The fran-

7. Emmanuel Beau de Loménie, *Les Responsabilités des dynasties bourgeoises* (4 vols.; Paris: Denoël, 1946–63), II, *passim.*

8. Minister of the interior to all prefects, July 3, 1877, in 2M 42, Archives départementales, Haute-Garonne, hereinafter cited as AD, appropriate department.

9. Various dispatches to the prefects during September and October, 1877, in F(7) 12681, Archives nationales, hereinafter cited as AN.

10. One republican pamphlet carried the following lines: "Nos mandataires ont été renvoyés sous prétexte de péril imaginaire. . . . Le véritable motif est sous-entendu. On le trouve dans le jeu d'une coalition monarchique formée depuis longtemps sous la direction du clergé dans le but de renverser la République, au profit d'une restauration impossible, dont le préambule serait inévitablement l'anarchie la plus épouvantable. . . . Après avoir renverser la République, chaque parti voudrait s'emparer de ses dépouilles. L'entente serait impossible et nous tomberions dans un chaos de dissensions intestines,

tic efforts of the regime in the last weeks of the campaign to replace local functionaries with its own men suggest as much. What better demonstration of the solidarity of businessmen, farmers, and their professional servants need we have than the decision of the prefect of the Haute-Garonne to dismiss an inspector of animal disease for purveying "hostile propaganda."[11]

To expose the source of social upheaval, the republicans returned to the attack that had served them splendidly in the recent past. "Republic or monarchy, that is the question which you are called upon to resolve," Jacques Gudin from Château-Chinon told his constituents. For "honest and hardworking" democrats only one answer was possible. Government people, called Bonapartists sometimes, clericals always, represented aristocracy and privilege, the Satan and Beelzebub of "commercial and industrial interests." Peasants were reminded of hard times under the *ancien régime*: serfdom, mortmain, and *droit du seigneur* (applied to both wife and daughter and shared with the curé!). The issue was joined between remaining "free citizens" or falling victims to the depredations of "dukes, barons, marquis, knights of the stock exchange and of the wet blanket, that bastard and sanctimonious aristocracy which dares to parade about as a ruling class."[12]

François Dubois from the Côte-d'Or proclaimed his readiness to stand on the first line of defense for the "great social interests." His neighbor, Louis Hugot, echoed these sentiments, adding an appeal for a "true conservative policy . . . which we need to get on with business." As they plumbed the meaning of those "great social interests," republicans reasserted their fundamental conservative outlook. Cyprien Girerd of Nevers recalled that before the *seize mai* "order reigned everywhere, moral as well as material order." He had opposed amnesty for Communards and did not apologize for it. They had committed "a crime against France." Pierre Rouveure listed among the

---

duquel sortirait la guerre civile la plus épouvantable qu'on ait vu surgir." Attorney for Saint-Gaudens to the attorney general of Toulouse, October 9, 1877, in 2M 42, AD, Haute-Garonne.

11. Prefect of the Haute-Garonne to the subprefect of Saint-Gaudens, October 3, 1877, *ibid.*

12. *République de la Nièvre*, October 2, 1877; *Yonne*, October 11, 1877; *Avenir de Gers* (Agen), October 10, 1877; *République des paysans*, October 4, 1877.

achievements of the Republic "the smashing of the Commune." As vigorously as they defended order against the social movement of the left, the republican bourgeoisie did not neglect its responsibilities to egalitarianism and economic freedom, its leadership in the struggle for "equality before the laws and the right to become a property owner."[13] The democratic myth reached exalted height at this time: "Do you not know that universal suffrage is the peaceful weapon which will save us, that it is a marvelous instrument with which all laborers, tradesmen, and workers can gain an improvement in their lot, without violence and disorder" and that "the Republic stands for an equal sharing in the government of the nation among all its children in proportion to their strength and their talents[?]"[14]

And so it went. Charles Rameau and Léon Journault from the Seine-et-Oise, Albert Cornil and Joseph Chantemille from Moulins, Armand Fourot from the Creuse, Henri Germain from Trévoux, Louis Gatineau from the Eure-et-Loir, Charles Cherpin from Saint-Étienne, Ernest Constans from Toulouse all contributed to marking out the ideological configuration of the Republic and restating its essential class foundations.[15] They had done so in an apparently curious fashion, campaigning heavily on the clerical issue while everyone agreed that questions of political economy were at stake.

The republican bourgeoisie found in the clerical issue the unifying factor essential to the solidarity of the republican coalition. Something more than momentary tactics was at work here. If the Republic meant anything at all, it served as the political manifestation and ideological focus of a class of entrepreneurs who had taken up the development of the industrial and agricultural sinews of the nation. Since clericalism stood for forces alien and apart from the nation and its representatives occupied an ideological position separating them from the national republican system, a campaign against clericalism was, in reality, a campaign to strengthen the political supremacy of the secular order of

13. *Progrès de la Côte-d'Or,* October 3, 1877; *République de la Nièvre,* October 9, 1877; *Réveil de l'Ardèche,* October 6, 1877; *Avenir de Gers* (Agen), October 3, 1877.
14. *République de la Corrèze,* October 14, 1877; *Union républicaine de l'Hérault,* October 2, 1877.
15. F(1c) III, Seine-et-Oise 7, Allier 3, Ain 3, Eure-et-Loir 5, Loire 4, Haute-Garonne 7, AN.

bourgeois property and the national market. The collaboration of a faction of clericals with the defenders of monopolies challenged the bourgeoisie materially as capitalists and ideologically as a secular, rational class whose cultural preoccupations were closely intertwined with their pursuit of markets and profits.

Monopoly and privilege, largess for the few and penury for the many, not only deeply offended democratic sensibilities, but undermined the material base and the social power of the capitalist class, in contradistinction to particular elements of it. To the extent that the big railroads and their excretion in the Government of Moral Order remained unchallenged if not unchecked, the republican promise of equality, entrepreneurial freedom, and the smothering of class antagonisms remained unfulfilled. Under such conditions, the social upheaval that the entire bourgeoisie feared hovered as a real possibility for the future. It is small wonder, then, that the privileges and arrogance of the big railroad companies had become the focus of the struggle to consolidate the Republic itself and that they appeared to be organically linked to the pretensions and policies of a distrusted cosmopolitan church.

In contemporary statements on the origins of the *seize mai* regime, clericalism remained an immensely popular and convenient slogan.[16] Henri Brisson, speaking for a parliamentary committee of inquiry that completed its work in 1879, traced the roots of the crisis to "the possession of formal power in the hands of a shady government which had plotted its actions in the anterooms of the Chamber." In the elections that followed, he noted Finance Minister Caillaux's impressment of local fiscal agents in the campaign for government candidates. Brisson did not contend that Caillaux had any particular clerical ax to grind;

---

16. *Alliance républicaine de la Saône-et-Loire*, May 19, 1877; Ernest Constans in the *Dépêche de Toulouse*, October 11, 1877: "Le caractère distinctif de ce cabinet, son signe distinctif, c'est le cléricalisme. C'est la question cléricale qui a fait naître la crise; c'est la question cléricale qui a ramené M. de Broglie." *République de la Nièvre*, May 19,1877; Joseph Reinach wrote later: "Le coup d'Etat parlementaire du 16 mai a été la réponse de Rome au discours de Gambetta sur le cléricalisme et à l'ordre du jour sur les menées ultramontaines." Joseph Reinach, *La Vie politique de Léon Gambetta* (Paris: Alcan, 1918), 57.

nor was Caillaux in the habit of engaging in political dirty work on someone else's behalf. Caillaux did not work to turn the country over to priests; worse, he had disrupted the conditions for "peace and industry."[17] Charles Floquet estimated that the Chamber of Deputies elected in 1876 displayed a marked and "overwhelmingly anticlerical complexion." But again, like Brisson, he left that subject quickly to focus on the fiscal reform projects that the republicans began to press for. Against such reforms, a coalition "of the privileged" formed. Lacking the votes, they conspired to overthrow the republican government illegally.[18]

Gambetta had made a career of exploiting the clerical specter. He delivered the latest installment in early May, in a speech that had all the appearances of another anticlerical diatribe. But appearances deceive. The Republic of the republicans, the *bons bourgeois* of France, would not tolerate outside agents meddling in its business. This situation produced "weakness [and] powerlessness" in the state. Clerical influence had insinuated itself into a position "against the power of the state, against the proper functioning of the state."[19] Why did Gambetta invoke the authority of "moral order"? The state acted as the executive arm of the ruling class, but had much wider social functions. It provided a vital national focus for those whose class position remained ambiguous—peasants and petty producers—and the institutional muscle necessary to consolidate national bourgeois class rule.[20] Gambetta had not forgotten the *nouvelles couches sociales* and the promise of material uplift that the Republic continued to hold for the future. State intervention in the expansion of public works appeared to deliver on that promise.

Was clericalism then the only enemy? Gambetta did not think so: "What we must do is call attention to and denounce the actions of a political faction operating behind the false mask of religious prin-

17. *Yonne,* May 11, March 15, 1879.
18. Floquet, *Discours et opinions,* I, 83–104.
19. Léon Gambetta, *Discours dans la chambre à propos de l'agitation cléricale* (Paris: n.p., 1877), May 4, 1877.
20. On the role of the state in ambiguous class situations, see Karl Marx, *The Eighteenth Brumaire of Louis Bonaparte* (numerous editions).

ciple."[21] This "political faction" engaged in various efforts to subvert the rational development of public works and other foundations of the industrial order. Whatever the ideological manifestations, the battle remained joined on fundamental questions of social policy.

Édouard Lockroy brought the clerical issue to bear directly on the struggle against railroad cartels. In his tract, *À bas le progrès!*, it will be recalled, he denounced monopolies in sharply populist tones. He did so in defense of the expansion of production and the security of property.[22] In March, 1878, when the Chamber of Deputies had taken up the debate interrupted by the events of the preceding year, Lockroy returned to the attack. He accused the "forces of reaction" of planning to deliver everything into the hands of the big companies.[23]

For Lockroy the lines were drawn and the pivotal issue clear: "Either the state will take possession of a certain number of rail lines or the big companies will increase their power in dividing up the spoils. It all comes down to this: is it or is it not necessary to extend, enlarge and fortify the monopoly of the big companies?" Like Gambetta, he fell back on state authority to rescue the economic foundations of political democracy or at least the democracy of small producers. Lockroy purported to uncover a community of interest between clericals and the financial oligarchy, which had joined together against "true" popular and national interests: "The monopoly of the big companies, the ultramontaine church, these are the two arms of forces conspiring to remove from the people power over their own affairs; to undermine the government of the country by the country; to fight unceasingly against the Republic. This congruence of aims explains many things. It explains the otherwise inexplicable alliance of bankers and *dévots*."[24] We should discount the conspiracy and pay attention to the antagonist: two manifestations of "aristocratic" power mobilized against the legitimate aspirations of capitalists, entrepreneurs, and hardworking producers. The corollary is to eliminate the aristocrats, the privileges, and the special interests, and the democratic political

21. *République française*, May 6, 1877.
22. See Chapter I, herein.
23. Robert Schnerb, *Rouher et le second empire* (Paris, 1938), 242.
24. *Rappel* (Paris), March 13, 1878.

economy will produce its own rewards. Seen in these terms, Lockroy's words lose the evanescent quality of the politician's rhetoric and take on the aspect of a serious ideological statement.

Compromise and Resolution: The Freycinet Plan

Charles de Freycinet, Léon Say, and Léon Gambetta met in the latter's quarters on January 8, 1878, to agree on the principles of the comprehensive public works plan later popularly known as the Freycinet Plan. Although at the time the meeting aroused little interest, it proved to be an event of considerable importance. In that room sat three men who embodied, so to speak, the concentrate of bourgeois and middle-class France. Freycinet, in background and associations, ranked as one of the most prominent politicians and bureaucrats of the industrial community. Say's position and status are clear, as are Gambetta's. All too easily, however, Gambetta emerges as the people's politician, the tribune of those from whose ranks he sprung: petty producers, petit bourgeois *commerçants*, small farmers. It was he who led the *nouvelles couches sociales* onto the national stage. But he did so not in order to challenge the ruling class but to support its claims to power. He and his closest collaborators, men like Spuller and Allain-Targé, consistently defended social policies and ideological positions consistent with the general spirit of the bourgeois world view. Gambetta's particular calling consisted of spreading that message through the ranks of the middle classes.[25] One who later joined his government while remaining a consistent critic of the Freycinet Plan, Jules Lesguillier, understood the practical industrial motives behind Gambetta's support of the plan. "He believed . . . that there was a vital interest to be served in generating the public works program with the maxi-

25. Pierre Sorlin, in his exceptionally intelligent *Waldeck-Rousseau* (Paris: Colin, 1966), attempts to sort out republican political groupings in class terms. Thus, the Gauche républicaine led by Jules Ferry and Richard Waddington represents the industrial *grande bourgeoisie*; while the Union républicaine, Gambetta's formation, speaks for the *petite bourgeoisie*. Sorlin makes these distinctions on the basis of the social origins of the politicians themselves. Now, they might have worked with different groups of people, big or little bourgeoisie, but they had a fundamental identity. Carrying Sorlin's logic into the contemporary scene, we would have to have made of Georges Pompidou, Auvergnat peasant, a politician of the *petite bourgeoisie*.

mum energy, in completing, on the broadest scale, France's industrial plant, and thus accelerating her revival."[26]

Léon Say later referred to the gathering as a "historic evening."[27] Judging from subsequent events, Say had every reason to be satisfied with its outcome. The Freycinet Plan in its final form provided for 23,000 kilometers of railroad lines to be constructed or taken over by private companies with the benefit of partial state subsidy. The network, when completed, would forge the final links in the national market. Freycinet's arrangement managed to satisfy the demands of national production without seriously eroding the position of the banking-railroad nexus. Most important, the financing was to be carried out in several stages and thus did not threaten to suddenly dump large amounts of government paper on the market, which would depress existing issues and drive down the price of state securities.

Paul Leroy-Beaulieu greeted the Freycinet Plan with an enthusiasm rarely seen in the gray columns of the *Économiste français*. Deliberately patterned after its English counterpart, the *Économiste* served and spoke for the community of Paris bankers. Its views, therefore, deserve serious attention. In effect, Leroy-Beaulieu confirmed the financial powers' benevolent reception of the plan, which signaled a hardening of the alliance between the most enlightened members of that community and the republican bourgeoisie.[28] Free traders and international bankers, whom the republicans had charged with callous disregard of the internal market, swung their massive financial weight behind its development. The "City" and the country embraced each other in a common enterprise.

Leroy-Beaulieu put on a display of his laissez-faire repertoire. He then made short work of the myth of free competition. On the one hand, he denounced "as absolutely false and singularly dangerous in practice the theory which demands that the state assume responsibility for national savings, that it sponsor investments for capitalists, and

26. Lesguillier, *La Question des chemins de fer*, 5.
27. Reinach, *La Vie politique*, 71.
28. First mention of the plan in approving terms came only two weeks after Freycinet had taken office and before Say, Gambetta, and Freycinet met on January 8, 1878. He must have known, quite correctly, that the defeat of the *seize maisards* cleared away the last obstacle to public works. *Économiste français*, December 29, 1877.

that it protect them against their inexperience, their gullibility, and their greed." On the other hand, he insisted that "it is nonetheless true that the state performs certain functions which expand with the progress of civilization."[29] In one stroke, Leroy-Beaulieu wrote off petty producers, consigning them to that special limbo reserved for men who fail to fulfill their destiny in the marketplace. Yet, with equal decisiveness he confirmed the principle of state action within the same marketplace. This was both special pleading and something more. For what he took away with a sharp thrust of his laissez-faire blade, he returned under the guise of the state's obligations in industrial society. In so doing, he made a contribution to the erection of an ideological fortress spacious enough to accommodate the bourgeoisie and the petty producers under the hegemony of the former.

Richard Waddington, the Rouen cotton magnate, in 1877 had entrusted to himself the definitive interpretation of the public will. "The people have spoken," he said, and demanded a new dispensation in railroads.[30] But who had spoken and what in fact had they said? Departmental councils met in regular semiannual sessions where they voted resolutions on national issues. As we listen to their voices, it becomes clear that they spoke in accents markedly different from those from whom Waddington took his cue. Although the councils regularly called for state intervention, it was on a limited basis, to bail out bankrupt local lines or to create new ones. Little or no sympathy appeared for a national state railway system. Local concerns focused on promoting conditions favorable to business. No one sought a violent disruption of the status quo. Local control of regional lines, necessary to fill in the gaps in the national market, did not seem incompatible with the continued existence and privileged financial position of the big companies. Voices strident, rhetorical, and ideological on the national stage became muted, calculating, and practical in these modest meetings of lawyers, farmers, and businessmen, where the rhythm of production, sales, and profit set the mood. We can make more sense

29. *Ibid.,* January 19, 1878.

30. On the question of waterways, for instance, see Réponse au questionnaire de la commission officielle pour le développement du commerce extérieur, 1874, Chambre de commerce de Honfleur, in F(12) 2487 (b), AN.

of the positions of men like Eléazer Pin and Joseph Cazot, deputies
from the Gard and leading members of its general council, when we
know that they sat on the board of directors of the Alais-Rhone-
Mediterranean Railroad alongside the president of the Avignon chamber of commerce and a metallurgical entrepreneur from Givors. We
may even credit Eugène Spuller's alleged financial interest in the
Flanders-Picardy Railway Company, subject of an acrimonious debate
in 1875.[31] These were men protecting their own investments, to be
sure; but they were also men tied into the network of provincial
businessmen, where preoccupation with railroads transcended direct
financial interest without necessarily being in contradiction to it.

A survey of departmental councils shows that none of them
supported wholesale state repurchase of all railways, for they recognized, in the words of the general council of the Loire-Inférieure, that
the financial burden consequent upon such an undertaking would
"weigh heavily on the taxpayers." The same unanimity prevailed on
the question of local lines, but in the opposite direction. Referring to
a host of small companies in financial trouble and yet essential to
business, the departmental notables called for state intervention in the
form of subsidies or, failing that, repurchase of lines subsequently to
be turned over to the new companies representing important industrial
interests.[32]

Practical considerations smothered the bigger, political questions.
From France's economic stepchild, the Massif central, came the plea
"to do justice to the poor regions . . . [with a modest] 180 kilometers."[33]
A request from the Creuse specified the need for a rail link between
Montluçon and Aurillac. There was, the petitioners reminded their
deputies, "a vast area in the center of France totally deprived of the
means of communication. It is an immense clearing surrounded by
a forest of railroads." The general council of the Loire worried over
the fate of a projected railroad connecting Roanne to Chalon-sur-Saône

---

31. *Annuaire des chemins de fer*; report of July 18, 1875, in B/a 1274, Archives
de la préfecture de police de la Seine, hereinafter cited as APP.
32. Délibérations des conseils généraux, 1879, 1880, Délibérations: Procès-verbaux
des séances des conseils généraux, Var, 1879, Loire, 1880, all in AD XIX 12, AN.
33. Procès-verbaux des séances, Corrèze, 1878, *ibid*.

and thence to the markets of eastern France. The state insisted on a departmental subsidy, which was not forthcoming due to a depleted treasury. Will this set a pattern, the councilors asked, and limit new railroads to those successful in obtaining subsidies or guarantees of interest? Freycinet's plan, of course, avoided that obstacle. It is no surprise that he became a sort of national hero in mufti. The following year, in 1881, Saint-Étienne's problems came up for discussion. Her business suffered, it was alleged, because of the P-L-M monopoly. The departmental councilors petitioned the government to build competing railways and canals connecting the region to the Atlantic and Channel ports, the Mediterranean, and Switzerland. But no suggestion emerged as to how this was to be financed outside the hegemony of the big companies.[34]

In every case certain positions became apparent: the chief business of the government of the Republic was to enlarge the scope of economic activity; the state should act but in a circumscribed manner; there were no principled objections to monopolies though much specific impatience with their abuses; a national system of public works, within which the companies were to operate, was the ultimate goal. Finally, it is striking that behind all of this discussion lay the assumption that the defeat of the *seize maisards* cleared the way for an alliance between the industrial bourgeoisie and those elements of high finance that had not clung to political positions absolutely incompatible with the social basis and cultural expression of the secular, industrial Republic.

Chambers of commerce took similar positions. Business suffered from the unfair practices of the big companies. Its leaders summoned the state to exercise its responsibilities, but in a moderate manner. Businessmen generally opposed massive state intervention with a fervor bespeaking their commitment to entrepreneurial freedom. Lyonnais merchants, for instance, did not like the implications "for a democratic society like ours" of the state "trespassing outside its natural boundaries . . . to get into the commercial and industrial business." The chambers of commerce of Limoges, Annonay, Tours, and Gray

34. Petition from the Creuse, April 29, 1878, in F(12) 4854, Procès-verbaux des séances, Loire, 1880, 1881, in AD XIX F12, AN.

preferred the jungle of competition to the imposed order of engineers, "those theoreticians . . . who exhibit a marked tendency toward oppressive regulation and a mathematical tyranny so absolutely contrary to the spirit of commercial and industrial enterprise."[35] Several years later, when the Conventions of 1883 had passed the Chamber of Deputies, provincial businessmen expressed satisfaction with the result. On the other hand, amid recounting their economic troubles, they remembered to include high freight rates among the causes of their miseries. Businessmen in the older textile centers of Saint-Quentin, Elbeuf, and Nîmes felt the pinch worst of all, but through all of that they clung stubbornly to their principled beliefs in free competition right down, we may assume, to the death.[36]

Here lies the central contradiction of the republican position. A political alliance of petty producers and substantial industrial bourgeois inevitably generated profound tensions, not the least being the tendency toward concentration, which while welcomed in industrial circles was a source of anxiety among those ill-equipped to survive in such a world. Appeals to free enterprise, the virtues of competition, and the dispersions of economic power spoke in deceiving accents to the latter.[37] Left to the tender mercies of the hidden hand, vulnerable small producers had little prospect of survival. Those in a stronger position, for whom the chambers of commerce spoke, recognized that a combination of increased efficiency and state surveillance would help to consolidate their position.[38]

On one level, the interests of a class of industrial bourgeois and a mass of petty producers converged. Both could anticipate benefits from the development of internal lines of communication. But the former was in a far better position to absorb the cost—in the form of taxes and differential rates—than was the latter. For the backwoods,

35. Véron Duverger, *Le Régime des chemins de fer français devant le parlement, 1871–1887* (Paris: Guillaumin, 1887), 94, 98–103.
36. Responses to questionnaires circulated by the Chamber of Deputies to determine the causes of economic depression, in C 3329, AN.
37. Petition from the Creuse, April 29, 1878, in F(12) 4854, *ibid.*
38. *Le Rachat des chemins de fer devant les chambres de commerce: Extrait du "Journal des chambres de commerce"* (Paris: n.p., 1880); none of the chambers of commerce wanted *rachat*; those of Lyon, Grenoble, and Limoges argued specifically against the myth of free competition and the open marketplace.

even if served by rail lines, water transport provided a more attractive and cheaper form of transportation. The arrangements of 1859 had implicitly promised to build new canals and to dredge old ones under state auspices. But, as both Allain-Targé and Yves Guyot pointed out, the big railroad companies moved quickly from their impregnable position to crush competitive canal companies by lowering freight rates only until the latter had been driven out of business.[39] Competition became a device to favor the most efficient producers. Papon admitted as much in his polemic against the big companies, falling back on "the laws of industry from which their organization naturally arises." He then turned a neat semantic trick to soften the edge of unpleasant reality: "They would be legitimate if they did not enjoy a privileged monopoly under state protection."[40] A more forthright assessment of reality came from Alphonse de Foville, *polytechnicien*. He saluted "the dominant character" of the current material transformations, "the progressive elimination of small industry for large." He expected manufacturers to profit "from the boost given to small capital which . . . will become less timid about associating and will not hesitate to undertake great industrial enterprises." Agriculture, in his view, was destined to take the same road. The quantity marketed determined profit; a process of natural selection would raise the most efficient producers on the ruin of the rest.[41]

Freycinet emerged as the pivotal figure during the critical period of transportation development.[42] Once established in power, he moved decisively to consolidate the authority of his public works ministry over the planning and financing of railroads, canals, and ports. To strengthen his position, Freycinet assembled the Conseil supérieur des voies de communication. Although largely ornamental and advisory in function, this body's membership reflected the solid bloc of in-

39. *Rappel* (Paris), March 10, 1878; Yves Guyot, *Le Manuel du parfait bonapartiste* (Paris: n.p., 1875).
40. Papon, *Proposition de loi.*
41. Alphonse de Foville, *La Transformation des moyens de transport et ses conséquences économiques* (Paris: Guillaumin, 1880), 247, 277–78.
42. Freycinet held the public works portfolio for two years, from late 1877 to late 1879. At the latter date, he formed his own government, giving up public works to Henri Varroy but maintaining close scrutiny of its affairs.

dustrial and mercantile bourgeoisie mobilized behind an extended program of public works and internal improvements.

Whatever political setbacks that fraction of the big bourgeoisie had suffered, its command of transportation remained to be reckoned with—or rather, accommodated to. Four of its most illustrious members joined the council: Rothschild, head of the Nord Railway Company; Vuitry, chairman of the P-L-M; Adolph d'Eichthal, head of the Midi Railroad; and Louis Béhic, chairman of the Steam Packets Company. The council membership also included the presidents of the chambers of commerce of Paris, Lille, Le Havre, Rouen, Nantes, Bordeaux, Marseille, Lyon, and Saint-Étienne. Finally, several senators and deputies rounded out the membership: Louis Béraldi, Nicholas Claude, Dupuy de Lôme, Ernest Feray, Louis Hubert-Delisle, Jean Baptiste Krantz, Jacques Palotte, Henri Varroy; Henri Allain-Targé, Paul Bethmont, Sadi Carnot, Jules Ferry, Henri Germain, Jean Lebaudy, Jules LeCesne, Richard Waddington, and Daniel Wilson.[43]

Some of these men we have already encountered, and they composed a mixed group of supporters and opponents of the railroad monopolies and the Freycinet Plan. Their agreement to serve on the council did not signal support of the plan. Yet, it appears that they did submit to the logic of a national system of public works, which the plan embodied, and with it, the necessity of doing business with the big companies. Four of them, Claude, Ferry, Krantz, and Varroy, had roots in the industrial department of the Vosges. Ferry's father and his brother Charles ran the family firm. Claude was himself a cotton manufacturer.[44] Krantz, a *polytechnicien*, worked in the Corps des ponts-et-chaussées, where he held engineering positions attached to various railroads. Varroy, also a *polytechnicien* and an old collaborator of Freycinet, had worked as an engineer in the Vosges.[45] Varroy came to the council with experience in the mechanics of transferring

43. Carton 3, Freycinet Papers, Bibliothèque de l'École polytechnique.
44. Léon Louis, *Le Département des Vosges* (4 vols.; Épinal: n.p., 1889), IV, 382.
45. This and other succeeding biographical information, except where otherwise noted, comes from A. Robert *et al., Dictionnaire des parlementaires* (5 vols.; Paris: Presses Universitaires de France, 1889), and L. Ribière, *Biographie des membres de l'Assemblée nationale* (Paris: Wittersheim, 1879).

railroads from private to state ownership. The convention of March 31, 1877, between the state and the Poitiers-Saumur line was drawn up by two referees representing the government and the company. The latter chose Varroy to negotiate on its behalf.[46]

Lebaudy made his fortune in sugar refining and was a luminary of the Paris chamber of commerce. LeCesne, a self-styled "radical," ran a large shipping firm in Le Havre. Béraldi represented Martinique in the Chamber and had previously reached high levels in the naval bureaucracy.[47] Dupuy de Lôme fit the mold of expert and friend of industry. He descended from a family of naval officers, trained in naval engineering in the École polytechnique, worked as a port architect, and became known as an advocate of French merchant-marine interests. Hubert-Delisle represented Bordeaux wine, had championed free trade since 1848 (when he supported Louis Cavaignac before switching to Louis Napoleon), and remained a Bonapartist strictly as a measure of his continued commitment to free trade. Jacques Palotte was the son of a *maître de forges* in the Yonne, held a degree in civil engineering, ran the Commentry blast furnace division of the Commentry-Châtillon complex, and now represented the mineral and metallurgical interests of the Creuse in the Senate. Richard Waddington, from Rouen, controlled one of the city's major cotton-producing enterprises. Feray owned the Oberkampf Cotton Mills in Essonnes, on the southern outskirts of Paris. Henri Germain, of course, founded and headed the Crédit lyonnais. Carnot, like the others, mixed business and politics, drawing on the family fortune, a great name, and his École polytechnique background.

The heavy representation of Vosges textiles confirms the primacy of that department's industrial interests. Nicholas Claude, Émile George, Jules Ferry, and, after 1881, Jules's brother Charles, formed a small but solid phalanx of militant industrial politicians within the republican coalition. George and Claude took forward positions in the growing agitation for tariff reform. They then passed the baton for

46. C 3180, AN.
47. Which means he was associated with colonies, since the naval and colonial offices were combined at that time.

the last lap to their fellow Vosgian, Jules Méline. In only a few departments did the assemblage of political figures reproduce so completely the industrial structure as in the Vosges. To the Ferrys, Claude, and George, we can add the names of Christian Kiener, senator, *filateur*, and broker in Épinal; his son-in-law, Victor Bresson, deputy, also a manufacturer of cotton thread; Eugène Jeanmaire, Épinal lawyer and the city's former republican mayor; and *his* son-in-law, Alfred Brugnot. In the Vosges, the exception proved the rule: the only deputy not connected to the cotton industry, Louis Buffet, collaborated with the Government of Moral Order.[48]

Vosges industry had a stake in the development of the national market far out of proportion to the department's size and population. Its cotton-spinning and cotton-weaving establishments depended heavily on the home market. High railroad rates, which permitted raw cotton to travel from Antwerp to Épinal more cheaply than from Le Havre, raised costs above an acceptable competitive level. Taxes on local freight shipments, the so-called *petite vitesse,* multiplied the burden, creating "a kind of protected market for those industries near the seacoast and the major navigable waterways at the expense of the industry of the east."[49] No voices were heard from the Vosges supporting the dispossession of the big companies. The *patronat* understood that the way to markets ran over rails and that some arrangement between the big companies and the state, to fix equitable rates and to build more railways, represented their best prospect. As their eyes turned toward external colonial markets, with protection as a necessary corollary, their concern for a comprehensive and efficient transportation system quickened.

Several *polytechniciens* sat on Freycinet's council, as we have noted in passing. On one level, they constituted a committee of experts useful for their contributions to the technical elaboration of the plan.

48. Louis, *Le Département des Vosges,* IV, 366–69. The transmission of political "seats" within families followed common business practices where firms were kept within the family. It also reminds us of the habits of the ruling entrepreneurs of upper Alsace, the original home of a large number of Vosges industrialists. Jules Ferry, among other things, was a Kestner.

49. Réponse au questionnaire de la commission officielle pour le développement du commerce extérieur, 1874, Chambre de commerce d'Épinal, in F(12) 2487(b), AN.

And so they were. But we should remember that the social function of the École polytechnique was to train cadres to serve the industrial bourgeoisie. Steeped in the positivist tradition of social engineering, *polytechniciens* moved effortlessly from one regime to another. That as many found a home in the bureaucracy of the Republic as had served the authoritarian Empire in itself says something about the Republic. Many entered politics, including Freycinet himself, Krantz, Varroy, Carnot, Caillaux, and others. They did not perform as a single unit or hold identical political views. Caillaux, for one, threw in with the enemies of republican democracy. He was handsomely rewarded with cabinet positions and railroad directorships. But their intellectual formation and outlook bound them together in ways obscured by their political allegiances. Ideologically, they had much in common, on whichever side of the Chamber of Deputies they chose to sit.[50]

Freycinet's initial presentation of his plan before the Chamber of Deputies on March 14, 1878, confirmed the extension of the state railroad system to include the bankrupt western lines. At the same time, it clearly excluded the expropriation of the six companies. He did not believe it wise, he said, to put the companies under the gun at the moment when they were about to undertake new construction. That new construction, he neglected to add, included large segments of regional lines under state subsidy. The repurchase of the western lines was justified in terms of the "national interest"; to be supported on the same basis was the cooperation of the state with the big companies.[51] Freycinet thus removed the question of general *rachat* from the level of abstraction to the context of national economic calculation.[52] Speaking directly to France's industrial and commercial requirements, he added: "I believe that I have shown you that what we have here is purely and simply a matter of putting an end to an intolerable state of affairs, of resolving a precarious situation which has worried a great number of interests, a great number of departments, which threatens

50. The social and industrial role of the École polytechnique deserves a major study. For information, but little insight, the most useful recent study is Jean-Pierre Callot, *Histoire de l'École polytechnique* (Paris: Presses modernes, 1958).
51. *JOC*, March 15, 1878; *Journal des débats*, March 15, 1878.
52. Freycinet to MacMahon, quoted in the *Journal des débats*, January 4, 1878.

the completion and exploitation of our rail network unless the state exercises direction." Furthermore, he delivered an implicit rebuke to those who put the interests of stockholders ahead of producers.[53]

Freycinet was only following the logic of points of view expressed previously, including the sentiments of the "radical" Allain-Targé, who had calculated that state repurchase of the western lines would save the treasury 200 million francs against the subsidy and guaranteed interest due the P-O Railroad. "Railroad rates can enhance prosperity or produce ruin. Should they remain exclusively under the control of the companies, which are chiefly interested in their stockholders? . . . We used to think [in 1859] that competition would lead to the reduction of rates. Competition happened. But the big companies lowered their rates only to undercut the canals. . . . As far as the public was concerned, no reduction occurred."[54]

The confirming vote taken at the end of the debate on this first phase of Freycinet's plan left the hard-line defenders of monopoly trapped in a political dead end. Most of them were die-hard Bonapartists or royalists who had mistaken the railroad monopolies for a manifestation of a corporate order. Objectively, their position had isolated them from the industrial community and led them to support cartels at the wrong moment in history.[55]

The storms of 1877 had given way to the cheery skies of 1878. The worst of the monopolists had been driven from power; and although they and their allies remained in firm control of the big companies, they were forced to bend to the republican view of the political economy. On the other side of the recently dismantled barricades, the republican bourgeoisie was eager to get on with the public works program. The clamor of the previous year died down in an atmosphere of sober reflection on the future of French commerce and industry and, by implication, of the Republic itself. The industrialists of the north looked forward to the completion of a whole network of new lines. They did not concern themselves with the nature of the financing or

53. *JOC,* March 15, 1878. This was in reply to such complaints by Cunéo d'Ornano and Eugène Rouher. Picard, *Les Chemins de fer,* III, 483–86.
54. *Rappel* (Paris), March 10, 1878.
55. *JOC,* March 15, 1878; *Avenir de Gers* (Agen), January 19, 1878.

the obvious strengthening of the Rothschilds' Company of the Nord.[56] Among the politicians serving northern industry, the enthusiasm for the Freycinet Plan knew no bounds. Classification of several local lines as *réseaux d'intérêt général* (qualifying them for priority and subsidies) promised the end of hard times in the coal and metallurgical industries. New loans would be a "heavy burden," but the higher cause of "patriotism permits no backsliding." They understood the business of the Republic: "The Republic must prove that by any standard it takes second place to no other regime."[57] Northern industrial politicians, as we have seen in the case of Jules Deregnaucourt and Gustave Masure, had developed a strong sense of class interest, which gave an unambiguous quality to their conception of republicanism.

Their counterparts in the Yonne applauded Freycinet's boldness and imagination. His plan, they said, promised public works on a grand scale and glory to the Republic. On the question of the "rivalry" between the people's rights and the big companies' freedom of action there could be only one resolution—in favor of the people. The companies' position was rationalized into an "intermediary" between public savings and public works investment. Although public credit appeared strong (the liberation loan stood as testimony to that fact), there was no reason to overwhelm the national debt by expropriating the big companies. Attacks on the plan they put down to the last gasps of the discredited *haute banque*–Bonapartist clique. The plan would prevail because it followed "strictly republican principles." Moreover, "putting off its execution [would] disturb important interests in many departments." Elsewhere it was noted that state repurchase of bankrupt companies would actually relieve the distress of small shareholders (who were not the same people as the *rentiers* of Paris). Repurchase on this limited basis would rescue them from further bilking by the cartel and avoid yet another "humiliating surrender for our treasury to the great detriment of commerce and industry."[58] Occasional grumblings about the high price of repurchase caused hardly a ripple

56. *Bulletin de la Société industrielle du Nord,* VI (1878), 400.
57. *Progrès du Nord,* January 7, 1878.
58. *Yonne,* March 12, 14, and 16, 1878; *Union républicaine du Cher,* January 17, 1878.

in the placid waters of consensus. Each person wanted more railroads for his particular region and Freycinet's modified monopoly showed the way.[59]

It seems, then, that Freycinet and other high politicians correctly estimated the "great enthusiasm for public works" abroad in the country. Freycinet understood the political message as well: "If the Republic shows its true nature by the execution of useful projects, if it proves, as it shall, that it is a government of order, peace, and industry [travail]," then it will have passed the decisive test.[60] In concrete terms, this meant that the Republic could not afford to leave the fate of "poor and disinherited regions" like those in south-central France to the whims of the big companies. Republican values and the political supremacy of the Republic's high politicians traveled on rails.[61] This accounts for the dramatic turnabout from the mood of the previous year, when the republican bourgeoisie was prepared to go to war over the issue of railroad monopolies.

Why did the "radicals" of 1877 rally behind the Freycinet Plan in 1878?[62] The railroads were something of a stalking-horse in the contest for political power in the industrial Republic. It was not that railroads were unimportant to a bourgeoisie bent upon consolidating the national market. But this bourgeoisie, veterans of the struggles of the late 1860s, survivors of the Commune whose challenge to order they smashed in the name of the Republic, made of the railroad issue a question of the triumph of their class rule against a reactionary faction. They could not afford to give any ground. The railroad cartel represented the most obvious and most universally detested example of an antidemocratic faction's high-handed behavior. The big railroad companies' collaboration in the precipitation of the *seize mai* coup exposed their position. The worst fears for the egalitarian marketplace and entrepreneurial freedom appeared confirmed by this conspiracy of aristocrats. The monopolists had managed to turn most of the coun-

59. Charles Gignoux, *Rouvier et les finances* (Paris: Gallimard, 1931), 66–100.
60. *Journal des économistes*, Ser. 4 (September, 1878), 426–27.
61. Sadi Carnot, *Rapport: Incorporation de divers chemins de fer d'intérêt local dans le réseau d'intérêt général* (Paris: n.p., 1878).
62. *Rappel* (Paris), January 29, 1878.

try against them, even those ordinarily well disposed to the principles of "moral order."[63] The republicans raised the alarm of "social peril" as they had previously capitalized on the minuet of the monarchists. Once that challenge had been turned back and railroad development proceeded according to "republican" (national) principles, the compromise inherent in the Freycinet Plan was received with equanimity. In the campaign of 1877, the anticlerical onslaught had sustained the coalition of industrial bourgeoisie and the middle-class masses. Having rallied the popular forces against monopolies, the high politicians of the Republic led them into battle to secure the republican fortress against the surviving enemies of the bourgeois secular order. Farmers, mechanics, small producers, and industrial capitalists: an unstable coalition that remained viable only in the presence of a common foe. To the extent that the *seize maisards* were turned back, the foe became more difficult to locate. The time was approaching when he would have to be invented.

Had the railroad issue split the French bourgeoisie as profoundly as the events of 1877 suggest, Freycinet could not have counted on the backing of princes of finance, port merchants, industrialists of the interior, and partisans of *rachat*. We would have expected them to pull in opposite directions. The fact is they did not. Hardened political positions, so near in memory, broke against the solid front of class solidarity. If we use Beau de Loménie's razor, we will have no trouble understanding what happened. According to the principles of money-interest determinism, the *haute finance* assessed the going price of the republican bourgeoisie and paid it. Unfortunately for us all, no ruling class has ever purchased its hegemony merely with cash across the counter—or under the table.[64]

Freycinet's plan appeared to coincide with the national industrial and market outlook of the bourgeoisie and the limited regional hori-

63. Interview with a rich Paris merchant who complained that the *seize maisards* sold out the interests of commerce to high finance, in B/a 929, APP.

64. Beau de Loménie, *Les Responsabilités des dynasties bourgeoises,* II, 35–40; Jean Lhomme, in *La Grande bourgeoisie au pouvoir* (Paris: Presses universitaires de France, 1960), offers a sociological sophisticated variation on Beau de Loménie's thesis. Lhomme does not agree that a simple money transaction took place. He provides a more elaborate, but no more helpful, model of *clientage*.

zons of petty producers. A combined program of railroad building, harbors, and canals covered all interests. Thus, a significant and potentially dangerous assault on the industrial order was thwarted. Specific companies, financed through state subsidy of the big companies (and thus subordinate to them), operated sections of the third network. At this level, the local bourgeoisie obtained some measure of control over the links to their markets. At the other end of the scale, national industrialists had their market of increased consumption. Indeed, local markets, once tied into the national system of transportation, extended their own outlets, developing at the same time the community of property owners at the base of the republican coalition. The entrepreneurial prospects of the *nouvelles couches*, under the new dispensation, now appeared secure. Freycinet expressed the satisfaction of a conscious servant of class interests: "The government, in announcing . . . the advent of a new era of national prosperity, has committed itself to providing a substantial boost to public works."[65]

I say "appeared to coincide" and "appeared secure" because French capitalists stood to gain a disproportionally larger share of national production than French petty producers. This disproportion could only follow from the tendencies toward concentration, which the Freycinet Plan encouraged, combined with the relatively inelastic nature of the national market. Several years later, as we shall see, this ambiguity produced the political ferment surrounding Gambetta's moment of power.

Between 1878 and the final confirmation of the Conventions of 1883 a series of consolidations took place in the regions served by the big companies. Mostly they involved the transfer of concessions from companies specially organized to link local urban centers to the big companies. As a result, the latter swallowed up many of the remaining independent secondary lines. Cartelization, therefore, was confirmed— but with a difference. The companies did not receive a free hand even though the terms of the consolidations secured their preponderant position. They committed themselves to exploiting regional lines already linked to their own and to building new ones. They no longer needed to send their rolling stock over circuitous routes to avoid the

65. Carton 3, Freycinet Papers.

rails of their competitors—an abuse frequently cited by provincial businessmen—since those competitors no longer existed. The state guaranteed their interest on invested capital in return for a stronger voice in fixing rates, especially on freight traveling from private to state rails. Competition thus disappeared from the railway landscape; in 1883, when the formalities took place, construction of the third network merely confirmed the accomplished fact.[66] France was to have her national transport system, with the state actively engaged and the companies alive and healthy.

From the point of view of those most actively involved in tapping the national market, this was the best solution. A spokesman for the Union nationale du commerce et de l'industrie deplored, but only in passing, the elimination of competition; although everyone agreed that competition constituted "one of the fundamental principles of universal life" and was responsible for "the greatest amount of progress," experience proved that a regime of strict freedom was not proper to railroads. The Freycinet Plan substituted a "legal monopoly" for the previous regime—a gratuitous sophism, given the facts of economic life.[67] There was something for the colonial lobby as well, as Freycinet himself pointed out. Railroads carried the commodities packaged in *mission civilisatrice* wrappings: "Civilization spreads and takes root along the paths of communication. Africa, lying open before us, most particularly demands our attention. We must make every effort to capture the vast lands drained by the Niger and the Congo. At this very moment . . . three expeditions are being dispatched from the central, the eastern, and the western regions of Algeria to explore the possibility of building a railway across the Sahara to the Sudan."[68] This connection between national economics and imperial expansion provided an instance where business and special pleading triumphed over specious principle: the very same "radical democrats," who flayed the opportunist republicans for knuckling under to aristocrats and the big

66. France, Ministère des travaux publics, *Recueil des conventions passées, de 1883 à 1886, entre l'état et les compagnies des chemins de fer* (Paris: Imprimerie nationale, 1887).

67. Charles Limousin, *Le Commerce et les chemins de fer* (Paris: Union nationale du commerce et de l'industrie, 1883), 16–90.

68. *France coloniale*, March 11, 1880.

bourgeoisie, consistently campaigned against expropriation of the big companies, because those companies symbolized the venture capital important to their imperial ambitions.[69]

Grand Ministère

One final act in the drama remained to be played out. With the advent of Gambetta's "*grand ministère*," full of promise for reform, the final disposition of the railroads appeared undetermined. The exclusion, or rather the self-exclusion, of Léon Say and Charles de Freycinet from the government and the appointment of Henri Allain-Targé to the Ministry of Finance seemed to point to a denouement that the big bourgeoisie feared above all else—general and total *rachat* of the six companies. Paul Leroy-Beaulieu, the bankers' weathervane, wrote articles warning of the grave perils facing the nation's credit should a program of *rachat* be instituted. After Gambetta's fall, his gloom vanished in cheery anticipation of Freycinet's *gouvernement d'affaires*.[70] One interpretation of the events of the winter of 1881–1882 categorically asserts that the masters of high finance subverted Gambetta's government in order to block his alleged plans to expropriate all private railway companies.[71] René Waldeck-Rousseau, who served as Gambetta's minister of the interior, offered testimony to support that claim. He blamed the fall of the government on the "oligarchies controlling great monopolies, which shake down our commerce, our industry, our agriculture, [and] which care nothing for the heavy burden they impose on our national production."[72]

Some evidence exists to support this view. Allain-Targé rediscovered his concern for the egalitarian national market. In a series of statements published in the late summer and autumn of 1881, he

69. *France populaire*, November 17, 1881. This newspaper was published by the same people who put out *France coloniale*. Their editor was Eugène Menier, cousin of the radical chocolate tycoon, Émile Menier. The latter owned most of the cocoa plantations in Nicaragua.
70. *Économiste français*, November 19 and 26, 1881, February 4, 1882.
71. Beau de Loménie, *Les Responsabilités des dynasties bourgeoises*, II, 62–75.
72. René Waldeck-Rousseau, *L'État et la liberté* (Paris: Fasquelle, 1893), 104–109. Speech given on July 14, 1882.

reverted to the sort of general attack on the railroad monopolies that had characterized his political position in 1877. Having provided the initial justification for the Freycinet Plan, he now repudiated it. Freycinet, now out of power, allowed himself the luxury of a total indictment of the regime of 1859, of the rule of a "barony of bankers." However, nothing in the new system, according to Allain-Targé, guarded against the perpetuation of the oligarchy's power. The state had committed itself to building a whole network of railways at public expense. What was to become of them if they were not to be exploited directly? He proposed construction of cheaper narrow-gage railways— that is, nothing less than a total upheaval in the transportation system, which would in effect seal off local markets from the national system.[73] Like all previous proposals to reconcile national market requirements with the elimination of bankers' capital, this idea ended up in the dustbin. Provincial bourgeois, who enthusiastically welcomed the promise of wider markets and prolific production, did not concern themselves with the ultimate financial arrangements. No government of the Republic that ignored this mood had much chance to survive.

At the same time, others considered close to Gambetta launched simultaneous attacks on the monopolies, but Charles Baïhaut and Alexandre Papon differed on the solutions offered. Baïhaut wanted the state to manage all public works and to buy outright the strategically central P-O Railroad. His arguments focused on the mechanics of coal distribution. English coal traveled to Paris more cheaply than French coal from the Nord and the Pas-de-Calais basin, and Belgian coal crossed the frontier at rates lower than those applied to shipping the native product from Valenciennes to Lille.[74] Historically, however, northern manufacturers absorbed the coal of both foreign countries while the profits from the French coalfields continued to rise.[75] In this case, national industry benefited from differential rates. Papon disinterred the argument for free competition. Pushing the doctrine of

73. *Union républicaine de Paris,* July 30, August 10, 1881.
74. Charles Baïhaut, *Rapport de la commission du troisième réseau: Convention pour rachat d'une partie de la compagnie Paris à Orléans* (Paris: Quantin, 1880).
75. E. Labrousse (ed.), *Aspects de la crise économique en France* (La Roche-sur-Yon: Imprimerie central de l'Ouest, 1956); Jean Bouvier *et al., Le Mouvement du profit en France au xix siècle* (Paris: Mouton, 1965).

the egalitarian marketplace to its logical conclusion, he claimed for all producers an equal opportunity in the market through competition for their business by small and large companies alike.[76]

Gambetta himself had become more than ever a pillar of the ruling class and a fervent spokesman for its national economic interests.[77] The tribune of solidarity and the champion of the *nouvelles couches* never cut loose from the essential class basis of the Republic. His entire career stood as testimony to that fact; his repudiation at the hands of the workers of Belleville only confirmed the obvious. Furthermore, Gambetta had enjoyed the favor of the republican bourgeoisie, which took pleasure in recording that he "had never ceased to articulate that fundamental idea of order, of harmony which the Republic embodies." This view seemed justified by the attacks calling him "as authoritarian and as retrograde as the crustiest of bourgeois doctrinaires." Nothing he said or did suggested that he contemplated a repudiation of the Freycinet Plan. He was expected to put the finishing touches on the public works program.[78] Beyond this, the presence of men like Eugène Spuller, David Raynal, Maurice Rouvier, Félix Faure, and René Waldeck-Rousseau in his cabinet hardly augered ill for French business interests. Joseph Magnin's appointment as governor of the Bank of France reinforced this tendency. A former metallurgist from the Côte-d'Or and a protectionist of long standing, Magnin brought the spirit of industrial capital to the highest spheres of French finance.[79] Neither did

---

76. Papon, *Proposition de loi.*

77. One definition of "Gambéttisme": "de repousser . . . les exagérations de paroles . . . et les effusions internationales qui engagent et compromettent tout . . . de résister à cette politique de pieds et poings liés dans laquelle songe à s'abriter une diplomatie sénile . . . de vouloir dans les chambres françaises un peu moins de particularisme, un peu moins d'intérêts privés, un peu plus de patriotisme . . . car les hommes ne sont rien et la France est toute. Non, nous ne sommes pas Gambéttistes, nous sommes Français! Nous voulons, pour ce pays, une politique de vaillance et de dignité . . . on n'y trouvera jamais que des preuves de patriotisme." *Paris,* July 2, 1881.

78. *Temps,* October 28, 1881; *Union républicaine de l'Hérault,* September 9, 1881; *Télégraphe,* November 17, 1881.

79. *Dépêche de Toulouse,* November 28, 1881. A government both democratic and clearly oriented toward business was what Gambetta's constituency expected of him. *Démocratie du centre* (Bourges), September 1, 1881; *Démocratie franc-comtoise* (Besançon), November 14 and 15, 1881; *Ami du peuple* (Lille), November 18, 1881; *Progrès du Nord,* November 18, 1881. Raynal, two years earlier, said he stood for "la politique nouvelle, basée sur la science et l'expérience, et non comme autrefois sur la tradition et la passion." Clipping from *National,* April 17, 1879, in B/a 1237, APP.

Allain-Targé at the Ministry of Finance pose a threat. Apart from the fact that he was notoriously ignorant of money matters,[80] Allain-Targé's condemnation of the "bourgeoisie" in favor of the "forces of democracy" recapitulated the first principles of entrepreneurial freedom and national economics basic to the industrial Republic.[81] He only reasserted the political supremacy of the industrial capitalist class, albeit in radical terms.

A rapid survey of the terrain on which the general elections of 1881 were fought reveals the strong conservative business-oriented tendencies in the republican coalition; it also exposes some of the contradictions in that coalition. As rumblings on the left began to be heard, the candidates of the republican bourgeoisie closed ranks under the banner of order and property. Although this was not a new development and was inherent in the nature of the Republic itself, as I have already argued, it effectively legitimized, in the name of republican order, the compromise sealed in the Freycinet Plan. The intraclass struggle, which had constituted the stuff of politics during the previous several years and had provoked radical attacks on monopolies by an essentially conservative bourgeoisie, dissipated under the impact of the movement from below. Changing circumstances solidified the alliance, latent since 1878, among a segment of the big financial bourgeoisie, substantial industrial capitalists, and as many small producers as could be carried along.

Men who called themselves "radical socialists" noted what had happened and expressed bitterness at its consequences. Émile Girodet, a small merchant in the Loire town of Bourg-Argental, unseated Émile Crozet-Fourneyron, whom he labeled "Gambetta's side-kick" and a "specialist in fake radical alliances." Girodet singled out Crozet-Fourneyron's role in the budget committee of the Chamber for special attack: "Everybody knows that the budget committee has crowned the parliamentary oligarchy with a barony of financiers which supports the alliance of all capitalists against the workers."[82] In the Corrèze, Pierre Maillard, a radical parachuted in from Paris, had no chance

80. Sorlin, *Waldeck-Rousseau,* 229.
81. *Union républicaine de Paris,* August 31, 1881.
82. Elections générales, 1881, Loire, St. Étienne II, in C 3508, AN.

against Auguste Lecherbonnier, pillar of the local farm and business community. While the latter rested on his record of supporting all useful public works and occasionally denounced the church, Maillard attacked a regime whose members "mortgaged themselves to industrial and financial enterprises."[83]

Although he lost a close contact, Olivier Ordinaire of Besançon carried the republican message clearly to the farmers and businessmen of the Doubs. "The lines are drawn," he announced, "between the policies of careful reform, of practical and serious results and the policies of utopias and chimeras. . . . on the one side [we have] the politics of violence and factionalism, on the other, *la politique nationale*, peace, progress, and liberty." He accused his opponent, Charles Beauquier, of "setting town against country." Ordinaire offered "not civil war" but more of the Republic's great achievements, especially public works. Significantly, Beauquier aligned himself not with the faction of radical democracy but with the old stalwarts of the Franche-Comté republican establishment, men like Juste Gagneur and Antoine Gaudy. Even Charles Gambon, who busied himself in the Nièvre with polemics against "opportunism" and the "retrograde Gambettist spirit," spoke of the dangers of American agricultural competition and pledged himself to promote "energetic measures to bring prosperity to our agriculture and industry."[84]

On occasion the egalitarian nationalism and the economic conservatism explicit in the republican ideology parted company, and the tensions inherent in a coalition embracing a class of capitalists and a class of petty producers came to the fore. In the Aube, for example, Marc Bouillier bolted the regular party organization to campaign as an "independent democratic republican" candidate. The organization man, Eugène Bacquios, was supported by the local Comité républicain progressiste. Their confrontation, in microcosm, pointed to the future reorientation of republican factional politics. Bouillier championed

83. *République de la Corrèze*, August 4 and 11, 1881; *Réveil de la Corrèze*, August 3, 4, and 17, 1881; élections générales, 1881, Corrèze, Brives I, in C 3504, AN.
84. *Démocratie franc-comtoise* (Besançon), September 2–4, 1881; élections générales, 1881, Doubs, Besançon I, pamphlet entitled *Beauquier ou Grévy*, in C 3506, AN; *Patriote de la Nièvre*, August 9, 1881.

the people against a "small bourgeois barony and a ruling class," which had promoted monarchism. This was 1877 all over again. He went on to establish his ideological position. It will sound a familiar chord: "Equality of rights, equality of duties. No more caste, no more privileges, no more aristocrats, no more bourgeois, no more proletarians; [instead] a single class of citizens, in a word, national unification through legal equality and measures to enable everyone to attain the necessities of life and to participate in political life. Property attained through honest labor. . . . Democracy is not demagogy, it is the entire nation, united in solidarity." His final words, in which he invoked the names of Gambetta, Spuller, Floquet, and Bert, took him to the heights of egalitarian nationalism: "I want a system of national education so that our children will learn about our laws, become accustomed to them, and respect them." Bacquios for his part said little of political content. His deeds and supporters spoke for him. He was a physician, active in local charities, including a home for infant children and a mutual aid association for hosiery workers, and backed by local capitalists, *rentiers*, assorted other bourgeois notables, and, not inconsequently, Jean Casimir-Périer.[85]

Both Bouillier and Bacquios shared a common ideological perspective. However, while Bouillier fastened on the democratic myth as the best hope of small producers, Bacquios accepted the settled order of things and took his place among those ready to participate in the political arrangements consistent with that order. Specifically, the representatives of the republican bourgeoisie were prepared to do business with finance capital in order to extend the sphere of capitalist production, while their more radical brethren pressed the arguments for egalitarianism ("every man a property owner," "no more classes") against the tendency toward concentration inherent in the republican system.

This disagreement exposed the fragility of the republican coalition. The interests of the provincial industrial and agrarian bourgeoisie and those of the *nouvelles couches* did not coincide. Nor did they share the same outlook. Whereas the Republic stood to guarantee the posses-

85. Elections générales, 1881, Aube, Troyes I, in C 3502, AN.

sions of all property owners, republican social and economic policy moved toward maximizing the gains of productive capital. Under these conditions, the republican bourgeoisie galvanized a mass movement (the "democracy" of all producers) against bankers and aristocrats. Once that battle was won, or at least the differences smothered in the Freycinet Plan, they had no reason to continue the struggle for the doctrinaire nostrums of radical democracy. In terms of their ideological position—that the Republic obliterated classes and made it possible for every man to become a capitalist—the fact of massive public works was vastly more important than the financial principles behind it.

Gambetta misunderstood or refused to understand the implications of a social policy that he had helped to mold. His vision of class reconciliation made sense within the context of a defense of the material order and, indeed, served that order. He saw in himself the culmination of "practical and businesslike politics," which liberated "the bourgeoisie from its terrors, its hostilities, and its antipathies."[86] Immediately upon taking power he put into motion a vague program of reform to be carried out in a series of bureaucratic hammer blows. This stab at Jacobin democracy ignored history, ignored the united front of the industrial bourgeoisie, and ignored the general conviction that a national economic program was best served by allowing capital its head.[87] Gambetta left himself vulnerable to attack because of the confusion surrounding his intentions. And the attack came from his friends as well as his enemies. A few sober words from Léon Say about railroads raised the alarm. France had been blessed by the Freycinet Plan with the foundations of a solid program of political economy "worthy of the Republic." A plan such as Papon had offered would be a disaster and

86. Joseph Reinach (ed.), *Discours et plaidoyers politiques de Gambetta* (11 vols.; Paris: n.p., 1881–85), IX, 401, speech at Ménilmontant, August 12, 1881.
87. Several years earlier, a democratic republican developed a somewhat more highfalutin argument on the same theme. E. H. Freeman argued that "démocratie est ce système de gouvernement . . . qui les [puissances] exercise dans l'intérêt de tous, sans distinction des classes . . . celui qui garantit le mieux à l'homme, par l'égalité devant la loi." Under these conditions, he went on, the state ought to play a purely negative role in maintaining order, but within the limits that the social order and its material foundations not be threatened by the uncontrolled exercise of state power. *De l'Etat, de son rôle dans la société démocratique* (Paris: Librairie démocratique, 1872).

would leave the entire transportation system in total disarray. If, as was said, Gambetta had gone out of his way to "make pledges of wisdom to the conservative and moderate factions in the country," from what other factions had he expected support?[88] The bankers might have conspired to bring him down, but they could not easily have succeeded had the republican bourgeoisie been inclined to rush to his rescue.

88. *Télégraphe*, January 22, 1882; *Temps*, January 12, 1882; *Voltaire*, January 6, 1882; *Union républicaine de Paris*, January 26, 1882.

Chapter V

Ⅴ Schools for the Republic

"SOCIETY CAN only function," wrote Émile Durkheim, "if there exists among its members a unity of purpose and outlook. Education perpetuates and reinforces that unity by imprinting upon the mind of the child the essential values upon which collective life rests. However, on the other hand, total cooperation in society would be impossible without a certain diversity. Education itself assures the persistence of that diversity through progressive specialization. Looked at from either aspect, education consists of the deliberate and methodical socialization of the younger generation."[1]

Henri Allain-Targé and Charles Floquet, whose interest in education paralleled that of Durkheim, could not have agreed more. In the late autumn of 1881 they published in their newspaper a summary of the latest report from the general inspection of primary education. They found in it two items especially encouraging: local bourgeois were redoubling their efforts to promote popular education through subsidies and foundations, and the number of students in lay schools was rising, whereas those in church schools declined. These facts represented the culmination of over a decade's activity to establish a socially integrative primary educational system. "The lay, obligatory, free school not only rests at the base of the Republic, but behind all social stability [sécurité sociale]."[2] Ernest Constans, who was to or-

1. Émile Durkheim, *Education et sociologie* (Paris: Presses universitaires de France, 1966), 91–92.
2. *Union républicaine de Paris*, November 14, 1881.

ganize the liquidation of the Boulangists, reviewed the accomplishments of the republican government for his constituents in Toulouse. He placed educational reform on the same high level of achievement as the recently concluded Tunisian protectorate—lavish praise indeed, considering the immense enthusiasm that greeted that modest imperial coup. Upon the foundation of the new educational system he projected the erection of "a great and prosperous" nation, fashioned by the skilled hands of a "generation of citizens imbued with the spirit of the *patrie* and of the Republic."[3] These views suggest an interpretation of republican educational policy accentuating its positive, socially integrative, and disciplinary purposes.

We shall be concerned only peripherally with the politics of educational reform. The outcome of the struggles in the Chamber of Deputies and in the Senate was never in doubt, although the timing of legislation depended upon shifting political developments. Of primary importance is the character of educational policy as it unfolded amid a growing awareness of its social dimensions. It developed in response to social conditions and reflected the central preoccupations of the industrial and agrarian bourgeoisie. Overriding concern for social order, industrial strength, and national solidarity provided the mainspring of educational theory and policy in the 1870s. In this context, anticlericalism and *revanchisme* appear as secondary, derivative factors, much in evidence in rhetoric, but less so in the hard, practical calculations that went into making social policy.

Primary education in general and that special branch of primary education for the lower classes known as *formation professionnelle* became fundamental parts of official policy; yet, paradoxically, informal, private initiatives rather than institutional arrangements proved decisive. By the time educational reforms had been written into law, fifteen years of private initiatives had already established their content. These initiatives developed from the close relationship of the perceptions of leading men in the French capitalist community and their political spokesmen. We must not be misled into thinking that educational reform was strictly a Protestant enterprise and thus not

3. *Démocratie franc-comtoise* (Besançon), October 1, 1881.

characteristic of the nation as a whole. True, leading figures within the bourgeoisie happened to be Protestants who brought a particular zeal to the struggle to secularize schools. But their religious culture reinforced, rather than determined, their social outlook, which derived essentially from their class position. There is irony in all of this: compared with the theorists of the new education, the soldiers for God in the schools emerged as defenders of humane learning and honorable tradition against the "progressive" materialism of their positivist-minded contemporaries.

Positivism as an Ideology of Social Integration

Educational reform, viewed as one aspect of social policy, was shaped by a distinctive class ideology and in turn went into the elaboration of that ideology. The architects of what should be called social education[4] defined themselves and were defined by their policies as bourgeois politicians. That is, they served, with varying degrees of commitment, an established economic and social order. Positivist doctrine most closely approximated a systematic effort to construct a world view consistent with the bourgeois order. It provided at the same time a veneer for class interests expressed more crudely in national unity and social solidarity. Thus, we must first look at the positivist ingredient in the formulation of republican social policy, not because the ideas preceded the action—they did not—but because republicans self-consciously moved within a reigning system of social values. The republicans smoothly blended ingredients, subsequently hardened into ideology, that followed from the material and cultural experiences they confronted in real social relations. Positivism and secularism, as components of republican ideology visible in the educational system, certainly were used to promote "national

4. I make no claims to having invented the term "social education." It is, however, infrequently found in the literature on education, in itself perhaps a warning that a new approach is called for. One place where the term does appear is in Georges Sorel, *Réflexions sur la violence* (London: n.p., 1916). Whatever the ultimate ideological bankruptcy of Sorel's position may be, he did provide flashes of insight, especially concerning the social function of education in bourgeois society.

moral unity."[5] But their employment in the cause of republican democracy depended upon their inherent connection to the general class character of the Republic and to the men who made the Republic in their own image. Indeed, much of what appeared as varieties of positivist expression in the post-Commune decade was in fact an elaborate orchestration of basic social themes into positivist harmonies.

In its original eighteenth-century, rationalist-empirical form, positivism expressed the unfolding class values and world view of a fraction of the revolutionary bourgeoisie. With its progressive triumph, positivism rose to the heights of established ideology.[6] Republican spokesmen for social education thus had a rich tradition from which to draw —a tradition that leaped the gulf from pious hope to effective reality only with the transformation of France from an aristocratic-bourgeois oligarchy into a producers' democracy.

We may begin with the Marquis de Condorcet, to indicate the genesis of social education as it appeared at the first light of the bourgeois dawn. That Condorcet's constructs had no immediate practical sequel should come as no surprise in view of the primitive state of the French internal market in his time. But his central theme would reappear later, thrown into sharp focus by the new men brought forth in a maturing industrial order:

It is important to afford the children of the poorer classes, who are the most numerous, the possibility of developing their talents. This is not only a means of insuring the country more citizens able to serve it, the sciences more men capable of contributing to their progress, but of also *reducing that inequality due to difference of wealth, and of bringing together the*

5. Harry Alpert, *Émile Durkheim and His Sociology* (New York: Columbia University Press, 1939), 29.

6. See Frank Hartung, "The Social Function of Positivism," *Philosophy of Science,* IV (1945), 120–33, and "The Sociology of Positivism," *Science and Society,* VIII (Autumn, 1944), 328–41; Robert A. Nisbet, "Conservatism and Sociology," *American Journal of Sociology,* LVIII (1952), 167–76. Hartung: "If the historical function of pre-Comtean positivism was to assist the bourgeoisie to dominance, one may say that the class function of Comtean positivism was to assist in consolidating that dominance, and that the class function of post-Comtean positivism is to assist in maintaining it" ("The Social Function of Positivism," 124). Hartung is one of the few sociologists, along with Nisbet and the late C. Wright Mills, who cast off the yoke of value-free sociometrics and cut through to the historical and social origins of sociology. His work has received none of the attention it deserves.

classes which this difference tends to separate. The natural order creates in society no other inequalities than those of wealth and education, and by extending education the effects of both of these causes of inequality will be lessened. The advantages of education, if no longer the exclusive privilege of opulence, will be less obvious, and consequently, less dangerous to equality.[7]

Condorcet's message echoed down through the decades. Jules Ferry raised him to the level of supreme authority on matters educational, especially since Condorcet had linked public instruction to forging national unity. Eugène Spuller preferred Auguste Comte, that "great thinker" who had proclaimed that "the time has come to replace tumultuous debates on rights with the serene contemplation of duties."[8]

Comte followed Condorcet in presenting the "question of education as fundamentally a political question."[9] But in a changed historical setting the prophet of liberty was eclipsed by the "prophet of reconciliation and reaction."[10] Paul Arbousse-Bastid denies the authoritarian implications of Comte's habit of measuring education's value against its service to organic social harmony; yet he concedes that, for Comte, "education equals submission to order" and that "education must always subordinate the development of intelligence to sociability."[11] Consequently, Comte had no use for critical political economy, which represented the last gasp of "revolutionary metaphysics," constituting

7. Marquis de Condorcet, *Rapport sur l'organisation générale de l'instruction publique, fait à l'Assemblée législative, le 20 avril, 1792* (n.p.: n.p., n.d.), 290.
8. Jules Ferry, *L'École gratuite, obligatoire et laïque* (Paris: n.p., 1881), speech delivered in the Chamber of Deputies, December 23, 1880; Eugène Spuller, *Société d'instruction populaire et d'éducation militaire et gymnastique* (Nancy: n.p., 1884), speech at a meeting of the Ligue de l'enseignement de la Meurthe-et-Moselle.
9. Paul Arbousse-Bastid, *La Doctrine de l'éducation universelle dans la philosophie d'Auguste Comte* (2 vols.; Paris: Presses universitaires de France, 1957), II, 608.
10. See John F. Laffey, "Auguste Comte: Prophet of Reconciliation and Reaction," *Science and Society*, XIX (1965), 44–65, for a full discussion of Comte's contribution to the theoretical foundations of the politics of reconciliation.
11. Arbousse-Bastid, *La Doctrine de l'éducation universelle*, I, 242, II, 653. Comte's most complete and reactionary statement of the social function of education appeared in *Discours sur l'ensemble du positivisme*, written under the impact of the 1848 revolution. His final work, *Appel aux conservateurs* written in 1855, placed him securely in the camp of reaction. "Je suis convaincu," he wrote, "que le positivisme ne tardera pas à être surtout invoqué au secours de l'ordre," a state of affairs which did not appear to distress him. Auguste Comte, *Correspondance inédite*, III, 62, quoted in Arbousse-Bastid, *La doctrine de l'éducation universelle*, II, 438.

a "permanent danger" as its false lessons "promote the hope of abolishing the fundamental institution of property." Needless to say, he had his own notions of how the political economy functioned, which reinforced his conservative position. He elevated the progressive division of labor between worker and owner to an axiom of geometrically irrefutable proportions from which he derived the reality of socialization, expressed in the natural solidarity of capital and labor, bankers and proletarians.[12]

With Émile Littré, positivism emerged from the Comtian mists to realize itself in the form of prescriptions for social therapy and ideological formulations in support of social order. Littré expressed his admiration for Thiers, who had proved his mettle by dealing ruthlessly with Communards and by revealing an insight into the deep conservatism of French bourgeois and farmers. For Littré, the notion of the conservative Republic expressed a plain fact of reality: democracy's existence depended upon social peace. Indeed, democracy justified itself by absorbing the social conflicts that had brought previous regimes to grief. He thus could pronounce harsh judgments on the past *classes dirigeantes* for being responsible for France's sclerotic society (a cause of revolutions) while coolly ignoring the class dimensions of democracy. "The social problem in France these days," he wrote, "reduces itself to a single imperative: prevent violence from above and violence from below from disrupting the orderly march of progress."[13]

Littré did not, however, plant himself Canute-like against the tides of change. He did seek to discipline, although not to dissolve, the anarchy of marketplace society with positive institutions of social integration. In this quest he assigned to education a leading role. As the democratic Republic, by definition, provided a "common ground" for peasants and workers to emancipate themselves, so its schools provided for the "upliftment of the laboring masses by introducing

12. Jean Cuisenier, "Auguste Comte et la sociologie économique," *Cahiers internationaux de la sociologie*, n.s., XXIV (1959), 126–31.
13. Émile Littré, "D'une influence de la philosophie positive en nos affaires," *La Philosophie positive*, XXI (1878), 56–61; Émile Littré, "Des Conditions du gouvernement en France" (review of a book by that name by Antonin Dubost), *La Philosophie positive*, XVI (1876), 169–70, 163.

them to a superior moral and intellectual system." Coupled to a system of carefully graded educational foundations, the Republic stands indestructible, defended by "the popular masses," who "welcome stability, tranquillity, and a business climate favorable to prosperity."[14]

"Nothing is more important at all levels of social relations," wrote Littré's collaborator Charles Robin, "than a common body of knowledge, whatever the diversity in vocation, position, or point of view." Positive education did not derive from abstract principles but was imposed by the realities of industrial life: the division of labor and mutual interdependence. The task of primary education, in particular, was to inculcate the values of "sociability," counteract the egoistic impulses inherent in the marketplace, and, at the same time, counsel submission to "the necessary relations linking each man to another," while training the youth to assume an immediate functional place in society. The prevailing social order provided abundant examples of the dominance of these necessary relations: "Agriculture produces, industry transforms, trade distributes, and banks create credit."[15]

Louis Narval, another Littréist, deplored rampant individualism for its destructive and degenerative consequences as had precipitated national collapse in places like Poland and Spain. France's "so-called ruling classes" had led her down the same dangerous path. The first business of education, therefore, was to demonstrate the "idiocy, the crime" of egoism and its threat to public order. Positive secular education taught solidarity and common moral principles. Narval pointed out that clerical education was no longer to be tolerated, not because of the existence of some clerical plot against the Republic, but because traditional religious principles no longer bore any functional relation to modern society. In the Middle Ages, an attack on the church was an attack on the social order. In the industrial world, the absence of moral solidarity exposed the social order similarly to attack.[16] With sociability,

14. Littré, "Des Conditions du gouvernement en France," 171–75; Émile Littré, "Question de sociologie pratique: Par quelle conduite la république française peut-elle consolider le succès qu'elle a obtenu?" *La Philosophie positive*, XXIII (1879), 297–307.

15. Charles Robin, "Des Rapports de l'éducation avec l'instruction," *La Philosophie positive*, XVII (1877), 165, 26–28, 44, 161.

16. Louis Narval, "Le Positivisme dans l'éducation," *La Philosophie positive*, XV (1875), 62–79, 195–217, XVI (1876), 127–43.

Robin repeated, came a clear "knowledge of the solidarity which binds all social functions" and which "promptly dissolves all the hatred and mistrust" apparent in human relations. The accumulated benefits for social order shone forth through the dark clouds of conflict and discord. "The peasant and the worker will learn to prefer the banker to the usurer; they will regard the property owner, the industrialist, the financier as merely servants of a certain order on whose existence depends all social progress; they will cease to regard them as thieves." [17]

Léon Gambetta, Eugène Spuller, Paul Bert, and Jules Ferry, high politicians of the Republic, all sat at Littré's feet. Charles de Freycinet's association with the Gambettist faction has been offered as evidence of the insinuation of the positivist approach into republican politics. Gambetta himself preferred the company and advice of men formed in the Polytechnique tradition of social engineering. [18]

Gambetta consistently dealt his political hands from a deck stacked in favor of prevailing social and industrial relationships—what he called the "nature of things." Defending his plans for comprehensive tax reform in 1876, which included the introduction of an income tax, he emphasized that his scheme best "corresponds to the reigning conditions of the social order." Pierre Deluns-Montaud, who was to become Gambetta's private secretary during the stillborn *grand ministère,* found in the latter's every political move "the fruitful application [to social policy] of the law of industry . . . the law of the division of labor." [19] Gambetta found in positivist doctrine that systematic elaboration of the principles of order and harmony without which democracy degenerated into anarchy. [20] For the sake of social order, society could

17. Robin, "Des Rapports," 163–64.
18. W. M. Simon, *European Positivism in the Nineteenth Century* (Ithaca: Cornell University Press, 1963), 154–55; John Eros, "The Positivist Generation of French Republicans," *Sociological Review,* III (1955), 255–73; A. Pierre Deluns-Montaud, "La Philosophie de Gambetta," *Revue politique et parlementaire,* XI (1897), 251–58 (Deluns-Montaud was Gambetta's private secretary during 1881–1882); A. Dupront, "Jules Ferry opposant à l'empire," *Revue historique,* CLXXVII (March-April, 1936), 356–69.
19. *République française,* October 16, 1876; Deluns-Montaud, "La Philosophie de Gambetta," 245.
20. John Eros, in his article cited above, succumbs to much the same sort of confusion as does Alpert. He sees the positivist influence realized in political behavior, especially in an alleged sense of modern political organization, "realism" as opposed to

not be left to run on its own. He spoke often of "disciplined democracy," a shorthand for institutions of social integration, association, solidarity.[21]

Accused of favoring a strong state, Gambetta admitted the fact and let slip the secret that the republican bourgeoisie had come to power and intended to stay in power within the confines of the existing state apparatus. He again appealed to social necessity, to the need to contain the centrifugal tendencies of capitalism by eliminating through state action its most abrasive character; in other words, he advocated the reinforcement of bourgeois hegemony by extending its values and opportunity. He recognized classes, but denied their antagonism, suggesting that only foolishness or wickedness stood in the way of "preparing and cementing the union of classes, of establishing the regeneration and greatness of France on a solid foundation of an alliance between the proletariat and the bourgeoisie." Thus Gambetta's ferocious offensive against "so-called conservatives," whom he held responsible for promoting social chaos as they held fast to an exclusiveness and rigidity, sowing the seeds of discord and revolution despite their pretensions to defend society. "For our part," he reminded a meeting of sponsors of the *bibliothèque populaire* of the eleventh arrondissement of Paris, "the source of our obsession with the extension of education is a commitment to *social defense.* . . . From now on, to shunt aside any part of our native talent from productive activity will constitute an act of sacrilege, impiety, and betrayal of the future role of France."[22]

"extremism" or "total solution" politics; opportunism thus amounted to nothing more than the application of science to politics. This is to miss the point by abstracting a mode of behavior from its social context. Thus in this way science becomes a value-free tool with no connection to ideology. Politics is the elaboration from a theoretical model in the context of a challenge engendered by a given set of social relations. Republicans, Gambetta included, behaved the way they did because of what they were, that is, the political outcroppings of an entrenched bourgeoisie whose roots penetrated deeply into the soil of France. It was this fact that gave positivist formulations their cogency, not the other way around.

21. Docteur Robinet, "Gambetta positiviste," *Revue occidentale, philosophique, sociale et politique*, X (1883), 209.

22. Léon Gambetta, *Discours à Romans* (Paris: n.p., 1876), 13–14; speech of July 30, 1873, quoted in *Gambetta* (Paris: n.p., 1882), a contemporary collection of speeches and miscellaneous Gambettiana; Extract from *République française*, January 30, 1877, in B/a 919, Archives de la préfecture de police de la Seine, hereinafter cited as APP.

Eugène Spuller took a harsher line. He dispensed with the traditional genuflections to liberty in favor of a realistic assessment of social reality and its implications for social policy. Spuller's radical critique of the July Monarchy and the Second Empire recapitulated their failure to evolve the mechanisms for national solidarity and social integration. Both regimes flaunted inequality and thus reduced their social base to nothing. François Guizot's education bill of 1833 he considered a beacon of enlightenment in a dark age, but even it was an obvious prop to support the dominance of a narrow ruling class. Big banking and landed property no longer monopolized the marketplace. They brought into the world smaller entrepreneurs whose appearance on the scene transformed bourgeois oligarchy into middle-class democracy. These new arrivals turned the weapons of a bourgeois value system against its originators. Entrepreneurial freedom demanded equality. Spuller stood for equality; but, "equality must be understood to mean the unification of different classes of French society."[23]

Spuller spoke frequently of *morale* in education, by which he meant the propagation of existing social values. All education, especially in the formative primary years, should be consistent with reigning social values so as to dissolve elements of class conflict within the higher synthesis of the *"corps social."* His emphasis remained consistently antilibertarian. He rejected the notion of social contract, for it set the primacy of the individual against the sense of man as a "being created to live in society."[24]

Spuller, however, needed no abstractions from political theory to make the case for social education. Political democracy imposed social discipline as it simultaneously provided the instrument of personal liberation. "No one can doubt that universal suffrage . . . has transformed the nation, in establishing for all time political equality, and has abolished forever revolutionary violence." But more than an act of faith was required. Whereas the vote was the great equalizer, universal education "will bring about a moral and social revolution." And, to

23. Eugène Spuller, *Éducation de la démocratie* (Paris: Alcan, 1892), 7, speech given in Paris on November 1, 1880; Eugène Spuller, *Conférences populaires* (2 vols.; Paris: Dreyfous, 1879–81), I, 275, speech given on February 3, 1879.
24. Spuller, *Société d'instruction populaire.*

ensure that order above all will reign, this reform will "not recognize class distinctions."[25] Ironically, Spuller rejected the philosophical roots of political liberty even as he welcomed their flowering in political democracy. This rejection hardly slowed him down, since he did not recognize the contradiction; nor, if he had, would it have concerned him. He cut through the knot in a way that would have brought mutterings of incomprehension to the lips of latter-day Lockeans who, like Stuart Mill, were wrapped up in efforts to adjust preindustrial philosophy to industrial reality. Spuller understood that as the national economic market, open to talent and energy, gave birth to political institutions molded in its own image, the requirements for social order became ever more pressing. A class that had entered into its inheritance, as had the French industrial and agrarian middle class, knew that the political conditions of its rule stood on shifting sands without parallel foundations of social stability. Education provided these foundations by establishing discipline, commitment to the (bourgeois) nation, and social peace.

Paul Bert, in the best positivist tradition, combined a fervent commitment to science with a sharp sense of the socializing mission of education. He did not, in fact, separate the two. Social education brought to reality the application of science to society. In the 1860s, while teaching physiology at the Collège de France, Bert had helped to found a weekly magazine devoted to the popularization of science. The first issue of the *Revue scientifique* focused on the subject "science and democracy." Its message proclaimed that "science . . . expects to become the regulator of society." Bert strongly defended the proposition that the "scientific method must be used to solve social problems" and that the scientific perspective determines how "people will be assigned to the place in society consistent with their aptitudes and ethnic origins." Science applied to education, even at the simplest primary level, served social solidarity. It liberated the spirit from those "absurd fears and inane beliefs" that prevented the child from recognizing and respecting the nation's laws. "From natural law to social

25. Spuller, *Éducation de la démocratie*, 30–31, speech given at Grenoble on September 27, 1884.

law does the progression move."[26] This unlimited regard for science, as a force for both social control and social uplift, suggests a link between three stages of Bert's own career: practicing scientist, active politician and educational reformer, and imperial proconsul.[27]

Bert had nothing but the most profound contempt for religious education. His comments on the morality of priests bordered on the salacious. His sarcasm knew no bounds. Whatever one might make of the psychological roots of Bert's notorious anticlericalism, we must point to its essential logic within his own frame of reference. Religion cut across science and was incompatible with it. Science itself gave form and coherence to the "religion of patriotism." As an expression of the mental perspective of the French bourgeoisie, science carried great value in enforcing a rigorous intellectual discipline within which "the love of country, respect for personal dignity, belief in progress, and commitment to social solidarity" held chief prominence. Religion provided no viable framework for the indoctrination of moral values and civic responsibility. An established state system transmitted basic public and private virtues without the crippling encumbrance of metaphysical or theological speculation. Such virtues he defined as duties to "family, society, *patrie*, fraternity, solidarity."[28]

Bert extended the social argument to support the urgency of obligatory education on the primary level. He did not find the arguments for "liberty" convincing, inasmuch as they masked the church's efforts to maintain its dead hand over education.[29] Alleged threats to the abso-

26. Léon Dubreuil, "Paul Bert et Gambetta," *Grande revue*, CXLVIII (1935), 639; "Rapport fait au nom de la commission chargée d'éxaminer la proposition de la loi de M. Barodet . . . sur l'instruction primaire, par M. Paul Bert," *Journal officiel de la république française: Chambre des députés, compte-rendu sténographique*, 1880, session extraordinaire, Annexe No. 1981, hereinafter cited as *JOC*.

27. Bert was no run-of-the-mill scientist. He published in a dozen fields, including chemistry, botany, geology, zoology, descriptive anatomy, comparative anatomy, and physiology. His career ended abruptly in Hanoi in 1886 where he died in the service of France as resident-general. A biography of this fascinating career remains to be written. Bert's personal dossier, in F(17) 22742, Archives nationales, hereinafter cited as AN.

28. Italics added. Paul Bert, *L'Instruction religieuse dans l'école: Conférence présidée par Gambetta*, August 28, 1881 (Paris: Picard-Bernheim, 1881), 13–22, 23; Paul Bert, *De l'éducation civique: Conférence du 6 août 1882* (Paris: Picard-Bernheim, 1883), 15, 19–20.

29. Paul Bert, *Discours parlementaires* (Paris: n.p., 1882), II, 138–44, speech in the Chamber of Deputies, March 17, 1879.

lute power of the *père de famille* over his children to dispose of them at will moved him not at all. In an industrial world, society could not afford to count on the common sense of the individual parent to develop the spirit of sociability in the young.[30] Bert attacked legislation passed in 1875, extending church privileges to higher education, on the grounds that such a move heightened the danger of social cleavage along class lines. In place of the disinterested (but socially utilitarian) pursuit of knowledge, the universities would cease to be "centers of intellectual unity and moral harmony" and would become battlefields where sectarian struggles would be fought.[31]

As early as 1870, Bert developed the social theme that he carried through to the end of his career as an educational reformer: "At the heart of every social question lies the necessity to provide popular education."[32] The justification for obligatory education, he repeated in 1880, rested on "reason of state," and this was a matter of social security.[33] To give the citizen the vote without proper indoctrination courted national disaster. To a bourgeois audience in Paris he put the matter bluntly: "In this century of universal suffrage, the sons of peasants and workers will be your masters tomorrow! Thus you should be the first to insist that they be properly educated." And consequently he expected the rich to contribute proportionally to school subsidies, for "education is a precondition for prosperity and social security."[34]

Whereas Gambetta pretended to preside over the evaporation of classes and Spuller prescribed moral discipline for those same nonexistent classes and Bert proclaimed the dictatorship of science, Ferry articulated a comprehensive argument for social education. Charles

30. Marx, in the first volume of *Capital*, discusses this problem fully.

31. Victor Basch, "Paul Bert et l'oeuvre scolaire de la république," *Grande revue*, XIII (1900), 614–15.

32. This statement he made while campaigning for a seat on the Yonne general council. Léon Dubreuil, "Les Origines immédiates des lois laïques," *Grande revue*, CXXXV (1931), 195.

33. "Rapport fait au nom de la commission," *JOC*, 1880, session extraordinaire, Annexe No. 1981. Bert: "Une nation n'étant pas une simple juxtaposition d'individus reliés par les intérêts matériels et des lois de police, mais une individualité collective, ayant ses raisons d'éxistence et ses principes de vie, il lui appartient . . . de veiller à ce que les citoyens soient élevés avec la connaissance et dans le respect de ces principes mêmes; sans quoi l'éducation publique ne serait qu'une préparation d'anarchie."

34. Bert, *De l'éducation civique*, 7; *ibid*.

Morazé maintains that the advent of Jules Ferry to power in 1880 marked the entrance of a major French industry, cotton textiles, into the highest councils of the Republic. This event, Morazé continues, has great symbolic meaning, for it identifies the coming of age of an industrial bourgeoisie at the expense of an older generation of agrarian gentry and bankers.[35] The point is well taken even if it ignores Augustin Pouyer-Quertier of Rouen cotton, Raoul Duval of the same city, and Jean Dollfuss of the Alsatian branch of the cotton industry, each of whom shared in the power of the Second Empire at different times. Morazé's thesis must be carried further. Ferry's ministry marked the consolidation and fulfillment of the principal drama of the 1870s: the enlargement of the governing base in France to include provincial manufacturers, industrious independent peasant-farmers, and even petty producers. These groups did not, however, replace the former bourgeois oligarchs so much as they forced a redistribution of power. Ferry's most notable achievement, as one of the politicians par excellence of this coalition, was to reconstruct primary education. The concomitant extension of bourgeois class values within the democratic Republic and the renovation of education did not occur by accident. No more accidental was Ferry's starring role or the perspective he brought to it.

Ferry's social outlook rested on the hard facts of industrial reality. He found in positivism a congenial method for working out the reconciliation between the tradition of liberty and the socializing thrust of industrial concentration. He accepted the class structure (he called them "hierarchies") of modern society as the inevitable consequence of the logic of production. As industrial society submitted to this hierarchical discipline, its members found bountiful compensation in "social harmony, in universal contentment" under the benevolent dispensation of industrial capitalism. Beyond this, the positivist approach enthroned facts against fantasy. Social progress depended on a "necessary return to reality which pushes aside the rationalist abstractions of economists as well as the apocalyptic mysticism of socialist systems."[36]

35. Charles Morazé, *The Triumph of the Middle Classes* (Cleveland: World, 1966), 341.
36. Dupront, "Jules Ferry opposant à l'empire," 366, 356–59.

In his quasi-academic writings much more than in his political speeches, Ferry's preoccupations come through with considerable force. Commenting on the positive philosophy of Marcel Roulleaux, he noted with vigorous approval the former's concern with "duties" in human social relations. In contrast, liberal political economy peddled the dangerous doctrine of human rights: "Individualism is an antisocial doctrine, insofar as it can neither explain nor master the complex of social relations. It is impossible to derive from the principle of individual right anything but the interminable conflict of individual egos and the fundamental negation of all social life." While the untrammeled assertion of individual rights provided the decisive impulse to drive the industrial machine forward, industry itself imposed its own laws of socialization and solidarity in contradiction of its own origins. But that contradiction was not to be transcended, only smothered. If "the concentration of capital is an established fact,"[37] as he insisted, society must submit while devising institutional arrangements to blunt its cutting edge against the social fabric. Ferry sought such arrangements in workers' associations and social education. Thus, having denounced the politics of individualism, he welcomed its industrial offspring while seeking to impose effective discipline on the energetic but unruly child.

On a page in his notebooks, Ferry copied the following lines from an article in the *Temps* (February 18, 1846): "Instruction develops and fortifies man's apprehension of his own dignity, which is to say consciousness of his rights and duties. Thus enlightened, man will count on reason and not on force to realize his aspirations."[38] Ferry worked to create the same conditions for social control through social education and was quick to concede that in the struggle between rights and duties, the latter demanded priority.

He had once scorned the Napoleonic centralized state, writing to Yves Guyot in 1869 that "to settle once and for all in France the problem of democratic liberty, we must demolish from top to bottom the institutions of the Year VIII."[39] But once the opponent of the Em-

37. Jules Ferry, *Discours et opinions* (7 vols.; Paris: Colin, 1893), I, 584, 587.
38. Dupront, "Jules Ferry opposant à l'empire," 368.
39. *Ibid.*, 371.

pire became the man of government, the melody changed. Democratic liberty, after all, reached its highest expression and fruition in a growing industrial structure. The state now must face its responsibilities to protect that industrial structure from the shocks of disorder, to integrate all producers, and to provide skilled workers properly schooled in their civic responsibilities. And, if industrial necessity were not enough, Ferry could always invoke the patriotic catechism, whose first rule disestablished religion in favor of a secular morality that turned aside the "frightful spectacle" of men who believed they served God by "betraying their country." Ferry delivered an even more serious indictment of past educational practices. The previous generation of education conducted under the spirit of the *loi Falloux* had left large numbers illiterate, useless to their society, and easy prey to peddlars of socialist patent medicines.[40]

Private Educational Initiatives

In the light of the views of Ferry and his associates, the Ligue de l'enseignement takes on a new and significant dimension. The league pursued programs consistent with current perceptions of social education. Popular libraries, adult education, pamphlets, and informal schools attached to military units all served to satisfy the dominant preoccupations with social solidarity and national unity. Under its banner were mobilized those who ruled France as well as those who ran France.[41] Entrepreneurs and lawyers brought to their work a confidence in the fruits of social education and an abiding concern for social discipline. The positivist-scientific spirit infused and helped shape their world view, within which assumptions about the nature of society and the requisites and limits of social reform were scarcely a matter for fundamental criticism.

Although the Ligue de l'enseignement did not take final shape as

40. Ferry, *L'École gratuite, obligatoire et laïque*, speeches delivered in the Chamber of Deputies, December 23 and 20, 1880.

41. The thought and the language come from V. G. Kiernan, *The Revolution of 1854 in Spanish History* (Oxford: Clarendon Press, 1965), 44, whose discussion of Spanish politics at an earlier time raises some interesting parallels.

a formal organization until its founding national congress in 1881, it brought together local societies that had been functioning for fifteen years. In 1866, Jean Macé, backed by Frédéric Engel-Dollfuss and other Alsatian textile magnates, founded the Société des bibliothèques communales du Haut-Rhin and the Société des bibliothèques rurales de Mulhouse.[42] Both organizations also benefited from support by the government administration behind a front organization known as the Société Franklin.[43]

Upper Alsace proved to be fertile ground in which to nourish Macé's tree of knowledge. His initiative and the paternalist philanthropies of the textile *patronat* coincided. For a generation the Société industrielle de Mulhouse had sponsored a wide variety of public benefactions. Education fit into its overriding concern for better-trained as well as socially responsible workers. Articles promoting obligatory primary education began to appear regularly in the *Industriel alsacien*, the society organ, in 1861. Primary schooling followed by apprentice schools added perfection of skills to a foundation of simple moral lessons, reading, writing, and arithmetic. They reserved secondary education for aspiring managers. As late as 1866, 50 percent of the chil-

42. *Bulletin de la Ligue française de l'enseignement*, I (1881), hereinafter cited as *BLFE*; Ferdinand Buisson, *Dictionnaire de pédagogie et de l'instruction primaire* (2 vols.; Paris: Hachette, 1888), II, 1588; Claude Fohlen, *L'Industrie textile au temps du second empire* (Paris: Plon, 1956), 71; R. Oberlé, *L'Enseignement à Mulhouse de 1789 à 1870* (Paris: Société d'editions des belles lettres, 1961), 252–53.

43. The Société Franklin subsidized and supervised the stocking of municipal libraries. Its board of directors knew no partisan politics. Republican Jules Simon served as vice-president. His collaborators included the Bonapartist Saint-Simonian banker Adolphe d'Eichthal, the liberal Jules Clamageran, the Catholic conservatives Auguste Cochin and Albert de Broglie, Jean Dollfuss of Mulhouse textiles, and the banker Henri Germain. Bibliothèques municipales, scolaires, populaires, 1850–1877, in F (1a) 632, AN. More than simply a philanthropic impulse called the Société Franklin into existence. Victor Duruy, Napoleon III's minister of education, had taken into account the growing need to supplement his efforts to universalize primary education on terms favorable to the government. He knew education to be a political weapon and was determined that that weapon be wielded by established authority. In the third arrondissement of Paris, the radical republicans Edmond Adam and Frédéric Morin had installed a popular library under the aegis of the Société des amis de l'instruction. They had great success on this scale and planned to expand into the provinces. The Société Franklin was designed to head off this and other similar projects. Prefect of police of the Seine to the secretary-general of the Ministry of the Interior, May 12, 1864, circular from the minister of the interior, April 8, 1864, in F(1a) 632, AN.

dren in the Mulhouse region remained without basic schooling. Macé's
project aimed to reduce that number while providing continuing education for adults. One Mulhouse manufacturer pledged six thousand
francs each year to repay the parents who sent their children to school
rather than to work.[44]

The first *bibliothèque communale* to achieve a measure of success was at Sainte-Marie-aux-Mines (Vosges) where a five-hundred-
volume lending library had been installed. The subscription list of
patrons reproduced in miniature the board of the Société industrielle
and the Mulhouse chamber of commerce: Charles Thierry-Meig,
Rissler-Kestner, Charles Diehl, and Jean Dollfuss. A practical concern with social mobility and labor discipline inspired the Alsatians.
Earlier preoccupations with abstract "pedagogical ideals" gave way to
overriding social considerations. They determined that "a specific form
of education ought to be tailored to each class in society." Apprentice
training, in particular, responded to social necessity. Industrial demands determined the price, which was gladly paid, "to develop the
skills of the working class is to consolidate the position of industry."[45]

Macé himself never took a hard political position. His perspective
on the social question, from which he derived his educational program,
cut across political lines and embraced deadly political enemies in a
common effort.[46] Affirming that "solidarity among all members of a
society is a fact which it is not permitted to deny," he dedicated himself
to its realization. Mass education followed necessarily from universal
suffrage if the social fabric were to remain intact. At stake was nothing
less than "the life or death of the nation." Macé likened his efforts to
a crusade with its attendant military overtones. He did not shrink from
the crudest imagery to make his point. Appealing for funds in 1866,
he said, "Why, since we are talking about overhauling our military
system, do we not organize an educational *landwehr* as an auxiliary to

44. A. Dessoye, *Jean Macé et la fondation de la Ligue de l'enseignement* (Paris:
Flammarion, 1883), 105. Dessoye was a member at that time of the council of the
league; Oberlé, *L'Enseignement à Mulhouse*, 83, 253.
45. Jean Macé, *Morale en action: Mouvement de propagande intellectuelle en
Alsace* (Paris: n.p., 1865), 48–49; Oberlé, *L'Enseignement à Mulhouse*, 251.
46. Spuller, *Éducation de la démocratie*, 179, speech at the Third Annual Congress
of the league in Reims, March, 1883.

the regular army. I cannot believe that public order would suffer in the process."[47]

The Ligue de l'enseignement suffered no interference from the government before 1870. Republicans and imperialists easily closed ranks to support social reconciliation and national harmony through education. Macé himself sat on the board of the Société Franklin. None of the early foundations ran afoul of the police, and in Metz the prefect pledged and delivered his full support. The prefect of the Marne noted with satisfaction that among the sponsors of the Ligue de l'enseignement of Reims he found the cream of the mercantile and business establishment, who supplied books to workers filled with the wonders of "morality, the ideals of family life . . . and the pleasures of the intellect."[48]

Catholic traditionalist enemies of the Empire and of the league found a deeply sinister meaning in the comfortable collaboration between the two. Jean de Moussac oddly linked the league to the First International as "discreet flatterers of the crowned socialist." But he counted on the class interests of the "democrats involved in the league, their independence, their moderation" (meaning their bourgeois perspective) to stifle the impulse to "embrace the grim utopias which the minister, Monsieur Duruy, and his master pursue."[49] Moussac's judgment suggests he was concerned much more for the social implications of the new education than for its antireligious thrust. He could thoroughly dislike what was going on but at the same time recognize its purposes and limits.

The league's consistent orientation toward serving industrial needs revealed itself at its inception. A *catalogue populaire*, which Macé drew up for Alsatian libraries, included books on railroads and the cotton and silk industries, several volumes on traders and missionaries in Africa and China, Barthélemy Saint-Hilaire's *Lettres sur l'Egypte*

47. Macé, *Morale en action*, 16–17; *Opinion nationale*, October 25, 1866, quoted in Dessoye, *Jean Macé*, 47–48.

48. List of sponsors of the Société Franklin pour la propagation des bibliothèques populaires, in F (Ia) 632, AN; Dessoye, *Jean Macé*, 70; several reports of the prefect of the Marne, 1867–1868, in F(17) 12527, AN.

49. Jean de Moussac, *La Ligue de l'enseignement* (Paris: Librairie de la "Société bibliographique," 1880), 24–25.

(a promotional pamphlet written on behalf of the Suez Canal Company), Thierry-Meig's *Six semaines en Afrique,* and selected classics of liberal political economy: Bastiat, Jean Baptiste Say, Michel Chevalier, Thiers, and Batbie (*Le Crédit populaire*). Macé did maintain scrupulous neutrality in religion. Both Catholic and Protestant Bibles appeared on the list.[50]

The league rapidly overflowed the boundaries of Alsace. At least a dozen *cercles* were founded elsewhere before 1870. For the most part, industrial and commercial centers led the way. In Épinal, Émile George, a lawyer closely tied into Vosges textile interests and later spokesman for protectionist interests, sponsored the Cercle spinalien in association with Nicholas Claude, textile entrepreneur, and Charles Ferry, Jules's brother.[51] The Cercle rouennais found supporters among that city's textile entrepreneurs, including Raoul Duval, Napoleon III's deputy in charge of patronage and election management in Normandy. Jules Siegfried led the way in Le Havre. Antonin Proust, Allain-Targé's son-in-law, later Gambetta's minister for arts and trades, founded a branch of the league in Niort.[52] The Cercle girondin at Bordeaux solicited funds from that city's commercial establishment, citing league experience in other cities, especially "the happy prospects for solidifying under our influence the working class" and the importance of the "creation of schools for the poorer classes."[53]

The rapid expansion of popular libraries, adult education courses, and locally sponsored lay primary schools became possible only with the intensive commitment of local bourgeois, politically republican, who alone were in a position to obtain the necessary financing either privately or from public funds where they controlled town government. At the same time, the parent society benefited occasionally from the largess of the rich. Émile Menier, the cocoa king, subscribed to the league for three thousand francs over and above what he donated an-

50. Macé, *Morale en action,* 235–63.
51. *BLFE,* II (1882), 350; Léon Louis, *Le Département des Vosges* (4 vols.; Épinal: n.p., 1889), IV, 382.
52. Buisson, *Dictionnaire,* II, 1591. Raoul Duval's presence seems surprising at first glance. But given the stated program of the league to promote the socialization of the people, Duval easily fit in. Besides, he was a Protestant.
53. Report of the attorney general of the Bordeaux appeals court to the minister of justice, December 16, 1868, in BB (18) 1795 (1), 9803 (A), AN.

nually. Local societies, of which there were over one hundred by 1880,[54] paved the way for the great reforms that were to follow; they set the tone and focused on the social, moral, and utilitarian aspects of education as viewed from the angle of practical necessity.

Private and local sources, mobilized in the numerous circles of the league, and not state bureaucrats or doctrinaire politicians, worked out the requirements of social education within the context of their own experiences. In Boulogne-sur-Mer, for instance, the local industrial arts council organized courses for working adults and established a popular library of 1,500 volumes. A total of 178 employers, from big shippers to retailers, contributed thousands of francs to the projects which the municipal council also subsidized to the amount of 400 francs. In Versailles, the popular library counted 14,000 volumes by 1877; by that date the number of annual borrowers had reached 17,000, representing an eight-fold increase from twelve years earlier.[55]

Few departments in France saw as much concentrated effort in privately sponsored education as the Yonne. Its bourgeoisie and the lawyers and politicians close to them threw their energies into public service through education. Paul Bert, born and brought up in their midst, freely acknowledged these influences. He recalled one Alexandre Dethou, a successful farmer near Auxerre, who started an *école d'apprentissage* on his property and from that experience developed an elaborate scheme for a national system of free and lay education. A firmer commitment was forthcoming from the Société de l'instruction populaire de l'Yonne, organized under the leadership of Hippolyte Ribière, a close political ally of Bert. Ribière had served the republican cause defending political criminals during the grim years of the Empire. Through Bert he became Gambetta's appointee to the prefecture of the Yonne after the fourth of September.[56] Ribière

54. Report of the rector of the Académie de Grenoble to the minister of education, January 26, 1874, report of the prefect of the Ain to the minister of education, July 12, 1875, in F(17) 12527, *ibid.; Progrès de Lyon*, June 8, April 15, 1872; *Progrès du Var* (Toulon), December 17, 1873; *BLFE*, I (1881), 73–76; Buisson, *Dictionnaire*, II, 1591.

55. Moussac, *La Ligue de l'enseignement*, 171n, 155.

56. Dubreuil, "Les Origines immédiates des lois laïques," 191–214; Dubreuil, "Paul Bert et Gambetta," 632–33.

defined education in socially functional terms. He called upon the responsible elements of Yonne society to mobilize all "citizens to struggle against the enemy within, ignorance, plague of our past, which, transformed, will become the patriotism of the future."[57]

A powerful pressure group counting two thousand members by 1875, the Société de l'instruction under Ribière operated under the assumption that the purpose of education was to reconcile the divisions that threatened to disrupt French society, the Commune being a recent bitter example of such divisions. Democracy made every man sovereign and the arbiter of governments; and since governments existed to be preserved, "we must be devoted to them and teach others to be as devoted themselves." Whether Ribière followed a line laid down by Bert or vice versa does not alter the significance of their position, which was, in the former's words, to invoke education in pursuit of "social peace."[58] Bert had earlier placed education at the very foundations of democracy. Its viability as an active force for social conservation and national regeneration rested on solidarity, which would, however, be a hollow slogan without the necessary commitment to the "destruction of social barriers."[59]

By the close of the decade, the Société de l'instruction populaire de l'Yonne had penetrated deep into the department's rural heartland. Its libraries became altars where peasants worshiped the cult of republican solidarity, accompanied by a liturgy in the form of sacred literature—Benjamin Franklin's *Moral Essays*, Victor Duruy's *Histoire de France*, Pierre Mignet's *Vie de Franklin*, Maynard's *Vie de Saint Vincent de Paul*—read and interpreted on Sunday mornings by missionaries from the city.[60]

At the dawn of the new decade, the organ of the Yonne repub-

57. File of the Société de l'instruction populaire de l'Yonne, in F(17) 12544, AN.
58. Ribière repeated with obvious accord some simple lessons drawn earlier by Bert about the passage from the *ancien régime* to republican France. Its message told of history providing the tools if only they were put to proper use: "L'Étude des anciens temps nous inspire le respect du notre . . . et nous enseigne la résignation, en présence de maux que le suffrage universel nous donne le moyen d'adoucir progressivement." Annual report for 1875 of the Société de l'instruction populaire de l'Yonne, *ibid.*
59. *Liberté de l'Yonne*, June 5, 1872; Basch, "Paul Bert et l'oeuvre scolaire," 610.
60. List of books distributed by the Société de l'instruction populaire de l'Yonne, in F(17) 12544, AN.

licans and business interests reviewed with satisfaction the achievements of the 1870s and pointed toward yet uncompleted practical tasks
of material amelioration, which, along with further efforts in popular
education, led to the highest end: "human solidarity." Victor Guichard,
president of the general council and a lawyer sometime associated
with the Suez Canal Company, focused his decennial review of the
state of politics on the unfinished business in education, which was
to get the church out of the schools. He likened the clergy to a fifth
column, a dagger aimed at the "heart of our youth as it seeks to instill
contempt for the glories and institutions of the *patrie*." Guichard,
let it be said, did not indulge in gratuitous priest baiting. Within his
frame of reference, he could see them only as a socially corrosive
element.[61]

The Bordeaux bourgeoisie, like its counterpart in Auxerre, brought
enlightenment to adult workers. The Société des amis de l'instruction
élémentaire represented the Ligue de l'enseignement in the Atlantic
port. Founded in 1867, the society's various adult education courses
were attracting fourteen thousand students by 1881. Workers, who
were admitted only upon recommendation, studied reading, writing,
arithmetic, and practical subjects such as hygiene. Its "popular" composition is attested to by a breakdown into vocations of those who
regularly attended courses. Clerks and low-level white-collar people
made up the largest single category, followed closely by skilled workers
in the metallurgy, printing, carpentry, and sugar-refining industries.[62]

Government officials, under both the Empire and the Republic,
who carefully watched the progress of such organizations, agreed
that its social utility proved impressive. Imbedded in the ordinary

61. *Yonne*, January 3, July 27, 1880, March 9, 1878. Guichard's grandson,
Pérouse, echoed these sentiments in his campaign for a seat on the general council: "Le
meilleur gage de la prospérité matérielle . . . est le développement intellectuel et le
progrès moral. . . . Je veux l'instruction obligatoire afin de donner à la France de jeunes
générations digne de suffrage universel et *devouées à la République*." *Yonne*, July 15,
1880, italics added. Pérouse had a professional acquaintance with scientific and positivist discipline and a special feeling for material prosperity; he was a *polytechnicien*,
member of the Corps des ponts-et-chaussées attached to the railroad section of the
Ministry of Public Works.

62. Report of the minister of education, January 4, 1881, annual report of the
Société des amis de l'instruction élémentaire de Bordeaux, 1877, both in F(17)
12539, AN.

curriculum were strategically placed homilies emphasizing one's "duties toward one's fellow man, society, and the family." The rector of the Académie de Bordeaux confessed to a high admiration for the group, and he was willing to see it continue to operate even though "members of the committee are well known for their 'exclusive' political opinions."[63]

He might have had in mind Amédée Larrieu, overseas shipper and democratic leader of the general council of the Gironde. But whatever Larrieu's political views, his social orientation as a member in high standing of the Bordeaux bourgeoisie should have given the rector no cause for discomfort. Jules Steeg, a Protestant pastor by trade and republican politician, also was active in local education as well as on the national scene.[64] Steeg held a series of conferences for adults, under the sponsorship of the Société de propagation de l'instruction du quartier Saint-Nicholas (Bordeaux), in which he encouraged the pursuit of worldly success through hard work. He drew his examples from the heroic revolutionary era, recalling men like Lazare Hoche, nephew of a fruit peddlar who rose rapidly to general once careers had opened to talents, and Louis David, "once reduced to abject poverty," who achieved spectacular artistic success by unceasing labor. "Because of what happened then," Steeg reminded his working-class audiences, "we all possess equal rights . . . and each of us is obliged to work for our country's glory, her freedom, her moral stature, and her prosperity."[65]

Coordination between league headquarters in Paris and local societies promoting communal schools and people's libraries rested in the hands of the Cercle parisien. The latter's sponsors featured a stellar cast of bourgeois republicans, ranging from the moderate to the radical: Henri Martin, Jules Clamageran, Henri Brisson, Hippolyte

---

63. Report on the activities of the Société des amis d'instruction de Bordeaux, 1868, rector of the Académie de Bordeaux to the minister of education, January 10, 1873, both *ibid.*

64. Steeg wrote one of the moral and civic instruction manuals approved by the Conseil supérieur de l'instruction publique for use in primary schools. Buisson, *Dictionnaire*, II, 1838.

65. Procès-verbal of a meeting of the Société de propagation de l'instruction du quartier Saint-Nicholas, May 8, 1881, in F(17) 12539, AN.

Carnot, Paul Challamel-Lacour, Nicholas Claude, Cyprien Girerd, Jacques Laisant, Émile Littré, Joseph Magnin, and Eugène Spuller. The ladies' auxiliary brought together yet more great names from the republican establishment: Dorian, Menard-Dorian, Kestner, Cornil, Kœchlin, Lazard, and Siegfried.[66]

By 1881, Macé could look with satisfaction upon the achievements of the Cercle parisien. One of its subsidiaries, the Société de sou des écoles laïques, collected funds to subsidize building rural schools and stocking libraries. Rural education, in Macé's view, expressed the apogee of the league's civilizing and socializing mission: "One village is nothing. But with universal suffrage, all the villages add up to France itself, because that's where we find the majority of the population." Too much of the available reading matter still flowed from château and presbytery. What sort of commitment to national unity, to republican institutions, those vehicles of order and progress, could be expected of a population steeped in the history of the "glorious deeds" of Vendée rebels and counterrevolutionary émigré gangs? Bad books made bad citizens. What was seen, perhaps in an exaggerated fashion, as a "mounting tide" of clericalism threatened to inundate the villages recently brought into the republican consensus. Books from the era of the *loi Falloux* remained at the core of primary school curricula. "Patriotism is frequently ignored, or worse, spat upon . . . [books] appear to have been written less to mold enlightened citizens respectful of the laws and institutions of their country than to raise a generation of servile clods." The day had passed when ignorance stood as a barrier against social disorder. The viability of the political economy rested on the constant expansion of a trained efficient body of producers. Education strengthened the social equilibrium by providing the tools for energetic and constructive activity adding to the social output.[67]

In the matter of books and religious content, careful attention was paid both to local sensibilities and to a sharp differentiation between

66. *BLFE*, I (1881), 4–6.
67. *Ibid.*, 341–81; *Démocratie franc-comtoise* (Besançon), January 2, 3, and 18, 1879; *Union républicaine de la Saône-et-Loire*, September 3, 1881; *Petit mâconnais*, September 23, 1881.

"theological or supernatural" doctrines and basic moral precepts, which might or might not be grounded in revealed religion. The tendency was to move away from religious underpinnings to *éducation morale*, which favored a secular, social framework. The notables of the Corrèze strongly supported some sort of religious training in public schools, fearing that without it the children would confront the world "having no sense of good and evil, no idea of the reciprocity of rights and duties" fundamental to good citizenship and social responsibility. Moral principles, they were convinced, also reinforced a sense of one's "duty to the *patrie*."[68]

In the Côte-d'Or, those who defended religion, in any form, stood condemned of "antipatriotism" and of being anxious only "to sow the seeds of discord and hatred while we all have need of solidarity and peace." The bourgeoisie of the Côte-d'Or, like its counterpart elsewhere, possessed a clear understanding of the social value of a secular morality and expressed confidence in its applicability. The bourgeois turned the clericals' arguments against them by insisting that clerical agitators, wherever found (and sometimes invented), were responsible for "creating disorder" leading to the "disruption of business."[69]

Expressing its views on Article 7, the general council of the Hérault (strong Protestant country) asserted its conviction that the law "constitutes, as things are now, an indispensable buttress of the social order [*sécurité sociale*]." The two popular libraries installed in the *mairie* of Béziers reflected the strong secular tone of the region. A single work by Chateaubriand in its catalog was lost among works by Louis Blanc, Jean Macé, Voltaire, Victor Hugo, and Jules Michelet. Befitting a coastal town, a copy of the *Voyages of Captain Cook* took first place in the display. The local *cercle* of the Ligue de l'enseignement had a strong radical flavor tempered by a sensible regard for the complexity of "social questions," which, as if then to deny that complexity, were to be solved by political means. "Socialism, that is the

68. Conseil général de la Corrèze, *Procès-verbaux des délibérations, 1880* (Brive: n.p., 1881).

69. Conseil général de la Côte-d'Or, *Procès-verbaux des délibérations,* first session, 1879 (Dijon: n.p., 1880); see also the records for the general councils of the Aisne, the Doubs, and the Puy-de-Dôme in the same series.

consideration of reforms against the systems of revolutionary anarchists."[70] The circle's counterpart in the Breton department of the Ille-et-Vilaine took the opposite position on the grounds that to enforce Article 7 would be to restrict the freedom of fathers to choose education for their children. Yet, beneath a surface broken by differences over religion, lay a bedrock of common concern for social education, which, in the words of the Bretons, "will safeguard the rights of civil society and of the state."[71]

An abiding concern for demonstrating the necessary link between a healthy marketplace, untroubled by social disturbances and alternative fantasies, and proper civic and moral indoctrination animated locally initiated education. Such was the view, for instance, of the Société contre l'ignorance de Clermont-Ferrand, whose statutes expressed its conviction that "a people can achieve material well-being without employing subversive tactics" so long as they "are docile and hardworking and constantly apply themselves to their own edification." The rector of the Académie de Grenoble, reporting in 1870 on the activities of the Société des amis de l'instruction populaire de Valence, willingly tolerated a touch of *opinion avancée* among its members because of their good work among the *classes laborieuses*. The local prefect, eternally vigilant against political deviation, refused to be concerned with possible political implications in the face of the obviously immense social good accomplished "in spreading enlightenment and instruction among working people."[72]

It is revealing to note how easily and naturally social education took its place among the great public works undertaken at the time.

---

70. Voeux des conseils généraux, Hérault, 1879, in AD XIX 12, AN; *Union républicaine de l'Hérault,* July 5, 1881; see also report on the Société de bienfaisance pour la propagation de l'instruction primaire et de l'éducation morale et religieuse d'Arpajon (Seine-et-Oise), in F (17) 12544, AN: "L'association, sans aucune caractère politique, et mené seulement par le désir d'améliorer en instruisant, s'efforce de propager, par la distribution de bons livres, les sentiments moraux et religieux."
71. Voeux des conseils généraux, Ille-et-Vilaine, 1879, in AD XIX 12, AN.
72. Société contre l'ignorance de Clermont-Ferrand, statutes, article 3, in F(17) 12541, rector of the Académie de Grenoble to the minister of education, April 11, 1870, prefect of the Drôme to the minister of education, March 3, 1870, in F(17) 12538, AN. A report from the prefect (now republican) filed nine years later indicated the group had not altered its mode of operation to adjust to a more congenial political environment.

As the extension of roads and railroads into the countryside brought the rural masses access to the national market, the parallel extension of schools brought to those same masses the skills, habits, and, above all, commitments with which they would be assimilated into that market and imbued with its values. Schools and railroads: "The first brings intelligence; the second prosperity."[73] Uniformity of consciousness and the extended market; these were the two forces for industrial progress, solidarity, and social order.

Education and Solidarity

At the heart of the program for social education lay the conviction that education provided the means for the disinherited to acquire a material stake in society. Instruction in useful skills coupled with an indoctrination into acceptable social values would equip the proletarian or the marginal farmer with the tools by which he could become a property owner. Thus perforce integrated into the bourgeois world, or at least at its edges on unequal terms, the worker no longer would find himself at war with that world. He would become its ardent defender. Gambetta called for the establishment of vocational and technical schools "in which legions of workers would be placed squarely on the road to becoming craftsmen, entrepreneurs, capitalists." The result he envisioned was nothing less than the "beginning of the solution of the social problems which weigh heavily on our consciousness." In the acquisition of a useful skill, the worker develops his "productive power: it is essential that his *capital manuel* . . . reinforced with his *capital intellectuel* become the wellsprings of leisure and wealth."[74]

Gambetta's pronounced validation of the infinite flexibility of the marketplace expressed a *petit bourgeois* illusion sufficiently grounded in reality to hold out the hope of a benefit to be gained. Henri Brisson understood equally well the political dimension of an educational

73. *Avenir de Gers* (Agen), January 26, 1878.
74. Gambetta, *Discours à Romans*, 24–27; Report of a speech delivered by Gambetta on June 15, 1878, at a meeting of the *bibliothèque populaire* of the thirteenth arrondissement, in B/a 921, APP.

reform determined by class interest. One of his favorite projects was to extend education in rural France beyond the rudiments offered in the primary schools. "We must make available," he insisted, "serious training courses for the sons and daughters of those small artisans, small farmers, and small landowners who make up the backbone and the cadres of our rural democracy."[75] Behind these slogans lurked a sharp sense of the imperatives called forth by the stabilization of a social system whose essential values could not be questioned.

For Jules Ferry the process of integration through education promised no disruption of the social status quo but, indeed, quite the opposite. *Pari passu* with the assimilation of useful skills, the sons of workers and the sons of bourgeois would become imbued with "that spirit of togetherness and that community of values which constitute the real force of democracy, by the initial *rapprochement* . . . which follows from the mingling of rich and poor on the same schoolroom benches." Ferry did not expect the poor to learn much more than their proper place in society. This impression is borne out in his harsh imagery. Inevitably the sheltered world of the classroom gave way to the nasty and brutish world of the marketplace, where man's place was determined by his class and not his intellectual gifts. Rich and poor were destined to follow divergent paths. That was in the nature of things. Ferry recognized, indeed welcomed, what he called "the historic law of modern industry," which decreed the "ever-widening separation of capital and labor and the inevitable and growing distinction between the function of the capitalist and that of the laborer."[76] The laborer could expect no immunity from such "laws."

Qualified efforts to homogenize all classes ended with primary studies. Beyond the level of the primary school, industrial necessity took over and imposed its own discipline. Ferry's decree of November 29, 1881, established a network of upper primary schools, which offered two-to-three-year terminal courses designed to provide for

75. Clipping from *Les Hommes d'aujourd'hui*, "Brisson," Année 3, No. 94, in B/a 981, *ibid.* Rochefort's *Intransigeant*, July 9, 1881, for once hit the mark when it referred to Brisson's point of view as "moralité politique genre Spuller."
76. Speech of April 10, 1870, quoted in Louis Legrand, *L'Influence du positivisme dans l'oeuvre scolaire de Jules Ferry* (Paris: Rivière, 1959), 115.

the "sons and daughters of farmers and artisans" some further general education with apprentice training. They reproduced under state auspices the apprentice schools, which had been the pride of entrepreneurial philanthropic efforts for the previous two decades. Ferry abandoned any pretense of social mobility. These schools, he wrote, "are not to scatter their students in all professional directions, but are to direct them arbitrarily toward those vocations to which they have been assigned by their birth."[77]

The system of upper primary schools grew out of a long and rather confused effort to institutionalize professional training. Until the early 1880s state action accounted for little progress in this field. Private and local initiatives filled the gap. Industrial centers, beginning during the Second Empire, sprouted professional and apprentice schools.[78] Generally speaking, and there were exceptions, the former served those destined for the lower white-collar and shopkeeping professions, while the latter, in great number, trained wageworkers to develop greater efficiency in their industrial calling. Ferdinand Buisson found the apprentice schools of significant social value, since they rendered the worker "better trained, *more devoted to his station*, and consequently harder working." The general level of morality and social achievement would be raised by the "raising up of the working classes."[79] For some, purely practical education was not enough. Octave Gréard looked to an educational scheme that "elevated the working youth above mere preoccupations with a craft" to considerations of a general nature, especially "how to be a success and increase one's opportunity for leisure." Mostly, however, the emphasis was on acquiring skills to produce more and therefore to earn more within a stated occupation. Considerations of social mobility went by the board. The Paris municipal council, by 1882, ran four apprentice schools for furniture making, construction work, and precision-tool making for men and home economics and secretarial skills for women. The

77. Records of the Conseil supérieur de l'instruction publique, in F(17) 12964, AN.
78. In Le Creusot, Mulhouse, Douai, Le Havre, La Ciotat, Besançon, and Brest, among others. There were 58 by 1894. Buisson, *Dictionnaire*, I, 96–97, II, 2453.
79. *Ibid.*, I, 96.

Chambre syndicale des tailleurs ran a course on pattern making and cloth cutting. Its graduates turned out to be better tailors and were supposed to command higher wages.[80] As in other aspects of education, the Ligue de l'enseignement crystallized and articulated middle-class consciousness of the pressing need for extended professional and apprentice training.

An in-depth report on the subject delivered at the Third National Congress of the league in 1883 by Arthur Mauroy, member of the Paris Conseil des prud'hommes, made explicit the industrial and social purposes of such education. Mauroy began with what he considered the indisputable assertion that "the state of commerce and industry is serious, very serious." Exports were dropping and the internal market could not be expected to take up the slack. France tottered on the brink of absolute dependency upon other countries. Specific industries through which she had previously established a mastery over external markets wallowed in depression; a general business crisis and untold social unrest threatened. Secular economic conditions were not entirely responsible for this state of affairs. Frenchmen habitually overestimated their capacity to compete with other countries and consequently took no steps to create the proper conditions to support the struggle. Explicitly rejecting protectionism to redress the balance, Mauroy believed only in reversing the "absolute insufficiency of our professional education."[81]

Much had been done in this area, indicating the path that had to be followed. Several dozen centers boasted professional schools by the end of the 1870s. Each school specialized in training skilled workers appropriate to the local industry. Nonvocational courses in *éducation civique et morale*, under control of the *patronat*, served special spiritual needs. Adults were not forgotten. They put their evenings to creative use in learning extra skills with instruction provided by the various

80. Octave Gréard, *Éducation et instruction, I: Enseignement primaire* (Paris: Hachette, 1885), 135; *Paris*, January 20, 1882.
81. Arthur Mauroy, "L'Enseignement professionel en France: Urgence absolue de son développement et rôle de la Ligue dans ce développement," *BLFE*, III (1883), 145–60.

sociétés industrielles around France.[82] The benefits to be gained by increasing the efficiency of the industrial plant became obvious. In addition, the nation as a whole reaped a social dividend; education furnished the key to unlock careers open to talents but, as Ferry and others made clear, within sharply defined limits. Industrial progress reinforced social solidarity by uniting all in the common patriotic effort. For Jules Simon, the bourgeois ideologue, necessity dictated the direction of education and neatly dovetailed with passion to spread science and enlightenment.[83]

Education subordinated to industrial requirements carried within it the solution to the social question. Workers, spending their leisure time in the classroom rather than the tavern, were insulated against "deplorable sentiments."[84] Furthermore, an education linked to the world of practicality and production, in which the worker found his newly acquired skills marketable, served to justify a solid commitment to that world and an easy acceptance of the social relations that characterized it. " 'To make the worker a new man, master of his fate, free, powerful enough to act for himself or join in collective efforts, what do we need? Schools, schools, and still more schools. ... It is through that effort that will be erased forever the depressing prospect of social war, whose echoes continue to reverberate.' "[85]

Alfred Deseilligny, a *grand bourgeois* who understood the meaning of social education, spoke in similar accents. He noted that unlettered workers were much more prone to violent strike action than those blessed with an education. Echoing Jules Siegfried as well as Ferry, Gambetta, Spuller, and Bert, he insisted that the "law which

82. *Ibid.*, 152; "Le Cercle parisien de la Ligue de l'enseignement," *Cahiers laïques* (September-December, 1958), 84.

83. "Le monde de la science sera-t-il fermé pour les ouvriers? Ils sont nés ouvriers, mais si parmi eux, il y a a un homme de génie, la société ne viendra-t-elle pas à son aide pour en faire jaillir l'étincelle, ne tendra-t-elle pas une échelle à ceux qui se sent capables de monter? Dégageons donc ceux-là de la masse et en faisant profiter l'individu, c'est le corps social tout entier qui bénéficiera . . . [industrie] cesse d'employer les hommes comme force naturelle et les utilise comme direction intellectuelle. La richesse d'un pays dépend désormais de la capacité de sa population." Jules Simon, *L'École* (12th ed.; Paris: n.p., 1893), 394–95. The first edition of this work was published in 1864.

84. Meaning subversive ideas. Mauroy, "L'Enseignement professionel," 157.

85. Leneveux, *Le Travail manuel en France*, quoted *ibid.*

made every man a voter has for its necessary corollary obligatory education." Without it, "we are left to fear that the era of revolutions has not yet passed." Spuller too worried about revolutions; however, they had their uses in awakening the bourgeoisie to its responsibilities. "Each of our great political and social crises, those of 1830, 1848, and 1871, have given birth to a movement for popular education," such as the Union française de la jeunesse, a sort of *jeunesse dorée* with a social mission, which filtered middle-class youth into working-class districts after the Commune to tutor those unable to attend school.[86]

But the education of workers, or even farmers, beyond the rudimentary skills required to sustain repetitive labor cut two ways. While becoming more efficient units of labor power, workers necessarily found their universe expanded. As they mastered instruction in the more complicated processes associated with the modern industrial plant, workers achieved at least a degree of sophistication and a heightened perception of the world within which they functioned. Thus, for their own sakes, they claimed and received the dispensation of *enseignement professionel*. This helps to illuminate, for instance, the educational program of the workers' delegation to the 1867 International Exposition at Brussels. This program placed the highest priority on a significantly expanded program of apprentice and professional training coupled with an introduction to subjects of general culture.[87] Much of what workers dreamed in the 1860s became reality in the subsequent decades. And that realization occurred under bourgeois auspices. Industrial necessity imposed a system of education that, while it became a sharpened instrument of social discipline, carried the cutting edge of social liberation.[88] This contradiction did not pass unnoticed, and its perception by the architects of social education accounts par-

86. Alfred Deseilligny, *De l'influence de l'éducation sur la moralité et le bien-être des classes laborieuses* (Paris: Hachette, 1868), 221–25; Eugène Spuller, *Ligue française de l'enseignement: Congrès départemental et régional tenu à Nancy, Novembre, 1883: conférence de M. Spuller* (Paris: n.p., 1884), 21.

87. Georges Duveau, *La Pensée ouvrière sur l'éducation pendant la seconde république et le second empire* (Paris: Editions domat montchrestien, 1946).

88. See Marx's penetrating comments in *Capital* (New York: Monthly Review Press, 1967), 1, 487–89.

tially for the heavy emphasis on *éducation morale* in primary-school and apprentice-training curricula.

Éducation morale subsumed under general principles a diverse assortment of didactic lessons, including the nature and responsibility of family, duties of the citizen, history of the nation and its institutions and political economy. Notwithstanding this diversity, the program of *éducation morale* outlined by the Conseil supérieur de l'instruction publique held together as a unit. Fundamental to all lessons and reading matter presented was the specific concentration on solidarity and sociability. According to Buisson, who had some say on such matters, the purpose of primary education was to teach not only basic skills but to develop the personality, character, and sociability of the child.[89]

In the absence of authoritarian institutions, more subtle forms of manipulation were required to develop a disciplined and enlightened citizenry. Teachers were expected to communicate above all respect for the state, the embodiment of national sovereignty, and its foundations in law, order, and property. Moral education founded on the "principles of natural reason" did not exclude directly the teaching of the principles of Christian morality so much as it made them irrelevant against the principles of social morality. Religion in the schools dissolved solidarity; the overriding concern should therefore be with "the duties which bring men together and not the dogmas which divide them." In this context, laic education received a curious definition designed to underline its social function: " 'Laic' is not the opposite of 'religious,' but of 'ecclesiastical'; laic religion has as much validity as ecclesiastical religion."[90]

At the core of the primary school curriculum, a course of "instruction civique, morale, et économie politique" held highest priority. Preschoolers learned patriotic songs, poems, and simple dialogues on

89. Ferdinand Buisson, "La Nouvelle éducation nationale," *La Foi laïque* (Paris: Hachette, 1891).

90. Conseil supérieur de l'instruction publique: enseignement moral, 38–39, in F(17) 12964, meeting of the Conseil supérieur de l'instruction publique, January 7, 1881, in F(17) 12962, AN.

patriotic and moral themes.[91] In the first cycle, including ages seven
to nine, students repeated by rote simple words and phrases, such as
"citizen," "soldier," "army," and "patrie," designed to elicit a sense
of the "idée nationale." Moral self-discipline was encouraged to arm
the children to "discover by themselves their errors and their wrongs."
Looking ahead to adult responsibilities, the children were warned
against the cardinal vices of sloth, idleness, drunkenness, disorder,
cruelty, and "gross appetites." For the ages nine to eleven, in the second
cycle, somewhat more sophisticated concepts were introduced. Civic
duties, such as the obligations to pay taxes and serve in the army,
came up for discussion. The teachings of that beloved bourgeois hero,
Benjamin Franklin, on matters of thrift and self-reliance were included side by side with a (curiously contradictory) maxim "not to
become obsessed with money and gain." At the level of the third and
final cycle, including ages eleven to thirteen, the course bore down
heavily on social morality, democracy as the embodiment of social
justice, and solidarity. Question and response characterized the typical
dialogue at this level: "What does a man owe to his country? Obedience to its laws, military service, discipline, respect for the flag, and
the prompt and full payment of taxes." Elementary clichés of "political
economy" rounded out the program: property, buying, selling, raw
materials, capital, work, association, and savings.[92]

Paul Bert wrote one of the handbooks used in the primary *éducation morale* course.[93] It may be taken as typical of the genre and tells
us much about its author, as we witness his own ideological position
unfold within the framework of a series of simple causeries destined for
the wide eyes and impressionable minds of primary school children.
Bert constructed the volume as a dialogue between his protagonist,
named Pierre, and the patient, rigorously logical anonymous teacher.

91. Buisson considered musical training extremely important. Each child since
he is equally French along with all others ought "tenir sa place dans le concert et dans le
choeur de la nation: ce qui fait l'âme d'une nation, ce sont des sentiments collectifs qui
ne se développent et ne s'entretiennent que s'ils s'expriment en commun." *La Foi laïque*,
21.
92. *Cours de l'enseignement moral* elaborated at the July 24, 1882, session of
the Conseil supérieur de l'instruction publique, in F(17) 12964, AN.
93. Buisson, *Dictionnaire*, II, 1838.

Pierre started off the discussion on the wrong foot, suggesting that devotion to the *patrie* did not represent the highest virtue. The teacher responded harshly to these "most hateful words" and went on to describe the achievements of the Republic in forging "la grande nation" out of formerly disparate and contending provinces. Whatsoever the nation required, the citizen gave freely. The state demanded the payment of taxes; the citizen paid happily in the knowledge that "taxes are necessary to support the army." Under the *ancien régime*, armies lived off the country, which was portrayed as a most disagreeable situation (accompanying this lesson was a nightmarish drawing of soldiers grabbing fowl, corn, and young peasant maidens).[94] Taxes also helped support prosperity through trade, providing the necessary funds to maintain and modernize French ports.[95]

An enumeration of civic duties followed but was reduced primarily to voting, through which the citizen exercised his sovereignty. "It is important to vote for upright men," the teacher admonished; and the determination of what constituted uprightness came from the study of history and civics and the reading of newspapers. At this point Pierre laughed. His grandfather, wise and cynical with age, dismissed newspaper reading as something only for bourgeois with time on their hands. Workers, such as Pierre's father, had no business indulging in such frivolities. This was dangerous advice, for workers who did not take seriously their civic duty to vote would lack commitment to the system and leave them vulnerable to the blandishments of subversives. Besides, in *grand-père*'s youth, "only the rich voted; today all workers vote as well, and if they don't read newspapers and don't know what is going on, they will leave themselves to be lead by the nose."[96]

Obedience to the law followed logically from the lawmaking process in which all men were involved at some level. Laws might

94. Paul Bert, *L'Instruction civique et morale à l'école* (Paris: n.p., 1881), 27, 29, 37–45.

95. "Eh bien, maître Pierre, par où passent le coton qui arrive d'Amérique et le vin qui s'en va en Angleterre? Par les *ports*. . . . Et s'il n'y avait pas de ports, nous n'aurions pas de coton et nous vendrions moins bien notre vin. Vous voyez bien que nous avons intérêt, au moins autant que les gens de Marseille et du Havre, à ce que leur port soit bien entretenu, et qu'il est juste que nous payons tous pour celà quelque petite somme, quelque impôt." *Ibid.*, 39, italics in the original.

96. *Ibid.*, 67–70.

be criticized, but must be obeyed all the same. Under the kings of France the people "could reasonably refuse to obey a law which emanated from a single head. One could even excuse popular uprisings and revolutions" under such conditions. But no more. Today "everybody rules, the entire nation speaks in the voice of universal suffrage. Against whom would one revolt? Against France? That would be treason!"[97]

Democracy, once established, functioned automatically to enhance the conditions for liberty and equality. All men, bound up in the unity of the nation, knew no artificial divisions; the triumph of the Revolution ended the era of classes. All men were now equal "in the pursuit of their fortune, as one sees every day the sons of workers enrich themselves by proper behavior, intelligence, and hard work." This was the lesson of equality to be learned well. "There is the brainless [écervelé] type who thinks that equality means that everybody possesses the same wealth so as to obliterate the differences between rich and poor."[98] Clearly, such nonsense, unless eliminated from the consciousness, made for dangerous thoughts and even more dangerous actions.

The adoption of Bert's primer completed the transformation of éducation morale from a religious to a secular base. Jules Simon was one who had recognized the necessity, but his brief tenure as minister of education in 1872 and 1873 had produced no significant alterations in primary education. We may put this down to a reluctance to alienate the Catholic right, which would have certainly precipitated his dismissal from office. His decision to undertake a modest revision of the secondary school curriculum, reducing the emphasis on classical Greek and Latin in favor of living languages, nearly had him removed.[99] Simon's hesitations reflected his concern to burn no bridges. Ambition triumphed over principle, but sufficient pressure from the provincial bourgeoisie, who proved to be the backbone of the educational reform movement, had not yet built up.

Simon at least laid foundations for one facet of social education.

97. Ibid., 77–78.
98. Ibid., 135–64, 120–23.
99. Georges Weill, Histoire de l'enseignement secondaire en France, 1802–1920 (Paris: Alcan, 1921), Chap. 8.

He appointed Émile Levasseur to review the state of history and geography teaching at all levels.[100] Levasseur was no random choice. His attitudes toward education, articulated later, followed in the republican tradition. Levasseur frankly identified primary education with political indoctrination. He endorsed the value of *enseignement civic* insofar as its lessons were "simple, clear, designed to encourage patriotism and taught respect for basic [republican] institutions." Levasseur did not expect, nor did he want, all men to become philosophers: "One has to have been close to the masses to appreciate the extent to which they are naïve about political affairs . . . only those of us properly trained have the necessary qualifications to deal with political matters and to lead the masses, who, because of their limited education and daily labors, are incapable of understanding the intricacies of politics."[101] It goes without saying that Levasseur did not contemplate correcting the "limitations" of the popular mentality in such a way as to nurture a critical intelligence.

Simon came under attack for allowing his timidity to sidetrack the necessary introduction of socially relevant materials that conformed to industrial reality. Primitive industrial society had permitted workers to grasp a sense of freedom and dignity that was no longer possible. The modern factory reproduced the horrors of Dante's Inferno: *lasciati ogni speranza.* In their despair, workers turned to drink and socialism. Such social dynamite could be defused only through the indoctrination of the basic principles of "political economy." Those principles taught not only how "wealth is produced and accumulated" but, more to the point, communicated the message that to destroy the political economy served no one and left both worker and capitalist bereft of means to sustain themselves. "We must teach the people, smitten with dreams of utopia, to recognize neutral, providential, and indestructible social laws, which, through a miraculous process, produce the prosperity of nations and the unbounded welfare of individuals." The writer condemned classical education for the laboring classes,

---

100. Paul Gerbod, "La Place de l'histoire dans l'enseignement secondaire de 1802 à 1880," *L'Information historique,* No. 3 (1965), 130.

101. Émile Levasseur, *La Population française* (Paris: n.p., 1892), III, 289–90.

because it taught socialism. "What was Sparta, after all, if not Lycurgus' version of a phalanstery?" Somewhere along the way, the initiate into the mysteries of political economy learned to turn it to his advantage, as the system promised, "to acquire a little capital" and thus to become one, in full consciousness, with the world of the marketplace. Democracy then realized its intended mission, in the "fusion of interests, the reconciliation of classes, unity in strength, and the salvation and renovation of the patrie."[102]

Buisson's commentary on the *caisses d'épargne scolaires* carried the message of how social education revealed the wonders of capitalism. "Learning to save" develops an appreciation of "one of the essential attributes of the civilized man." There was nothing like an introduction to one of the basic exercises in political economy to produce a full consciousness of its benefits. "In this way the most miserable laborers will assure for themselves their future well-being and perhaps even their fortune."[103]

A Case in Point: Jules Siegfried

Jules Siegfried stands out among many *grand bourgeois* entrepreneurs who devoted themselves to philanthropy and its offshoot, social education. Siegfried rose to prominence as a businessman and community leader in Le Havre, the center of his cotton brokerage establishment. However, he served his apprenticeship in Mulhouse. There he learned the fundamentals of social responsibility in the best of schools —the tightly knit community of Protestant textile manufacturers. Through his mother, a Blech, he entered a world whose twin preoccupations with industrial achievement and good works were reflected in every aspect of economic, social, and cultural life. Since its inception in the 1820s, the Société industrielle de Mulhouse, organ of that region's *grand patronat*, led France in both technical innovation

---

102. C. Lebrun, *Lettre à M. le ministre de l'instruction publique et des cultes sur l'économie politique et le socialisme, le 30 novembre 1871* (Paris: Chevalier, 1871), 3, 7, 11, 20.

103. Buisson, *Dictionnaire*, I, 305–307.

and philanthropic endeavors on behalf of the less fortunate classes.[104]

In 1865, Jules and his brother Jacques proposed the foundation of an *école supérieure de commerce* in Mulhouse. It began operations in 1868 under the patronage of the Société industrielle.[105] In this instance the brothers Siegfried were concerned with training cadres for an intensified French commercial effort overseas. The question of markets for French industrial products reinforced the broad social interpretation of education. Jules drew attention to the coming struggle: "French industry, so well set up in terms of resources, has shown a justifiable uneasiness over the serious weaknesses in our commercial organization, especially as it concerns exports; it senses instinctively the absolute necessity to open up new markets, without which it faces the erosion of its prosperity."[106]

Jacques Siegfried made a world tour in 1868 to seek opportunities for French business in France's own colonies and elsewhere. He discovered for himself the limitless potentialities of the Far East, China as well as Indochina, which might easily be made into a great market for French capital. Investment expansion outside Europe, Siegfried insisted, "is becoming more and more the prime condition of a nation's power." He urged the government (the report was addressed to the minister for commerce and agriculture) to encourage the training of merchants, bankers, and factors in the mechanics of overseas trade. In an aside, he noted the communal political structure in Cochinchina, in which local notables exercised preponderant authority. Frenchmen, he continued, should not move to undermine local political autonomy. "In terms of our political position we should encourage the natives to involve themselves in local government rather than in the affairs of the country as a whole." A few years after Siegfried's visit, an

104. André Siegfried, *Mes souvenirs de la troisième république: Mon père et son temps: Jules Siegfried, 1836–1922* (Paris: Presses universitaires de France, 1946), 5–10; Georges Duveau, *La vie ouvrière en France sous le second empire* (Paris: Gallimard, 1946); Oberlé, *L'Enseignement à Mulhouse*.

105. Jules and Jacques Siegfried, *Mémoire au sujet de la fondation à Mulhouse d'une école de commerce, présentée à la Société industrielle de Mulhouse, 1865* (Paris: n.p., 1884).

106. *Bulletin de la Société industrielle de Mulhouse*, XXXIX (1869), 16.

opening wedge was made into the transformation of a traditional society and the absorption of a native elite into the French system. The Ligue de l'enseignement set up shop in Saigon, stating its purpose to be "the diffusion of instruction throughout the country and the dissemination among the natives of the essentials of French civilization." Its membership included four hundred Frenchmen resident in Cochinchina, forty Annamese, four Chinese, and the king of Cambodia.[107]

In the meantime, Jules Siegfried spent the years of the American Civil War in Bombay where he amassed a large fortune buying and selling cotton. He got out with his money just before the bottom dropped out of the Bombay market with the reopening of the southern American ports. On his return to Le Havre, Siegfried plunged immediately into civic affairs. He joined the chamber of commerce and obtained election to the municipal council. Simultaneously, in a gesture to his native region, he donated 100,000 francs to the Société industrielle de Mulhouse to establish a "cercle pour travailleurs." This was the first of many such philanthropies through which Siegfried expressed his paternal regard for the "welfare of the people, all those humble and modest folk whom he called 'les petits gens.' "[108]

Jules's Protestantism complemented the strong sense of social responsibility learned in the world of Mulhouse business. His son André closely links his father's pursuit of entrepreneurial success with the moral commitment expressing it. Jules held as the highest value the duty "to serve God and to collaborate in His work on earth." He was gripped by a "deep sense of his obligations toward his fellow man which he placed on the same high level as those he owed to God." Siegfried's perception of the duties of the capitalist toward the worker, however, derived less from his religious calling than from a practical regard for the strengths and weaknesses of democracy. He was fond of quoting Lord Randolph Churchill's celebrated epigram: "If you want to make the people conservative, give them something to conserve." It was so much the better if the religious theme harmonized with the

107. Jacques Siegfried, *Seize mois autour du monde* (Paris: Hetzel, 1869), 298–347; *BLFE*, I (1881), 612–13.
108. Siegfried, *Mes souvenirs de la troisième république*, 15–20, 30–37, 39; Moussac, *La Ligue de l'enseignement*, 185.

social. His social program focused on elevating the material and moral position of the worker to a level of genuine dignity, so as to consolidate the family and thus society. Leading a syndicate of businessmen in Le Havre, Siegfried organized workers' housing societies, which built tenement blocks. Monthly rent was credited toward purchase of a house or flat, where workers, settled in a "clean and healthy domicile, with their well-cared-for families," thereby avoided "the café and the disruptive agitations on the streets."[109]

Siegfried was one of the founders of the Le Havre circle of the Ligue de l'enseignement in 1868 and of the Cercle Franklin in the same city in 1874. Each ministered to the social, cultural, and educational needs of the popular classes so as to provide the training and habits of mind necessary to integrate the people into society. He admitted the strong influence of Jules Simon's approach to social problems, spelled out in the latter's book *L'Ouvrière*. Simon rebutted the prevailing notion that considered "labor as a form of slavery." "Nothing of the kind," he insisted. "Ignorance is the only slavery, because slaves are victims of their passions while reason confers power and freedom."[110]

Following the collapse of the Second Empire, Siegfried became a republican. On September 4, 1870, the mayor of Le Havre, Henri Guillemard, flanked by Siegfried on one side and Félix Faure on the other, proclaimed the Republic.[111] Siegfried's views, however, had not changed. His social orientation remained fixed. His son without irony called him a "conservative democrat."[112] The Ligue de l'enseignement became the primary vehicle through which Siegfried and other members of the Le Havre bourgeoisie confronted the social question. Under the Republic, the task took on a special urgency. "Considering that

109. Siegfried, *Mes souvenirs de la troisième république*, 7–8, 39–46.
110. *Ibid.*, 48; Buisson, *Dictionnaire*, II, 1591; Émile Levasseur, *Questions ouvrières et industrielles en France sous la troisième république* (Paris: Rousseau, 1907), 811; Moussac, *La Ligue de l'enseignement*, 185; Jules Simon, *L'Ouvrière* (Paris: n.p., 1867), 434. There were numerous later editions.
111. Faure at this date was a lesser luminary in the Le Havre business firmament and collaborated closely with the Siegfried brothers. He, like Jacques, undertook a tour in search of markets at the behest of the imperial government. Félix Faure, *Du Commerce français dans le Levant et de son développement possible: Rapport à son excellence le ministre du commerce et de l'agriculture* (Le Havre: Santallier, 1870).
112. Siegfried, *Mes souvenirs de la troisième république*, 40.

political freedom under the Republic makes the nation, more than ever, master of its own destiny . . . it is of the greatest importance that each citizen be properly instructed and carefully schooled so as to express himself on [the nation's] future in the most intelligent manner possible. [We] regard it as our duty to state that obligatory primary education is a measure of public safety."[113]

As elsewhere in France, the bourgeoisie of Le Havre recoiled from the shock of the war and the Commune determined to advance the cause of national power and social peace through education. The municipal council in 1871 appropriated 1,200,000 francs to build several lay primary schools. Since the schools were to be nonconfessional, government obstruction prevented construction until 1876. Three years later, Jules Siegfried, now mayor of the city, officiated at the opening of four schools. His remarks on those occasions illuminate a characteristic view of social education.[114]

The Prussian schoolmaster doubled as the gymnastics instructor, and that lesson was not lost on the French. Siegfried placed the value of physical education in a context broader than its military application; or, more precisely, he recognized military power to be one expression of a healthy, well-knit society. That society, he asserted, functioned through the constant striving of individuals—that "struggle for existence in which every man is summoned to engage." For "the largest number of individuals, physical strength" represented their most important and, frequently, their only asset. Thus followed the social need for that force to be sharpened and disciplined so that its bearers might prove useful citizens. "If we consider," he continued, "the struggle of nation against nation, which is accelerating sharply, happily not on the battlefield but in the peaceful competition of production," the physical resources of the population weigh heavily in the balance. A healthy people was a productive people, applying their energies to the physical and intellectual tasks needed to secure the industrial foundations of

113. Circular of the Ligue de l'enseignement du Havre, March 7, 1871, signed by Jules Siegfried, in F(17) 12527, AN.

114. *L'Éducation dans les écoles communales du Havre: Discours prononcé par M. Jules Siegfried, maire de la ville du Havre, les 28 septembre et 5 octobre* (Le Havre: n.p., 1879), 3–5.

the Republic. Among the social benefits that would accrue, not the least was the solidarity of citizens behind their government: "Certainly parents will experience a great joy and satisfaction in seeing the care with which their children are educated and will pay homage to the democratic and republican government to which they owe these outstanding benefits."[115]

Moral education, intellectual education, and professional education in close articulation with physical education stood as the four corners of primary education. Moral education combined a secular morality with traditional religious principles to reinforce social solidarity. "Our lay teachers will instruct our children to love God and their neighbor" and "to love their country and work for its glory." Within a basically secular curriculum, the primary schools of Le Havre included didactic religious training: the Old and New Testaments, the history of the saints, the Catholic catechism, and preparation for first communion. Considered in the context of social education, the inclusion of Catholic religious training in schools sponsored by Protestant bourgeois should not strike us as odd or inconsistent. Catholic religion formed part of the great tradition of France. Thus its propagation within a secular school system "was indispensable, since it inculcated in the child precise knowledge and a healthy respect for the great principles on which all civilized societies rest."[116] In the pursuit of social order founded on an enlightened and respectful citizenry, reflexive hostility to religion had no place. Religious training, integrated into a comprehensive moral and intellectual system, buttressed rather than undermined positive solidarity.

For the sons of the working class, *formation professionnelle* completed the cycle. In his discussion of this subject, Siegfried revealed a concern for the division and the discipline of labor as well as for questions of social mobility. Apprentice schools followed programs laid down by the "entrepreneurs of the city" who "fed" work into the school shops. Following three years of study, fully formed apprentices took their places within the craft or business for which they had been trained

115. *Ibid.*, 6, 7.
116. *Ibid.*, 9, 13–15, 11.

(at the expense of the municipality). In such a manner Le Havre industry and commerce guaranteed to itself a steady supply of carefully allocated labor. Mobility was encouraged, but within well-defined limits corresponding to the requirements of industry. The schools "train not merely ordinary workers, but workers who will rise easily to the level of foreman and supervisor. Openings for outstanding work-ers and foremen are appearing all the time in larger numbers; they are sought after, not only in France, but in far-off lands." Beneath the obvious concern of entrepreneurs to have at their disposal a disciplined and efficient labor force lay a more fundamental consideration: "The industrial struggle is daily becoming more fierce, not only between individual and individual, but between nation and nation; in order to sustain the struggle on favorable terms, it has become ever the more necessary to have knowledgeable and well-trained workers."[117]

This viewpoint sheds some light on the mentality of what has been called, in the historical literature, "social imperialism": the linkage of national prosperity to success in the *lutte industrielle* and to forg-ing a laboring class equipped morally, intellectually, and physically to sustain that struggle.[118] Lacking the means or the will to employ coercive methods to that end (even if such an alternative were not absurd in the context), men like Siegfried sought through education to fulfill the demands of social solidarity and national economic power. It was, they recognized, of little value to merely chant the usual litanies celebrating the high principles and moral superiority of the bourgeois Republic. To hedge the future of the domestic political economy against unforeseen shocks required a sustained effort to mobilize the working class and the multitude of small property owners behind national industrial goals. Education, delivered formally in the schools and informally in the ateliers, became a potent weapon

117. *Ibid.*, 23, 20.
118. On this subject, for England see Bernard Semmel, *Imperialism and Social Reform* (London: Unwin, 1960), and G. D. H. Cole and Raymond Postgate, *The Common People* (4th ed.; London: Methuen, 1949), Chap. 33. Nothing of the scope of Semmel's work exists for France. I have made a stab at an outline of the subject elsewhere: Sanford H. Elwitt, "French Imperialism and Social Policy: The Case of Tunisia," *Science and Society*, XXXI, No. 2 (Spring, 1967), 129–48. *Cf.* Chapter VII herein.

in the hands of industrialists to translate the values and aims of a fraction of society into the values and aims of society as a whole. In this manner would the promise of democracy be realized and the established social order achieve a full measure of permanence.

Nationalism and Militarism in Education

Among the many stalwarts of the movement for social education throughout France, Freemason affiliations were commonplace. This fact has often been made too much of, leading to a single-minded concentration on anticlericalism as the mainspring of educational reform. All too easily this view reduces itself to seeing the process of social education as a sinister conspiracy planned in the dark and secret inner recesses of Masonic temples. That will not do. Freemasonry formed one element in a complex of social institutions distinctive to bourgeois France. It existed parallel to and intertwined with chambers of commerce, societies for agricultural improvement, and a variety of philanthropic associations devoted to education.[119] Freemasonry was an expression, but only one expression, of a broader and deeper cultural phenomenon.

Edmond Tiersot, one of a host of republican politicians who held membership in a Masonic lodge, in 1853 defined the principles of Masonry as harmony with the "flag of France," that is, in terms of national solidarity. His commitment to the transformation of France into a "country of citizens and thinkers instead of a population mired in superstition" evokes a spirit wholly alien to simply reflexive anticlericalism. In this spirit, Tiersot and his brethren of the Masonic lodge of Bourg-en-Bresse established private schools in the 1850s for "moral and civic education," financed popular libraries, and mobilized departmental notables behind the Société pour l'instruction primaire. Education carried out at this level by private citizens, at a time when the spirit of the *loi Falloux* dominated official policy, clearly aimed at concrete social objectives and deliberate indoctrination: "Social ques-

119. See, for instance, the *Journal de commerce maritime et des colonies* (Le Havre) for 1879–1880 and the *Tribune coloniale* (Versailles) for 1878.

tions ought not to take precedence above political questions." The same people moved on other, parallel fronts toward their goal of social amelioration. They floated a project to fund a *banque populaire* to provide cheap credit for small entrepreneurs and producers as well as for workers who aspired to enter those ranks. With their social action on the track, the Bourg Freemasons established themselves firmly in the Ain republican leadership and formed a solid barrier against social upheaval in the dark days of 1871.[120] They acted consistently with their class interests and responsibilities, of which their Masonic affiliation was only one expression.

In Nantes, a Mason presided over the Comité républicain, which in turn worked closely with the Cercle Franklin, also tied into Masonic lodges through common personnel. The establishment of the Ligue de l'enseignement in Nantes following the Franco-Prussian War sparked a concerted effort by Masonic lodges to sponsor schools. Venerable Charles Laisant, future radical deputy and Boulangist, joined his lodge, Free Conscience, with the merchants and shipowners of the Peace and Union lodge to organize popular libraries. Laisant was a *polytechnicien*, engineering officer, and mathematician following in the footsteps of his father, who had been known around Nantes in 1848 as a *radical avancé*. Laisant later distinguished himself as a harsh critic of railroad monopolies.[121] A product of the scientific-positivist nexus reigning in the École polytechnique, at home in the world of overseas commerce, and a bourgeois democrat, Laisant moved along a well-trod path in the company of more celebrated republican reformers like Jules Ferry and Paul Bert. His Masonic affiliation was neither incidental nor central to his secular life. He came to it naturally, as an adjunct to his social and cultural formation.

A bitterly hostile account of Masonic activity in the Nièvre supplies further evidence of the brotherhood's social action in education. In addition to providing annual subsidies to the Ligue de l'enseignement, the Masonic lodge of Nevers made gifts of savings accounts to

120. A. Trolliet, *Histoire de la loge maçonnique l'Amitié fraternelle, Bourg, 1828–1928* (Bourg: Page, 1928), 120, 124–33.

121. Henri Librec [H. Billy], *La Franc-maçonnerie dans la Loire-Inférieure, 1749–1948* (Nantes: n.p., 1949), 57; *JOC*, March 16, 1877.

outstanding graduates of lay primary schools. Masons considered these donations as investments "to encourage the lucky recipients [to develop] a passion for work and the spirit of thrift."[122] This was not uncommon; Masons in Mulhouse undertook an identical project in 1864. Education, not seen as an end in itself, provided the moral underpinnings for a heightened sense of patriotism and led the Masons to support patriotic groups such as the Ligue des patriotes and gymnastic societies. In 1881, they joined in the foundation of a Comité du propagande maçonnique de l'oeuvre de l'éducation civique et militaire de la jeunesse française. In the Cévennes, Masons followed suit and took advantage of the expansion of the Ligue de l'enseignement to get into the business of civic education. Concern for social peace and solidarity, evident in educational efforts, spilled over into attempts to forge links with workers. The Masons of the Nièvre joined their brothers throughout France to lobby for the law of 1884 legalizing associations. Their enemies understood well the motives behind their patronage of the working class. "Will the Masons succeed in dominating the *syndicats* and the *compagnonnages?* We doubt it, because the proletariat rightly regard the lodge as a bourgeois institution."[123]

Freemasonry's anticlerical tone appeared as a function, not the driving force, of national education linked to social utility. Invocations of solidarity from Masonic sources—"all men are brothers and bound together in solidarity"[124]—expressed in slogan form the central ideological formula of postrevolutionary France. To the extent that education provided the moral underpinning of a common culture, which could unify all Frenchmen, in opposition to the material forces conspiring to destroy that unity, secularization was a necessary corollary to education.

What could be a better expression of the principle of unity, itself

122. From the *Châine d'union*, quoted in *La Franc-maçonnerie dans la Nièvre* (Nevers: n.p., 1885), 37.

123. Oberlé, *L'Enseignement à Mulhouse*, 245; *La Franc-maçonnerie dans la Nièvre*, 40–41, 44; Daniel Ligou, *Frédéric Desmons et la franc-maçonnerie sous la troisième république* (Paris: Gedalge, 1966), 64.

124. From the Progrès lodge in Paris, in *Démocratie*, December 12, 1869, quoted in I. Tchernoff, *Le Parti républicain au coup d'état et sous le second empire* (Paris: n.p., 1906), 323.

a very vague notion, than the mythology and sentiments of patriotism made concrete in rigorously didactic lessons? Clearly such steps could not be taken apart from secularization. Religion posed its most serious threat by purveying a false notion of the "nature of things." "Belief in the intervention of angels, of saints, of other heavenly beings; belief in the power of miracles to change the course of wars and politics; all of this leads to the most absolute indifference toward patriotism."[125] Unarmed with an appreciation of the realities of life, scientifically cataloged, the individual could not fulfill his civic responsibilities and march happily to his prescribed destiny.

A population educated in the bosom of the church, a people infected, in Gambetta's words, "with a hatred for modern France, with a hatred for the principles of justice on which rests our national law," was bound to produce an antinational fifth column, exercising its destructive capacities to sow the "seeds of discord and division" and subvert the natural solidarity of the nation.[126] It was pointed out that teaching-order practice frequently was to separate the rich and the poor in the schoolroom, thus perpetuating class distinctions and reinforcing class consciousness. As Jules Ferry never tired of reiterating, the "great necessity" was "to suppress class distinctions" and to "gather together, on the school benches, youths who will find themselves in a short while later mustered together under the colors of the *patrie*."[127] During the debate in the Chamber on secularization of primary education, Édouard Lockroy argued for the immediate disestablishment of all congregations. He failed to gain his point but succeeded in making the case without resorting to a violent, unreasoning anticlericalism. The congregations, he argued, presented a "real danger," which he characterized as a "social peril" since religious instruction corrupted "those who represent the future of France."[128] Patriotism, however, did not begin and end with rhetoric. A significant aspect of social

125. Robin, "Des Rapports," 186–87.

126. *République française*, February 9, 1876; Gambetta, *Discours à Romans*, 5–7.

127. *Tribune coloniale*, July 27, 1878; Jules Ferry, "Discours sur l'égalité d'éducation," delivered in the Salle Molière on April 10, 1870, quoted in Legrand, *L'Influence du positivisme*, 221; Ferry, *L'École gratuite, obligatoire et laïque*, 8.

128. Quoted in Alexandre Israel, *L'École de la république: La Grande oeuvre de Jules Ferry* (Paris: Hachette, 1931), 89.

education was the broad-scale introduction of military training and martial motifs into the young Frenchmen's consciousness.

With a full decade of achievement in sponsoring popular libraries and education societies behind them, the notables of the Ligue de l'enseignement turned their attention to specific tasks of military and civic education. Spuller referred to this effort as the *"cause national"* and pronounced it the true vocation of the league.[129] Local federations encouraged the development of uniform standards of military instruction and brought teachers under their direction. This they could do easily, inasmuch as mayors, municipal councilors, and other bourgeois notables dominated the federations. Where teachers demonstrated incompetence to meet their tasks, the league recruited retired officers to teach military subjects, caring little for the backgrounds or worldly political biases of former military men. Rural communities, where the patriotic ethic had not yet penetrated, received disproportionate attention. Rifles and uniforms were furnished. A new patriotic song reverberated among the hills and plains of rural France: "Garde aux Vosges," a painfully obvious parallel to the German "Wacht am Rhein."[130]

At the beginning of the new decade, the league's First National Congress heard an impassioned plea for more military and civic education from Émile George. Senator from the Vosges, George stood in relation to Vosges textiles as Jules Siegfried did to Le Havre commerce. George began by performing the required ritual: bowing in the direction of the eastern frontier and recalling with stirring emotion the futile bravery of French arms in the war of 1870. He then got down to business. Bravery was not enough, as the Germans had amply demonstrated. The French lacked organization and a properly instructed soldiery, both of which the Germans had possessed in abundance. The Ligue de l'enseignement had only to follow the general line apparent in its past work, to put its considerable leverage and prestige behind military education for every youth above the age of thirteen, and the situation would not repeat itself. The foundations

---

129. Spuller, *Éducation de la démocratie*, 189–90.
130. *BLFE*, II (1882), 369–71.

already existed in the local initiatives; coordination would rapidly follow. Beyond the immediate practical end, military education fulfilled a special social function, George went on. Military exercises, already organized in scattered cantons, grouped together young people from several communes, representing a cross section of classes that performed in unison. The cantonal committees of organization, offshoots of league federations, grouped together local bourgeois notables. At these sessions "all the youth of the communes, rich and poor, assembled at regular intervals to take part in uniform exercise, recapturing the spirit of the school, will learn mutual respect and affection . . . at the end of a certain period of time of constant contact, *national ties will be strengthened,* to the great profit of the army and of the nation."[131]

Military training in schools and in paramilitary formations had occupied the sons of the European bourgeoisie since the beginning of the century. *Turnvater* Jahn's hysterical exertions represented an early and not altogether extreme form. The Czech nationalists organized their Sokols to the same purpose. In each instance, the measured cadence of uniformed youths, the camaraderie of the barracks, the chanting of patriotic hymns while performing calisthenic exercises tightened social bonds.

The French experience followed in this tradition. Condorcet included in his prescription for educational reform civic training for soldiers and military training for civilians. Gambetta's ideal of the "new Frenchman," molded in republican schools, included much more than simply basic mental skills: "I want him to act and to fight. At the side of the teacher, the physical instructor and the soldier must stand; so that our children, who will be our soldiers as well as our future citizens, can handle a sword, shoot a rifle, carry out long marches, sleep under the stars, and endure bravely all conceivable hardships for the nation." Spuller cursed those who would abolish the army, "a detestable dream," while assigning to military education a fundamental role in civic indoctrination. Privately sponsored military societies led the way, generating "genuinely elevated feelings" among

131. *Ibid.,* I (1881), 353–67, italics in original.

children and "teaching the highest values of civic duty—even martyrdom."[132]

Paul Bert elevated military education to the level of high policy in national defense. He ridiculed pacifist and socialist peddlars of internationalist solidarity. He mocked the idea that modern technology, finance, and communications made national frontiers obsolete. On the contrary, the ripening of industrial society required redoubled efforts on behalf of national integration and social solidarity. Bert waxed positively lyrical, conjuring visions of "little soldiers" marching in close ranks, "shoulders thrust back supporting a rifle, officers in the lead, with the *tricolore* above them rippling in a stiff breeze." Military education, above all, taught discipline, "respect for the law," and obedience to prescribed social duties. He quoted with approval Paul Déroulède: "Bankers understand as we should that the best protection for their vaults against potential intruders remains a sharp sword."[133]

This was a strange conjunction: Paul Bert, radical democrat and key figure in the formulation of republican social policy, cabinet minister, respected scientist, and Paul Déroulède, rabble-rouser, loudmouthed nationalist, hatemonger, professional putschist, and self-annointed gravedigger of the Republic. But for all his solid scientific substance, Bert yielded not an inch to Déroulède on matters pertaining to what he defined as national goals. The fact that Bert's hot-blooded patriotism sprang from a cool assessment of social and industrial realities demonstrates how the apparently healthy growth of social education produced the grotesque flowers of a strident nationalism. Bourgeois democrats, acting within a class-determined set of assumptions, did not hesitate to embrace a passionate and sometimes violent nationalism to support positive solidarity. That they did so made a Déroulède superfluous. Furthermore, we must not read Déroulède's later career back into this earlier period. The Ligue des patriotes, notwithstanding its ultimate destiny as a gang of thugs,

132. Condorcet, *Rapport sur l'organisation générale de l'instruction publique*, 283; Joseph Reinach (ed.), *Discours et plaidoyers politiques de Gambetta* (11 vols.; Paris: n.p., 1881–85), II, 23–24, speech in Bordeaux, June 26, 1871; Spuller, *Ligue française de l'enseignement*, 25–50.

133. Bert, *De l'éducation civique*, 19–25; Bert, *Discours parlementaires*, II, 393–94.

began, like the Ligue de l'enseignement, as a privately and handsomely financed lobby and pressure group to promote shooting clubs, gymnastic societies, and paramilitary squads of the sort that Paul Bert had urged.[134] The roster of the charter members of the Ligue des patriotes included the most impeccable array of notables, including Gambetta, who always flaunted his passion for things military, and Félix Faure, whose baggage included not incidentally the largess and prestige of the Le Havre bourgeoisie.[135] Ferdinand Buisson by 1879 had already established himself as a noted theorist of social education. The first edition of his *Dictionnaire pédagogique* appeared soon after his appointment as director-general of primary education under Ferry. Buisson stood second only to Déroulède as vice-president of the Ligue des patriotes.[136]

Local circles of the Ligue des patriotes and the Ligue de l'enseignement worked together closely or were intertwined in function and membership. Several shooting clubs and military and gymnastic societies sprang up under joint sponsorship in the mid-1870s. By 1885 there were 172 circles bearing names reminiscent of Freemasonry: National, Fraternelle, Réveil, Patriote, Tricolore, Martiale, Amis du progrès. Only in the Norman and Breton west did the military societies fail to penetrate. There the struggle between class-conscious bourgeois and backwoods gentry had not yet been decided.[137]

The Association nationale des tireurs de France et d'Algérie was formed in 1875 under the patronage of some of the brightest stars in the republican firmament: Gambetta, Carnot, Simon, Auguste Scheurer-Kestner, and Spuller. From early 1882, a Paris coordinating body known as the Sociétés de tir served as a propaganda mill and clearinghouse for local units. Its founding message explicitly linked

134. *Ibid.; Drapeau*, December 29, 1881.
135. Faure, like Paul Bert and Jules Siegfried, coupled an interest in colonies and trade with a strong commitment to popular education. E. Maillard, *Le Président Félix Faure* (Paris: Librairie historique des provinces, 1897), 20.
136. Daniel Halévy, *Trois épreuves* (Paris: Plon, 1938), 113–14. Halévy wrote this pamphlet on the road from national mysticism to national socialism. He referred to Buisson as a "pacifist," citing as evidence the fact that Buisson appeared to follow the line of the Grand-Orient de France, which "annonce et annoncera toujours la grande paix humaine." Halévy, wittingly or not, mistook a cliché of solidarism for pacifism.
137. F(17) 12539, AN.

civic and military education. "In the schools we prepare the youth of France for their duties toward society and the family; we are only completing their education by preparing them to defend the homeland."[138]

The Union des sociétés de gymnastique constituted at Bordeaux in 1880 drew on the resources of both the Ligue de l'enseignement and the Ligue des patriotes. "Its goal was characterized in a simple triad: *patrie, courage, moralité.*" One of its most valued volunteer workers was Félix Faure. The society sponsored national and regional fetes of gymnastic displays and competitions, all of a quasi-military nature and all dedicated to the "exaltation of patriotism." Jules Galland of the Société gymnastique de Cambrai surveyed with satisfaction his group's efforts to promote patriotism. He specifically recalled the example of *Turnvater* Jahn as one spiritual ancestor of the French gymnastic movement. From the resolutions adopted during the semiannual sessions of scattered general councils came the repetition of similar themes. Even in those areas where religious education had not been discredited, the national purpose eclipsed sectarian squabbles. The general council of the Corrèze publicized the following resolution: "We must educate our children in a nationalist and patriotic catechism, tied closely to a military ethic. . . . At the side of the teacher . . . our children will have a military instructor who shall teach them respect and discipline."[139]

Official recognition of military education followed private action. On January 25, 1882, a military education committee attached to the Ministry of Education met and laid plans to finance military instruction units attached to communal schools. The Ministry of War was to supply retired officers and noncommissioned officers to supervise drills and parades. The ministry further announced its intention to commission songs and books for the project. The minister of education referred perfunctorily to the obvious advantages of military education should "citizens be called upon to make the supreme sacrifice."

138. *Drapeau,* December 29, 1881, January 5, 1882.
139. Undated report to the minister of education, fine arts, and culture, report of the rector of the Académie de Poitiers to the minister of education, fine arts, and culture, report of 1883, all in F(17) 12539, AN; voeux des conseils généraux, Rhône, Cher, 1881, in AD XIX 12, AN; Conseil général de la Corrèze, *Procès-verbaux des délibérations, 1880* (Brive: n.p., 1881).

More important were its social benefits, which counterbalanced the tendency toward liberty and individualism produced by democracy and universal suffrage and developed discipline, respect for law, and a high moral level. The minister, of course, was Paul Bert. Members of the committee included Buisson, Faure, and Déroulède.[140]

Bourgeois Cultural Conquest

The movement for social education did not proceed from triumph to successive triumph without retreats forced by external pressures. During the four years' reign by the Government of Moral Order, the police and the educational bureaucracy worked hard to contain the movement. The school-building program in Le Havre did not develop momentum until after 1876.[141] The Société de l'instruction républicaine based in Paris was finally suppressed on August 27, 1877, after months of harassment, even though it had enjoyed legal status as a *société anonyme de capital variable*. Not to be confused with the various circles of the Ligue de l'enseignement known as *sociétés de l'instruction républicaine*, the Paris group included many of the men associated with the league. Its activities covered the political side of the social education movement, especially the production of pamphlets aimed at the rural population: "The society strives to replace chauvinism and superstition with a patriotic and republican mentality. It wants to penetrate the consciousness of our rural cottagers with the imagery of the great steps forward made in the direction of political and social progress and of the heroic acts of the great and the humble."[142]

Under the first Broglie government, from 1873 to 1874, the police bore down heavily on private lay educational foundations. Orders circulated to all prefects and rectors in late December, 1873, by Minister of Education Fourtou laid down the hard line to be applied. Action followed. Its character confirms the social thrust of education organized by the industrial and agrarian bourgeoisie. The Comice agricole de Narbonne requested permission to organize informal

140. *Drapeau*, February 2, 1882.
141. See above, footnote 33.
142. *BLFE*, I (1881), 150–250.

classes for teachers in the rudiments of modern agricultural technology. These lessons were then to be transmitted to their students in farming communities. The prefect feared political repercussions, which is to say that his allies among the rural gentry preferred ignorance to enlightenment in the fields. Permission was denied. The same fate awaited the Société des écoles laïques du premier arrondissement in Paris. The society had been organized in 1872 as a legal entity with an initial capital of ten thousand francs, divided into two hundred shares of fifty francs each. Its organizers included five wholesalers from the Sebastopol-Halles quarter, an unnamed *rentier*, and the managers of the two *grands magasins* of the neighborhood, Samaritaine and Au Louvre. The society's schools for boys and girls appeared to threaten the monopoly over the minds of both students and teachers held by the state educational apparatus. The report by the prefect of police certainly viewed the matter in those terms, charging the society with fostering the creation of "sharp minds . . . and preparing the future enemies of order." Oddly enough, the founding statement of the society does not appear to bear any relationship to the prefect's assessment. Its concern was with the traditional aims of social education: "The companionship of the school . . . is the best way, or at least the easiest, to bring together the different classes of society and to erase social divisions." [143]

Thus, a movement for social education that consciously strove to "erase social divisions" and create the intellectual foundations of industrial discipline provoked a counterattack in defense of "order." Viewed politically, the apparent paradox disappears. Since the republicans used their educational foundations to consolidate their power, the frankly antirepublican Government of Moral Order used its considerable administrative power to attempt to smash the educational movement. But the attempt failed miserably. No similar suppression had occurred under the Empire, a government of "order" if there ever was one. The story becomes clear in a comment on education made in 1873 by Armand Audiganne, a sharp and thorough observer of the

143. André Delcourt, "Les Associations parisiennes de propagande en faveur de l'enseignement populaire dans les premières années de la troisième république," *L'Actualité de l'histoire*, No. 4 (April, 1953), 8–20.

social and industrial scene: "Soon we will witness the disappearance of the distinctions between city and country, between work in the fields and work in the workshops, between workers and bourgeois; we will be left with only two distinct societies, the old and the new, which is to say the old and the new regimes." Audiganne went on to characterize the society that emerged from the Revolution of 1789 as one dominated by "new interests," that is, "industrial interests."[144] Neither Audiganne nor anyone following his argument need embrace a "red and black" model of French society. An industrial bourgeoisie hardly qualifies as "red." Nor can we conclude simply that the struggle brought forth once again the ancient antagonists, Catholics and anti-clericals. For, as we have seen, Catholic religious training in a secular context was not excluded from the new schools.

Republican social educational policy unfolded within the limits of a class ideology, of which positivism, the dictates of industrial discipline, and the preoccupation with solidarity and social peace were the expression. Freemasonry, for all its rococo ornamentation, simply realized the logic of this position in the worship of the religion of progress. The personnel of the Government of Moral Order, even though they were all or nearly all *grand bourgeois*, knew themselves to be of a very different mental cast than the republican bourgeoisie with whom they had to contend. The former struggled to maintain a rigid and traditional conception of society and to live the reality of the early nineteenth century against all objective pressures to the contrary. They accepted and hoped to perpetuate a situation in which distinctions of town and country and bourgeois and worker prevailed. They saw no reason to deny what was for them a living reality in the name of industrial necessity.

In terms of the wider class interests of the bourgeoisie, the republicans pursued a more coherent and ultimately more viable line. For they knew, and said often enough, that consciousness of class distinctions and not the reality of such distinctions themselves threatened to tear apart the social fabric. Beyond that, their own class interests, which

144. Armand Audiganne, *Le Travail et l'industrie en France* (Paris: n.p., 1873), 18.

they defined quite rightly as the national interest, propelled them to
pursue a radical educational policy in the name of social conservation.
Their experience told them that the progress of industrial capitalism
depended upon its accessibility to wider domestic markets and a disciplined labor force. Thus it was in their own interests that distinctions
of town and country be obliterated and that *enseignement professionel*
be given high priority. Jules Simon kept industrial interests upper-
most in mind. He, for one, was willing to embrace the principles of
social mobility because it suited national economic policy. He argued
for wider educational horizons for workers, not so much to enhance
their dignity as human beings (which is the way Paul Bert would have
argued), but because the accelerating complexities inherent in the
division of labor fastened the worker to one spot unless he had some
general knowledge of the nature of the machine.[145] Republicans risked
the chance that education could be turned against them, for the promise of social mobility could never be fulfilled and the instruction of
workers led to the kind of consciousness that they were determined to
stifle. But military education and limited mobility for the sons of the
petite bourgeoisie to some extent neutralized that threat.

Secondary questions of religion could not be permitted to wrench
the process of social education off the track. Positive instruction in the
mechanics of a secular, material world replaced the previous emphasis
on speculative knowledge. Men like Paul Bert sought through education to raise man to a higher level of consciousness of the dignity of
self. But to what extent this goal represented a doctrinaire philosophic
position is debatable. The rhetoric of the philosophs only disguised,
and not too well at that, the tough, practical calculations of shrewd
bourgeois ideologues. The arguments of the Catholics that obligatory
lay education could not be suffered to infringe upon the absolute authority of the *père de famille* held no meaning for the proponents of
social education and not because they were largely Protestants or free-
thinkers. In terms of the industrial character of society, stripping the
père de famille of his authority represented a necessary and progressive
step. It prevented him from sending his children to work when they

145. Simon, *L'École*, Pt. 4, Chap. 4.

ought to be in school learning the skills and social habits that would make them more effective and docile members of the labor force. Whatever the humanitarian or doctrinaire motives embedded in this view, they remained secondary and must be related to the general outlook of a large fraction of the industrial bourgeoisie.

I say "large fraction" because bourgeois with a traditional and narrow outlook did not disappear and, during these early years of the Republic, managed to make life temporarily miserable for the republican bourgeoisie. Their class position was, on the surface, indistinguishable from that of their political enemies. For instance, Christophe Mony, the hard-line Catholic managing director of the Commentry-Châtillon Iron and Steel Works, led the struggle in the department of the Allier against lay schools and controlled his workers with an absolute paternal authority.[146] He cannot be said to have been any less a *grand bourgeois* than Jules Siegfried, Émile George, or Jules Ferry. What distinguished the others from a Mony was not their formal class position, but their class outlook, its breadth, we might even say its vision, and its consistency with social reality. Therein lies the difference between the "old" and the "new" of which Audiganne wrote.

Paul Bert exposed the abyss that separated men like himself from the Catholic traditionalists of the right. During the Chamber debate in 1880 on obligatory primary education, Bert pointed to what can only be called the confrontation of two cultural worlds: one which held in high regard the "sentiments of civic dignity," the other committed to the "sentiments of Christian humility." Spokesmen from the right in effect confirmed Bert's view. They conceded nothing to the republicans on the social question, but preferred to deal with it in traditional ways. Charles Chesnelong in the Senate rested his case on the grounds not of Christian sentimentality but of an opposing world view: "We hear a great deal about social solidarity; we are told that this principle of solidarity ought to replace the old principle of Christian charity which today appears to be old-fashioned and out-of-date."[147] Between Chesnelong and Bert, between the stalwarts of tradition and

146. Jean-François Viple, *Sociologie politique de l'Allier* (Paris: n.p., 1967), 41.
147. Quoted in Israel, *L'École de la république*, 16, 40.

the spokesmen of the provincial bourgeoisie, no compromise position existed.

The Catholic bourgeoisie had made their alliances with the backwoods gentry, who had always relied on the curés for their local power. The *instituteur*, in league with the republican bourgeoisie and the professions, threatened that power, indeed threatened a way of life. In these terms the struggle was carried on—a struggle not merely over the spoils accruing from political power, but between rival cultures. In these early years of the Republic before socialism became a political force, Frenchmen of property could afford the luxury of splitting ranks over how best to deal with the social question. Basically in agreement on social policy, they differed, sometimes profoundly, about how it was to be developed and in what context (industrial or traditional) education would be molded. Not until the late 1880s and early 1890s did changing conditions produce a closing of the ranks. It might be suggested that the appearance of socialism simultaneously with the proclamation of the *esprit nouveau* was no accident.

Chapter VI

National Economics: Tariffs

DURING MUCH of the nineteenth century, French producers enjoyed a protected internal market insulated by high tariffs against foreign competition. The commercial policy of the Second Empire, however, broke with this tradition and introduced moderate free trade. The Cobden-Chevalier Treaty of 1860 between France and Britain began the trend. Napoleon III's regime negotiated a series of bilateral trade agreements that reduced import duties on textiles, manufactured goods, and some agricultural products. All of these treaties provided for sliding scales that gave the French some flexibility, but deprived France of the complete freedom to establish unilaterally a general tariff without the consent of her trade partners. Napoleon III's stated motive for lowering tariffs, especially vis-à-vis British manufacturers who could undersell French textile producers on the latter's home ground, was to force the French to modernize, cut costs, adopt the latest technology, and thus compete on an equal footing at home and in the world market. He promised substantial credits to facilitate modernization and concentration. The credits did not, however, materialize in any way proportional to domestic industrial requirements. French capital continued to flow abroad in search of greener pastures, keeping domestic interest rates high.

More aggressive capitalists found themselves cut off in two directions from realizing greater profits. On the one hand, they lacked security in the internal market (which, being largely rural, had its limits) with the specter of cheap British goods looming on the horizon.

On the other hand, the capital that would be available to forge the sinews (rails, canals, highways) of a national market, which could transform a collection of regional markets into a national market, went elsewhere. Thus, many of the same people who protested against railroad monopolies and high finance fought free trade as well.

Free trade versus protection became a political issue in the 1860s, and the regime's policy alienated many of its previously loyal supporters, especially in the textile industry. Chapter I has outlined some of the political consequences. Thiers' regime gave strong indications of preparing to reverse the previous policy, as it dragged its feet on the renegotiation of the treaties of the 1860s. However, the Government of Moral Order continued free trade. Thus, by 1877 when the republicans consolidated their power, the tariff issue remained to be resolved. Several years of protectionist pressure resulted in the General Tariff of 1881. Although by no means a reversion to high protection, the 1881 measure reflected a marked trend toward economic nationalism that culminated in the Méline Tariff of 1892.

Protecting the National Market

The tension between intraclass conflict and fundamental bourgeois solidarity, manifest in the politics of railroads and education, also was reflected in the struggle over tariff reform that began in the late 1870s. Although specific economic issues were at stake, broader questions of social policy intruded: the relationship between capitalist and petty producer; class struggle between employers and workers; and the purpose and thrust of French imperialism. Those who advocated protection frequently argued within a context of national economics, whose outlines already had taken shape. That program included the extension of rails, schools, and empire. Behind the strictly business-oriented questions of trade relationships and the formulation of a suitable antidote to the ravages of the great depression, lay the deeper issues of social policies and ideological solidarity proper to a consolidation of the republican system. Since that system balanced delicately between widening capitalist production and the self-conscious efforts of the republican bourgeoisie to maintain a stable social order, the construction of a coherent tariff structure proved to be no simple matter.[1]

The French "commercial crisis," as it was known, constituted a regional manifestation of a worldwide depression in capitalist production. By 1877, general agreement held that French industry suffered from overproduction and falling prices. Unlike the British and, to a lesser extent, the Americans, French entrepreneurs could not export their miseries. Indeed, evidence mounted up to suggest that France lay helpless before efforts by Britain to dump its inventories outside its frontiers.[2]

According to a good deal of testimony from businessmen and chambers of commerce, the political uncertainty surrounding the events of the *seize mai* had aggravated the crisis. "All security has disappeared," read a widely circulated petition to the Chamber of Deputies. MacMahon, it continued, should recognize that "all the industrialists, merchants, and laborers" will hold his regime responsible for the "ruin of the nation." Alfred Delesalle, a cotton cloth manufacturer from Lille, complained that his industry had taken a series of hard blows resulting from the political ups and downs of 1877. His words were echoed by the chamber of commerce of Reims, a delegation of wool and cotton manufacturers from the Aisne, and the "leading merchants of the city of Nevers," who recounted the hardships endured by small businessmen fallen into the debt of their wholesale suppliers.[3] Another petition with 4,498 signatures of businessmen from a dozen departments scattered throughout the country

1. See Chapter I.
2. Nicholas Claude, *Enquête commerciale et industrielle du Sénat: Déposition de M. Claude* (Paris: n.p., 1878); Voeux des conseils généraux rélatifs au commerce, in F (12) 4841 and situation industrielle des départements, Somme, troisième trimestre, 1879, in F(12) 4541, Archives nationales, hereinafter cited as AN; A. Fougerousse, "La Crise industrielle en France," *La Réforme sociale* (October 1, 1884), 289–307. The general council of the Nord dated the decline from 1875.
3. Crise industrielle, 1877–1878, petition subscribed to by businessmen from L'Abresle (Rhône), Romans (Drôme), Tulle (Corrèze), Paris, Montbéliard (Doubs), Mauzé (Deux-Sèvres), Saint-Michel (Vendée), and Toucy (Yonne), in F(12) 6171, AN; Sénat, Commission du tarif général des douanes, *Enquête sur les souffrances du commerce et de l'industrie et sur les moyens d'y porter remède,* transcript of sessions on December 8, 11, and 18, 1877, and January 24, 1878, hereinafter cited as Sénat, *Enquête.*

testified that the current malaise stemmed directly from "political uncertainties." They turned their judgment into a statement for the Republic: "The executive power has totally disregarded the results of the elections of October 14 and interpreted the Constitution in a wholly antiparliamentary spirit." Republicans made political capital where they could. Paul Bert and Charles Lepère of the Yonne tabled a petition from "184 industrialists and merchants of Auxerre . . . who, [they alleged] since the sixteenth of May, had experienced a crisis of incalculable gravity." Jules Grévy, president of the Chamber of Deputies, delivered a stack of petitions to the minister of agriculture and commerce, Pierre Teisserenc de Bort, with a personal note warning him that "a great number of merchants . . . are convinced that the cause of their misery may be traced to the political uncertainty that weighs so heavily on the nation."[4]

These expressions recall the mobilized opposition against the Government of Moral Order by the republican bourgeoisie on the railroad issue. Most businessmen coupled their expressions of anxiety over falling prices and constricted markets with an expectation that more railroads would contribute to their salvation. The Comité industriel et commercial of Normandy, representing chiefly cotton entrepreneurs, applauded Freycinet for "taking the initiative on projects whose realization will have beneficial consequences." But few in the industrial community believed that protective action should end there. Nicholas Claude, the Vosges cotton senator and a major national republican figure, raised the prospect of "moderate protection" of internal markets to supplement the cost reductions expected from the completion of the third rail network.[5]

The conjunction of the beginning of the tariff protection campaign with the struggle over railroads dramatized the concerns of the industrial bourgeoisie, whose relatively weak position in the world market propelled them to seek to expand the internal market.[6] In

4. Petitions received on December 8, 1877, in F(12) 6171, Jules Grévy to the minister of agriculture and commerce, March 16, 1878, in F(12) 4854, AN.
5. Sénat, *Enquête*, Annexe No. 8; Claude, *Enquête commerciale et industrielle*.
6. Petition from the chamber of commerce of Chalons-sur-Sâone, February 27, 1878, in F(12) 6171, AN.

the contemporary political context, industrialists inclined to the republican position and made of tariff reform a political issue that fed into the intraclass conflict that had characterized the *seize mai* crisis. Once again the industrial bourgeoisie's ambition to rule directly in its own interests exposed the socioeconomic basis for the constitutional conflicts of the mid-1870s.

The leading promoter of protection, the *Industriel français*, expressed its suspicion that the Government of Moral Order had planned to renew the Anglo-French commercial treaty without discussion, thus demonstrating its ties to a Bonapartist oligarchy of monopolists and confirming that the "tendencies of doctrinaire free trade" were incompatible with an "essentially democratic cause, the cause of industry." As for the arguments for free trade advanced by men like Isaac Péreire, they amounted to the deceptions of a monopolist and an international financier whose railroads and Transatlantic Steamship Company represented the antithesis of "truly free and national" industry. Such apologists for free trade were "cosmopolitans" wedded to an antipatriotic and antidemocratic illusion of the "community of nations" and scornful of the "homeland" and of the "national interest." A communication from the wool industry of Saint-Quentin, which included one hundred employers and forty thousand workers, to the general council of the Aisne linked free trade with "monarchist" principles typical of an "aristocratic society," whose laws "always favor the upper classes and capital."[7] By "capital" they meant finance capital. Once again surfaced the antagonism that industrial capitalists felt vis-à-vis their class brethren in command of the organs of banking and credit. Industry was "democratic" and "national" whereas capital was "aristocratic" and "cosmopolitan." Spokesmen for the manufacturers in Le Havre complained that French vulnerability to English competition resulted less from the former's comparative inefficiency, a favorite free-trade argument, than from a lack of capital at reasonable interest rates. [8]

7. *Industriel français*, November 1, August 9, October 4, 1877, July 11, August 29, 1878.

8. *Journal du Havre*, quoted *ibid.*, August 16, 1877. De la Germonière, of Rouen, argued that "les rélations entre les industriels normands et les commissionnaires du

This sort of rhetoric suggests that the debate between free traders and protectionists sounded the depths of opposing conceptions of the social order. The subsequent struggle did not remain free of serious ideological confrontation. As in the controversy over railroads, the dissipation of the *seize mai* crisis reduced the temperature of the confrontation without eliminating it. The egalitarian, nationalist, and solidarist doctrines of republican democracy took on wider meaning when applied to industrial policy. Indeed, the republican ideological position became more precisely defined in industrial terms and in all that this implied: tariffs, empire, and approaches to the working class. At the same time, the crisis in capitalist production forced the republican bourgeoisie to trim its ideological sails against the crosswinds of conflicting interests arising from the worlds of petty production, agriculture, and finance. Although nationalist economics gathered a large number of adherents to its standard, compromise with other points of view became necessary: compromise anchored in the solidarity of all forms of capital, in which the quest for a stable social-industrial order proved to be the determining factor.

The crisis in production that developed during the mid-1870s penetrated to the deepest layers of French society. It struck with the most force against the textile and metallurgical industries, which accounted for a major portion of France's industrial plant, measured in the number of workers employed and the quantity of fixed capital.[9] The agricultural crisis followed several years later, thereby deepening the trough of consumer demand. The disparity between the two sectors of the economy helps account for the fact that farmers' pressure for protection did not coincide with that of the industrialists.

The initial impulse for protection came from the cotton thread manufacturers concentrated in the north, in Normandy, in the east,

---

Havre sont journalières, les intérêts se touchent: ce grand port possède des capitaux; s'il le croyait avantageux, ne chercherait-il pas à placer son argent dans l'industrie avec laquelle il est en contact si intime? Eh bien, pourrait-on citer beaucoup de maisons havraises s'intéressant à nos usines? Non! La souffrance de notre industrie est donc incontestable." Sénat, *Enquête*, 49.

9. France, Bureau de la statistique générale, *Annuaire statistique, 1879* (Paris: Imprimerie nationale, 1881), 300–303, 314–17, *Annuaire statistique, 1880* (Paris: Imprimerie nationale, 1882), 328–29.

and in the Paris basin.[10] Entrepreneurs in these areas discovered that the first symptoms of a progressive economic disease took the form of a sharp decline in sales. Bankruptcies and layoffs followed in rapid succession. In 1875, the prefect's quarterly report for the Somme boasted of the robust condition of the local cotton industry. By 1879, the market had collapsed, forcing spinning firms to "sell at a loss." Twenty firms had gone under or were absorbed in the four-year period with a parallel decline of 31 percent in the number of workers employed. The same observation held for other large concentrations of textile production such as Mortagne and La Ferté-Macé in the Orne and Romorantin in the Loir-et-Cher. Several cotton-spinning and cotton-weaving plants in Louviers and Évreux (Eure) either closed down or temporarily laid off all their workers. The local impact was substantial, inasmuch as these factories each averaged 250 workers employed. The wool industry in the same region felt the effects of the general stagnation, although to a less dramatic degree. Employment remained stable while the number of enterprises declined. Wool entrepreneurs appeared to be maintaining workers in part-time employment to preserve the public peace. Unlike their counterparts in cotton manufacturing, wool producers did not hold foreign, especially British, competition responsible for their poor condition. Wool cloth by this time had become France's leading export product, and Britain had become an important customer. Consequently, the industrial bourgeoisie of the major centers of wool production, Reims, Tarare, Roubaix, and Péronne in the Somme, resisted protection.[11]

The discontent among provincial producers created by the crisis found expression in a massive effort to lobby against renewal of the commercial treaties. This reflected the general view that only by slamming the door to outside competition would French industry be

10. The departments in question included the Nord, the Pas-de-Calais, the Somme, the Seine-Inférieure, the Eure, the Aisne, the Vosges, and the Seine-et-Oise.
11. Situation industrielle, Somme, troisième trimestre, 1875, troisième trimestre, 1877, troisième trimestre, 1879, in F(12) 4541, situation industrielle, Eure, troisième trimestre, 1879, in F(12) 4500, situation industrielle, Orne, troisième trimestre, 1881, in F(12) 4537, situation industrielle, Loir-et-Cher, quatrième trimestre, 1878, statement of organization of the Association pour la défense de la liberté commerciale, in F(12) 6385, AN.

rescued from permanent stagnation. Everyone produced his own statistics to show that the level of textile-goods imports had increased steadily since 1820 and especially markedly since 1873. Nicholas Claude pleaded the case of the Vosges *patronat*, whose internal sales had declined as the result of a substantial increase in British imports that had tripled in the five years following 1873. Independent statistical surveys bore him out.[12] Against this sort of information, the free-trade argument, that France preserved an overwhelmingly favorable balance of trade with Britain, appeared weak and unconvincing. Not only did that balance reflect the specialized manufactures in luxury goods organized on the basis of petty production, but much of what Britain imported she reexported overseas, thereby protecting her own national industries.[13]

Auguste Lalance, an Alsatian businessman-propagandist reflecting on the situation, pointed out to his compatriot Auguste Scheurer-Kestner that France had little to fear from tariff retaliation against her luxury industries, which could hold their own on the basis of high quality craftsmanship. But the wave of the future lay clearly in mass manufacturing in which the British held a commanding position. Lalance foresaw a progressive deterioration in the position of domestic petty production under the pressure of more efficient large units. Its social consequences disturbed him, for with widely dispersed small industries "every intelligent worker has a chance to become an employer." However, concentration followed the "law of progress" and was "inevitable."[14] Within the limits imposed by these "laws," however, much could be done. Protection of major industries necessarily spilled over into all branches of production so that some semblance of social equilibrium might be preserved. Protected industries would retain their quasi-monopolistic position within the internal market, and their labor-intensive character occupied workers on the job, making them less likely to be recruited for the war of labor against capital.

12. Claude, *Enquête commerciale et industrielle; Industriel français*, June 14, 1877, figures taken from the quarterly reports of the Ministry of Agriculture and Commerce.
13. *Journal des économistes*, Ser. 4 (September 15, 1878), 306–32.
14. Auguste Lalance to Auguste Scheurer-Kestner, January 16, 1879, Scheurer-Kestner Papers, in 276 AP 2, AN.

Thus, the republican bourgeoisie moved toward a grand scheme that provided protection for its vital interests in the factories and on the streets.[15]

A program of national economics made for some curious alliances on both sides of the question. During 1878, leading members of the financial bourgeoisie organized a free-trade lobby to "oppose any increase in tariffs" and to support the system of commercial treaties. Adolph d'Eichthal, the Saint-Simonian banker, served as the association's president. He was seconded by an array of vice-presidents representing the chambers of commerce of Reims, Lyon, Saint-Étienne, Boulogne-sur-Mer, Marseille, Paris, Bordeaux, and Tarare. The board included several important Paris commercial figures such as Alexandre Lebaudy, the sugar refiner, Alexandre Clapier and Maurice Rouvier, the political voices of Marseille commercial interests, and several members of the Conseil supérieur du commerce et de l'industrie. The latter body had been stacked against representatives of textiles and metallurgy. According to Paul Leroy-Beaulieu, who was in a position to know, the banking brothers Fould, Henri and Léon, provided the chief impetus behind the organization.[16]

The free-trade lobby, then, did not totally reproduce the anti-democratic "cosmopolitan" alliance that the republican bourgeoisie had beaten back in 1877. The *haute bourgeoisie financière* was nevertheless well represented. Several of its political chiefs from the Second Empire reappeared, men like Eugène Rouher and Pierre Magne. The latter was noted for his sympathy toward an economic orientation "open to international" ties.[17] But Clapier, Rouvier, and Lebaudy were not men of reaction, nor did the businessmen from several big industrial centers believe they had betrayed the Republic of the bourgeoisie by agitating for free trade. The Eichthals and the Foulds appeared

15. Chambre des députés, *Commission sur le tarif général des douanes: Procès-verbaux des séances,* testimony of Martelet, representative of the Association nationale de l'industrie française and a director of Denain-Anzin, June 15, 1878, hereinafter cited as Chambre, *Commission.*

16. *France coloniale,* October 23, 1879; F(12) 6385, AN; *Économiste français,* June 8, 1878; *Journal du commerce maritime et des colonies* (Le Havre), January 23, February 22, 1880.

17. Charles Gignoux, *Rouvier et les finances* (Paris: Gallimard, 1931), 51.

to speak their language. Eichthal worried about agriculture, which, he said, "embodied our hallowed tradition of equality" and which needed freedom of trade so that small producers would seek to rise and become farmer-capitalists. Fould said he was concerned about the narrowed consumer market that would surely follow the elevation of customs duties.[18]

Alexandre Clapier attempted to harmonize the republican ideological position on equality, entrepreneurial freedom, and a national industrial policy with free trade. Whatever the outcome of the tariff question, the integrity of the Republic remained the chief consideration: "Any deep division between the political system and industry [will] provoke apathy and discontent and will result in the internal struggles which lead inexorably to revolution." He did not expect free trade to usher in an era of universal peace and prosperity, internal order, and class reconciliation, as some of its more fervent advocates asserted. Free trade did promise, in his view, "to facilitate the entente between employers and workers through the application of equitable settlements, to stimulate the productive activity of workers, [and] to elicit increases in wages." For Clapier as well as for republican economic nationalists, trade policy was above all a question of social policy. Clapier's colleague from Marseille, the radical Maurice Rouvier, took a doctrinaire laissez-faire stance, warning against any tampering with the "natural laws that govern the production, the distribution, and the consumption of wealth." He turned the egalitarian argument against the protectionists. Higher tariffs would benefit only the biggest industrial and agricultural capitalists, leaving the rest to struggle along on their insufficient capital. Rouvier did not appear to be troubled by the fact that he was unwilling to permit petty producers to fall victim to the very "natural laws" that he had enshrined.[19]

18. Chambre des députés, *Extrait du Journal official du 28 novembre 1878, Association pour la défense de la liberté industrielle et commerciale: Déposition auprès de la Commission du tarif général des douanes* (Paris: n.p., 1879), 3–32.

19. Alexandre Clapier, *Le Tarif général des douanes et les traités de commerce* (Paris: Bureau de la Revue britannique, 1879), *passim*; Maurice Rouvier, *Discours sur le projet de loi rélatif à l'établissement du tarif général des douanes* (Paris: Wittersheim, 1880), 4–16.

An equally imposing array of industrial notables organized the forces of tariff protection. The Association nationale de l'industrie française featured as its president Alexandre Jullien, head of the forges and foundries of Terrenoire. Jullien had been a leading figure in the Bonapartist political machine in the Loire during the Second Empire. At that time his business had been riding a wave of prosperity. Now with such items as rails for American railroads in slack demand and with the prospect of new French railroad building projected in the Freycinet Plan, he had become a stanch protectionist.[20] The directors of the association included a cross section of French industrialists, whose establishments ranged in size from the Denain-Anzin complex and the Japy Watch and Hardware Company to moderate-sized forges, foundries, and textile mills. They came from all corners of the nation to contribute their voices and support to the protectionist cause: ship-builders from Le Havre and Bordeaux; machinery manufacturers from Lille, Essonnes, Saint-Ouen, and Paris; mining entrepreneurs from the Midi, Rive-de-Gier, Nord, and Pas-de-Calais; metallurgists from Com-mentry-Fourchambault, Allevard, Marseille, the Ariège, Blanzy, and Commentry-Châtillon; and the ubiquitous textile men from Elbeuf, Rouen, Lille, Essonnes, and Saint-Quentin. The chambers of commerce of Épinal and Saint-Dié adhered to the association en bloc.[21]

Representatives from the association and from the chambers of commerce paraded steadily before Senate and Chamber committees constituted to receive testimony on the economic situation. What they heard was to be assimilated in proposals for treaty renewals and the General Tariff. The composition of neither the Senate nor the Chamber committee revealed a marked tendency toward either side of the issue. However, the presence of certain key figures provided a clue to which way the wind was blowing. Augustin Pouyer-Quertier, the boisterous self-made millionaire Rouen cotton magnate, headed the Senate committee. He had been a protectionist since 1860 and on that basis joined Thiers' Provisional Government of the Republic in 1871.

20. Sénat, *Enquête*, February 16, 1878.
21. *Industriel français*, March 21, 1878; *Journal des économistes*, Ser. 4 (August 1, 1878), 266; Chambre, *Commission*, June 15, 1878.

Jules Brame of the Nord was vice-president of the committee, which included strong protectionists like Ernest Feray of Essonnes; Pierre Teisserenc de Bort, who had served as minister of agriculture and commerce following the collapse of the *seize mai* regime; the free trader Louis Hubert-Delisle of Bordeaux; the engineer-industrialist Dupuy de Lôme; and Charles Chesnelong, a big royalist landowner. The Chamber's committee was led by François Malézieux from Saint-Quentin, a town whose textile manufacturers contributed substantially to the agitation for protection. Jules Méline, the future hero of protection from the Vosges, was vice-president. Secretaries of the committee included the free traders Lebaudy and Rouvier and the protectionists Pierre Legrand and François de Mahy. The latter represented colonial interests in his capacity as deputy from the island of Réunion and had made a reputation as an ideological democrat. The committee was divided equally between protectionists and free traders, with Richard Waddington and Eugène Rouher in symbolic command of either side.[22]

Every industry in France that did not depend upon a supply of foreign raw materials or semifinished goods, such as some branches of cotton cloth production, or upon a large export market, such as finished wool and silk goods, joined the movement for tariff revision. In some cases, the chief concerns focused on maintaining large numbers of workers on the job. This was particularly true for the Vosges cotton industry, where cheap water power drove mills in which hundreds of workers labored under a single roof. Vosges industrialists did not employ a large amount of steam horsepower, certainly no more than "backward" Normandy and one-third that of the Nord; they did not need to—a point that raises doubts about such measures of capitalist development. Northern industry, in contrast, faced the crisis with a heavy burden of idle machinery and workers. Everywhere, previous commitments to machinery, what Nicholas Claude called "the excessive development of the means of production," linked textile producers to their counterparts in mining and metallurgy.[23]

22. Chambre, *Commission*, December 20, 1879; A. Robert *et al.*, *Dictionnaire des parlementaires* (5 vols.; Paris: Presses universitaires de France, 1889), IV, 223–24.
23. Bureau de la statistique générale, *Annuaire statistique, 1893*, 370–71; *Industriel français*, January 17, 1878.

Some of the nation's largest iron and steel complexes, whose political weight could not be discounted, lent their active support to the protectionist campaign. The metallurgists of Longwy in the Ardennes recounted "twenty years" of imports that had cut into their market. "We hope," they petitioned, "that the government will take whatever steps are necessary to preserve the French market for national industry." Perhaps they had in mind the 150 million francs' worth of imports, mainly coal, iron, and steel, that annually passed through the railroad junction of Jeumont on the Belgian border. Antoine Martelet, of Denain-Anzin, spoke for "all the great industries of France united in solidarity" behind efforts to protect the national market. Firms large and small, he alleged, trembled in fear of ruinous competition, the social consequences of which had already been noticed in trade imbalances and falling profits. He warned that without protective measures French industrialists would be forced to screw up the level of exploitation on a labor force already severely tested. The threat of a "plague of strikes . . . deadly to public order" hung in the air.[24]

Paul Schneider, coal mine operator in the Aveyron and brother of Schneider of Le Creusot, raised the familiar question of transportation costs. Insufficient canals had been built since promises of them had been made in 1861. A ton of coal shipped from Douai to Paris continued to cost more than a ton shipped from Newcastle to Bordeaux. He suggested that the French bourgeois' generous social conscience, in the form of workers' benefits, added to the disparity. He expected protective tariffs to constitute the price paid to maintain employment and steady wages. Without making the threat explicit, Schneider speculated darkly on the consequences of one million workers, according to his estimate, and their families (including those in coal and ancillary industries) driven to poverty by a serious slump in mining and metallurgy.[25]

Northern industrialists did not limit their efforts to appearances

24. Sénat, Enquête, February 16 and 19, 1878; Tableau général du commerce de la France avec ses colonies et les puissances étrangères pendant l'année 1878 (Paris: Imprimerie nationale, 1879), 110; Chambre, Commission, June 15, 1878.

25. Chambre, Commission, Déposition de la section de l'Association française représentant l'industrie houillière, June 21 and 22, 1878.

before parliamentary committees. Even before the committees were constituted, they organized a conference with the leading republicans of the area, Gustave Masure, Jules Brame, and Martin Kolb-Bernard, to remind them of their responsibilities. The latter recognized the solidarity of all industrial politicians and proceeded to organize an informal protectionist bloc including deputies and senators from all industrial departments. They constituted nearly 50 percent of the Chamber and managed, in June, 1878, to delay ratification of a Franco-Italian commercial treaty signed the previous year. Jules Méline sponsored the measure to postpone ratification. This event marked the beginning of his fifteen-year campaign to achieve high protection.[26]

This association of northern industrialists was one link in a nation-wide chain of associations galvanized by the bourgeoisie for political action to determine industrial policy. The north took the lead insofar as its complement of textile plants, mines, and blast furnaces constituted the highest degree of industrial concentration in France. Its chambers of commerce were the most active in the political arena. The businessmen of Lille, Roubaix, Tourcoing, Douai, Valenciennes, Amiens, and Dunkirk recognized a common stake in "national industry" and found eager allies in other parts of France. Industrialists in the Seine-Inférieure and the Eure took up the theme of social peril inherent in the industrial crisis. They were joined by the associations of cotton producers in the Vosges and the Aisne who repeated the warnings of a "crisis in worker relations" should they fail to maintain their markets.[27]

Norman industry appeared to be particularly vulnerable to the "economic revolution," as the chamber of commerce of Elbeuf described it, overtaking French industry. According to Senator Stanislas Cordier of Rouen, his region's cotton-weaving industry had shifted markedly from domestic handloom production to mechanized weaving. Because the progressive concentration of machines created an equally concentrated population of proletarians, agricultural labor

---

26. *Industriel français,* November 1, 1877; *Journal officiel de la république française: Chambre des députés, compte-rendu sténographique,* June 8, 1878, hereinafter cited as *JOC.*
27. *Industriel français,* May 5, September 6, 1877.

could no longer absorb the large numbers of workers laid off during periods of low production, and handloom weavers found themselves in a state of chronic underemployment. Under these conditions Norman capitalists showed understandable reluctance to close their mills, having lost their safety valve. Senator Henri Wallon of the Comité industriel et commercial of Normandy, reflecting on these conditions, concluded that free trade threatened the "national interest" and the "interests of the people."[28]

To suggest that the industrial bourgeoisie mobilized a common front on the tariff question would be misleading. Nor did all protectionists argue from a "republican" position as is conventionally understood. Rather the reverse happened. A further refinement of the character of the Republic and its socioeconomic constitution emerged from these events. Furthermore, as a class movement to establish the Republic on solid grounds of industrial prosperity and social solidarity, the forces of bourgeois interest, on whichever side they fought, demonstrated remarkable cohesion. Two deputies and glass producers, Pétrus Richarme of the Loire and Alfred Girard of the Nord, reacted to foreign competition in opposite ways. Richarme welcomed the introduction of new techniques from Germany and totally modernized his plant in Rive-de-Gier. He expected the installation of new equipment to reduce his capital costs in depreciation, to cheapen the price of his bottles, making them more attractive in the market, and thereby to create more jobs. Girard argued that his branch of the industry could not afford competition and that maintaining the employment level of the dense population of workers in Valenciennes required decisive protective measures in the "political interest" of all industrial producers.[29] Each addressed himself to the profound question of the relations between capital and labor; each provided his own solution. Neither doubted that the chief business of the Republic consisted of moving quickly and decisively to institute his preferred mode of socioeconomic policy.

28. *Ibid.,* June 13, 1878; Sénat, *Enquête,* February 19, 1878, déposition de la chambre de commerce de Rouen; *Industriel français,* June 28, 1877, January 17, 1878.
29. Chambre des députés, *Commission du tarif général des douanes: Procès-verbaux des séances,* November 21, 1878, in AD XIX F25, AN.

Cities divided according to industry, but never on the aims of industrial policy. Metallurgists from Saint-Étienne were highly protectionist, whereas their counterparts in cotton cloth finishing benefited from low tariffs on cotton thread and sheeting (*draperies*). Both insisted that their way constituted the smoothest path to social peace. In Roubaix the issue was joined between cotton producers operating under the gun of British competition and wool producers who sold heavily on the export market. However, both sides agreed on the necessity for the state to undertake a decisive industrial policy to preserve "the public peace" and to make it unnecessary for Roubaisian industry to embark upon the dangerous course of wage reductions and layoffs. Not all wool industries were export oriented. The chamber of commerce at Elbeuf questioned Rouvier, when he was minister of commerce and colonies in late 1881, on what protective measures for wool he was prepared to support. His noncommittal response did not please them.[30]

Port cities in general supported free trade as it was in their obvious interest to do so. But some deviations occurred. Bordeaux stood firm. Its republican leader, mayor, and future deputy, François Lalande, reminded Freycinet when the latter visited Bordeaux in 1878 that her trade also formed part of "national industry" and that her workers depended upon that trade.[31] Lalande was particularly concerned about renewing the Franco-American trade treaty, which was in jeopardy, and to that end he mobilized the Bordeaux *patronat* behind the Comité franco-américain. Bordeaux also fought unsuccessfully against the reintegration of French colonies into the metropolitan tariff structure.

Only Bordeaux, Le Havre, and Marseille participated massively in foreign trade. Other ports, like Nantes, engaged in extensive shipbuilding that had not prospered. Again foreign competition emerged as the culprit, although just how protective tariffs would have promoted indigenous shipbuilding remains unclear. The chamber of

30. Chambre, *Commission*, May 7, 1878; *Industriel français*, July 12 and 19, 1877; Chambre des députés, *Procès-verbaux de la commission du tarif général des douanes: Réponses des chambres de commerce*, Marseille, in C 3223, AN; *Démocratie franc-comtoise* (Besançon), June 2, 1879; *Télégraphe*, December 9, 1881.
31. *Journal des économistes*, Ser. 4 (October 15, 1878), 141–46.

commerce of Lorient spoke in sharply protectionist terms as it viewed the decline of French exports passing through the city's harbor: "All of our industries are in a state of grave crisis; in order for them to sustain the struggle they will begin to have to lower the wages of workers, which is a serious and dangerous business." Little distinguished the response of the bourgeoisie of Lorient from that of Lille, Épinal, and Saint-Dié.[32]

The alliance of finance capital and shipping interests against protection received unexpected support from "radical" elements within the republican coalition. On the railroad issue they had been at each other's throats as the latter defended the egalitarian marketplace against monopoly. They appeared to oppose protection on the same grounds. Actually, a convenient rendezvous of economic interest and ideological principle took place. Maurice Rouvier's position needs no further explanation. Representatives from the south, where the wine business reigned supreme, joined him. The chief radical organ of Languedoc, the *Dépêche de Toulouse*, made no secret of its reasons for denouncing protection, but gilded the lily with an elaborate ideological statement on the dangers to democratic liberties posed by certain industrial interests. Voices from the Midi joined in, claiming to speak for the entire rural economy of France.[33] Noël Madier de Montjau, an old Montagnard from 1848 and a carping critic of conservative tendencies within the republican political establishment, inclined toward free trade because he believed it to be "democratic." But he represented a silk-growing region recently devastated by phylloxera and consequently demanded protection for his farmer constituents. They were, he said, "members of the great national family," and their miseries were a harbinger of a general social crisis destined to victimize both employers and workers.[34] Madier the radical was no stranger to bourgeois thinking. He was perfectly prepared to allow

---

32. *Industriel français*, June 20 and 27, 1878, September 20, 1877; *Réponses des chambres de commerce*, Lorient, May 15, 1878, Lille, April 25, 1878, in C 3223, AN.

33. *Dépêche de Toulouse*, July 9, 1881; *Union républicaine de l'Hérault*, October 4, 1881.

34. Chambre des députés, *Commission du tarif général des douanes*, testimony of Noël Madier de Montjau, December 6, 1878, in AD XIX F25, AN.

concentration to take its course as long as his constituents received protection for their property.

The most curious of radicals occupied an elegant townhouse in Paris near the Parc Monçeau. Émile Menier had inherited from his father a flourishing chocolate-manufacturing business that he had expanded. The factory on the eastern outskirts of Paris employed three hundred to four hundred workers. Vast cocoa plantations in Nicaragua supplied the raw materials.[35] Needless to say, he enthusiastically advocated colonial expansion. Menier headed the Comité franco-américain that agitated for the renewal of trade treaties with the United States.[36] He plunged into radical politics in the early 1870s, financing several newspapers, like the *Tribune* of Bordeaux, that combined hard-line democratic slogans with vigorous support of the bourgeois system in France and overseas. His most ambitious venture, the *Réforme économique*, a biweekly magazine, was staffed by the radicals Yves Guyot and Charles Boysset of Mâcon (the deputy of the *grands crus bourgognes*). The journal consistently coupled attacks on protection with demands for the democratization of the Republic. It welcomed also the development of workers' associations and expected them to "enlighten" the proletariat on the "immutable laws of political economy."[37]

Menier used the "principles of advanced democracy" the way other entrepreneurs used fringe benefits—to tighten the bonds of loyalty between capital and labor. "He welcomed socialist principles" that for him meant gathering together all his workers in a "great family." In a celebration of his achievements on the occasion of his death, Eugène Menier, a cousin and colonial propagandist, put Menier squarely in the tradition to which he belonged: He "represents the solidarity of big business with the Republic; through his efforts, the Republic found a secure place among those interests.[38] Émile Menier's own

35. Report of November 18, 1872, in B/a 1179, Archives de la préfecture de police de la Seine, hereinafter cited as APP.
36. *Avenir de Rennes*, August 8, 1878; *Union nationale du commerce et de l'industrie* (Paris), August 28, 1880.
37. Report of November 8, 1872, report of November 10, 1875, in B/a 1179, APP; *Réforme économique*, Ser. 3, III (1880), 354.
38. *France coloniale*, February 24, 1881.

theoretical contributions to the elaboration of republican ideology remained consistent with his class position. He defended the institution of universal suffrage with great energy. It "constitutes the most serious guarantee of security" imaginable. "It represents the right of everyone to peacefully influence the destiny of his country . . . [and] it replaces violent responses to the solution of political and social problems with peaceful action."[39] As a radical Menier made an outstanding contribution to the defense of the bourgeois order. Indeed, he accepted the unstated premise that the primacy of capital in the hands of enlightened democrats constituted the best guarantee for that order. Despite his political eccentricities, Menier easily accommodated to the Ferrys and Gambettas. If anything, he and his fellow radicals surpassed the leading politicians of the Republic in their uncritical and somewhat simple-minded reliance upon the hidden hand. They had no social program to speak of and, in their contention that workers had a stake in maximum entrepreneurial freedom, veered closely to the position of the financial bourgeoisie. It is a mystery how these men ever became known as men of the left.

Economic nationalism occasionally encountered resistance from quarters not identified with big bourgeois radicalism. Gambetta and his associates expressed their initial reaction in the crudest predestinarian pseudo-Darwinism: "Production should be cut back, and that can only be accomplished by the liquidation of a certain number of enterprises. . . . The weakest, of course, the most poorly located, the most inadequately equipped, the worst managed, the poorest. But how will we know them? They will reveal themselves through testing and struggle, by the struggle for existence . . . which provides the natural corrective to great industrial mistakes."[40] These were sentiments worthy of the immortal Guizot and evidence of a certain confusion, prompting a police agent to remark on Gambetta's hesitancy to commit himself on matters of political economy that it was "a task considerably more demanding than making speeches against the ene-

39. Émile Menier, *L'Impôt sur le capital* (2 vols.; Paris: Dubuisson, 1875), I, 402–408.
40. *République française*, April 17, 1878.

mies of the Republic."[41] The confusion reflected the poverty of formulas upon which some republicans had come to depend and that had
served them adequately in conditions where the political lines were
clearly drawn. It reflected also a tension between the democratic
egalitarianism of the republican bourgeoisie and its class basis. The
crisis in production gave evidence of turning into a general social
crisis in which petty producers would be forced to the wall and the
working class driven to raise the stakes in the struggle between
capital and labor. These considerations raised certain hard questions,
among them the business of the Republic to perpetuate the conditions
of security for small producers. For the latter the elevation of tariff
barriers made no apparent sense, since it would allow more efficient
industrialists to drive the small producers out of the market and strip
them of any residual control over prices on articles of consumption.
Gambetta's confusion, then, reflected the unstable alliance between
industrial capital and petty production that had previously made
possible the political successes of the republican bourgeoisie.

However, no amount of rhetorical sleight of hand could make the
class foundations of the Republic disappear, and its more perceptive
ideologue politicians understood this. Writing of the death of Camille
de Montalivet, a leading senator of the conservative bourgeoisie,
Spuller eulogized the man's contribution to the formation of the
"conservative republican party" and to the support of big business
for the Republic. Spuller issued an invitation to "independent and
intelligent conservatives . . . to mark out the terrain on which they
may render a service to the nation."[42] He thus confirmed the primacy
of class solidarity underlying the foundations of the Republic and
drew attention to the fact that in any contest of priorities industrial
interests would prevail.

It was by no means clear that a thoroughgoing program of
economic nationalism, embodying a protective tariff, would benefit
anyone but capitalist producers, enabling them to establish com-

41. Report of May 21, 1878, in B/a 921, APP.
42. Clipping from *République française,* January 7, 1880, Scheurer-Kestner
Papers, in 276 AP 1, AN.

modity prices without the fear of foreigners underselling them. We may concede at least the whisper of truth in Leroy-Beaulieu's self-serving assertion that behind the movement for protection stood cotton and metallurgical producers, whose vision did not extend beyond their balance sheets and who were intent upon preserving a quasi-monopolistic position in the domestic market.[43] The Mélines, the Waddingtons, the Masures, the Dautresmes, and the Claudes translated these interests into national economic terms. Jules Ferry gave ideological coherence and attempted to show how the national republican system guaranteed social equilibrium. These men and others like them had made the Republic an expression of their class outlook and were engaged in building a stable bourgeois system. They argued consistently and cogently for a national economic policy that, in their terms, promised security for petty producers as well as themselves. However, they proved unable to carry the capitalists of the ports and export industries with them, to say nothing of the "radical" elements in their party. More importantly, the bulk of French farmers, themselves only beginning to enter the market, remained unmoved. The united front of property owners seemed to be on the verge of collapse. As is usual in such situations, the antagonists struck a compromise to preserve the solidarity of the republican bourgeoisie.

When protection came to France, it arrived under the pressure from agricultural interests whose conditions had deteriorated during the early 1880s. Little was heard from that sector of the economy during the period discussed here. The voices for agricultural protection in the late 1870s came from the fringes of that world. "Manure . . . is the standard of the wealth of nations," announced Léon Vingtain, a former deputy and farmer from the Loir-et-Cher. He spoke for sheep raisers, whose contribution to the raw material of textiles was supplemented by the production of manure and who fought a rearguard action against the importation of foreign raw wool.[44] Raw wool constituted France's number-one import, and the wool cloth producers of Roubaix, Tarare, Reims, and Saint-Étienne

43. *Économiste français,* June 24, 1882.
44. Sénat, *Enquête,* deposition of the Comité industriel de Flers (Orne), February 5, 1878; Chambre, *Commission,* June 12, 1878.

led the opposition to protection among manufacturers.[45] Marginal and exotic products suddenly became essential to national survival in the view of their producers. Potato growers who sold their crops to manufacturers of potato starch wanted high tariffs on corn starch. Cattlemen dealing in hides expressed alarm at the high rate of imports of their commodity. In the latter case they faced the power of port manufacturers dealing in the preparation, for export, of imported hides and skins. Félix Faure of Le Havre was one such businessman.[46]

The only organized effort for agricultural protection parallel to the work of the Association nationale de l'industrie française was made by the Société des agriculteurs de France. Its membership list read like an *Almanach de Gotha* of titled gentlemen farmers. Big landowners from the west provided the leadership in the campaign for agricultural protection. In contrast to the rest of France, Norman and Breton departments included a high percentage of landholdings organized on the basis of *culture indirecte*, leaseholding and share-cropping, rather than *culture directe*, owner cultivation.[47]

In its agitation and propaganda for protection the Société des agriculteurs attempted to camouflage its *grand seigneur* complexion under a dense foliage of rural democracy and entrepreneurial freedom. Its leaders revealed themselves to be practical businessmen who had nothing in common with backwoods gentry. Their professed sensitivity to the social implications of tariff policy paralleled similar perceptions found among the industrial interests of the republican bourgeoisie. The president of the society in 1879, Monicault, warned of the widening abyss separating industrial from agricultural production. He projected a bleak vision of thousands of small cultivators driven from their lands under the twin blows of foreign competition and the high cost of capital for improvements. He frankly preferred autarchy to increased dependence on foreign food, with good reason, since his class constituted the major supplier of animal

45. Imports of raw wool doubled between 1870 and 1873 and continued to rise thereafter. *Industriel français*, October 25, 1877.

46. Various petitions to the Chamber of Deputies and to the Senate, in F(12) 4841, 4854, AN.

47. *Bulletin de la Société des agriculteurs*, XVIII (1881), 301–303; France, Ministère de l'agriculture, *Statistique agricole de France* (Nancy: n.p., 1877), 324.

and grain commodities to the domestic market. In a direct appeal to the solidarity of France's industrial and agricultural producers, the society's president in 1881, the Marquis de Dampierre, raised the specter of social upheaval: "When one sows by the handful the seeds of antagonism in the fields of material interests, one risks reaping an evil harvest."[48]

No political alliance emerged from the intersection of industrial bourgeois and protectionist farmers on the tariff question. Rouvier mocked the Société des agriculteurs de France, calling it a *société royale* controlled by big capitalist farmers who had nothing to offer to democratic enterprise. Clapier considered the entire protectionist movement to be the work of cotton magnates and landowners in Normandy and Brittany.[49] He was mostly correct, at least about the farmers, whose interests did not coincide with the mass of rural producers. The former produced for a wide market; the latter did not. The bourgeoisie had ridden a popular crest to power and could not jeopardize its ideological position by an alliance with aristocratic reaction. The principle thrust of its tariff campaign had been to demonstrate that the national republican system incorporated effective barriers to the social consequences of concentration. Republican bourgeois offered protection to petty producers who stood to become the first victims of concentration. However, these initial forays into the field of economic nationalism rested on the position that the solution to the production crisis was to raise the prices of manufactured commodities relative to agricultural produce. As long as rural producers made up the bulk of the internal market and did not share the industrialists' anxieties, the campaign to protect the Republic's social fabric by protecting her national industries failed to score a victory.

For most farmers their interests as commodity producers did not undergo a severe test; nor could they be expected to accept an arrangement whereby differential protection for manufactured goods locked them into a captive market in which their own commodities

48. Chambre des députés, *Commission du tarif général des douanes,* testimony of E. de Monicault, February 24, 1879, in AD XIX F25, AN; *Bulletin de la Société des agriculteurs,* XIV (1879), 330–42, XVIII (1881), 259–74.
49. Rouvier, *Discours, passim;* Clapier, *Le Tarif général, passim.*

sold at world prices driven downward by the abundance of foreign wheat. Likewise, those industrial bourgeois pressing for protection could not ignore the fact that, in the words of Maurice Lévy-Leboyer, "industry remained . . . the tributary of agriculture" insofar as markets were concerned.[50] The poorest wheat harvest since the year of the Commune was produced in 1879; however, the heavy import of wheat did not depress the price on the internal market. Demand easily matched supply. It appeared that, for all the talk about foreign competition, rural producers at this moment did not suffer the effects of that competition.[51]

Rural France, we have often been told, constituted a community of independent small producers. The statistics bear this out. Farms of less than 10 hectares (one hectare equals 2.47 acres) extent made up 85 percent of all holdings. They rested in "the hands . . . of that class of hardworking and thrifty peasant cultivators of which France is so rightfully proud." So stated the authors of the 1886 report on the rural economy. But that placid perspective had another side. They went on to point out that units surpassing forty hectares in size made up nearly one-half the total arable land.[52] This suggests that a substantial number of farmer-capitalists, small in terms of the total rural population but significant in terms of agricultural production, occupied an increasingly important place on the rural landscape. When the crisis in agricultural production struck in the early 1880s, this class of rural bourgeois joined forces with their industrial brethren to renew the pressures for tariff protection. Until that time came, the political alliance of farmers and the industrial bourgeoisie that had seen the Republic through its most critical days had no existence on the tariff question.

50. Maurice Lévy-Leboyer, "La Croissance économique en France au xix siècle," *Annales: E.S.C.,* No. 4 (July-August, 1968), 788–808.
51. In 1879, for instance, imports of wheat reached their highest levels ever. The mean wholesale price per hectolitre stood halfway between the highest and lowest prices recorded for the preceding twenty-five years. It must be remembered in this connection that until the late 1870s high transportation costs made the shipping of bulk food products across the oceans uneconomical. Bureau de la statistique générale, *Annuaire statistique, 1880,* 290–91, *Annuaire statistique, 1882,* 290–91; Paul Bairoch, *Agriculture and the Industrial Revolution* (London: Collins, 1969), 50.
52. Bureau de la statistique générale, *Annuaire statistique, 1886,* 293–97.

The crisis in agricultural production that began in 1882 squeezed marginal farmers. The dissolution of a large number of small holdings appeared to threaten the ideological solidarity of capitalist property and private property, upon which the republican bourgeoisie had built its alliance with the *nouvelles couches*. Some saw the future clearly even before the crisis burst upon the country. In 1879, the farmers and businessmen assembled in the general council of the Nord disdained the "promises and empty encouragements" doled out to agriculture. In this second largest of all wheat-producing departments, the ruling class of industrial capitalists were especially sensitive to the delicate balance between the two worlds of town and country. They worried less about feeding their workers than opening the floodgates to massive movements of population away from the villages. This would have reduced ready supplies of cheap seasonal labor and fueled the engine of class antagonism between capital and labor.[53]

Objective developments tended to reinforce their anxieties. The Nord's high wheat yield reflected the department's ability to feed its industrial proletariat with its own resources. However, while industrial and coal production experienced a boom between 1862 and 1882, wheat production dropped by nearly 25 percent. The market price for arable land increased at a rate faster than that in any other area during the same period. Small farms continued to dominate, much more so than in most other departments, but the percentage of farms exploited by tenants and hired labor was comparatively very high (nearly 33 percent). The net result was to put a premium on agricultural capital, shift production away from market crops such as wheat and other grains, and promote the cultivation of cash crops, especially sugar beets, directly tied into manufacturing. Western regions of high grain production, the Vendée and the Mayenne in particular, took up the slack, increasing their yields and also witnessing a rapid rise in the market value of land. Not every industrial area followed the pattern apparent in the Nord. In the Allier, home of the great metallurgical complexes of Commentry-Châtillon and Montluçon, wheat production

53. Procès-verbal de la séance du Conseil général du Nord, 1879, in AD XIX I12, AN.

increased significantly in the same period, accompanied by a boom in the price of land. Here again, as in the Nord, *culture indirecte* constituted a relatively high percentage of the total number of agricultural exploitations.[54]

Only the bottom layers of the *nouvelles couches* took the heaviest blows delivered by the crisis insofar as they could not sustain themselves on the land. The burgeoning rural bourgeoisie did not lose their land; on the contrary, they began to demand protection for their steadily increasing investments.

In contradiction to their professed anxieties about the potential disruption of the social equilibrium, the industrialists of the Nord, at least, did in fact argue for an economic policy that satisfied both industrial and agricultural capital. They could share the optimism of Léon Sibrac of Bordeaux, who expected protection to produce agricultural prosperity in the long run as rural producers became secure in their markets. His economics perhaps is open to question, but no one concerned with the social foundations of the Republic could dispute his major thesis: "Democratic republican government finds its most solid support in small landed proprietors, for whom the raising of grain is the indispensable element of industry and security."[55]

No one abandoned the effort to arrive at "security and industry," but honest men disputed the road to take. The committee of the Chamber of Deputies delivered an ambiguous report full of platitudes at the end of 1879. It found, to no one's surprise, national production to be of vital interest to the Republic and warned of the approaching industrial struggle. Significantly, the committee noted that French tariffs stood much lower than had those of other nations at the threshold of capitalist transformation, such as the Cromwellian Protectorate, Britain under the younger William Pitt, and contemporary America.[56] The new tariffs of 1881 neither endorsed free trade nor embraced protection. They reflected, on the one hand, the split between economic nationalists and liberals and, on the other, the deep concern among all

54. Ministère de l'agriculture, *Statistique agricole, 1884*, 266–67, 294–96, Table X.
55. Léon Sibrac, *Étude sur la crise agricole: La République des paysans* (Bordeaux: Ragot, 1884), 11–23.
56. *JOC*, Annexe au procès-verbal de la séance du 20 décembre 1879.

factions of the republican bourgeoisie for the social consequences of concentration and the consequent liquidation of petty production. France remained suspended for a decade between the modified free trade established in 1860 and the aggressive protectionism embodied in the Méline Tariff of 1892.

Solidarity: Labor in the National Market

The crisis in production affected not only markets, inventories, and profits. Its social impact took equal place among the preoccupations of employers, for they had to face the potentially explosive consequences of falling wages and rising unemployment. They could ill afford to be complacent about the impact of the crisis on the working classes, who by the late 1870s had displayed renewed energy in organizing their own class formations.[57]

This is not the place to discuss the history of French workers in the first decade of the Republic—a story that remains unwritten. We are concerned here only with the initiatives and the responses of the republican bourgeoisie as they measured the social dimensions of the crisis. Discussion in previous chapters introduced the subject and established the republican ideological position. We need recall only that they preached the solidarity of capital and labor and sought to smother class distinctions under the common citizenship of all Frenchmen. At this time, confronted with the possibility of class warfare provoked by an economic crisis, they acted within their previously established solidarist framework.

These next several pages chart that action, which intersected with the campaign for tariff protection. Intraclass conflict, a major element in the battles over railroads and schools, did not dominate the political scene in the story that follows. That should come as no surprise. Both the "old" bourgeoisie (those whom the republicans referred to as "aristocrats") and the republican bourgeoisie shared common class

57. A. Montet, "Le Mouvement ouvrier à Paris du lendemain de la commune au premier congrès syndical en 1876," *Mouvement social,* No. 58 (January-March, 1967), 3–41; *Séances du Congrès ouvrier de France,* 1876, pp. 109–68, 201–72, 313–70, 1878, pp. 76–273, 405, 472, 1879, pp. 296–447, 655–709.

concerns. Nevertheless, the latter group took the lead and showed the most flexibility in dealing with the social question.

During the mid-1870s, employers, shaken by the experience of the Commune and fearful that its spirit might spread to industrial areas, used repression where they could, combined with paternalism: providing for their workers schools, lodging, nourishment, and moral indoctrination. Employers deplored the rising tide of associations and the formation of *chambres syndicales* among workers, and they believed that their own efforts contributed to the solidity of the Republic and to the fulfillment of its egalitarian ideals. Cotton producers in the Vosges noted with concern the tendency of workers to abandon their roots in the land to concentrate in mill towns. They urged measures to reverse the drift from agricultural regions, a drift that they believed produced a decline in moral standards. Businessmen in the Nièvre stated that "if agricultural work remains linked to industrial labor, we believe that the morality of labor would be enhanced." In each case the industrial bourgeoisie preferred to sacrifice the depressive effect on wages produced by a reserve army of labor in favor of conditions that appeared to sustain social order. In truth, the sacrifice was not all that great, for it was preferable that workers temporarily laid off have a piece of land to fall back on rather than to mill about in the streets. The least complacency about the future of relations between capital and labor came from the textile centers: the Vosges, the north, Saint-Quentin, Normandy, and the upper Loire. The chamber of commerce of Roanne urged measures to capitalize on the workers' alleged "love of property" to reduce the fever of class antagonism. In heavily agricultural areas, like the Vendée which produced more wheat than any other department, farmers employing labor on a regular basis reproduced the attitudes of the industrial bourgeoisie.[58]

By the latter part of the decade the crisis in production and the growing acceptability of national economics forced a reconsideration of the relations between capital and labor that went beyond repression and paternalism and yet combined elements of both. Eugène Tallon,

---

58. *Annales de l'Assemblée nationale*, XLI, 295–323, hereinafter cited as *Annales*; Ministère de l'agriculture, *Statistique agricole, 1879*, 247.

a conservative republican manufacturer from Clermont-Ferrand who
served on the Conseil supérieur du travail des enfants, argued in 1877
that the conception of "absolute freedom of labor" was a false and
dangerous abstraction, which, in reality, translated into the "absolute
freedom to be powerless, isolated, and miserable." The failure of some
of his class brethren to recognize "the modern industrial world," dominated by the "tensions of competition, the expansion of machinery, and
the spread of large enterprises," would estrange workers from the
republican system, he believed. Tallon welcomed the creation of independent workers' associations as a means to "solidly cement the
union of classes." Without prompt action, he warned, the atmosphere
would darken with conflict, as rumblings of class warfare reverberated
in a social climate already characterized by "two peoples living side by
side, regarding each other, on the one hand with suspicion, on the
other with anxiety, each filled with feelings of bitterness and antagonism."[59] Allain-Targé had sounded the same language, and he was
to become the chief architect of the parliamentary bill on associations
that became law in 1884.

Employers, particularly in textiles, had reason to fear the consequences for social peace of the crisis in production. Beginning in 1879,
a wave of strikes swept France at an accelerating rate. Official sources
recorded fifteen for the first quarter of 1879 and sixty-three for the
same period of 1882. Workers in textiles, especially in the various
branches of the cloth-weaving industry now largely mechanized, accounted for a large proportion of the strikers. Of the principal textile-
producing regions, the Vosges stood out as the theater of conflict in
1879. Saint-Quentin, Roubaix, and Saint-Étienne also witnessed several strikes. By 1882, the focus of strike action had shifted to the north.
These struggles of capital and labor focused mostly on workers' demands for higher wages, at a time when employers claimed they could
not sustain higher labor costs. In a few instances, the strikes persisted
for months, as in Vienne, where four thousand workers in the woolen
cloth industry stood off a coalition of sixty-five employers for five

59. Eugène Tallon, *La Vie morale et intellectuelle des ouvriers* (Paris: Plon,
1877), 2–45, 59, 63–67, 110–16.

months. The strike ended only when the workers' strike fund had become exhausted. More commonly the issues were settled in a few days through a combination of threats and administrative pressure against workers and a few exemplary dismissals of their leaders. In some cases employers agreed to raise wages while they compensated themselves by shortening the workday and reducing their contributions to insurance and pension funds.[60]

These experiences only proved that industrial conflicts resolved in such a manner constituted no solutions at all. Most important, they did not enhance the interests of the industrial bourgeoisie, who could ill afford sporadic disruptions of their operations at a time when they were struggling to maintain production and retain their markets. An approach that protected both the bourgeoisie's investment in capital and labor offered, if not the ultimate solution, more promise than existing arrangements. Solidarity through association thus appeared more attractive strictly on the grounds of class interest.

A social program, framed to relax worker-employer tensions, attempted to soften the crisis. Legalization of workers' associations— which would place workers on an equal footing with employers, convince workers of the capitalists' flexibility, and provide workers with a sense of common responsibility in the process of capitalist social production—appeared more and more attractive. Gradually, the most fervent exponents of solidarity led a coalition including hard-line paternalists and progressive republican reformers to support the legalization of independent workers' associations. That outcome proved less ironic than it appears; class collaboration under the fiction of an equality restrained within legal limits not only maintained the fact of bourgeois class rule, but established the mechanics to settle industrial disputes, making strikes unnecessary. The banker Paul Laffitte envisioned what might even be termed corporatist formations:

We have witnessed and we will continue to witness battles between capital and labor which are just as harmful to labor as they are to capital. Who then knows what might be accomplished by an association of employers

60. Grèves, 1879–1882, in F(12*) 5749, AN.

and an association of workers which, inspired by the same spirit of conciliation, would bring together the two parties in an atmosphere of steadiness
and of peace? . . . perhaps, then, the day will arrive when industry will
constitute a huge army in which everyone from the supreme commander
down to the lowest recruit will share the same interests, the same sense of
responsibility, and the same aspirations.[61]

Charles de Freycinet, chief engineer of the Republic, lent the impressive weight of his influence to reinforce the arguments for solidarity and protection. In September, 1878, he toured the northern
industrial region to promote his public works program. A year of
protectionist agitation had preceded his arrival, and that agitation had
frequently focused on the dangers of class conflict stemming from the
crisis in production. Alfred Delesalle, who often spoke for the employers of Lille, denounced free traders for irresponsibility on the social question and for peddling programs that threatened to dissolve
the solidarity of capital and labor. "The 1860 reforms . . . have
slammed the door" on proletarian upward mobility. Freycinet made
no secret of his concern for the social question and dismissed out of
hand a social policy that did not take serious account of the relations
between capital and labor. At Lille he affirmed the "duty of a republican government . . . to promote the well-being of the working classes, to guarantee them wages, and to protect them as much as possible
from the disasters of unemployment." Continuing to Douai, he com-
plimented the workers of Denain for their restraint and discipline and
exhorted workers in the Anzin coalfields, who had recently shown a
menacing militancy, to emulate their comrades and retain confidence
in the Republic. At a banquet hosted by the local bourgeoisie, Freycinet exuded confidence and sympathy and spoke of solidarity: "Let us
drink to the end of the crisis, to the rejuvenation of industry, to its
revival through the alliance and mutual confidence of capital and labor."[62] His words echoed beyond the north and reflected a general
consensus of social purpose: "To achieve the closest solidarity and

61. Paul Laffitte, "Les Corporations et les chambres syndicales d'ouvriers," *Revue
bleue,* No. 49 (June 2, 1877), 1163.
62. *Industriel français,* November 15, 1877, September 19, 1878.

mutuality between capital and labor"; to neutralize workers' political
formations by encouraging association, the best "guarantee of social
peace"; to develop the "human solidarity" of citizens against the di-
visiveness of separate class identity; and to defeat socialism by enlightened state and employer social action.[63]

Leading exponents of national economics, the protectionist faction
of the industrial bourgeoisie, did not need to be told of the importance
of the solidarity of capital and labor. They faced the stark reality of
deteriorating market conditions, which had begun to produce a decline
in the rate of profit. For them, higher tariffs would serve not only to
blunt the edge of the crisis, but also would provide shelter against the
storms of class struggle. "In these difficult times," Nicholas Claude
told the April, 1878, meeting of the Vosges general council, "it is all
the more essential to provide for the security of labor and to protect
our workers against unemployment." Later in the same year Claude
warned that if the free traders prevail "they will have succeeded in delivering a crippling blow to the Republic, incensing our working
people who will be reduced to starvation once our plants are forced
to shut down."[64] Claude's counterparts in Normandy already began
to take action. Spinning and weaving plants in the Le Havre region
and in the city itself cut their work week from six to five days with
threats of further reductions without any wage compensations. The
merchants and industrialists of Le Havre followed the tendencies to a
menacing denouement: commodity prices continued to rise, negating
the benefits produced by the rise in real wages since 1860. Their "industries, exposed to cutthroat foreign competition, which will ruin
them," will collapse, followed by "tremendous damage to our prosperity and to the domestic tranquillity." Two years later, while the
economic debate still raged, the bourgeoisie of Le Havre recalled how
the big bourgeoisie clustered around MacMahon had attempted to

63. "Les Grèves et la question sociale," *Journal des économistes,* IX (March,
1878), 186; *Union républicaine de la Saône-et-Loire,* September 1, 1881; *Progrès du
Nord,* October 26, 1881; *Démocratie franc-comtoise* (Besançon), October 3, 1881;
Avenir clermontois, December 9, 1881.
64. *Progrès du Nord,* February 4, 1878; *Industriel français,* April 9, 1878;
Mémorial des Vosges, October 22, 1878.

sabotage the interests of national industry by blocking all efforts to raise tariffs.[65]

Free trade, the protectionists agreed, generated forces that drove employers and workers into further conflict. Naturally, the former expected the latter to absorb the worst blows, but not without exacting a price. Thus, a nationalist economic policy in their view realistically confronted the "heavy responsibilities that [encompass] the whole question of public order." The government of the *seize mai,* in its abject surrender to big bourgeois liberalism, criminally evaded those responsibilities. Fourtou, MacMahon's minister of the interior and chief manager of the government's political affairs, had promised "security for business." Instead, from the textile and metallurgical entrepreneurs' point of view, the opposite appeared to be the case. Delegations from the coal-producing areas of the Gard and the Loire (La Grand' Combe and the Saint-Étienne basin, respectively) reminded Marie de Meaux, minister for agriculture and commerce, that "we have under our tutelage a numerous and active working population; we cannot stand by while our stake in a substantial capital investment is compromised." In each case, rates of profit sharply declined from the exceptionally high levels reached in the early 1870s. The Loire Mines Company, which dominated production in the Saint-Étienne basin, experienced a precipitous drop in production, from which it did not recover until the mid-1890s. In contrast, the mines of La Grand' Combe continued to increase production and maintain a steadily employed labor force, apparently counting on exploitation of its deep seams and the forthcoming return to republican (*i.e.,* industrial) government to see them through the crisis. More enlightened policies were expected of a republican government, which by definition was closely attuned to the interests of "national industry, which is to say the interests of the laboring classes."[66]

Although no one in France argued directly that tariff revenues

65. *Industriel français,* July 25, 1878; *Journal du Havre,* May 2, 1878; *Journal du commerce maritime et des colonies* (Le Havre), April 2, 1880.
66. *Industriel français,* July 12, August 16 and 23, 1877, March 21, 1878; Jean Bouvier *et al., Le Mouvement du profit en France au xix siècle* (Paris: Mouton, 1965), 379, 404, 407; *Soleil* (Paris), March 12, 1878.

might constitute a fund to be expended on social reform, as was the case in England during Joseph Chamberlain's tariff reform campaign,[67] French protectionists at least attempted to make the case that the republican system, managed by an industrial bourgeoisie deeply committed to the egalitarian tradition, promised social reform on the basis of national solidarity. The reactionary-clerical bloc, on the other hand, stood behind "aristocratic" and antipopular policies. Gustave Masure, addressing "the workers of the Nord," urged them to rally to the Republic. On the occasion of François Raspail's death, Masure hailed the "great popular leader" for his leadership in social reform and summoned bourgeois republicans and workers to conquer new terrain "through wisdom, calm measures, respect for the law, and commitment to duty."[68] Masure echoed the sentiments of the Lille textile *patronat*, the machinery industrialists associated with them, and the coal mine operators of the Nord and Pas-de-Calais basin. Although the latter sustained foreign competition effortlessly and were to improve their position when the canal network to Paris was completed, they supported their textile brethren. Their support not only gave evidence of class solidarity, but the determinants of business as well. "The companies of the Nord and the Pas-de-Calais [drew] the major part of their shareholders and directors from . . . the bourgeoisie of the towns of Cambrai, Valenciennes, and Lille-Roubaix-Tourcoing" and their capital from local banks, such as the Crédit du Nord.[69]

Intensification of work with the purpose of cutting costs represented another way in which French entrepreneurs attempted to meet their competition. The Société industrielle of Amiens devoted serious study to the problem of the workers' tendency to extend their Sunday holiday through Monday. Its report was written by Maxime Lecomte, himself a lawyer representing northern interests and soon to become a deputy from the department of the Nord. *Le chômage de lundi* not only left plants shorthanded, but separated workers from the discipline

67. See, for Britain, the pioneering work of Bernard Semmel, *Imperialism and Social Reform* (London: Unwin, 1960).
68. *Progrès du Nord*, January 21, February 19, 1878.
69. Marcel Gillet, "The Coal Age and the Rise of Coalfields in the North and the Pas-de-Calais," in François Crouzet *et al.* (eds.), *Essays in European Economic History* (London: Arnold, 1969), 198.

of the factory. Unsupervised leisure time promoted bad habits: laziness and drunkenness. "The atelier routine suffers disorganization, true enough, but what is more serious, the cohesion of the working-class family is profoundly shaken." Lecomte had little faith in the success of direct disciplinary action unless coordinated by "all the principal industrialists of the region." He considered education to be the best weapon against *le chômage de lundi,* education directing workers onto the path of sobriety and responsibility and education in the virtues of thrift. "By saving will the worker raise himself. It will allow him to work, not only longer (thereby increasing his wages), but more effectively and under improved conditions. By convincing the workers to save and by creating the necessary facilities, [employers] will inspire them with a passion for order and economy." Lecomte referred specifically to workers' savings channeled into funds from which employers would draw investment capital, promoting as well the solidarity of capital and labor in a common enterprise. Proudly he concluded that such an effort constituted the "highest expression of patriotism, progress, harmony," and social peace.[70]

In a move that seemed to point in a direction opposite from that taken by Lecomte, several leading republican politicians of the textile industry pressed for a reduction in the working day. The bill introduced initially in 1880 by Richard Waddington, Gustave Masure, Pierre Legrand, and Auguste Dautresme provided for a limit of ten hours in the six-day week in all establishments employing more than twenty-five persons. Waddington, whose cotton plants in the Rouen region were second in size only to those of Pouyer-Quertier and whose workers called his factories "capitalist prisons," made much of his paternal commitments. He expected workers to use their time for rest, instruction, and recreation—all under the guidance of the patron. On strict economic grounds, the politicians of northern and Norman textiles argued that a controlled reduction in work time would permit more efficient utilization of fixed capital and thus arm them with a weapon against foreign competition.

Dissenting voices condemning the movement that linked solidar-

70. *Industriel français,* September 6, 13, and 27, October 4, 1877.

ity and protection were heard. Not unexpectedly, they arose from the ranks of free traders. Arthur Mangin, writing in Leroy-Beaulieu's *Économiste français,* denounced the whole movement toward reform, calling it a marriage of "protectionism and socialism." He foresaw the widening shadow of state intervention in the political economy and the implementation of the ten-hour day followed quickly by worker agitation for further reductions and higher wages. In fact, Mangin alleged, the textile tycoons' only purpose was to drive small producers out of business, to replace competition with concentration and oligopoly. They pretended to fear external competition while in reality they coveted control of the internal market.[71] Yves Guyot, who ghost-wrote Émile Menier's radical tracts, feared that such measures would strike at the heart of the industrial system itself. He anticipated workers retreating to a narrow corporatism reminiscent of the transition to capitalist industry, "falling into the errors of protectionism," and "turning their backs on the machine." As for the numerous and poorest classes, they would become victims of a system of high protection that maintained artificially high prices on articles of mass consumption. Universal suffrage without cheap goods, at best, meant nothing and, at worse, was a cruel joke. Resurrecting the argument once used to defend the Cobden-Chevalier Treaty of 1860, one commentator welcomed the inevitable "birth and development of the huge factory, big manufacturing and the impossibility of capital-poor firms to sustain the feverish struggle, in a word, the crushing of petty production."[72]

Free traders argued consistently that the untrammeled movement of commodities across France's borders provided the most secure hedge against social unrest. Free trade stimulated business, boosted agriculture, and thus produced high levels of employment and wages. Economic indicators, however, pointed in the opposite direction and especially revealed a tendency toward concentration that the free traders themselves appeared to welcome.[73] These facts tended to link a national policy of industrial protection with a parallel movement

71. *Économiste français,* June 24, 1882.
72. *Réforme économique,* Ser. 3, III (1880), 354; *Temps,* August 28, 1881.
73. Yves Guyot, *La Libre-échange et le travail* (Paris: Alcan, 1883).

toward social reform. A policy of protection implicitly followed; it was not the socialism of the collective action by workers against capital, but the "socialism" embodied in the national solidarity of capital and labor. What liberals called "protectionism and socialism" in fact constituted a widespread effort by provincial capitalists to defend their command of social production, the foundation, as one of them put it, of "our republican system."[74]

Thus, entrepreneurs did not abandon their resistance to independent workers' associations or retreat from the most coercive devices of paternalism just because of the growing power of the organized working class. On the contrary, the regularization of employer-employee relations constituted a significant step forward toward ending the "war against capitalists" carried on by "certain political sects" that strove for the conquest of political power. "The laboring classes must recognize that [strikes and other forms of class confrontation] inevitably will plunge them into misery and undermine the prosperity of the nation. . . . The association of capital and labor is an inescapable necessity [that will] enhance the more profitable utilization of our productive forces." Association also had a practical application beyond solidifying the solidarity of capital and labor. Protectionists emphasized the rising costs of labor as a major contributing factor to the crisis they endured. The wholesale elimination of jobs would gain them only a Pyrrhic victory as massive unemployment threatened to unleash social warfare.[75] The Paris chamber of commerce, which had opposed the movement favoring tariff retaliation, nevertheless urged businessmen to develop the internal market. To do so successfully in the face of foreign competition required concerted efforts to keep down the price of labor. The chamber called for more benevolent paternal-

---

74. *Enquête parlementaire sur la crise économique et sur la situation industrielle, commerciale, et agricole en France, 1884*, in C 3223, réponses des chambres de commerce de Saint-Quentin, Grenoble, Montpellier, Elbeuf, in C 3329, AN; Jacquet, a republican, attacking Gambon, a radical, in *République de Nevers*, July 16, 1881.

75. *Enquête parlementaire*, in C 3223, réponse de la chambre de commerce d'Angoulême, in C 3329, petition to the Chamber of Deputies from 130 municipal councilors, merchants, and industrialists of Niort, December 8, 1877, in F (12) 6171, AN.

ism to sugar the pill, including pension benefits and encouraging workers to develop a stake in enterprises, as a means of "eliminating ... the antagonism that prevails between labor and capital."[76]

Eugène Spuller made the same point directly to the businessmen of Paris in 1880: "Let your hearts beat in harmony with the great heart of France ... because the most vital and pressing interests of the nation demand order, peace, and the reconciliation of classes." Gambetta, unlike Spuller, did not advocate an unambiguous nationalist economic policy. Nevertheless, he articulated the general bourgeois class position on the solidarity of capital and labor, and he made the direct connection between the "intimate union of classes" and a new burst of capitalist energy. He forcefully urged businessmen to abandon their marketplace mentality in favor of national social action to fortify national production. Gambetta understood that the "union of classes" constituted a powerful weapon in defense of the bourgeois social order. He declared that freedom of association assured "guarantees that a liberal regime must accept, guarantees that will bring labor and capital face to face, no longer as antagonists, as rivals and implacable combatants consumed with hatred, but ... as two forces destined to fuse their energies" for the vitality of French production.[77]

The politicians did not content themselves with words. One example may be taken as typical. René Waldeck-Rousseau made contact in 1876 with Joseph Barberet, a Paris baker promoting reformist syndicalist associations with employer support. Waldeck-Rousseau launched his career as a lawyer representing various business interests in Rennes and Nantes. His move to Paris and subsequent election as a deputy for the Ille-et-Vilaine marked a leap forward in his political and financial fortunes. Waldeck-Rousseau's social outlook may be summarized in Pierre Sorlin's apt phrase: "faire entrer le prolétariat

76. *Moniteur officiel du commerce*, August 9, 1883.
77. Eugène Spuller, *Éducation de la démocratie* (Paris: Alcan, 1892), 27, speech delivered on November 1, 1880; Joseph Reinach (ed.), *Discours et plaidoyers politiques de Gambetta* (11 vols.; Paris: n.p., 1881–85), IX, 172–75, speech delivered at the banquet of the Chambres syndicales de l'union du commerce et de l'industrie, March 25, 1881; Léon Gambetta, *Discours à l'assemblée générale de la société l'union du commerce, prononcé le 20 mars 1881* (Paris: Union nationale du commerce, 1881), 15.

dans la bourgeoisie."[78] He believed firmly and seriously in solidarity, in the Republic's destiny to inaugurate an era of class reconciliation under the guidance of the ruling bourgeoisie, and in the unlimited opportunities awaiting anyone who took "the high road of hard work." No narrow reactionary, Waldeck-Rousseau argued with his best lawyer's logic in 1881 for the railroad commissionaires' right to a secure contract, denied them by the railroad companies. He was joined in this effort by several leading republicans, among them Allain-Targé, Germain Casse, Constans, the textile contingent of Dautresme, Masure, Ferry, Legrand, Waddington, and by Joseph Cazot of Nîmes—himself the principal stockholder in a local railroad.[79]

Waldeck-Rousseau's patronage of Barberet did not happen by accident. The latter had been working since 1873 to integrate workers into the republican system. He fought every effort by Parisian working-class leaders to separate workers into a class movement. Barberet and his associates "patronized the workers' movement in order to retain their influence in these circles, but they shied away from anything that resembled class separation and, a fortiori, the idea of class struggle, the consequences of which would be to detach workers from the bourgeoisie, whether conservative or radical."[80] He negotiated a government subsidy for a contingent of moderate workers to attend the International Exposition in Philadelphia in 1876. They returned locked in bitter combat with an independent workers' group that had published, "in the name of all French workers," a "declaration of war of the proletariat against the bourgeoisie, a war for the very existence of our class." Their manifesto ended: "War against individualism! War against capitalism!"[81] Barberet confronted these same people two

78. Pierre Sorlin's excellent biography, *Waldeck-Rousseau* (Paris: Colin, 1966), especially Chap. 5, should be consulted on the details of Waldeck-Rousseau's social program.

79. René Waldeck-Rousseau, *L'État et la liberté* (Paris: Fasquelle, 1893), 3, speech delivered on September 29, 1879; René Waldeck-Rousseau, *Questions sociales* (Paris: Fasquelle, 1895), 3–18; *JOC*, March 3, 1881; Procès-verbaux de la commission chargée du projet de loi tendant à regler les rapports entre les compagnies de chemins de fer et leurs agents commissionés, séance du 24 mars 1880, in C 3179, AN.

80. Montet, "Le Mouvement ouvrier à Paris," 17; Joseph Barberet, *La Bataille des intérêts* (Paris: Cinqualbre, 1879), 155–210, 380–82.

81. Benoît Malon, "Le Mouvement syndical de 1872 à 1878," *Revue socialiste* (October, 1886), 868–75, 880–82.

years later, at the Lyon session of the Congrès ouvrier, and again at Marseille the following year, where he led the losing struggle by the mutualists and Proudhonists against Jules Guesde's collectivists. His republican friends did not forget him, for he remained useful. Ernest Constans, minister of the interior under Jules Ferry in 1881, appointed Barberet to direct administrative surveillance of *sociétés profession-nelles* in his ministry. When Waldeck-Rousseau succeeded Constans later in the year, Barberet remained at his post.[82]

Barberet's political collaboration with the republicans no doubt was founded on his conviction that his way constituted the best hope for improving the lot of workers. Nevertheless, he could not avoid falling into ideological collaboration with men who, like himself, opposed the big bourgeoisie while never ceasing to defend the Republic's social foundations in the bourgeois order.

The law on associations of 1884 that followed the class consensus underwent a four-year gestation period. Several versions passed the Chamber of Deputies only to be rejected by the Senate. The latter's actions generally have been cited to illustrate that body's inflexibly reactionary character, but, since 1879, the Senate had been "republican" by all counts.[83] The paradox is more apparent than real. "Republicans," which included everyone who was not an out-and-out monarchist, never marched in lockstep on every issue. Furthermore, we should recall that the procedure devised to elect senators favored rural and small-town petty producers who remained separate from the mainstream of capitalist production—if they did not see it as a positive threat. Thus they did not favor measures to stabilize the capitalist order, especially measures singling out workers for special consideration. Certainly the law threatened to drive a wedge between capitalists and petty producers. However, it did not directly tax the pocketbooks of the latter, so the alliance remained intact.

Henri Allain-Targé contributed the most to the formulation of the bill that became law, in modified form, in 1884. His social views

82. M. Egrot and J. Maitron (eds.), *Dictionnaire biographique du mouvement ouvrier français* (6 vols. to date; Paris: Editions ouvrières, 1969–), IV, 183–84.

83. See, for example, Jean Lhomme, *La Grande bourgeoisie au pouvoir* (Paris: Presses universitaires de France, 1960), Pt. 3.

need no further elaboration except to report his violent hostility to all forms of socialist collectivism. He denounced socialism as the expression of doctrines contrary to the spirit of France, better suited to "Asiatics" and to "Moslem and Slavic peoples."[84] Charles Floquet and Joseph Cazot supported Allain-Targé's efforts. Floquet told his Paris constituents in 1879 that "the social revolution was accomplished in 1792." He looked forward to an era of class reconciliation under republican democracy when social questions "will be settled by the peaceful and determined efforts of the democratic electorate."[85] Cazot, as early as 1876, warned of the difficulties involved in achieving measurable social progress: "Every gain registered by the concentrated action of capital produces the contradictory subjection of the impoverished masses." He urged businessmen to study the writings of Proudhon on workers' associations and cooperatives and heralded the dawn of "the solidarization of the total population on the basis of liberty and equality."[86] Another version of the law on association, sponsored by Laroche-Joubert, made its point in the bluntest terms: "Association . . . represents both our benevolence and our commitment to systematic regulation: benevolence, because it will . . . produce an improvement in the lives of the greatest number; systematic regulation, because this powerful instrument of progress . . . will remain securely under our control and not become a dangerous weapon in the hands of unscrupulous men."[87]

Allain-Targé's report went beyond a simple summary of the discussions of the committee for which he was secretary and *rapporteur*. It bore the individual stamp of his mind and confirmed him as a leading architect of republican social ideology, to which his earlier work had already borne witness. In the report he combined the essential ingredients of the republican program: the solidarity of capital

---

84. *Union républicaine de Paris,* August 22, 1881.

85. Charles Floquet, *Discours et opinions* (2 vols.; Paris: Dervaux, 1885), I, 251–52.

86. Report of June 9, 1876, on Cazot's speech to the Masonic lodge, Alsace-Lorraine, in B/a 1004, APP; Projet de loi sur les syndicats professionnels proposé par Cazot et Tirard, November 22, 1880, in C 3290, d. 1951, AN.

87. Proposition de loi sur les associations et sociétés proposée par Laroche-Joubert, March 19, 1880, in C 3290, AN.

and labor, social defense, a nationalist economic perspective, and a realistic appraisal of the logic of industrial concentration.

He made the obvious point that independent workers' associations already existed in large numbers as did associations of employers. However, whereas the latter operated freely, the former existed under the "constant threat" of dissolution and administrative repression. Liberated from their "isolation" and free to pursue the "amelioration of their condition," workers would abandon the strike as a weapon of class warfare. "Experience has shown that wherever workers' *syndicats* exist [and are tolerated] strikes are rare or, [when they occur], are of brief duration." Thus, removing the heavy hand of police surveillance with the repeal of the notorious Articles 231 and 234 of the penal code constituted an act of appeasement and an important step toward establishing social peace. Whatever arguments had been marshaled against freedom of association and whatever resistance that policy had encountered were forced to submit before the fact that associations were inspired by "peaceful goals, aspirations to order and equilibrium . . . [and] represented a repudiation of violent and revolutionary tactics." Social order under the Republic demanded that those workers who "seek to free themselves from vague theories and utopian notions in favor of taking the practical road to social improvement" be supported with the full force of legislative power.[88]

Allain-Targé made no concessions to the spirit of small enterprise. He welcomed the domination of industry by "steam" and "the machine" and accepted the implications for progressive industrial concentration. The task remained to arm "national industry against the fierce competition" generated by other nations. The periodic crises produced by this "vicious competition" would wipe out the small factory. "It has become increasingly necessary to concentrate and to mobilize all productive resources and great masses of capital." Workers themselves were to be "mobilized, concentrated, and disciplined in mass formations for action on the industrial battlefield." National industry and the

---

88. Annexe à la séance du 15 mars 1881, Rapport fait au nom de la commission chargée d'éxaminer le projet de loi rélatif aux syndicats professionnels, par M. Allain-Targé, *JOC.*

necessity to avoid "political perils" to the Republic demanded as much. "Finally, is not any other policy [that refuses to recognize the right of association] subversive of the pressing economic, industrial, and commercial interests of France?" [89]

Allain-Targé's text received wide publicity in the republican press. In one place large chunks of his report were reproduced, followed by a concise assessment of its primary social purpose: "Association is indispensable for reestablishing the equilibrium between the two elements of production [capital and labor]. It will provide the best guarantee of republican stability." [90]

Liberalized association represented a triumph for the French working class insofar as it was liberated from direct police sanctions over its own organizations. (This advance should not be confused with the continued willingness of the state to use the police and the army to smash strikes.) Liberalized association also and contradictorily represented the maturation of the ideological wisdom of the French bourgeoisie, again insofar as it recognized and was willing to implement means to enforce the solidarity of capital and labor and thus to defend the republican system on solid grounds. We must also recognize, as the republican bourgeoisie recognized, that the bourgeoisie had other weapons in its arsenal, that the liberalization of the laws on association occurred simultaneously with the extension of the railroad system, the reform of primary education, the movement toward protection, and, finally, a heightened commitment to overseas empire.

89. *Ibid.*, May 17, 1881.
90. Clipping from *Indépendent*, March 16, 1881, in B/a 929, APP.

Chapter VII

⟦ *Social*
⟦ *Imperialism*

FRENCH OVERSEAS EXPANSION had a history that spanned many generations preceding the birth of the Third Republic. In the modern industrial age the acquisition of colonies and the export of capital became enlarged in scope and took on a qualitatively different aspect. Economic expansion beyond the frontiers of France began to accelerate dramatically in the years covered in this study. Specifically, from the late 1860s to the middle 1880s, French development of West and Equatorial Africa, Southeast Asia, and the Maghreb became significant imperial enterprises. From the Senegal to Tonkin, merchants, bankers, planters, and soldiers marched forward to stake out new territories and to consolidate old ones. These events provide the backdrop for the following examination of the social determinants of imperialism and their relationship to the consolidation of the Republic. The discussion starts from the premise that imperialism, like charity, begins at home.

Imperialism, Lenin wrote, represents the highest stage of capitalism and reaches its peak when finance capital conquers the commanding heights of the political economy. At that point, the progressive export of capital becomes necessary to the survival of capitalism itself.[1] France provides a variation on this model, without necessarily proving an exception to it. The export of capital takes on many forms. Finance capital remained strong (indeed gained strength) within the French

1. V. I. Lenin, *Imperialism: The Highest Stage of Capitalism* (numerous editions, first published in 1915).

economy even though the big financial bourgeoisie were forced to surrender political ground. French banks had exported capital for several decades before the Third Republic and would continue to do so, in the form of government loans, investments in foreign railroads, and the like. France's financial sector formed one element, one might say even an element apart, of the republican socioeconomic system.

In our period, the crisis in production threatened the stability of that system and particularly the social balance upon which it rested. Capitalism no longer existed, in Eric Hobsbawm's words, "as a super-structure erected on the immovable base of peasantry and petty bour-geoisie."[2] Capitalism, as a mode of social production, had taken center stage and yet continued to coexist with petty production. The working class also occupied a portion of that stage and, from the bourgeois point of view, added a new dimension to the crisis. Thus, in examining the republican conception of empire and republican imperialism in action, I will emphasize the social aspect of the story. That explains my use of the term "social imperialism" to underscore a policy designed to buttress the republican system, while not downgrading the role of profit seeking in French imperialism. There is no question of "prestige" or "glory" apart from the social context. In any event, for the Far East at least, John Laffey has effectively demolished the argument for prestige and glory as motivations for French imperial expansion.[3]

Reference was made earlier to social imperialism in the context of Jules Siegfried's enterprises in educational reform. As one of the great merchants of France, his imperial interests come as no surprise and have already been described.[4] However, Siegfried also possessed close business and family ties to the industrial regions of the east, and he was a member in high standing of the established republican bour-geoisie. Not so Victor Hugo, who nevertheless provided the most

2. Eric J. Hobsbawm, *The Age of Revolution* (London: Weidenfeld & Nicolson, 1962), 178.
3. John Laffey, "The Roots of French Imperialism: The Case of Lyon," *French Historical Studies*, VI (Spring, 1969), 78–93; John Laffey, "Les Racines de l'impérial-isme français dans l'extrême orient," *Revue d'histoire moderne et contemporaine*, XVI (April-June, 1969), 282–300.
4. See Chapter V herein.

rhetorically ornate explication of social imperialism (in this one instance, I leave the quotation in French, for it loses everything in translation) :

Au dix-neuvième siècle, le blanc a fait du noir un homme; au vingtième siècle, l'Europe fera de l'Afrique nouvelle, rendre la vieille Afrique maniable à la civilization, tel est le problème, l'Europe le résoudra. Allez peuples! emparez-vous de cette terre. Prenez-là. A qui? À personne. Prenez cette terre à Dieu. Dieu donne la terre aux hommes. Dieu offre l'Afrique à l'Europe. Prenez-là. Où les rois apporteraient la guerre, apportez la concorde. Prenez-là, non par le canon, mais par la charrue; non par le sabre, mais par le commerce; non par la bataille, mais par l'industrie; non par la conquête, mais par la fraternité. Versez votre trop-plein dans cette Afrique, et du même coup résolvez vos questions sociales, changez vos prolétaires en propriétaires; allez, faites, faites des routes, faites des ports, faites des villes, croissez, cultivez, colonisez, multipliez; et que, sur cette terre, de plus en plus dégagée des prêtres et des princes, l'esprit divin s'affirme par la paix et l'esprit humain par la liberté.[5]

Siegfried, a conservative gentleman, would not have put the matter in such language, at least not publicly. But he would have agreed with its spirit.

As would have many others, for imperialism exerted a unifying force across a broad front, from the republican bourgeois industrialists and their spokesmen to the sometime radical voices of petty production. A few hard-line liberals, like Yves Guyot, held out, not so much as opponents of empire as critics of social imperialism and its offspring— metropolitan-colonial integration.[6] Leroy-Beaulieu, in 1881, appeared to have changed his mind from 1870, when he had argued against *colonies de peuplement* in *La Colonisation chez les peuples modernes*. He now argued for the conquest, annexation, and development of Tonkin.[7] Frédéric Le Play's disciples, showing, for a change, good bourgeois sense, expressed excitement over the French penetration

5. *Union nationale du commerce et de l'industrie* (Paris), May 8, 1880, speech before a group of Paris businessmen, May 19, 1879.
6. *Réforme économique*, Ser. 3, I (1879), 111–17, 174–80; Louis Kerrilis, "De la colonisation française," *Journal des économistes* (February, 1881), 263–86.
7. *Économiste français*, August 20, 1881.

into Africa.[8] On the radical side, Georges Clemenceau and Georges Périn, leaders in the attack against Jules Ferry's Tunisian policy, earned the special mention by a leading colonial propaganda organ as "old friends of the colonies."[9]

Profit seeking naturally dominated the politics of imperialism for the republican bourgeoisie, for example, as in the involvement of Jean David and Louis Robert-Dehault, who was the senator from the Haute-Marne and mayor of Saint-Dizier, in the *Messagéries fluviales de la Cochinchine*, and in Joseph Cazot's presence on the board of the Crédit mobilier.[10] Nevertheless, considerations of social order always followed as another element in the total complex of relations connected to capitalist social production. One journalist, a strong supporter of Gambetta, made a modest proposal. He suggested sending all French children on public welfare to work in Algeria: "They should be sent when they reach the age of twelve and given some training in farming skills. Then they will be placed on selected farms, thus taking up the slack in the number of available agricultural proletarians. When they marry, they will receive some land of their own, along with a small loan to begin its development as a paying proposition."[11]

Social Imperialism Defined

For a full statement on social imperialism, we must look closely at Jules Ferry, who emerged in the late 1870s as its principal ideologist and a leading proponent of economic nationalism. During his political apprenticeship in the previous years, Ferry had developed the underpinnings of a theoretical position that came to life in the programs for education and extended empire. Ferry did not stand out in the great debates on railroads or on tariff revision. However, he would have been

8. *Réforme sociale* (February 15, 1884), 175–76.
9. *France coloniale*, January 8, 1880.
10. *France populaire*, September 27, 1881; Jean Ganiage, *Les Origines du protectorat français en Tunisie* (Paris: Presses universitaires de France, 1959), 657.
11. *Paris*, July 9, 1881. We have no way of knowing whether the author of the preceding had been familiar with Edward Gibbon Wakefield's *The Art of Colonization*, published in 1835. However, the proposal bears a striking resemblance to Wakefield's schemes for populating England's "white" colonies, especially Canada. Then again, the similarity may merely reflect conventional wisdom.

the first to recognize that a coherent social policy for the Republic necessarily included all these elements in a closely articulated order. Ferry's perspective derived from his formation among the textile bourgeoisie of the east. His experience produced a sharp intellectual appreciation of the social dimensions of the modern industrial order. He confronted the challenge of social upheaval with a comprehensive program for educational reform.[12] His forays into political economy struck a somewhat different note, deploring on the one hand the process of capitalist concentration while on the other seeking the keys to untroubled bourgeois class rule within the terms set by that process of concentration. Ferry, like so many of his associates, viewed the Republic as a fortress of social order.

In *La Concentration industrielle* (1870) Ferry recalled the struggle of the industrial bourgeoisie to liberate itself from the "despotism of big capital." Under the umbrella of a powerful state apparatus, a "capitalist oligarchy" had launched France onto the path of capitalist enterprise through the exercise of monopoly and concentration. The oligarchy's achievements in the accumulation of capital did not stand the test of social utility. It proved "incapable of providing the leaders, the traditions, the examples to [our] hardworking society, incapable of establishing from generation to generation that continuity in factories and in business establishments that constitutes the strength of genuinely industrial nations." Liberty, to these capitalists, remained imprisoned within the bonds of self-interest and never extended to the national economy. The Revolution did nothing to correct matters. Its doctrinaire application of libertarian principles ruled out for a generation the productive association of entrepreneurs. Big capital remained supreme, backed up by the monopoly power of the Bank of France. Small entrepreneurs found themselves hemmed in by a poverty of capital and by high rates of interest. When the challenge to the French from across the Channel became irresistible, their choices were reduced to competing on the world market at a disadvantage, accelerating the process of concentration to lower costs, or maintaining the labor-intensive character of French industry with its attendant

12. See Chapter V herein.

social costs. Ferry illustrated the social consequences of technical transformation by reference to the industry closest to him, textile production. He cited the testimony of Jules Brame of Lille: "From domestic production, from handweaving which supplements agricultural work, we must move to concentrated labor, to the socialization of the weaving process . . . to a system of large units utilizing mechanical and efficient methods of production." None of this was reversible, and with the disappearance of the "struggle of competition" under conditions in which "collective direction replaced individual action," the class of industrial entrepreneurs found in their hands the responsibility for directing social affairs. Ferry summoned them to meet those responsibilities. "The challenge of modern industry amounts to the following: To open the way for the masses to achieve the full benefits of social life, and, consequently, to reduce continually the costs of production, to put within their reach material comfort that becomes progressively cheaper to acquire."[13]

Ferry's other important work of this period, Les Comptes fantastiques d'Haussmann, cast the same argument in polemical form. He attacked Baron Georges d'Haussmann's demolition of the old Paris for its disruptive social consequences. The prefect had systematically dismantled "the Paris of artists and philosophers . . . where the artisan . . . lives cheek by jowl with the financier," he had raised monuments to "triumphant vulgarity," and in the process he had broken the bonds uniting classes, whose physical intimacy in the traditional environment had engendered a spirit of social solidarity.[14] Ferry underlined the inadequacy of the libertarian tradition of 1789 that had canonized the dogmatic assertion of individual rights and the "shattering of social life." But he did not propose to deploy effective countermeasures against the free working out of the economic system. He accepted what he called "the inevitable law of modern industry: the progressive differentiation between capital and labor and the growing distinction

13. Jules Ferry, "La Concentration industrielle," Discours et opinions de Jules Ferry (7 vols.; Paris: Colin, 1891), VII, 500–35.
14. Jules Ferry, Les Comptes fantastiques d'Haussmann (Paris: Chevalier, 1868), 8.

between the role of the capitalist and that of the worker."[15] Seeking corrections that would not disturb the established socioeconomic order, Ferry prescribed universal secular education and an aggressive colonial policy. The elements of disintegration unleashed by the forces of social change were not to be attacked at their sources, but rather sublimated and exported.

Several years later, while defending his imperial policy as a whole, Ferry summarized the logic of his thought and made the definitive statement for social imperialism. As he viewed it, imperialism was the "offspring of modern industrial development." The crisis in production, which to him constituted a social crisis, could be averted only through colonial expansion. What follows has been quoted often, to the point that it has nearly reached the exalted status of a cliché, but we must listen again:

The protectionist system is like a steam engine without an escape valve, if it is not complemented by a careful and serious colonial policy. The great amount of capital committed to our industrial plant works only to diminish the profits from that capital, and the consequence will be to depress the wages of labor. . . . Social peace, in this industrial age, is tied to the expansion of markets. . . . Consumption in Europe has reached the point of saturation; we must develop new masses of consumers in other parts of the world; [for if we do not] we will concede the doom of modern society and prepare for the dawn of the twentieth century a social upheaval of cataclysmic proportions whose ultimate consequences no man today can predict.[16]

Even before the crisis in production made its initial measurable impact, industrialists raised their voices for a coherent imperial policy. By 1874, the chambers of commerce in the chief textile-producing regions of the north, Normandy, and the east launched a campaign to develop more aggressive imperial policies. Rouen cotton producers, whose exports went "almost exclusively to Algeria," demanded special

15. Quoted in Louis Legrand, *L'Influence du positivisme dans l'oeuvre scolaire de Jules Ferry* (Paris: Rivière, 1959), 125–26, 211.
16. Jules Ferry, *Le Tonkin et la mère-patrie: Témoignages et documents* (Paris: Havard, 1890), 38–43.

protection there and in other less active colonial entrepôts. The wool producers of Elbeuf feared that their markets in America, Germany, and the Near East would shrink, leaving them with overproduction and redundant workers. They, as did the entrepreneurs of Lille and the cotton manufacturers of the Vosges, looked to aggressive imperial expansion, especially in the further development of Algeria, to provide a safety valve for production. Lille businessmen added a bid for state action to encourage education in foreign languages, geography, and the techniques of international trade.[17] As the protectionist movement grew, republican policy moved toward a tighter integration of France's most favored colony Algeria into the metropolitan economic structure. This view translated itself into pressure to merge Algerian tariffs with those of France and was intended to produce a larger protected market within which French production, partially insulated against the shocks of the crisis, would sustain its profits and levels of employment. As the liberal Yves Guyot noted with bitterness and anger, such action summoned up a program of national economics on all levels.[18]

The coming of the crisis multiplied and amplified the pressure for a protected metropolitan-colonial political economy. When the bourgeoisie spoke of "assimilation," this is generally what they meant. Napoleon III's imperial policy had functioned in reverse, which was consistent with his commitment to free trade. His tariff regime gave neither colonial products preference in the French market nor French products in colonial markets.[19] Louis Napoleon also reversed the process known as *cantonnement indigène*, an administrative device used to separate the Arabs from their lands to pave the way for European colonists to seize those lands for themselves. One of the first decrees of the republican regime on Algeria reinstituted the preimperial policy and placed all lands under French civil law. Its formal purpose was to

17. Réponses au questionnaire de la commission officielle pour le développement du commerce extérieur, in F(12) 2487 (b), Archives nationales, hereinafter cited as AN.

18. Yves Guyot, *Lettres sur la politique coloniale* (Paris: Reinwald, 1885), 339.

19. Arthur Girault, *The Colonial Tariff Policy of France* (Oxford: Clarendon Press, 1916), 66–80, notes one exception to the rule: colonial sugar. French beet sugar producers forced the state to rescind its preferential status. That happened on January 1, 1870, the day before Émile Ollivier came to power and signaled a conservative turn to imperial trade policy.

facilitate commerce between Arab and European; in fact, it encouraged the plunder of the former by the latter.[20] The movement toward tariff assimilation expressed what Arthur Girault called the "traditional tendencies of the republican party" and formed part of the general protectionist movement that he dates, rather late, from 1883.[21] It included the development of protected markets for a wide range of commodities, ranking from metal products to articles of personal consumption, such as clothing and food.[22]

Those "traditional tendencies" of which Girault wrote constituted the republican formulation of social imperialism and national economics. Colonial exploitation contributed to the solution of the socioeconomic crisis and, by implication, recognized the comparative inelasticity of the domestic market. Unanimity on both counts prevailed among a wide range of entrepreneurs, and it is particularly significant how consistently they linked empire to domestic problems of production and social relations. Once the national movement toward protection became evident by 1881, the next logical step was to look toward extended empire. Roubaix, Saint-Quentin, and Elbeuf claimed that only development of those markets combined with tariff assimilation would protect their industries and preserve the social balance sustained by them. The Elbeuvians expressed anger that the government should even question their relations with "their" workers, suggesting the government should turn that bureaucratic energy in other, more fruitful, directions. The manufacturers of Louviers, Thiers, Cambrai, Montbéliard, Laval, and Abbeville voiced variations on the same theme—a

20. Arthur Girault, *Principes de la colonisation* (4 vols.; Paris: Larose, 1927), IV, 374–81.

21. Girault then muddies the waters of a perfectly sound argument by stating that tariff assimilation also represented the fulfillment of the "democratic" principles of equality beween the French and the colonial peoples. Industrial production interests and domestic social concerns always dominated the work of the republican imperialists. Their notion of equality had to do with the expansion of the regime of private property so as to smooth the way for capitalist exploitation of the colonies. Girault, *Colonial Tariff Policy*, 81–85.

22. The biscuit bakers of Calais complained bitterly about British competitors underselling their product in North Africa and demanded that "imports of biscuits into Algeria be subject to the same duties as are imposed on them entering France." *Industriel français*, July 4, 1878; Louis Bernard, *Essai sur le commerce de Marseille* (Marseille: Chez l'auteur, 1887), 338.

theme that dwelt heavily on the social implications of the crisis, on the relations between capital and labor. Even in ports such as Nantes and Marseille, where protection never generated enthusiasm, tariff assimilation had its champions, liberal imperialists who recognized that metropolitan-colonial integration, especially in the case of Algeria and Indochina, was not incompatible with modified free trade.

J. B. Trystram, president of the chamber of commerce of Dunkirk, vice-president of the Nord general council, and a major republican leader in that area, did not count himself among the stalwarts of national economics. However, he worried about the falling rate of profit and the glut of goods. He continually fought protection, calculating that the path to increased trade (and thus increased production and employment) lay along bilateral trade treaties, "more French commercial representation abroad," and the encouragement of emigration to the colonies, especially to North Africa. Thus were free trade and social imperialism inseparably joined, suggesting that all proponents of imperialism shared an identical class outlook and argued only over details. Nevertheless, protection and imperial preference generally marched together in close ranks: "The decline of our exports to the colonies provides . . . a convincing refutation of free-trade theories . . . this decline demonstrates our inferiority in production compared to other countries."[23]

The foregoing statement constitutes a confession of relative weakness, to be sure, but not one that might be construed to support the proposition that the French bourgeois lacked an "entrepreneurial spirit." Rather, it reflects both the limitations of a domestic market dominated by petty producers and the hard realities of political life that dictated the alliance of the republican bourgeoisie with those same producers. How much better for the peasants of Algeria, Tunisia, Egypt, and Indochina to subsidize with their labor the survival of the peasants of France!

23. Réponses des chambres de commerce, chambre de commerce d'Elbeuf, in C 3329, Régime douanière des colonies, 1845–1890, in F(12) 6290, chambre de commerce de Saint-Quentin, chambre de commerce du Mans, in F(12) 4841, chambre de commerce de Nantes, Conseil général du Nord, in F(12) 6290, AN; Bernard, *Essai sur le commerce*, 344.

Northern industrialists commanded the strongest sector of French productive capital. Both free traders and protectionists could be found among them, the former in Roubaix where wool exports continued to increase, the latter in Lille-Tourcoing whose cotton production bore the brunt of the crisis. Metallurgy, mining, and sugar-beet production rounded out the complex. Social conservatives and good republicans all, they mobilized together to seek solutions to the crisis in production. Quite naturally, they turned their eyes toward empire. By 1879, in contrast to earlier years, northern capitalists developed a strong and sustained interest in metropolitan-colonial integration.[24]

They deplored the increased colonial trade handled by the British and feared the worst as the British introduced steamships, thereby increasing their tonnage capacity per ship by three or four times. Port interests could only applaud their demand for a program to increase the tonnage capacity of the French merchant marine, another indication of the bourgeois solidarity that imperialism engendered. But that constituted only a secondary consideration. Northern businessmen were quick to comprehend the relationships linking the solution to domestic social and economic problems with the thorough exploitation of the colonies. They focused on Algeria.[25]

The businessmen of the north had considerable experience in balancing agricultural and industrial labor, private property and capitalist property. They also understood the power of the cash nexus in the creation of consumers. Assimilation to them meant the systematic "expropriation" of arable lands remaining in Arab hands. Its purpose was to provide for greater colon settlements, whose industrial needs would be supplied by the metropolitan manufacturers, specifically of textiles, iron and steel goods, and processed sugar, all northern specialties. In return the businessmen expected the more intelligent and efficient Europeans of Algeria to produce for export to France grains, raw wool, and alfa, a flaxlike grass important in the production of coarse cloth such as corduroy. Although northern capitalists self-consciously

24. Publications of the Société industrielle du Nord and issues of the *Progrès du Nord* prior to the late 1870s for the most part ignored imperial activity.
25. *Bulletin de la Société industrielle du Nord*, VII (1879), 113.

spoke of "expropriation," the process they envisioned proved less harsh in practice. They merely expected that the elimination of collective ownership within Arab communities would automatically produce a transfer of lands to the superiorly ambitious Europeans:

The prompt and definitive establishment of property relations among the Arabs is of even greater importance than the extension of our lands. . . . When the Arabs become *individual*, and no longer collective, proprietors of the land, they will naturally sell large parcels to the Europeans. Slowly but surely, a large portion of high quality land will pass into the hands of the latter, and agricultural colonization will develop on a scale hitherto unknown.[26]

Northern capitalists did not appear to make a distinction between the expansion of small holdings and of large latifundia. If anything, they preferred small holdings to increase, being concerned less with heavy capital investment in agriculture than with the extension of private property beyond French boundaries, but always in the interests of their own substantial capitalist apparatus. Others, like Jules Ferry, emphasized the importance of extensive capital investments in North Africa. However, the distinction is unimportant, for the single goal remained to buttress the republican social system through its extension and reproduction in the French empire. Radicals, like Alfred Talandier of Paris, attacked Ferry for supporting "plutocrats" against "small capitalists." They failed to notice the symbiotic relationship between the two and ignored the necessity for capital export to develop the colonies for the benefit of France, which they enthusiastically promoted.[27]

As this evidence suggests, many "radicals" on the left of the domestic political spectrum turned into fervent imperialists when they focused their attention beyond the national frontiers. No one defended imperial interests with more energy than Eugène Menier. His career provides a model for the radical imperialist. Menier's father, grandson of a 1793 Montagnard, owned a shipping supply company with headquarters in Bordeaux and branches in Madras and Pon-

26. *Ibid.*, 59–100, quotation on 65–66.
27. Talandier quoted in Martin Aldao, *Les Idées coloniales de Jules Ferry* (Paris: n.p., 1933), 93.

dichéry. He also owned plantation land on the island of Réunion. Eugène launched his political career in the defense of Paris during the Prussian siege. He remained in the city to take part in the Commune, for which he paid with seven months' imprisonment. He then turned to lobbying for colonial interests, financing and editing two newspapers, the *France coloniale* and *France populaire*, the latter a self-proclaimed organ of "moderate and liberal radicalism," frequently critical of the Gambetta-Ferry nexus for its alleged "opportunism" and for dragging its feet on institutional (not social) reform. Menier advocated the standard radical demands: abolition of the Senate, total and immediate separation of church and state, civil divorce, and a popularly conscripted army with no built-in exceptions for the rich and educated. He added to these common elements a new and significant ingredient, the extension of the colonial system.[28]

Menier supported the reigning assimilationist doctrines as applied to Algeria. This involved not only tariff assimilation, which he swallowed even though he was a free trader, but opening up native lands to French exploitation. He projected a complete vision of social imperialism that combined the extension of opportunities for private property with large-scale commercial development. It is no coincidence that these two elements of political economy, petty production and capitalist enterprise, formed the basis for the republican system in France itself. To support the expansion of French-owned private property in Algeria, the *France populaire* ran a campaign offering one hectare of "first-rate arable land" in the department of Alger to any Frenchman willing to emigrate. The accompanying promotion extolled the limitless potentialities for gain: "The land carries immense value for the future; the destinies of France are certain in opening wide the opportunities for agricultural, industrial, and civilizing action in [the exploitation] of the immense riches of all Africa."[29] Menier's attacks on finance capital's penetration into Algeria recall the republican assault on the railroad companies. He characterized the Crédit foncier algérien, a bank formed to buy up huge chunks of real

28. *France populaire*, May 23, June 18, August 2, 1881; *France coloniale*, August 4, 1881.
29. *France coloniale*, May 12, 1881.

estate for speculation, as an enterprise in "thievery" that "has no other purpose than to exploit cruelly and recklessly a country which, in the near future, must become equal to the task of providing for the necessary expansion of France. . . . The consequence will be to smash our small local banks, whose initiatives have been most productive, which take care of local needs and satisfy the legitimate interests of commerce and industry."[30]

Menier projected a vision of an extended metropolitan-colonial system to "Tunisia, Cambodia, Annam, Tonkin, and beyond where French influence will expand without interference; France's colonial policy ought to take first place on the agenda of the nation's business . . . and we can take credit for establishing the foundations for this increase in the influence of the republican idea." He made no distinction between secular "civilization," France's special dispensation, and business. Indeed, the implantation of the former paved the way for successful commercial exploitation. Clerical influence in French Guiana had opposed public education and stifled the spread of "liberal ideas" after emancipation in 1848. The colony had moved quickly along the path of ruin as the natives, sunk in apathy and superstition, were drained of the energy and resisted the initiative to become effective workers in cultivating the colony's agriculture. He repeated the same for Guadeloupe. It seemed that the church, in its struggle against the "republican idea," revealed the essence of that idea, which was to spiritually emancipate native labor to prepare them for service to French capital.[31]

Plans were already under way to democratize established colonies, particularly in the West Indies, along French lines. What the monastic orders accomplished in Canada during the *ancien régime* the republican missionaries hoped to surpass in the Caribbean. This meant the promotion of diversified agriculture and the introduction of universal secular education. Both were designed to increase the small farmer's independence (as in France) and to camouflage class-color barriers. The *Tribune coloniale,* in its own words the organ "of French democracy overseas," proposed that cane sugar production in Guade-

30. *Ibid.,* February 12, March 12 and 26, 1880.
31. *Ibid.,* May 1, 1879, June 30, 1881, January 6, 1882.

loupe and Martinique be reduced and the acreage given over to food-producing farms of limited size. Cane sugar production, the *Tribune* contended, was in the long run economically suicidal because of the favored position of the beet sugar producers in France. But there was an even more cogent reason that had nothing to do with the economics of agriculture. Food production "easily accommodated itself to the division of property."[32] Thus would the greengrocer's paradise flourish in many climes.

On matters of education, the *Tribune coloniale* was ferociously anticlerical. The congregations who controlled the schools in Guadeloupe were charged with fomenting racial prejudice, accentuating "distinctions of skin color," and arousing undemocratic class consciousness among their pupils.[33] A strong policy of militarization and secularization was in order, as had been attempted briefly in Martinique in 1848 when military rule was established along with the first *lycée national*. Military service reinforced education, adding patriotism to solidarity. "The school and the army, do they not truly provide the strongest bonds between youngsters of the same country?"[34]

A favorite project of radical imperialists was the Trans-Saharan Railroad, which was to link the Algerian ports with the western Sudan and, ultimately, Dakar in the Senegal. The planners of the Trans-Saharan plotted its course to take the railroad through the western deserts and oases of Algeria, where French troops had been engaged in a series of skirmishes with the native Arab population. The latter had stubbornly maintained their "feudal" social structure, resisting the plunder of their holdings and the transformation of their lands into private property under the republican system—thus striking a blow against "assimilation." With the railroad would arrive colonists and businessmen to open the way for the native population "to receive its first contact with civilization in the shape of industry and technology; the opening up of modern transport facilities [will hasten] the creation of commercial contacts based upon the products of the soil

32. *Tribune coloniale*, March 17, July 20, 1878.
33. *Ibid.*, July 27, 1878.
34. *Ibid.*, November 23, 1878.

and nourished by its extensive exploitation."[35] One "product of the soil" in which the French showed strong interest was alfa.

Eugène Menier did most of the promotion and propaganda for the railroad, including the organization of various lobbies. At a meeting of the Société pour le progrès des sciences sociales, where republican businessmen gathered to discuss social questions and political economy, Menier delivered an address on the importance of the Trans-Saharan. All present agreed that it represented an important enterprise to enhance national production. Among Menier's enthusiastic listeners was Nicholas Claude, the textile senator from the Vosges.[36]

Gazeau de Vautibault, general secretary for the International Geographical Congress of 1878 and high official in the Société agricole de France, also became actively involved in Trans-Saharan promotion. He imagined a fabulous commercial expansion that promised even more fabulous social rewards. The railroad, Gazeau claimed, will provide "the happiest solution" to the Republic's social, moral, material, and political problems. "France will discover an enormous outlet for her unproductive capital. The accelerating industrial crisis will be arrested as . . . our excess products flow toward the vast and unlimited market provided by the eighty million inhabitants of the Sudan." The railroad also promised great domestic social benefits as the unemployed, the *déclassés*, and the adventurers flooded the area, thus relieving the Republic of the burden of their presence. Businessmen in turn would be released from the anxiety of retaliatory tariffs as they channeled their resources toward this new frontier, which Gazeau compared to the American West after 1869. Finally, he proposed that the railroad be awarded a monopoly to sell salt to the natives, which would produce the necessary revenues to pay off the cost of building the line (estimated at 400 million francs) and expose the indigenous population directly and dramatically to the benefits of French civilization by providing them with cheap salt.[37] Whatever the problems of building such a railroad, the project followed closely the pattern of republican

35. *France populaire*, July 11, 1881.
36. *France coloniale*, April 22, 1880.
37. Gazeau de Vautibault, *Le Trans-saharien* (Paris: Perois, 1879), 1–24.

consolidation through a combination of imperial expansion and social integration. Gazeau himself had argued earlier that it was the chief mission of the Republic to do so, by mobilizing national resources and generating prosperous national production. This worthy effort separated the Republic from previous regimes, notably the Second Empire, that had preserved "monarchical institutions" based upon the "anti-republican" spirit of "privilege, monopoly, and financial speculation," which conspired to suppress the legitimate aspirations of the "working and commercial classes." The solidarity of capital and labor remained unstated, but firmly implied.[38]

Between 1879 and 1881, a governmental Commission supérieure du trans-saharien existed, but its studies led nowhere.[39] Time and energy might have been conserved had it paid close attention to estimates made by General Louis Faidherbe fifteen years earlier. Faidherbe kept a sharp eye open for commercial potentialities in Senegal and the western Sudan while he served as governor-general in the region. He dismissed a railroad as a pipedream and encouraged instead the development of agricultural commodities to be shipped by sea from the West African coast to Bordeaux.[40] Trade figures for the early 1880s, while the industrial crisis was in full swing, validated Faidherbe's instincts. France imported from Senegal twenty-one million francs' worth of raw materials, mainly peanuts, peanut oil, and gum. She exported seven million francs' worth of manufactured goods, including salted meat, cotton cloth, silk cloth, and wines.[41]

Although promotion of the Trans-Saharan Railroad remained a

38. Gazeau de Vautibault, *La République et prospérité* (Paris: Librairie libérale, 1874).
39. M. Dubois and A. Terrier, *Un Siècle d'expansion coloniale* (Paris: Challamel, 1901), 438–40, 469–70.
40. Louis Faidherbe, "L'Avenir du Sahara et du Soudan," *Revue maritime et coloniale*, XXXI (1863), 245–48. Faidherbe "réussit . . . à transformer complètement le Sénégal [dans] une colonie vivante et riche, disposant de ressources considérables." A. Terrier and C. Mousey, *L'Oeuvre de la troisième république en Afrique occidentale* (Paris: Larose, 1910), 26–31. A. S. Kanya-Forstner's study of the military side of French penetration into western equatorial Africa, *The Conquest of the Western Sudan* (Cambridge: Cambridge University Press, 1969), does not, I think, do justice to Faidherbe's commercial interests and involvements.
41. France, Ministère de la marine et des colonies, *Statistiques coloniales pour 1882* (Paris: Imprimerie nationale, 1884), 44.

minor affair on the periphery of French colonial efforts, the formulation of and the arguments for the project revealed how imperialists linked empire to domestic social relations. Also revealed was the fundamental bourgeois perspective of political "radicals," who in some ways displayed the imperialist spirit more forcefully and energetically than the leading (and more conservative and nationalist) politicians of the Republic. The iron horse never penetrated the Saharan wastes. However unsuccessful the project turned out to be, its planning and justification constituted a significant example of social imperialism at work.

Tunisia: Social Imperialism in Action

The Trans-Saharan fiasco did not hamper the further development of Algeria, which was integrated into the metropolitan tariff structure in 1884. Concurrently, the French imperial appetite hungered for further expansion within North Africa. Tunisia appeared to present the obvious target, for there was some truth to the assertion that it constituted "an extension of Algeria." More important, it possessed a fertile field for extensive agricultural development with its "hardworking" population and "fertile soil," needing only infusions of French capital, discipline, and efficient farming methods to make the land blossom with "lucrative exploitations." Tunisia, announced Jules Ferry, "must be considered as . . . a colony for capital export."[42] The following rather lengthy account of the Tunisian story would appear to be unjustified by the relatively minor role that country played in the total French imperial structure. However, it serves admirably well to illustrate republican social policy in its imperialist aspect—in other words, social imperialism in action.

In 1881, while president of the Council of Ministers of the Republic, Ferry launched a military expedition into Tunisia and imposed on that African principality a French protectorate. As a reward for his

42. Bernard, *Essai sur le commerce*, 337–38; Aldao, *Les Idées coloniales*, 97–99.

bold action, Ferry and his cabinet were overthrown in the Chamber of Deputies on November 9, 1881. In this sequence of events, the historian of French Tunisian policy, Jean Ganiage, discerns the roots of an "active anticolonialist tradition" and the "depth of the anticolonialist movement."[43] The precipitating factor leading to Ferry's fall was the revelation in the Chamber that certain financial interests, including prominent politicians such as Ferry's brother Charles, had a large stake in Tunisia that the government felt obliged to protect. Clemenceau, Camille Pelletan, Henri Maret, and others exploited the issue to launch a general attack on Ferry, Gambetta, and the *politique opportuniste*. Henri Rochefort, from his lofty perch in the gutter, hurled obscene epithets at the ruling political establishment.

A focus on such rhetoric diverts attention from the key revelation of the Tunisian controversy in 1881. The debate brought out widespread support for a policy of intervention. *L'affaire tunisienne* was the product of neither a bankers' conspiracy nor an accidental collision of random events. The French neither stumbled onto the extended empire in North Africa nor were they hoodwinked by a small clique of financial masterminds. The sudden imposition of the Tunisian protectorate came perhaps as a surprise. But nearly everyone supported the acquisition and defended the policy, if not the government that had acted. We must not make the mistake of interpreting the November 9 vote against Ferry as a vote against expansionism. Even on the left, critics attacked the action but not the assumptions behind the action. Many deputies who voted for Gambetta's *ordre du jour* (which Ferry refused to accept despite its bland language) that brought down the government did so with the intent to dissociate themselves from Ferry without repudiating the colonial policy that Ferry represented. Gambetta had carefully framed his *ordre du jour* to express approval of the government's behavior while at the same time disengaging from it. In early December, when Gambetta asked for additional credits to pursue the military expedition, the antiimperial opposition of November melted away. A few royalists and Bonapartists voted "no" from

43. Ganiage, *Les Origines du protectorat*, 699.

force of habit. Among the left-wing radicals, Clemenceau, Pelletan, and Georges Périn abstained.[44]

Close examination of the shock waves generated by the Tunisian affair and of the arguments surrounding it does not reveal the "depth of the anticolonialist movement," but its opposite. The imperialist responses to the crisis in production settled the issue. Even those who did not recognize the opportunities for capital investment rose to defend the policy and did so in terms of the social benefits to be gained. The republican social ideology, articulated in so many ways on different occasions in the 1870s, returned to provide the ideological justification for the Tunisian protectorate.[45]

The reason for the French presence in Tunisia is not disputed. Tunisia had interested small groups of French investors for many years, particularly *haute banque* interests who saw in this ill-governed outpost of the Ottoman Empire a capital export market ripe for the plucking. Their Italian counterparts were interested too, and it was a question of who would gain the first solid foothold in the court of the bey of Tunis. A syndicate led by the Gouins and Mallets won the race against the Italians by tying up the Tunisian national debt. They managed to extract a promise of French governmental support for their considerable financial commitment. When a marauding band of tribesmen, known as the Kroumirs, threatened to topple the bey's shaky government, raided the Algerian frontier, and thus struck fear into the pocketbooks of the bankers, the call went out for French troops; and they were delivered. But the government insisted that the bey sign an agreement giving the French mastery over Tunisia's financial affairs. That agreement, the Treaty of Bardo, established a de facto French protectorate. French troops from Algeria crossed the frontier in the spring of 1881 and spent the next twelve months reducing the Kroumirs.

Much criticism of the expedition was concerned with the manner in which it was carried out, specifically the commitment of a substan-

44. L. H. X., *La Politique française en Tunisie: Le Protectorat et ses origines* (Paris: n.p., 1891), 311.
45. *Yonne*, November 10, 1881; *Union républicaine de Paris*, September 4, 1881; *Avenir clermontois*, December 19, 1881; *Union républicaine du Cher*, October 12, 1881.

tial body of troops whose logistical support and auxiliary services appeared less than adequate for the job. A brief flurry of criticism toward Ferry and the war minister, General Joseph Farre, in September, 1881, centered on the apparent laxity in military preparation. Even in newspapers traditionally bound to the government, ghastly stories of disease, negligence of the wounded, and severe shortages of food raised doubts about the high command's competence.[46] But in all cases, such reports were linked to positive affirmations of the military expedition's importance in terms of its domestic social value.

Many welcomed the Tunisian expedition for the revitalizing effect it would have on France's martial spirit. Among the republican bourgeois, patriotic élan ranked high on their scale of desirable social virtues. Thus, a military demonstration, whatever its practical results in Africa, would carry enormous value by stiffening the spines of the French and restoring self-confidence. Jean Grosjean wrote to his former business associate in Mulhouse, Auguste Scheurer-Kestner: "I am positively delighted with the course of events in Tunisia. For better or for worse, we are taking to the battlefield again and we can see that the French soldier still knows how to fight and that the republican government is not a government beset by fear of combat."[47] There existed, as Claude Digeon has pointed out, a profound malaise that had gripped politicians and intellectuals following the defeat of 1870 and the civil war in Paris.[48] French superiority in arms, which had not been seriously questioned for a century, had suddenly evaporated—to be replaced by the nightmare of Sedan, Metz, and the futile heroism of the Army of the Loire. That disaster, furthermore, seemed to be at least partially responsible for the terrible events in Paris the following spring.

Tunisia offered the first opportunity since 1871 to test French arms. While victory was not as total as defeat had been and the ragged Berber tribesmen were in no way comparable to the well-trained

46. *Indépendant du Var*, September 18, October 9, 1881.
47. Grosjean to Auguste Scheurer-Kestner, April 7, 1881, Scheurer-Kestner Papers, in 276 AP 2, AN.
48. Claude Digeon, *La Crise allemande de la pensée française, 1871–1914* (Paris: Presses universitaires de France, 1959), Chaps. 4 and 5.

Prussian infantry, the army had responded to the demand to "loudly proclaim" that France was no longer "a nation humiliated and impotent."[49] The most brilliantly executed war games could not match a genuine campaign for building morale and sharpening the army's tactical edge. There was nothing like "shooting at a real enemy" to dramatize the army's "sublime mission."[50] From the radical newspaper *Mot d'ordre* came a statement that put together, in one neat package, business, the republican system, and national honor: "The heartfelt support of all Frenchmen accompany our brave soldiers, carriers of individual liberty and commercial security, marching under the flag of the Republic to accomplish the final pacification. . . . This is no question of dynastic war [drawing the contrast, altogether unwarranted, with Napoleon III's imperialism], nor of the adventure of some pretender [Mexico?] . . . civilization itself faces a threat from the Tunisian pirates. We are not engaged in a war of conquest; we insist only on respect for our territory, our compatriots, and our businessmen."[51]

For the Republic, the army was an appendage of the social organism whose utility transcended narrow military functions. Equal in importance to the *école laïque*, the army provided a stage on which the citizen acted out solidarity and patriotism. Professional soldiers, such as General Alexandre Guillemaut, agreed: "In a country as avid for equality as ours . . . the army must not be composed solely of the disinherited, and to lessen the peril of future civil war, the rich must not let the poor do their fighting. Further, if rich and poor associate together in the ranks, they will develop mutual esteem and reciprocal feelings—and out of this union and solidarity will emerge a firmly established social order."[52] That message got across even to conservative notables who swallowed their repugnance for the *levée en masse* in recognition of the social utility of universal military service. At the pinnacle of the great whiggery of France, Daniel Halévy noted that the "bourgeoisie happily delivered their young men to the company

49. *République de Nevers*, April 9, 1881.
50. *République française*, June 26, 1881, quoted in J. F. E. Robinet, *La Politique positive et la question tunisienne* (Paris: n.p., 1881), 10n.
51. Quoted in *Union républicaine de Paris*, April 5, 1881.
52. Assemblée nationale, *Annales de l'Assemblée nationale*, May 28, 1872.

of workers and peasants in the barracks."[53] Gambetta's parliamentary private secretary, Pierre Deluns-Montaud, reported the former's passion for the profession of arms. Gambetta held a "profound belief in the uplifting qualities of war," in which the people, mobilized under the colors of the Republic, would express in noble deeds their patriotism and civic spirit.[54] *Civisme* functioned as a centripetal force in a society seeking integration; and *civisme* demanded of the citizen only one thing: submission to the duties imposed by the republican state. The army, stripped of its antisocial, exclusive, praetorian trappings, took its proper place as the "right arm" of the state. Fulfillment of the citizen's obligations to France required the fulfillment of all "civic duties"; and no obligation superseded participation in and support of the military establishment.[55]

There was cool realism behind all this rhetoric, the realism of acutely sensitive political ideologues who grasped the critical importance of the times they lived in, recognized the deadly threat to order and social peace raised by challenges to the bourgeois order, and successfully (for a time) held the battlements of the social status quo. This is not to suggest that the Tunisian campaign was launched, deliberately, to galvanize popular patriotism. The process was more complex and subtle. Popular patriotism was neither a direct cause nor an effect of Tunisia. Rather, it was an ingredient of an ideological mix that made Tunisia acceptable to Frenchmen who had been taught to recognize the

53. Daniel Halévy, *Trois épreuves* (Paris: Plon, 1938), 67. This represented an advance beyond the traditional position expressed by Thiers who argued that "it was not safe to put a gun on the shoulder of every socialist." A. F. Kovacs, "French Military Institutions Before the Franco-Prussian War," *American Historical Review*, LI (1946), 217. Thiers believed that the chief purpose of an army was to maintain domestic order. He had, of course, considerable experience along those lines.

54. A. Pierre Deluns-Montaud, "La Philosophie de Gambetta," *Revue politique et parlementaire*, XI (1897), 259.

55. Léon Gambetta, "Discours pour l'anniversaire de Hoche," June 24, 1872, quoted in Henri Genevois, *Les Enseignements de Gambetta* (Paris: n.p., 1895), 117; Joseph Reinach (ed.), *Discours et plaidoyers politiques de Gambetta* (11 vols.; Paris: n.p., 1881–85), VIII, 237. Gambetta surely would have endorsed the definition of *civisme* that appeared in Charles Bailleul's 1842 *Dictionnaire critique du langage politique, gouvernemental, civil, administratif, et judiciaire*: "Se prouve par l'accomplissement de tous les devoirs qu'impose la société, et non par cette éloquence de carrefour et de banquets qui n'appartient qu'aux charlatans et factieux." Jean Dubois, *Le Vocabulaire politique et social en France de 1869 à 1872* (Paris: Larousse, n.d.), 246.

value of a colonial expedition in the positive results of social integration and class reconciliation which, it was said, followed in its wake.[56]

Mission civilisatrice had long been the favorite pious slogan used to camouflage the plunder of other peoples—and not by the French alone. The expansionist impulses in French democracy had not been expressed so forcefully since Jacques Brissot's saber-rattling oratory in the Convention. Under republican auspices, *mission civilisatrice* was given a new dimension to include exporting both French capital and political institutions. These were investments that promised to return handsome social dividends. For Tunisia, the civilizing enterprise could only have the most beneficent consequences. Its population would come to recognize the reality of French power in North Africa, cease to be "obstacles" to its extension, become "brothers" in the glorious enterprise, and elevate themselves, through legal and institutional reform, to the "moral stature of Europeans." Gambetta envisioned a world community of Frenchmen, the "aggrandizement of France overseas, without distinction of color, of class, and of caste."[57] The democratic myth indeed served many purposes. Visions of the Mediterranean as a "French lake" were conjured up under the guise of promoting democracy to the ends of the earth.[58]

Rational discourse suffered once the cause of colonialism became the cause of popular democracy and social order. Considering the relatively minor financial stakes involved, from which few could be expected to profit, enthusiasm for the protectorate was out of proportion to its immediate material benefits, a fact that becomes intelligible only in light of the immense social interest in colonialism. That was the reality to which all arguments, whether of principle or expediency, submitted.

Thus, the Tunisian debate in the summer and autumn of 1881 precipitated a lurid display of naked chauvinism. The republican press demanded a Carthaginian peace for the "African thieves" who flaunted their contempt for the flag.[59] Whoever dared to expose the expedition

56. Léon Gambetta, *Discours à Romans* (Paris: n.p., 1876), 15–17.
57. *France populaire,* May 8 and 16, 1881.
58. *Républicain de la Loire et de la Haute-Loire,* October 4 and 10, 1881.
59. *Démocratie franc-comtoise,* November 12, 1881.

as the work of "speculators" stood accused of peddling "antipatriotic gossip" in the face of a challenge to French prestige.[60] Honest criticism of the logistical arrangements for the military campaign was barely tolerated, and the slightest suggestion of corruption drew hysterical charges of treason against those who raised such questions in public. They were the accomplices of "reactionaries," whose only purpose was to undermine confidence in the Republic. Behind each critical word lurked a sinister "antipatriotic campaign pressed forward with such enthusiasm as to make the Germans explode in laughter."[61] At the annual session of the Loire general council, a routine meeting was suddenly interrupted when a member of the republican majority rose to deliver a passionate plea that the council take a stand on Tunisia to demonstrate its concern for the "honor of the flag." He was ruled out of order by the president to the accompaniment of loud applause for the speech.[62]

Here, as elsewhere, rhetoric illuminates ideology and provides a clue to real preoccupations. It is insufficient to conclude that the natural reflex of Frenchmen was to support their army. The cause of Tunisia was a republican cause, with all the undertones this suggests. It was the national republican coalition, the rock of stability, whose established position stood the test. If, as Gambetta had asserted, "France and the republican party are one and the same," support for the regime's actions took on an overriding importance.[63] If the Republic represented the best, indeed, the only hope for defending the established order, its alternative was not some other regime, but savage internecine conflict ending in social revolution.

Every major theme developed by the republican bourgeoisie in the preceding decade was aired in the short, violent debate on Tunisia in November, which led to the overthrow of Ferry's government. Few of the critics on the extreme left challenged the social ideology on which justification for the policy ultimately rested. The most telling

60. *Union républicaine du Cher*, October 12, 1881.
61. *Union républicaine de l'Hérault*, September 20, 1881.
62. Conseil général de la Loire, *Procès-verbaux des délibérations* (Saint-Étienne: n.p., 1881).
63. Gambetta, *Discours à Romans*, 5.

points were made not by those who dwelt on the shady financial operations, but by those who saw expansion as a corrosive, corruptive influence on French democracy. Jean Turigny sensed a device for dodging
social reform. In an article rimmed in heavy black, Turigny mourned
the French dead in Africa and denounced such wars as fit only for
Germans. They were "murder on a grand scale" producing the "slaughter of thousands." Social reform at home was what was required. Once
the Republic had put its own house in order, it would conquer the
world through the irresistible force of its moral superiority.[64] Yves
Guyot suggested that a favorite republican slogan, *la république, c'est
la paix*, sounded somewhat hollow. Colonialism was a "flagrant contradiction" of the requirements of the peasant Republic, which asked only
for peace and low taxes. Guyot agreed with the Gambettists that the
business of government was to legislate the "appeasement of social
discord," but he accused the Chamber of sidestepping its responsibilities by dabbling in adventurism. He did not consider, or at least did
not comment on, the possibility that adventurism itself supplied a
means to appease social discord.[65]

Conscious perhaps of their vulnerability to charges of antipatriotism, the most outspoken left-wing critics did not permit their ex-
posure of the financial speculations behind the Tunisian imbroglio to
overflow into a general denunciation of imperialism itself. Clemenceau, in fact, challenged Ferry to produce evidence of commercial
opportunities or a strategic military position available in Tunisia. He
did not agree that Tunisia was the "key to Algeria." Clemenceau met
Ferry on the very ground the latter chose, thus implicitly accepting
the republican thesis on colonialism.[66] Alfred Naquet limited his attack
on Ferry to a matter of parliamentary procedure. He was not prepared
to condemn the government for acting in "defense of French interests;

64. *Patriote de la Nièvre*, November 3, 1881.
65. Guyot, *Lettres sur la politique coloniale*, 294–95; Yves Guyot, "M. Gambetta
and the French Elections," *Contemporary Review*, XL (October, 1881), 41.
66. Ganiage, *Les Origines du protectorat*, 682. He quotes Clemenceau apparently
without appreciating the significance of his words. The key passage is: "Je ne vois pas là
l'institution de grands débouchés pour notre commerce, la création de comptoirs ou
d'établissements industriels, rien, en un mot, qui ressemble à la *légitime exploitation du
sol tunisien*." *Union républicaine de la Saône-et-Loire*, November 9, 1881, italics added.

foreign business establishments and colonies are necessary to a great people and they must be protected." Unforgivable in his view was that "the national flag was committed" without the approval of the Chamber. Naquet did not imply that the Chamber, once consulted, would not have risen to its patriotic duty. Like Clemenceau, he accepted the legitimacy of expansion and criticized only the means by which the policy was carried out. There was not the slightest whiff of anticolonialism in his oratory.[67]

Ferry's statements in the Chamber concentrated on fundamentals. He dismissed, rather too lightly, the accusations of financial manipulation as irrelevant to the question. There was, in his eyes, an infinitely more serious issue involving the heart of republican social policy. At stake was the viability of the democratic Republic. We can understand Ferry's apocalyptic rhetoric. The life of his government and his own considerable political reputation hung in the balance. But we should recall that from the very outset of his career, Ferry fastened on the conservative Republic as a necessary precondition of social peace and order.[68]

The events he had set into motion in Tunisia, Ferry explained in the Chamber on November 5, followed faithfully the direction taken by established "national policy." The "causes of the Tunisian expedition" could not be separated from "national causes" and "patriotic necessity."[69] Repudiation of the protectorate implied negative consequences far beyond a temporary setback to French power in the struggle for empire. "Patriotic necessity" did not refer to the potential damage to French prestige in international politics, however important this might be. Rather it referred to the implications for future social order, that is, a question of social policy, which made support for the expedition a patriotic necessity. The foundations of democracy rested on the bedrock of class solidarity interlaced with thick veins of

---

67. *Rappel* (Paris), November 9, 1881. Maillard, another radical acting true to form, attacked the government because "its weakness gravely compromised colonial interests in Algeria." *Réveil de la Corrèze*, August 3, 1881.

68. A. Dupront, "Jules Ferry opposant à l'empire," *Revue historique*, CLXXVII (March-April, 1936), 352–74.

69. *République française*, November 7, 1881.

patriotism. This was the myth from which republican social ideology took its original inspiration, and massive quantities of intellectual energy were spent in the effort to endow that ideology with an impregnable logic—a logic that swept from the board hesitations, doubts, and second thoughts. Having spawned the ideological construction that legitimized and rationalized conservative social policy, republicans could not repudiate one aspect of that policy, Ferry reminded them, without betraying their own position and looking quite foolish in the bargain.[70] Given this kind of logic, Ferry could in all earnestness deride the left-wingers for wearing their patriotism on their sleeves. With their glazed eyes locked in a fixed stare "on the blue line of the Vosges" they failed to appreciate the potentialities for national power and intensified solidarity in colonial undertakings. "The real issue in this debate," Gambetta repeated after he had succeeded Ferry as president of the council, "is whether we have a foreign colonial policy, whether we accept the time-honored tradition of our country, whether we accept our responsibilities, or whether we will betray our history."[71]

Headlining its review of the Tunisian episode with the revealing phrase, "la politique nationale," the *Voltaire* laid heavy emphasis on the social benefits of expansion:

The common sense and patriotism of our frontier citizens have for many years convinced them to support a broad, tough, yet prudent foreign policy. But perhaps the people of the interior, without foreign contacts, need to develop a broader outlook. Justice requires, also, that the national spirit be toughened and that our fellow citizens not be discouraged from going to foreign lands where they will get rich, from where they will accumulate wealth in which we all shall share, and to which they carry aloft the glory of France.[72]

As a military exercise, as a demonstration of French national vitality, and as evidence of vigorous French initiative in international affairs, the Tunisian expedition certainly performed a necessary function. But what was to be gained was not so much glory on distant battlefields as reassurance at home of the viability of the Republic.

70. *Ibid.*
71. *Ibid.*, December 3, 1881.
72. *Voltaire*, January 11, 1882.

For more than a decade, republicans had promised peace and order. "Without the Republic," Gambetta warned, "there remains only internal conflict, party factionalism, anarchy, and disorder; and disorder means the finish of France."[73] Delivery on the promise required a united front of the "dynamic forces" in France, whose allegiance was not to party or faction but to *nationalité française,* of which the Republic was the "impregnable rampart."[74]

Gambetta succeeded Ferry to power, and although his cabinet led a short, nasty, and brutish life, it continued Ferry's work and his commitment to social imperialism. As we have seen, Gambetta always considered imperial consolidation and expansion to be cornerstones of republican national policy. He committed himself to consummating Ferry's initiative in Tunisia. He continued Freycinet's policy of military disengagement from Egypt, thus acquiescing to British primacy on the banks of the Suez Canal. This made sense in imperial terms for several reasons: France had no reason to fear losing her considerable investments in Egypt, because the British did not threaten them; the focus of the French empire was elsewhere, in northern and western Africa; and French merchants did a considerable business shipping in British bottoms.[75] Spuller certainly exaggerated Gambetta's pioneering work in imperialist agitation when he claimed that Ferry took his imperial outlook from "Gambetta's direct inspiration." Nevertheless, Spuller spoke Gambettist language when he claimed, in 1893, that in the previous era a commitment to empire "had penetrated to the deepest layers [*couches*] of the population."[76]

Gambetta's cabinet was filled with representatives of the ports and other imperial interests. We need only list Waldeck-Rousseau, whose interest in empire and social reform qualifies him as a social imperialist of the first rank; his protégé Félix Martin-Feuillée of

73. *République française,* February 9, 1876.
74. Eugène Spuller, *Discours à l'inauguration du monument de Gambetta, place du Carrousel, 13 juillet 1888* (Paris: n.p., 1888), 11–12.
75. *Paris,* January 6, 1882; Jean Jacques Weiss, *Combat constitutionnel, 1868–1886* (Paris: n.p., 1893), 253–98. The information on Franco-British shipping collaboration comes from John Laffey, "The Roots of French Imperialism in the Nineteenth Century," paper delivered at a conference held at Sir George Williams University, May 1, 1970.
76. Eugène Spuller, *La Tradition républicaine* (Paris: n.p., 1893), speech delivered to the Association nationale républicaine, June 29, 1893.

Rennes; David Raynal of Bordeaux; Maurice Rouvier of Marseille, who began his career there with the commercial banking house of Zafiropoulo; and Félix Faure of Le Havre. Rouvier headed the Ministry of Commerce and Colonies, marking the first time that the colonial bureaucracy had been separated from the Ministry of Marine.[77] Faure served directly under Rouvier. Paul Bert also joined the cabinet, and although his chief duties concerned education, he was well known as an advocate of colonial assimilation and a national policy directed toward metropolitan-colonial integration.

Following the fall of the cabinet, Bert accepted the presidency of the Société protectrice des colons de Constantine. He fully supported with, one might judge, unseemly enthusiasm the plunder of Algerian lands and forests for the benefit of European colonists; he encouraged colons to agitate to place Muslim communities under Draconian administrative control; and he publicly proclaimed that he was a "chauvinist by nature and unmoved by humanitarian poses." Apart from their common views on nationalist education, Bert and Gambetta spoke a similar language on imperial matters. The latter had stated in 1876: "Republicans have rejected the illusion that Algeria constitutes a country separate from France." Bert received his ultimate reward. In 1886 he became resident-general in Hanoi, where he died of malaria shortly after taking office.[78]

Félix Faure's entrance onto the stage of national politics at this time merits special comment. He parlayed a modest hide-importing business into a major leather-producing enterprise, selling his products in France and abroad. He thus had interests in both domestic production and foreign trade. Faure's success earned him an entree into the inner circles of the Le Havre bourgeoisie where, by the late 1860s, he had become chief lieutenant to Jules Siegfried and one of the city's

77. Hard-line assimilationists would not welcome such a move, for it merely represented a shift in bureaucratic responsibility without moving the colonies an inch closer toward "absolute assimilation with France"—that is, the attachment of all colonial affairs to the Ministry of the Interior. *France coloniale*, February 13, 1879.

78. Jean Jolly (ed.), *Dictionnaire des parlementaires français* (7 vols. to date; Paris: Presses universitaires de France, 1960–), I, 25; Charles Robert Ageron, *Les Algériens musulmans et la France, 1871–1919* (2 vols.; Paris: Presses universitaires de France, 1968), I, 235, 425, 430.

leading republican politicians. Faure marked himself early as an imperial propagandist and a promoter of its social benefits. He traveled through the Near East in 1870 and returned excited by the prospects of rich commercial opportunities awaiting French industrial and commercial capital. He urged Frenchmen to move into the Russian market, disparaging those who had qualms about doing business with a regime apparently unmoved by the currents of "social progress." Not only did a government that had emancipated sixty million serfs at one stroke deserve more sympathetic attention, but, whatever the case, fixed doctrinal positions ought not to interfere with the realization of promising business opportunities. Faure did not argue only for the special interests of Le Havre. He pointed out that the port's development would provide a direct link between the north, "the most important region of France from the point of view of industrial concentration," and the markets of the Mediterranean littoral. This applied especially to the wool and cotton trades, the latter being "Le Havre's principal export commodity." Finally, Faure proposed to counter the protectionist position, which argued for development of the internal market, by increasing the flow of French wool to her empire through the port of Le Havre. His clearly implied point was that imperialist ventures need not divide protectionists from free traders, that, on the contrary, the ventures provide cement to solidify the interests of both factions.[79]

Gambetta made another, less direct contribution to the imperialist movement by sponsoring the political career of Eugène Étienne. First elected deputy for Oran in 1881, Étienne began his ministerial career in 1887 under Maurice Rouvier as undersecretary of state for colonies in the Ministry of Marine and Colonies. Étienne by that time had emerged as the leading spokesman for colon interests and for a vigorous national imperial policy.

Étienne and Gambetta met in 1869 in Marseille, where the former worked for Zafiropoulo (Rouvier's employer) and "firmly took his

---

79. Félix Faure, *Du Commerce français dans le Levant et de son développement possible: Rapport à son excellence le ministre du commerce et de l'agriculture* (Le Havre: Santallier, 1870), 16–65; Félix Faure, *Le Havre: Son commerce, son industrie, sa navigation* (Le Havre: Santallier, 1869), 21.

place in the bourgeois circles of the great port." Rouvier by that time
had begun his upward climb in Marseille politics and attached Étienne
to his staff. They both played leading roles in the republican campaign
of 1869, covering Gambetta's radical flank. They operated out of the
offices of Gustave Naquet's radical newspaper, *Peuple*. We recall
Naquet's role in attacking workers' factions for raising their voices
against Gambetta's alliance with the Marseille bourgeoisie. Gambetta
brought Étienne to Paris in 1876, obtained an appointment for him
as commercial attaché to the fledgling State Railway Company, and,
finally, sponsored his candidacy in Oran in 1881. The two traveled
together frequently during that election year, especially to port cities
like Le Havre, where Gambetta was met "magnificently" by Jules
Siegfried. Despite the fact that he moved in such exalted circles,
Étienne considered himself a radical to the end of his career, and we
have no reason to doubt his sincerity. Indeed, Étienne's devout radicalism simply reinforces the argument that radicals frequently marched
side by side with, and sometimes led, the republican bourgeoisie in the
great imperial adventure. Étienne took pride above all in the alleged
close collaboration of European proprietors and Arab workers, a mark,
he said, of "tranquil labor and social peace."[80]

Étienne's reference to social peace provides a fitting conclusion to
this final episode in the making of the Republic. In their continuing
dedication to construct a stable bourgeois system, the republican leaders
recognized the importance of maintaining social peace. As long as
this remained a constant preoccupation, the alliance of capitalists and
petty producers remained a constant necessity. Perhaps these imperatives help to explain why the era of the Republic did not mark the
triumph of highly concentrated capitalist production that occurred
elsewhere in the latter part of the nineteenth century. Perhaps, even,
this was a matter of conscious choice. But here we leave fact for
speculation. The effect of political decisions on the future structure
of French production could be determined only by a study beyond the
scope and purpose of this book.

80. R. Villot, *Eugène Étienne, 1844–1921* (Oran: Fouque, 1951), 17–54, 107–109,
114–15.

Conclusion

CERTAIN DISTINCT MUTATIONS appeared during our period without, however, disrupting its essential unity. In the years preceding 1877, the emerging republican leadership constructed an ideological position embracing the unity of all producers. Their labors bore fruit during the subsequent years, which witnessed clear manifestations of the triumph of bourgeois class rule.

During the years of preparation, the republican bourgeoisie mounted a successful assault against the Empire (which had brought it into existence), staked out a distinctive ideological position consistent with the material and social concerns of capitalist producers, and consolidated a broad political base on the basis of common interests linking all forms of property. The republican message emphasized the unity of property, equality in the market place, and smothering of class distinctions. Hence, republicans took ideological positions against those big bourgeois and "aristocrats" whose exercise of political power appeared to thwart entrepreneurial freedom and had produced, in Spuller's words, "two enemy nations" and an explosive "class antagonism." They offered "political equality" as the stepping-stone to "order and prosperity" and to the enlargement of the rights of property.

The theme of class reconciliation, which later took on coherent form as *solidarité*, recurred often in those years. "Only the Republic can effect the harmonious reconciliation [of classes] and respect for the rights of property." So said Gambetta, who urged the bourgeoisie to concentrate their forces against "utopians and dreamers, [who] shower the masses with unrealizable promises, incoherent and illogical programs, aiming at the division of classes, fomenting discord between one and the other." César Bertholon echoed him: "We can . . . face without danger social questions. It is no longer a question of overthrowing the existing order." Gustave Masure put the matter even more bluntly: "The bosses . . . should follow closely every turn in the path of social change and should seek to forge links among all interests." We recall that Masure's *Progrès du Nord* circulated in Lille-Roubaix-Tourcoing, where "the bosses" commanded considerable capitalist property.

Culminating in the *seize mai*, the republicans fought on two fronts: against big bourgeois oligarchs and against independent workers' movements. They shifted their forces according to time and circumstance, but for the most part they leveled their heaviest guns against the oligarchs. Bonapartists, Orleanists, and monarchists of whatever complexion took on the aspect of an oppressive "class" apparently dedicated to blocking fulfillment of the small producer's modest aspirations: access to a wider market, relief from the tyranny of the tax collector, cheap credit, and education for his children. All of this has been explored and need not detain us, but a brief comment on the irony imbedded in this aspect of the story is called for. It should be apparent that the oppressive "class" did not constitute a class at all, but rather a fraction of the larger capitalist community. Its special interests produced a distinct outlook that, had it prevailed, most certainly would have hastened the "doom of modern society" and the "social upheaval" that concerned Jules Ferry. Thus, the republican bourgeoisie had to make war against them—warfare that remained, nevertheless, intraclass struggle. The irony rests in the fact that in the struggle the republicans enlisted massive auxiliary support from the world of petty production, whose inhabitants did not fully enjoy the rewards of victory.

These considerations in themselves can account for the radical rhetoric that bourgeois republicans frequently rehearsed. But we cannot leave matters there. This "radicalism" was both sweeping and circumscribed in its political nature, ruthlessly excluding any radical social content that challenged the fundamentals of the existing order. Republican democracy did indeed constitute a "radical" solution. Capitalists and petty producers alike sincerely embraced it with equal fervor, if from significantly different perspectives. Precisely for that reason and because the social question was deliberately muted, republican democracy served splendidly as an ideological instrument of class rule. The republican bourgeoisie inherited universal suffrage, welcomed it, used it, and turned it to their political advantage. Allain-Targé's "democratic myth" would have made no sense at all had it not produced deeply sympathetic vibrations among property owners. The realization of his vision of a community open to all hardworking *travailleurs* appeared to be worth the price it necessarily exacted: recognition of and subordination to bourgeois class rule.

As for the workers of France, their existence as a separate class was repeatedly denied. Each denial only confirmed the fact of their existence. Republicans, when they spoke of "reconciliation," meant integration if possible, suppression when necessary. We need only recall their efforts to rally workers to their radical political program, their strikebreaking in 1869, their silence during the liquidation of the Commune, and the bitter denunciations of the Communards by the peasants and farmers of the Savoie. Therein lay another bond between capitalists and petty producers.

The second half of our period, the years of consolidation, marked a new departure that, paradoxically, followed from the ideological constructions formed during the years of preparation. The republican bourgeoisie had to make good on their claims to root out oligarchic and aristocratic elements that had frustrated the full flowering of egalitarian democracy or, as Jules Lesguillier had warned in his pamphlet on railroads, suffer the consequences. At the same time, they could not afford to burn their bridges totally with the big bourgeoisie, with whom they shared a general class solidarity. Freycinet's public works program appeared to promise precisely the sinews of that national democratic market that constituted the essential material base of a stable bourgeois system. It proved to be more and less than that. The public works plan initiated in 1878 solidified the position of capitalist production by opening up to it new internal markets. It did not lavish the same bounties on petty production—especially its rural sector—which paid the price.

The resolution of the *seize mai* crisis in terms favorable to the republicans necessarily preceded the adumbration of the Freycinet Plan. An interpretation based upon the principle of *cui bono* might suggest that the republicans deliberately forced the hands of Mac-Mahon and his supporters. For in the crucible of struggle against monopoly and privilege, which appeared from the outside as a fight to the death, the republican bourgeoisie demonstrated with renewed radical energy its willingness to fight for the open marketplace and entrepreneurial freedom. This struggle also demonstrated that one fraction of the French bourgeoisie would not hesitate to drive to the sacrificial altar the short-range interests of another. When Freycinet and others demanded that the nation once and for all wrench itself free from the grip of the *féodalité financière*, they both expressed sincere conviction and took an opportunistic political position. They reasserted the republican bourgeoisie's claim to social and political supremacy. They also knew that the political power of the big bourgeoisie who controlled the railroads had to be broken so that they could then do business with them. Hence, the attack on the railroad monopolies revealed in action all the complexities of the republican social ideology developed earlier.

Once having made their point, the republican leadership then unveiled the Freycinet Plan, projected the benefits for the national market, and, of course, took all the credit for the plan's heroic efforts on behalf of the totality of the French business community. The elections of both 1876 and 1877 had made clear the chief interests of that community. The Freycinet Plan also made possible a loosening of the political alliance between capitalists and petty producers. For in the end, if we look at the fine print, the compromise embedded in the plan represented something less than the total capitulation of the big companies. Aristocratic reaction had been crushed, the alliance of the plutocrats and the *dévots* (as Lockroy had put it) had been broken, and republican democracy had prevailed. That was enough. The hidden hand became free to work its wonders—or so it seemed.

I emphasize the essentially laissez-faire thrust of the public works program to dramatize the fact that it did not work as expected. It did not halt the falling rate of profit and prices. The "liberal" and the "nationalist" bourgeoisie, free traders and protectionists, found the ground upon which they had met anything but stable. The national transportation system did not significantly reduce the pressure for a sweeping nationalistic economic program that included raising tariffs. If anything, the reverse occurred, as the inelasticity of the French internal market was brutally exposed. The question remained as to who would control that market. The Comité industriel et commercial of Normandy (*i.e.,* cotton producers) suggested as early as 1878 what became a reality: Freycinet's programs constituted an enormous step forward, but would not suffice. Nicholas Claude of Épinal made the same point several times. Nor could the politicians of capitalist production forget their allies in the world of petty production, for whom railways, canals, and roads fed into their regions a host of commodities that competed with their own as producers or, conversely, filled their markets with protected domestic goods for which they were forced to pay inflated prices. This explains why protection had to await the decisive pressure of agrarian capital. Petty producers, for their part, lost both ways—victims of the classic "scissors" crisis.

We must note at this juncture the recrudescence of a republican radicalism whose spokesmen surfaced in significant numbers in the elections of 1881. A full analysis of this phenomenon is outside the scope of this book, so I will only suggest that such radicalism sprang from those elements in the world of petty production that understood the capitalist thrust of the Freycinet Plan and rebelled against it. The "Barodets" (electoral statements) of 1881 bear this out. Yet this "radicalism" recapitulated the rhetoric and remained within the limits established by bourgeois ideologues: witness Girodet's attack on the "alliance of all capitalists" and Bouillier's vision of "no more bourgeois, no more proletarians; [instead] a single class of citizens . . .

united in solidarity." Other "radicals" went even further down that road and translated such social aspirations into a single-minded pursuit of imperial expansion.

Educational reform offered, on another level, a way out by transferring to the "cultural front" (the words are Antonio Gramsci's) the struggle to assert bourgeois power while providing a place in society for *les petits*. Education's purposes, ideological underpinnings, and consequences marked another step forward in the consolidation of the bourgeois Republic. I have placed some emphasis on positivist elements embedded in republican educational theory, but only to underline its class origins and purposes. Let us make no mistake. Theoretical constructions must not be taken lightly; they provided essential ideological garb to clothe the hard, practical calculations of bourgeois politicians. Social peace and *solidarité* constituted no idle rhetorical flourishes. They spoke immediately and directly to society's demands. Social peace covered a broad front of social relations, not only the specific relations between labor and capital. It expressed the bourgeoisie's determination to construct a stable republican system embracing all classes. While free and secular primary education promised upward mobility to the children of farmers and artisans and even occasionally to those of workers, educational policy focused unswervingly on its central purpose: to enforce, through indoctrination and national solidarity (and, if necessary, a strident nationalism) the ideological hegemony of the bourgeoisie. For that class, social peace and solidarity did not represent some theoretical abstraction, but cried out for immediate fulfillment.

Jules Ferry agreed with other republican leaders that the execution of the third network and the establishment of universal primary education were necessary to the consolidation of the Republic. He took an even more aggressive stance on imperialism, viewing expansion as the strongest pillar supporting the republican social order. Whether his judgment proved correct or false is beside the point. Imperialism, as a manifestation of bourgeois social policy supported by its distinctive ideology, followed the path of republican policy laid out in the preceding decade. It served to consolidate class rule and to insulate the political economy against the shocks generated by the great depression.

We may distinguish two aspects of imperialism, each closely related to the other. Ferry, his associates in the textile-producing regions of the east and north, and the leaders of the metallurgical industries promoted imperialism principally as a vehicle to lock up markets for French commodities and capital. This conception was closely linked to protectionism. Sharing that outlook were others who, although free traders, possessed similar concerns about markets and hoped that expansion would make protection unnecessary. They came mainly from the ports and the world of finance: Jules Siegfried, Félix Faure, Jules LeCesne, Maurice Rouvier, and the bankers' publicist Paul Leroy-Beaulieu.

The other aspect of imperialism emphasized colonies of settlement, focusing chiefly on Algeria as a place where small production could flourish at the expense of the native population. Eugène Étienne, protégé of both Gambetta and Rouvier, represented this view. He was joined by the "radicals" associated with the *France coloniale*, *France populaire*, and *Tribune coloniale*. Radical imperialism, then, was distinguished from market and capital-export imperialism by its reproduction of the social values of France's petty producers. But one could not live without the other. Étienne and Menier had close associations with bourgeois commercial and financial circles. They supported the Tunisian expedition because it appeared to be a natural extension of Algeria, just as Ferry foresaw great prospects in Tunisia for big capital investments. While Menier denounced the big bankers and the monopolies in a manner reminiscent of the republicans' radical attacks on the big companies, he promoted the Trans-Saharan Railroad, a project that demanded more than petty cash for its financing. Furthermore, the suggestion of the Société industrielle du Nord that native land in Algeria be transferred to Europeans by hook or crook followed closely the agitation by radical imperialists.

Paul Bert may serve to illustrate the link between the two imperialist tendencies. He contributed immensely to the elaboration of republican social ideology. Although formally committed to radical democracy, he practiced and preached bourgeois social values. Much in the style of Gambetta, Bert identified his ideological attachment to egalitarian democracy with what was best for the bourgeois system. Eugène Étienne, deputy from Oran, celebrated, certainly prematurely, the achievement of "social peace" in Algeria. Paul Bert, honorary president of the Société protectrice des colons de Constantine, did his part to achieve the same goal in France.

We ought not to place too much emphasis on the differences between the two tendencies. Colonies that provided opportunities for settlement also created new markets for metropolitan manufacturers and financiers. The manufacturers especially had a substantial interest in colonial expansion. As William Appleman Williams has pointed out frequently, a relatively inefficient industrial nation such as France required colonies that functioned as protected markets. Unlike efficient industrial nations, such as the United States and Germany, which did very well running "informal" empires, France could not compete in the international marketplace. To put it more bluntly: the viability and perpetuation of the system itself, at a time of depression and increasing working-class militancy, were at stake. A stable bourgeois socioeconomic order could not be expected to survive such blows without an imperial outlet.

Charles-Robert Ageron, in his recent article "Gambetta et la reprise de l'expansion coloniale" in the *Revue française d'histoire d'outre-mer*, LIX (April–June, 1972), 165–204, argues that "colonial policy constituted Gambetta's political testament to the Third Republic" and that Gambetta viewed colonization as an essential element in the *"solution of the social question"* (Ageron's emphasis). There is certainly no arguing with that, as long as we understand that Gambetta combined elements of both aspects of imperialism in an unstable mixture and did not, as his fate demonstrated, come close to appreciating the relationship between social imperialism and protectionism. Ferry, for his part, did. Gambetta neither invented nor fully comprehended the implications of social imperialism, although he clearly advanced policies associated with it. The lesson to be learned, and here lies the essence of his "political testament," is that the champion of the *nouvelles couches* paved the way for imperial expansion and thus, by direct extension, contributed to the consolidation of the bourgeois system at home.

Solidarité became a catchword for measures used to integrate the workers into the nation. We have witnessed the many-sided response of the republican bourgeoisie to independent workers' movements. For the most part, their formulas and their active efforts differed little from those of their "radical" brethren. After all, Léon Bourgeois, who fell from power in 1895 for his radical income tax proposal, made of *solidarité* a complete ideological statement. He had antecedents—and successors.

One of the latter was Georges Clemenceau, who stood straight and inflexible as the embodiment of pure "radicalism" and who harassed a generation of republican governments. Clemenceau first came to ministerial office in 1905 as minister of the interior, "France's chief cop," and became president of the council and minister of the interior in 1906. He devoted those years to breaking strikes with cold and ruthless efficiency. Simultaneously, in 1906, he included in his cabinet, for the first time in the Third Republic, a minister of labor and social welfare, thereby offering both the mailed fist and the outstretched hand. In effect, Clemenceau's social policy followed closely that of those republican bourgeois for whom he had displayed the utmost contempt. He justified his repressive actions in terms of the defense of France, which is to say the preservation of national solidarity, at a time when the clouds of war had begun to gather on the horizon. Those special circumstances did not confront the republican bourgeoisie of our period. Nevertheless, solidarist ideology, in whatever specific context, remained an essential component of a social ideology integral to perpetuation of bourgeois class rule. Clemenceau certainly would have scorned the suggestion that he acted within a class-determined framework, and there would be no doubt as to his sincerity. However, when it came to the exercise of power, he, like his political opponents, invoked solidarity in defense of the social order. In the application of social policy, Clemenceau proved himself to be a man of both movement and order.

Finally, to illustrate the endurance of the republican system, I can draw on a personal experience: an interview in 1961 with Maître D. Ordinaire, who practices corporate law in Paris. Ordinaire reminisced with me about his family, its modest peasant origins in the Franche-Comté, and its rapid ascent up the social ladder. His grandfather Dionys Ordinaire had been an important republican leader in the Doubs during the 1870s and had represented that department in the Chamber from 1880 to 1896. His father Maurice Ordinaire had served the same department in the Senate from 1913 to 1934, sitting on the right. Grandfather and father, Maître Ordinaire assured me, had held identical political views, even though they had sat on opposite sides of their respective chambers—views that he himself shared, presumably including, since he talked so much of it, a hard-line commitment to *Algérie française*.

This is a single example from which, certainly, no generalizations can be drawn. Nevertheless, as I listened to Ordinaire speak of the continuity symbolized in three generations of his family, I could not help but reflect on my intuition (and it was only that in 1961) that those who had made the Republic were themselves made of solid and durable material. Judgments about honor and corruption aside, that conclusion has stood up. It follows from the achievements of men who operated within a specific class-determined framework, who set out to accomplish a task, and who did their job well. We need not share either their outlook or their purpose. We are obliged, however grudgingly, to grant them our respect.

Note on Sources

THE FOLLOWING brief bibliographical note will serve to organize and classify the most important documentary foundations of this study. Not presented is a complete itemized and detailed bibliography, nor is any secondary material included. These may be found in the footnotes appended to each chapter.

Archival sources provided the core of my documentation. The collections in the French Archives nationales especially useful for this study include the following: the F(12) classification on details concerning the economy, particularly the series Situation industrielle des départements, F(12) 6171 and 6220–22 on the industrial crisis and the tariff, F(12*) 5749 on strikes from 1879 to 1882, and F(12) 4841, Voeux des conseils généraux rélatifs au commerce. The classification F(17) provides indispensable information on education, particularly regarding private and local initiatives. The series C collection includes all parliamentary records aside from the daily debates, namely, electoral statistics, campaign literature, reports of parliamentary committees, and official inquiries into the state of the economy. Within the C series I found these to be the most useful: C 3326–72, *Enquête parlementaire sur la crise économique et sur la situation industrielle, commerciale, et agricole en France, 1884*; C 3223, *Procès-verbaux de la commission du tarif général des douanes: Réponses des chambres de commerce*; and C 3392, *Projets et propositions de loi rélatifs aux syndicats ouvriers, 1881–1885*. The F(1) and the F(7) classifications, *politique générale* and *police politique*, respectively, include dossiers on individual officials and on some political movements. Two helpful segments of the AD XIX series are the F25, *Procès-verbaux des séances de la commission du tarif général des douanes, 1878–1880*, which supplements the material in C 3223, and the I1, *Procès-verbaux des séances des conseils généraux, 1839–1895*, an incomplete collection but mostly complete for the 1870s. In the BB series, which represents the files of the Ministry of Justice, I used BB(18) on the elections of 1869 and BB(24) 847 on the 1877 elections. Helpful, too, was the F(18) series on the departmental press and its volume of circulation and ownership. Finally, I consulted several private collections, most importantly the correspondence of Jules Simon (87 AP) and of Auguste Scheurer-Kestner (276 AP).

Several collections of departmental archives, all in the M series covering local political affairs mainly through the reports of prefects and subprefects, opened the way to some incursions into local history. They include the archives of the departments of the Drôme, the Haute-Garonne, the Hérault, the Isère, the Loire, the Nord, the Var, and the Vaucluse.

The archives of the Paris Prefecture of Police, specifically the B/a series, reward the researcher in inverse proportion to their quantity, which is massive. The Paris police kept (and keep) detailed records on the comings and goings of all active politicians, public figures, alleged agitators, etc. The extent to which the records are complete varies immensely. The accuracy of these reports must always be suspect since the channels of information used by police agents—domestics, concierges, mistresses, waiters, and casual informers—do not constitute the most impeccable of sources. It is not unusual for two agents to contradict each other on the movements of their quarry. The mass of trivia residing in these files is, however, worth going through for the occasional revealing report and even unsubstantiated rumors. In one way, the police archives are a researcher's delight, because its clerks clipped (and continue to clip) every major Paris newspaper and many from the provinces of material relating to every person on whom the police kept a dossier. Generally, these clippings report on or give the text of political speeches. Spot checks proved these files of clippings to be mostly complete in their coverage. Thus, frequently I was spared the grueling task of tracking down in the daily press the public utterances of national political figures.

Many local issues reflected national concerns. The cadres of the republican bourgeoisie did not live in Paris. Industrialists, merchants, and farmers worked their own local territory. Their public faces emerged from the pages of the dozens of local and regional newspapers that published consistently once effective censorship had been ended. I will make no attempt to list them *in toto*, except to note that I read selectively in over one hundred newspapers on the key issues of the time. These newspapers do not all appear in the footnotes, for frequently opinion from place to place on one or another issue varied only slightly. To have cited them all would have constituted senseless padding. Some of them, however, deserve special mention: *Avenir du Gers, Avenir clermontois, Dépêche de Toulouse, République de la Nièvre*, which changed its title to *République de Nevers* in 1878, *Démocratie franc-comtoise, République de la Corrèze, Union républicaine du Midi, République de la Loire, République des paysans* (Saint-Étienne), *Progrès du Nord, Gazette des paysans* (Beauvais), *Alliance républicaine de la Saône-et-Loire, Mémorial des Vosges, Progrès de la Somme*, and *Yonne*.

Historians argue over the validity of using newspapers at all in the reconstruction of the past. Many histories of France have provided ammunition for the negative side of the debate, insofar as the big Paris dailies often serve as the exclusive sources for the goings-on in the halls and corridors of the Chamber of Deputies and the Senate. These histories thus rest on the rumors, innuendoes, and allegations that frequently constitute the heart of such reporting. As the footnotes show, I used such sources sparingly, as I did not study the zigzags of day-to-day national politics. However, in the effort to develop a picture of republican social ideology and social policy, I found local and regional newspapers to be immensely fruitful sources.

Newspaper collections constitute only one of the resources of the Bibliothèque nationale in Paris. Its pamphlet collection provides a rich and easily accessible mine of information and opinion. For the purposes of this book, tracts dealing with railroads, tariffs, the social question, and education proved to be especially valuable. The footnotes refer only to those pamphlets that figured directly in the narrative. I sampled many others on the same subjects and left aside those peripheral or irrelevant to the main thrust of my argument. I shall echo Daniel Halévy's advice given in his little handbook, *Pour l'étude de l'histoire de la troisième république,* by calling attention to the great quantity of such material that remains to be studied. The manuscript collection in the Bibliothèque nationale, classified as Nouvelles aquisitions françaises (for the modern period), offers bits and pieces of evidence that supplement the basic material referred to above. Included are the typescript memoirs of Scheurer-Kestner, the Joseph Reinach Papers devoted mostly to letters and clippings relating to Gambetta, and the correspondence of Adolphe Thiers.

Printed sources, aside from pamphlets and newspapers, that proved most valuable included the following: the statistical annuals for the late 1870s and the early 1880s; special statistical compilations such as the *Statistique industrielle* for 1866 and the *Statistique agricole* of 1884; the *Dictionnaire des parlementaires* of A. Robert and his collaborators and the continuation of that project under the direction of Jean Jolly; the speeches and writings of Gambetta, Ferry, Waldeck-Rousseau, Floquet, Spuller, Allain-Targé, Pierre Joigneaux, and numerous lesser-known figures. Several of the reports of parliamentary committees on the tariff, railroads, and worker-employer relations, which were printed as annexes to the *Journal officiel* and exist in manuscript in the C series, also were printed separately, making them on occasion more accessible than the raw archives.

Index